Wisconsin Where They Row

Wisconsin Where They ROW

×

A History of Varsity Rowing
at the University of Wisconsin

Bradley F. Taylor

THE UNIVERSITY OF WISCONSIN PRESS

The University of Wisconsin Press
1930 Monroe Street
Madison, Wisconsin 53711

www.wisc.edu/wisconsinpress/

3 Henrietta Street
London WC2E 8LU, England

Copyright © 2005
The Board of Regents of the University of Wisconsin System
All rights reserved

5   4   3   2   1

Printed in the United States of America

Book design by Jane Tenenbaum

Library of Congress Cataloging-in-Publication Data

Taylor, Bradley F.
Wisconsin where they row : a history of varsity rowing at the
University of Wisconsin / Bradley F. Taylor.
p. cm.
Includes bibliographical references and index.
ISBN 0-299-20530-4 (hardcover : alk. paper)
1. University of Wisconsin—Madison—Rowing—History. 2. University of Wisconsin—Rowing—History. I. Title.
GV807.U57T39 2005
797.12'3'0977583—dc22

2004025626

This book was inspired by and is dedicated to:

my late uncle Lloyd R. Taylor, UW coxswain in 1923–24;

the open 4+ gold medal boating of 2000 IRAs, the members of which were: John Taylor (coxswain in the bowloader), Peter Vitko (bow), Mike Anderson, Rudy Rudert, and Mike Stahlman (stroke);

the varsity eight gold medal boating of 2002 Eastern Sprints and silver medal of 2002 IRA, the members of which were: Pete Nagle (bow), Sam McLennan (2-seat), Brian McDonough (3), Pete Giese (4), Micah Boyd (5), Dan Mueller (6), Beau Hoopman (7 and Captain), Paul Daniels (stroke) and John Taylor (coxswain); and

my wife, Fran Taylor.

Oh, sing me a song of college days
That tells me where I may go;
Chicago for her standards high,
Purdue for jolly boys,
Northwestern for her pretty girls,
Wisconsin where they row.*

*The lyric is a Wisconsin adaptation, believed to have been written in the 1920s, of the song "Sing a Song of College Days" published, without credit for either the words or the music, in the *Northwestern University Song Book,* edited by Donald G. Robertson, first published in 1917, and revised in 1919. The Northwestern song itself has roots of phraseology and cadence from a poem written in 1908 in the *Woman's College Journal* of the Woman's College of Baltimore (now Goucher College). The poem described the three editors—Laura Hutchins, Helen Buoy, and Nanne Weakley—of the *Journal*'s newly formed "department for its correspondents." Ms. Hutchins attended both the Woman's College of Baltimore and Northwestern University (see www.goucher.edu/library/robin.kalends.proph.htm as of March 31, 2003).

*This book has been gifted by the author to the University of Wisconsin Foundation.
Proceeds will go to the Foundation's permanent endowment fund,
The Mike Murphy Endowment Fund for Men's Crew.*

*Donors interested in contributing to the Murphy Fund or other funds benefiting
the men's and women's rowing programs should contact the
Director of Development for Athletics, UW Foundation,
P.O. Box 8860, Madison, Wis. 53708-8860 or call 1-800-443-6162.*

The following individuals and organizations have contributed to the publication of this book:

Paul and Mary Berge

Marla Boender

James H. Bowen, captain 1959

Mark Boyle

Paul H. and Nancy G. Burnett, in honor of Ed Burnett

Patrick J. Casey, 1954–1957

Joseph Robert Cincotta '87

Frank and Constance Clark

James and Lisa Cummings, in honor of our daughter, Meghan Cummings, 2000–2004

Jim and Katy Dyreby

Capt. Paul O. Eckhardt Jr., '33, and son Peter

Allan Erickson

*Robert and Mary Ann Espeseth Sr., in memory of 1951 crew teammates:
Del Barrett, Jim Healy, R. Y. Nelson, Pete Wackman, Doc Daentl, and Coach Norm Sonju*

David A. and Kimberly B. Evenson

Carlyle Fay

William "Golden Boy" Filip '88

John and Lynne Geweke, in memory of Alan Geweke

Thompson Christian Godfrey

Elmer A. Goetsch, in honor of Joel Richard Bock, 1996–2000

Jackson E. Goffman

Edward T. Golding

Dennis W. Hamill

Howard T. Heun, '36, and Donald R. Heun, '37, former captains of the Men's Team

John and Cathleen Hockers

Duane W. and Mary Ann Hopp, in memory of Norm Sonju

John H. and Ruth R. Huneke, in honor of John Taylor

Barbara Anderson, Mary Hurst, Diana Isenring, Craig Taylor,
and their families, in honor of their father, Lloyd R. Taylor, '24

Gene Huske, Men's Crew 1952–1957

Joe and Mary Lee Irwin

Duncan Robb Kennedy

Michael V. and Karen M. Kosky

Marie Towle Krause and Donald Krause, #7 Varsity '38–'39 crew

Ron and Jayne Kuehn

Jim Kurtz

Kathleen Galles Lhost

Stewart Gray MacDonald Jr.

Manke Enterprises—Mark and Neil Manke

Rose Marchuk, in honor of husband, Dan, and daughters Jennifer, Megan, and Stephanie Marchuk

Sarah Marty '97, in honor of the 1995–96 inaugural Lightweight Women's team

Timothy C. and Beth A. Mickelson

James T. and Mary Moran

Ted and Lynne Moreau, in memory of Richard Moreau, '43

Dale and Mary Ellen Mueller, in honor of
Eric Mueller, '94, Timothy Mueller, '96, Daniel Mueller, '03

David F. Nelson

Judy Nelson, in memory of Robert "R. Y." Nelson, captain '52

Oak Bank—Fitchburg

Konrad C. Opitz and Kay Jablonic Opitz

John Osborn, Men's Crew, 1969–1973

Roger Payne

James and Elizabeth Pick

Ben and Lee Porter

George A. and Doris W. Rea

Frederick A. Robertson

Robert and Barbara Rottman

Howard and Amy Lambrecht Ruddell

Louis S. Schueller Jr.

Stephen J. Shenkenberg

Marc and Mary Shuter

Ira Sandon Simpson and Aidan Robert Simpson, a future rower

Dennis D. Skogen

Matthew Stevenson Smith

The Sonju Daughters, in memory of their father, Norm Sonju

Carol J. Storm, in memory of David Storm

Brad and Fran Taylor, in memory of Doug Taylor

Dorothy W. Taylor

John O. Taylor, in memory of Jim Shuter

Kris Thorsness, in memory of my father, David Thorsness

Thomas and Mildred Toombs, in honor of Chris H. Anspach

Larry Trotter

James Urban

Julie Van Cleave

Roderick and Margaret Wagner

Dean R. Walker

Thomas Weil

Robert and Ruth Wierdsma

Nelson and Katy Williams

Charles and Carolyn Williams

Willard "Bill" Witte

Wisconsin Energy Corporation Foundation

Chubb & Son, Inc.

Wisconsin Alumni Association

National "W" Club

Contents

List of Illustrations	xiii
Acknowledgments	xv
Introduction	xvii
Prologue—UW History and Wisconsin Rowing, 1848–1925	3
1 **The First Race as a "Varsity"—Oconomowoc in 1892**	13
2 **UW President Adams Makes Crew a Priority**	19
3 **The Badgers' First Collegiate Opponent—Yale in 1896**	28
4 **The Berry Crate Crew of 1899**	34
5 **Wisconsin's First IRA Victory in 1900**	40
6 **Last of the Sculler Coaches—Ten Eyck and Vail**	44
UW History—1925–1946	62
7 **Never Giving Up—Coaches Murphy to Walz**	64
UW History—1946–2004	87
8 **Sonju Solidifies the Program**	90
9 **"Jabo" Takes Over**	124
10 **Chris Clark Assumes the Helm**	171
11 **The Pioneer Years of Badger Women's Crew**	190
12 **Mimier Named Women's Crew Coach**	199
13 **Sue Ela—First Full-Time Women's Head Coach**	223
14 **The Competition Becomes Fierce!**	257
Last Piece	276
Appendixes	
1. "W" Winners	281
2. UW Captains	297
3. Boatings of the UW Ten Eyck Trophy Victories	301
Notes	315
Bibliography	323
Index	325

Illustrations

1. View of Washburn Observatory and Lake Mendota, 4
2. View of Bascom Hill, 6–7
3. View of Agricultural Campus, 9
4. The Red Gym, 10
5. Commodore Peck's house, 16
6. 1892 varsity crew, 17
7. UW president Charles Kendall Adams, 19
8. Cornell crew coach Charles E. Courtney, 20
9. Boathouse with Red Gym, 21
10. First UW crew coach Amos Marston, 22
11. UW coach Andrew O'Dea, 23
12. Yahara River practice, 25
13. Yale Frosh vs. Wisconsin program cover—1896, 29
14. UW coach Curran C. McConville, 33
15. 1896 UW Varsity 8, 33
16. Hudson River course diagram, 35
17. The Berry Crate crew, 38
18. 1900 UW Frosh 8, 43
19. UW coach "Ned" Ten Eyck, 44
20. The three Ten Eycks, 45
21. 1907 UW Frosh 8, 47
22. Jack Wilce, 48
23. UW coach Harry Emerson "Dad" Vail, 50
24. Charles M. Pollock, 51
25. 1913 Poughkeepsie Regatta, 54
26. James Francis Augustine Pyre, 56
27. "Rusty" Callow, 60
28. Bascom Hill, 63
29. UW coach George W. "Mike" Murphy, 64
30. UW president Glenn Frank, 66
31. Paul O. Eckhardt, Jr., 68
32. UW coach Ralph Hunn, 70
33. Syracuse coach Jim Ten Eyck, 73
34. UW coach Allen W. "Skip" Walz, 74
35. Observation train at the Poughkeepsie Regatta, 75
36. Carl Holtz, 76
37. UW coach George Rea, 78
38. UW rigger and coach Curt Drewes, 79
39. 1946 UW Varsity 8 Finish, 80
40. 1946 UW Varsity 8 Eastern Sprints Winners—displaying shirts won, 81
41. Carillon Tower, 87
42. Memorial Union Terrace, 88–89
43. Coach Norm Sonju, 91
44. 1949 Yale noses out UW for victory on the Housatonic River, 96
45. Marietta course on the Ohio River, 102
46. 1951 UW Varsity 8 finish at Marietta, 104
47. 1959 Varsity 8 Winners of IRA, 112
48. 1964 Freshmen 8, 116
49. 1966 Varsity 8, 119
50. UW coach Randy Jablonic, 124
51. 2nd Varsity 8 finish, 1972 IRAs, 132
52. 1972 UW Frosh 8, 132
53. Ten Eyck Trophy, 133
54. Tim Mickelson, 133
55. 1973 2nd Varsity 8 team, 135
56. 1973 Varsity 8 team, 136
57. Head of the Charles course diagram, 137
58. 1974 Varsity 8, 138
59. 1974 2nd Varsity 8, 138
60. 1975 Varsity 8, 141
61. Jim Dyreby, Jr., 142
62. Lou Schueller, Jr., 143
63. Robert Espeseth, Jr., 143
64. 1979 Freshman 8, 146
65. 1983 Freshman 8, 147
66. 1985 Freshman 8, 152

67. 1986 2nd Varsity 8, 155
68. 1986 Varsity 8, national champions, 156
69. 1986 Men's/Women's national champions, 157
70. 1987 2nd Varsity 8, 158
71. Jabo and Steve Hatton, 161
72. 1990 Varsity 8, 163
73. Chris Clark, 171
74. 2000 Freshman 8, 174
75. 2001 2nd Varsity 8, 177
76. 2002 Varsity 8, 178
77. 2002 Team Ten Eyck photo, 180
78. Temporary crew quarters, 187
79. Beau Hoopman, 189
80. Early UW women rowers, 1896, 191
81. Two sorority crews, 1934, 193
82. Kathy Wutke, 193
83. Doug Neil, Curt Drewes, and Randy Jablonic, 196
84. 1972 Varsity 8, 199
85. Jay Mimier and Nat Case, 200
86. Badger Carie Graves, three-time U.S. Olympian, 204
87. 1975 Novice 8, 209
88. 1975 Varsity 8, NWRA champions, 212
89. 1976 Varsity 8, 214
80. Three Badgers on U.S. Olympic Team, 1976, 216
91. 1979 Novice 8, 220
92. 1979 2nd Varsity 8, 221
93. Sue Ela, 223
94. 1980 2nd Varsity 8, 225
95. 1984 Varsity 8, 233
96. 1985 Novice 8, 236
97. 1986 Varsity 8, 237
98. 1986 2nd Varsity 8, 237
99. 1995 women's crew, 248
100. Mary Browning, 257
101. 1999 Royal Henley Regatta entry from UW, 258
102. Maren Watson LaLiberty, 260
103. 2001 Lightweight 8, Head of the Charles winners, 266
104. 2004 Lightweight 8, IRA winners, 274
105. Bebe Bryans, 275

Acknowledgments

Writing a story of the 114 years of UW's college crew history, with its annually revolving rosters, reminds one of the story told by the late Lee Atwater (President G. H. W. Bush's air guitar–playing campaign manager) about his writing a school book report on a phone book, "Lots of characters, but the plot's a little thin."

The gathering of rosters, not to mention over 100 years of race results and descriptions, times, boatings, and anecdotes, requires the help and support of many people and sources. The Web site eBay has been a source of quite a few Poughkeepsie Regatta and IRA programs, as well as many UW photos and memorabilia. From the 1890s until World War II, the *New York Times* carried extensive coverage of college crew. After that, the local papers of rowing venues became the source of detailed race accounts. Wisconsin Crew Corporation Newsletters, dating from the late 1930s, provided many details and the UW's own sports media guides, beginning around the same period, added facts to the Badger rowing story.

Library sources included the Memorial, Steenbock, and Mills Libraries at the University of Wisconsin in Madison, Wis.; the Sterling Library at Yale University in New Haven, Conn.; the Mystic Seaport Library in Mystic, Conn.; the Navy Library in Annapolis, Md., and community libraries in Oconomowoc, Wis.; Worcester, Mass.; Seattle, Wash.; Minneapolis and St. Paul, Minn.; Cincinnati, Ohio, and Syracuse, N.Y., among others.

A special thanks to UW archivists Steve Masar, Bernie Schermetzler, and Steve Sundell for their making access as easy as possible; to Clayton Chapman for all his early help finding Poughkeepsie Regatta/IRA statistics; to Wisconsin crew coaches Randy "Jabo" Jablonic, Chris Clark, Sue Ela, Maren LaLiberty, and Jamie Whalen for their crew knowledge and support; to Tim Storm and Art Hove for their editorial inputs; to Mrs. "R. Y." (Judy) Nelson, for gathering and mounting in scrapbooks all those news clippings and photos on Wisconsin's crews; to Mrs. Duane (Joy) Daentl for her gifts of IRA programs, photos, and clippings; to Carlyle "Bud" Fay for his donation of his Big Ten Conference Medal to the new boathouse's history exhibit; to Mrs. James (Ruth) Healy for the donation her late husband's 1951 varsity eight IRA gold medal (in the 7-seat) to the Kohl Center sports history exhibit; to Carl (UW '47) and Jean Holtz for their donation of the Allen W. "Skip" Walz UW National "W" Club plaque and other material to the new boathouse's history exhibit; to Jim Moran (5-seat) for the donation of his 1951 IRA gold medal; to George Rea for contributing his uncle Will Gibson's 1899 second place "Strawberry Crate" race medal; to Lou Schueller for gifting two Head of the Charles gold medals and his nearly unique collection of four IRA golds in the eights; and especially to Paul O. Eckhardt, Jr. (UW '33), for his memorabilia, historical research, and energetic encouragement, and to many others too numerous to mention.

At the UW Foundation, appreciation is expressed to Mark Lefebvre for his early encouragement of the crew's history and for his introduction to the UW Press; to Wayne Hansen for his completely unexpected assistance in researching the individual biographies of those in the 1892 varsity; and to Trent Jackson and Stephanie Franklin for coordinating donor correspondence with the UW Press.

Thanks to the professional team at the UW Press for their long term support—to Raphael Kadushin for his early direction; to Sheila Moermond for her multiyear contributions of help and advice; to Sheila

Leary for development and sales support; to Badger rower on the first Lightweight crew Sarah Marty (UW '97), who while at the UW Press, provided her tireless and dedicated help in development activities and updating the women's list of "W" winners in crew; and to Sue Breckenridge for her good nature and expertise in leading the editing of the final product.

Ultimately, thanks to my wife, Fran, for enabling, in the broadest sense, the realization of this project.

Note to future researchers: All materials gathered—including UW Crew newsletters, over 60 of the roughly 100 IRA programs (1895–2004) and several thousand mostly digitized photos—are to be given (in 25 or more archival boxes) to the Memorial (text) and Steenbock (images) Libraries of the University of Wisconsin–Madison.

Alumni and supporters should send men's and women's UW crew-related materials, such as regatta programs, clippings, scrapbooks, memorabilia, and photos (labeled, if at all possible) to: Archivist, B134 Memorial Library, 728 State Street, Madison, Wis. 53706.

Note to readers: While sincere care has been taken in the researching of this project in many libraries and from hundreds of clippings and other sources, the details over many years as to boatings, results, times, locations, dates, correct spellings, and other data are always subject to unintended error. This author regrets any and all such oversights.

Photographs: Unless otherwise indicated, the photos herein are from the archives of the libraries of the University of Wisconsin, the UW Athletic Communications Office (many team photos are by former UW coxswain Duane Hopp (UW '55) with the UW Media Center from the early 1950s to 1986) or the newsletters of the Wisconsin Rowing Association (or its predecessor, the Wisconsin Crew Corporation).

While accounts from newspapers and other contemporaneous writings of sportswriters add greatly to race descriptions as presumably first-hand, on-the-scene reports in the vernacular of the day, inaccuracies often occur. Stroke rates, boatings, and other details may turn out to be incorrect because of simple errors, the excitement of the race, last minute boating changes, and other reasons.

As this book goes to press, it is with deep sadness that we note the passing, on February 2, 2005, of Badger rower, coach, and supporter Dick Tipple (UW '50). The author is sincerely grateful to Dick for his constant willingness to share his experiences and memories in support of the telling of the UW crew story.

Introduction

College rowing is a special sport. Crew (most commonly, the rowing competition in eight-oared racing shells) is the University of Wisconsin's oldest sport. At the varsity sport level today, 20 percent of all men and women student-athletes at UW are rowers!

Since 1892, thousands of wide-eyed athletes—many of them outstanding former Wisconsin high school performers in other sports—have largely been drawn from UW class registration lines, with the question, "Would you like to go out for crew?" Often with no prior rowing experience, the men and women accepting the challenge at UW have produced an amazing list of athletic achievements:

— 14 Ten Eyck Trophies (the overall team award in the men's heavyweight events), more than any other college, at the IRAs
— over 60 national and/or IRA men's and women's championships in eight-oared and small boat events
— 24 U.S. men and women Olympians

This book celebrates the history of this long line of student-athletes, and their parents, coaches, and supporters.

Good college rowers have excellent cardiovascular systems, sometimes from birth but always from hard work. Unlike other sports requiring similar cardiovascular development and endurance, such as swimming and long-distance running, college crew is a team sport. Good individual strength and technique must be delivered in concert with an entire boat's harmonic rhythm and pace. At the same moment, physical brutality is forced gracefully into perfectly synchronous motion—an orchestra of eight.

Many elements attract college men and women to the sport of crew. Publicity is not one of them. "If you want to see your name in the newspaper, go out for football," was the gruff advice given each fall to the University of Wisconsin freshmen rowers by head crew coach Norm Sonju, who led the Badger crews from 1946 to 1968. It's the love of the sport, the joy of competition, the challenge of mastering personal discipline, and the strong bonds of friendship that form the bedrock of each rower's commitment.

For some, like Sue Ela (UW '75) the attraction started with a feeling of the senses being aroused—perhaps watching from a boathouse rooftop—as she took in and processed that first observation of the unique grace of a shell slowly rowing away from the dock and out into the vastness of Lake Mendota. For Ron Kuehn (UW '68), the attraction was the chance to continue one's high school athletic career in a college sport at the Division I level.

For others, it was the wraparound panorama of landscape, in the fall or the spring, from the seat of a shell in the middle of a still-water lake or slow-moving river. Many are attracted to rowing by what the sport teaches them about themselves and others—achieving discipline of mind and schedule, or the battle endured to understand and overcome physical pain and develop the mental toughness that comes from its mastery. Still others feed off the special camaraderie developed through twice-a-day practices in a unique fraternity of oarsmen or women with the same dedicated teammates.

For everyone, however, one part of the sport's attraction is the emotional high one feels when eight rowers slip into that special rhythm of shared power and grace that, on the drive, literally accelerates and lifts the hull's contour seamlessly through the water.

The late Rusty Callow, a Washington rower and crew coach at three great universities, was asked, "Why crew?" His answer, written around 1965, was a three-page essay, the essence of which described his ideal rower as the one doesn't ask, "What's in it for me?" but rather, "What can I give?" The old coach also reminded his questioner, "Remember, there are no quarters, halves, timeouts, or substitutions." Callow went on to say that the long practices and the inability to quit before the finish line

> cannot help but build the participants' respect and admiration, each for the other . . . [from which] comes the sheer physical joy that an oarsman experiences when a boat is swinging, the spacing lengthens out, and the called-for silent "ten" or "twenty" hard strokes melds eight men and a coxswain into a single, wholly unified, struggling, competitive activity.

Author Robert F. Kelley, in his own essay, "That's Poughkeepsie" in the *1941 Poughkeepsie Regatta Program*, sought to characterize the significance of the national regatta to the college men who rowed in the annual event. Kelley wrote:

> The satisfaction of pulling an oar when you were in great physical shape, the shell coming to life beneath you and the crew fitting in as one man—it is a peculiar and unique sensation not to be described.

Oarsmen are generally highly oriented toward achievement—at their sport and at their academics. The first Big Ten Medal—given annually at each university to one individual[1] demonstrating "the greatest proficiency in athletics and scholarship—was first awarded at UW in 1915 to a rower. Over the nine-and-one-half year period prior to publication of this history, the men's crew accomplished the first- or second-best GPA rankings among the 12 men's sports at UW–Madison in 14 of the 19 semesters. The record has been similar for the men and the women rowers for many years at Wisconsin and undoubtedly for rowers at other schools across the nation. Many serious, academically-focused students find something special and attractive about rowing.

Crew has been associated with elitism because of its historical origins at Oxford, Cambridge, Harvard, and Yale. The notion of elitism is extended by this nonrevenue sport's centuries-old dependence on financial support from former rowers and supporters, but this is not to say elitism defines the sport. The socially elite athlete, if unaccustomed to making his or her own way, will find rowing a difficult dose of very hard work. An elitist's arrogance actually gets in the way of discovering the depths of one's mental capabilities to understand and manage the physical and mental challenges of rowing. In fact, the best rowers may be what at Wisconsin is known as the "blue collar" athlete—one possessing a strong work ethic, excellent physical attributes, and a clear, disciplined mind.

Worth noting is that the men's program at Wisconsin—now well over 100 years old—is different from most other college programs with similarly long rowing traditions. Frozen lakes, ever-tight budgets, an absence of athletic scholarships (or the Ivy League's varietal blend of "earmarked" applications for athletes and unlimited financial aid) leads to a rather basic recruiting process at UW. Untrained, midwestern novices characterize the sport in Madison.

Unlike college crew programs fed by prep schools and scholarship-recruited international rowers, men's crew at Wisconsin, up to now, has found its novices among students already enrolled on its own campus. Recruiting is often accomplished within a mile of the boathouse and within several weeks of the beginning fall semester. Historically, most Badger rowers have been Wisconsin athletes with no prior rowing experience, but possessing the athleticism, the work ethic and the love of outdoor physical activity.

Dedication and career success are the characteristics first noticed among rowers around the country. Heads of business, doctors, lawyers, bankers, judges, teachers, and other professionals of all types come out of American college rowing programs. In a sports world filled with controversies around graduation rates, greater participation of university president's in hiring coaches, pro draft eligibility, and the debate around college football's Bowl Championship Series ("BCS") play-off rankings, college rowing retains much that has kept the sport attractive to individual athletes over the years—amateurism, accessibility to walk-ons, camaraderie, potential for national team and Olympic participation, and a natural affinity with excellent students.

This is the Wisconsin story of more than 100 years of varsity crew, its several thousand oarsmen and oarswomen, and a program that placed Badger men on each of the last ten—and Badger women on seven of the last eight—U.S. Olympic squads through 2004.

For Wisconsin's women, varsity rowing advanced from the interest of one individual in forming a new women's club sport in the spring of 1972 to a national open (i.e., not "college-only") championship as a varsity crew only three years later, in 1975. Fourteen oarswomen from Wisconsin have become U.S. Olympians—since 1976, when women's rowing first became an Olympic event.

It is the objective of this history that the rowing legacy and strength of character built these many years at Wisconsin and elsewhere be protected and nurtured for the benefit of many future generations of athletes in this sport.

Wisconsin Where They Row

Prologue — UW History and Wisconsin Rowing, 1848–1925

The Early Days of UW and Sports on Campus, 1848–1892

The history of the University of Wisconsin began on the same day statehood was granted—May 29, 1848. The Wisconsin Constitution contemplated the establishment of a university, and in October of 1848 the regents named the university's first president, John H. Lathrop, the then president of the University of Missouri.

The college took shape over the next decade on College Hill, about one-half mile west of the capital on the former outskirts of the town of Madison. By the 1870s, an expanding community led to the gradual closing of the distance between campus and the community.[1]

The university granted its first degrees in 1853 to Levi Booth and Charles T. Wakeley. By commencement day of 1861 (when nine men graduated), the university had enough graduates to see the founding of the Wisconsin Alumni Association.[2] Another milestone for the school came in 1862, when the U.S. Congress passed the Morrill Act, providing lands to be later sold with the objective of creating long-term endowments in support of the school's operating costs—thus the origin of the university as a "land-grant college."

The tumultuous effects of the Civil War directly impacted the student population from 1861 to 1865, not only because Wisconsin contributed so many soldiers to the cause—90,000 men or about one in five of the state's male population were sent to the front—but also because the state's major military training camp occupied a large area a half-mile from, and within the full view of, the university campus on the hill. A hospital and prison for Confederate soldiers were also on the site.

The worst impact of the war on the university was the decline in enrollment—from roughly eighty in 1860–61 to nearly forty in 1864—as most students enlisted and several were detained at home to fill the places of older family members in the service. Some thirty men from the University of Wisconsin perished in the Civil War and are remembered in the Memorial Union. Following the end of Civil War, some men re-entered the university and enrollment turned upward. At the time of the first nonintramural college sports contests at the university—the baseball games of 1870—enrollment rose from less than 200 in 1869 to around 500 in 1871.

View of Washburn Observatory and Lake Mendota, c. 1884. Courtesy of University of Wisconsin–Madison Archives ("UW–Madison Archives"), Series 9. Photo by R. W. Curtis.

John Sterling—president of the university from 1861 to 1867 (which period overlapped that of the Civil War)—was replaced by Paul Chadbourne, a professor from Williams College. Three years later, Chadbourne resigned to return to Williams as their head and was succeeded on June 30, 1871, by John H. Twombly, a Methodist minister from Massachusetts. Twombly's administration is given little note in most histories of the school. J. F. A. Pyre, in *Wisconsin,* described Twombly: "The new President proved to be a large-boned evangelical of a pushing type, of insignificant scholarship and without social delicacy."[3] The Board of Regents, who found him to be too independent, soon replaced him.

The first evidence of crew at the University of Wisconsin was noted in a 1912 letter from alumnus C. B. Bradish, who wrote of his father's telling him that "he rowed on the first crew Wisconsin ever had" in 1874. Baseball preceded crew as the first sport at the university when, on April 30, 1870, the university team, organized as the Mendotas, played their first nonintramural opponent and outscored the Capital City Club, 53–8.

In the year of the first crew at Wisconsin, Arthur Hove, in his book *The University of Wisconsin: A Pictorial History,* described the seniors of the Class of 1874 as "twenty-six men and fourteen women."[4] The campus by this time was 235 acres along the southwestern shore of Lake Mendota, so water sports, such as boating and fishing, were accessible and familiar to the students at UW.

Although the university was already twenty-five years old in 1874, sports teams were just then being organized on campus. With small classes and few facilities heretofore, the earliest athletic activities took advantage of the campus's natural landscape of open fields and proximity to beautiful Lake Mendota on which shores stretched the university campus and the town of Madison.

In the year of the first crew's appearance, John Bascom had succeeded the three-year UW presidency of Twombly. Bascom—like Chadbourne, previously associated with Williams College—and the university's student body, many of whom were "of the ruling class or economically advanced class,"[5] were known to look to the East Coast schools for educational and social trends.

Crew had become popular at several of the Ivy League schools in the 1850s and '60s. The first intercollegiate sporting contest in the United States was a student-organized crew race between Harvard and Yale in 1852—a competition that continues to this day, making it the oldest collegiate sports rivalry in the United States.

The sport of rowing began to grow at the university in the 1870s and '80s. The economic depression of the 1870s made the student purchases of boats an intermittent affair, but the formation of fraternities in the late 1870s and '80s propelled the sport into an increasingly active intramural program. Crews were formed for intraclass races (freshmen vs. sophomores, etc.) as well as for intracollege contests (the law school vs. the engineering school, for example).

Some students with the financial means were able to acquire their own recreational equipment, including boats, guns (for hunting), farming tools, and fishing tackle. Students collectively were often a source of significant funds in support of sporting activities, including new shells and travel budgets for the crew, a large portion of the capital costs of the first boathouse (1892–93), and even funding of the $1.5 million construction of the Memorial Union (completed in 1928).

Competitive rowing was also in evidence elsewhere in the state. *Picturesque America,* the American Heritage publication of 1874, illustrated coxed fours competing in weekend races among the wharves and waterways of the Milwaukee River. As in many other of the nation's ports, the oarsmen and boats, used to bring cargo from the large ocean going and Great Lakes' ships to the storage warehouses on shore, often spent weekends competing to see which crews were the fastest.

Notwithstanding the increased student interest in athletics, president Bascom devoted a substantial passage in his baccalaureate sermon, "The Seat of Sin" (1876), to a condemnation of "athletic sports, college regattas and ball games," indicating that he foresaw and deprecated their introduction at Wisconsin.[6] As the competition increased and other schools' teams came to Madison, some of the vices of betting and drinking, which President Bascom had been afraid of, were known to occur.

In 1881 the regents acquired the Lower Campus—the center of which area today would be the open walks and grass between the Wisconsin State Historical Society and the Memorial Library—to provide "convenient and appropriate grounds for gymnastic and kindred exercises."[7] The field immediately became used for competition in baseball. The State Fair Grounds at Camp Randall were also used for baseball games.

Boating entries from many organizations began an annual tradition of "Class Day" races on Lake Mendota. Beginning in 1885, such student activities were captured in the student yearbook, *The Trochos* (a Greek approximation for the word *Badger*), which later became *The Badger* in 1889. *The Trochos* of 1885 listed the names of the rowers and coxswain of the winning Phi Kappa Psi entry in the coxed six-oared entry on Class Day in 1883. Don Kopriva and Jim Mott, in an outline history of UW sports, *On Wisconsin! The History of Badger Athletics,* wrote,

> Crew continued to grow in popularity on the campus with the founding of the Madison Boat Club in 1886. Its sponsors—six professors—were united in their belief that "the natural opportunities for boating at the University are unrivaled by those at any other college in the country."[8]

John Bascom, the university's fifth president, resigned effective in 1887, again the result of tension between the president and the regents. Bascom's successor, Thomas Crowder Chamberlain, brought no eastern credentials to his new position. Rather, he came with a solid midwestern background—having been born in Illinois and educated at Beloit College—and carried an "impeccable scholarly reputation" from a career as a field geologist.[9]

While his tenure was relatively short, Chamberlain successfully promoted several new ideas in education including allowing students to take elective courses, encouraging graduate study as a stimulant for research, and bringing the university, through increased publications, into contact with the university's natural constituency—the citizens of Wisconsin. He also lent a reluctant hand to improving conditions to support student athletics.[10]

In 1889, several students with previous experience in competitive rowing transferred to UW. They brought with them a doubles shell, which became a big attraction. Among those students was W. T. Saucerman, who became instrumental in a new boat club established in the winter of 1891.[11] President Chamberlain resigned in 1892 to become the head of the geology department at the University of Chicago, and sports continued to blossom on the UW campus, as Pyre described:

> Intercollegiate athletics came in with a rush after 1890. Within three or four years football, rowing and the field and track contests became the distinctive college games, overshadowing baseball and tennis, which had flourished the decade before.

View of Bascom Hill, 1885. Courtesy UW–Madison Archives, Image x2-5542.

College football was probably first played between Princeton and Rutgers in 1869. Thereafter, the sport prospered in the eastern colleges. Michigan sent a team east to play Harvard and other colleges in 1881. The honorary All-American football team was first selected in 1889, giving additional publicity to the sport and fanning spectator interest. Regarding football at Wisconsin, Hove wrote:

> Football appeared in 1889 as part of a broadening of the intercollegiate athletic program. College sports were on the rise and soon became enormously popular among students and townspeople.

In that first football game, UW lost 27–0 to the Calumet Club. Alvin Kletsch was thus the first "official" coach in UW history.

In 1891 the merger of the baseball, football, and tennis associations with the University Boat Club resulted in the first University of Wisconsin Athletic Association. All students of the university were automatically members, but management responsibility for all the athletics offered at Wisconsin was vested in a board of directors consisting of twelve students, three faculty members, and one alumnus.[12]

Pyre, writing about crew at UW, gave this description of the sport he personally knew so well:

> The most daring undergraduate conceit of those days was the introduction of eight-oar racing. Rowing is the most arduous of college sports and the most difficult to finance. The nearest college rival was Ithaca and indeed, eventually, Wisconsin had to go beyond the Alleghenies for competition. The enterprise owed its inception in the last analysis to the perennial challenge of Lake Mendota, but in the first instance to the enthusiasm and perseverance of C. C. Case ('93), who, from the hour he entered college, missed no opportunity to gain disciples for the sport of his fancy.
>
> In the spring of 1892 a pair of eight-oar gigs was purchased with money secured by subscription and a class regatta was held. The next spring an abandoned paper shell was purchased from Harvard and a crew composed largely of football athletes was put in practice.[13]

In the spring of 1892 the *Daily Cardinal* began publication, providing a sense of identity for the expanding student body as well as announcing and recording campus events. In addition, the newspaper, a detailed chronicler of much of university life into the twenty-first century, served to stimulate the student populations' growing interest in sports on campus.

The Camp Randall military camp land served, after the Civil War, as the State Fair Grounds until the university purchased the entire site for both a war memorial and for athletic fields in 1893. Camp Randall football stadium stands today on the ground of the former military camp.

View of Agricultural Campus, early 1900. Courtesy UW–Madison Archives Series 7.

The arrival of Charles Kendall Adams as president of the university in the fall of 1892 marked a growth spurt, not only in the university's enrollment and physical facilities but also in the level of interest in intercollegiate athletics. To find the funds needed to expand a campus pressed by increasing enrollments, Kendall used all his skills to generate broad support for his program. Foremost among his efforts was maintaining an effective and cordial relationship with the state legislature. In support of athletics at Wisconsin, Adams went to many of the games and "was always willing to give the players a pep talk between halves of a football game."[14]

Interest in athletics came from his prior experience as president of Cornell College. Adams had a sincere interest in and an appreciation for what intercollegiate athletics could bring to the spirit of the student body and the townspeople. He also knew what athletic success could bring to the national and international reputation of a university. Crew and football at Wisconsin were of particular interest to Adams: crew had been well developed at Cornell, where the campus sat astride the ten-plus mile long Lake Cayuga; rowing had begun at Cornell in 1870.

Under Cornell's head crew coach Charles E. Courtney—who became legendary during his thirty-five-year span (1885–1920) for his consistently successful crews—the name of Cornell College came to be known around the world.[15] The ascendancy of Adams to the presidency of Cornell in July 1885 coincided closely in time with Courtney's assumption of the head crew-coaching job at Cornell in the same year.

ARMORY AND GYMNASIUM, UNIVERSITY OF WISCONSIN.   MADISON, WIS.

The Red Gym, c. 1907.
Courtesy UW–Madison
Archives, Series 9.

From College to University, as Rowing Takes Root, 1892–1925

The era approximately spanned by the university administrations from Adams (1892–1901) through Edward A. Birge (1918–1925) was one of a consolidation of the maturity of the institution; it had evolved from a college to a university by the time Adams came to Wisconsin. A school of solid academic stature and graduate programs, enrollment mushroomed and the university's reputation and influence extended "far beyond the confines of the state by the end of the century."[16]

During this same era, Wisconsin rowing emerged as an important intercollegiate sport at Wisconsin. Adams's arrival in Madison, in the fall of 1892, followed by just a month the first race by a Wisconsin crew against an off-campus opponent—the historic race against the Chicago Navy on Lac La Belle in the resort town of Oconomowoc, Wisconsin.

In 1895, the year after Adams put his quill to the Regent's Report and wrote the now famous phrase of the "sifting and winnowing" at Wisconsin, three eastern colleges organized the initial race of the Poughkeepsie Regatta, later known as the Intercollegiate Rowing Association's (or IRA) national college regatta. As the only rowing college in the Midwest, the Badgers had to travel a long way east to find a worthy crew opponent. Their first intercollegiate contest was against the Yale freshmen on Lake Saltonstall in Connecticut in 1896.

On the train ride home on June 20, 1986, the Wisconsin rowers stopped in Poughkeepsie, New York, and watched four crews practice for the Poughkeepsie Regatta, held six days later on the Hudson River. The *New York Times* reported, "Manager [Oscar] Rohn said that under no circumstances could his crew enter the race, because they had made overtures months ago, but the colleges were unwilling to admit them."[17] The Badgers would attend for the first time the following year.

In 1899, the fifth year of the Poughkeepsie Regatta, the Badger crew landed all over the front page of the *New York Times* in their now famous "Berry Crate Race." A year later, the Badger freshmen brought home the first gold medal from the national college rowing regatta of 1900.

For much of the next quarter century, under the tutelage of coaches O'Dea, Ten Eyck, and Vail, the sport of crew at Wisconsin consolidated its sporadic schedules in the 1890s with annual trips east, fund-raising routines, and a few more races each season with midwestern boat clubs.

Edward A. Birge followed Adams as acting president, from 1900 to 1903, when Adams fell too ill to manage. Charles R. Van Hise was named president in 1904 and led the institution until his untimely death in November of 1918. World War I was under way and many aspects of American life seemed to be on hold. (Crew at Wisconsin had been suspended since the summer of 1914, when the medical faculty concluded that rowing, especially for four miles, was dangerous to one's health.) Van Hise had had the support of his classmate of 1879, Wisconsin Governor Robert M. La Follette. The two of them shared a feeling that the university should lend its resources to the development of the state, a concept that would soon lead to the "Wisconsin Idea."

Edward Birge returned to the university's presidency, following Van Hise's unexpected death, from December 1918 until 1925. Birge's administration, as before, set a transitional tone, awaiting the identification of a younger, more energetic replacement. The transition lasted seven years.

In the interim, crew was reinstituted in 1920, when the faculty agreed to renewed competition between outside clubs and colleges, so long as the distances were less than four miles.

1

The First Race as a "Varsity"— Oconomowoc in 1892

"Rower's ready?" BANG![1]

The crack of the starter's gun rolled out across Lac La Belle.

"One . . . two . . . three . . . four!" the Chicago Navy's coxswain cadenced aloud as his mature oarsmen began the powerful, chopping strokes required for a fast start. In the eight alongside the Chicagoans, the surge of energy through the muscles of the university boys quickly replaced the jitters they'd felt during the start count. The race was on.

The two eight-oared shells heaved down the course toward a small buoy three-quarters of a mile away. The out-and-back course, common in the day, was laid out east-to-west-to-east on Lac La Belle. The line serving as both the start and the finish were just off the lake's eastern shore, near the summer home of Oconomowoc Yacht Club Commodore Ferdinand Peck, a co-organizer along with the Chicago Navy's commodore of the day's regatta. (A Chicago businessman, Peck promoted the design and construction of the Chicago Auditorium Building in the early 1890's—for a time the largest and tallest building in Chicago.)

The Chicago Navy was made up of eleven boat clubs—the Farragut, Delaware, Pullman Athletic, Social Athletic, Union, Iroquois, Ogden, Ontario, Evanston, Catlin, and Quintard. (Several of these clubs would come together after the turn of the century—actually June 8, 1910—to form the Lincoln Park Boat Club of Chicago.) These eleven boat clubs wanted to hold their sixth annual regatta outside of Chicago. Commodore Peck of the Oconomowoc Yacht Club had received the proposal to hold the regatta on Lac La Belle in the July 11 letter from Dewitt Cregier, commodore of the Chicago Navy and former Chicago mayor (1889–1891). Peck quickly accepted. How the Badger crew—the only competitors that day from outside the clubs of the Chicago Navy—came to be invited to this summer regatta is a matter of speculation. It is probable the Navy looked over the likely entrants to the seventeen events of the day and found too many men competing in too many races to be able to fill out two complete boats of eight with enough rested oarsmen. Inviting the boys from the university would solve that.

Jim Henderson, 2-seat in the Chicago Navy eight and a summer member of the Catlin Boat Club, is thought to be the same "James Henderson" listed in *The University Badger Yearbook of 1894* as a member of Wisconsin's 1891–92 intramural crew during the school year. When Chicago's regatta planners made it known a noteworthy opponent was needed for the featured "eight-oared gig" race in August, Chicagoan Henderson probably gave Commodore Cregier the address in Madison of Badger crew captain C. C. "Jimmy" Case.

The invitation—with the Chicago Navy's undoubtedly offering to pick up the Badger's traveling expenses—was then mailed to Madison in late July or early August. Upon opening the Cregier invitation from the Chicago Navy, Case—and soon his teammates—realized their first opponent had been found from outside the limitations of intramural competition.

The year was 1892. The time was 3:30 on the afternoon of August 27 in Oconomowoc, Wisconsin, a popular summer resort village for Chicagoans. Oconomowoc, roughly halfway between Madison and Milwaukee, rests on the shores of the beautiful Lac La Belle.

Cheers from the crowd of 5,000—which included Wisconsin Governor George W. Peck (no apparent relation to Commodore Peck)—soon chased the starter gun's sharp report across the water. Most of the spectators had come by train to Oconomowoc from Madison, Milwaukee, and Chicago. At least five newspapers covered the full day regatta—a boating competition limited exclusively to the eleven boat clubs that made up the Chicago Navy, except for an eight-oared race.

Only the ninth event—"the eight-oared gig" race—included competition from outside the Chicago Navy's eleven clubs. In this race, the eight best rowers from the University of Wisconsin's heretofore-intramural sport of crew were pitted against a "picked crew" of the eight best from the Chicago Navy. Men against kids, the Chicago supporters had told themselves. They hoped the Navy's winning margin wouldn't be too embarrassing for the "university boys."

A composite account of the race would have read:

The Chicago Navy boat jumped ahead with a quicker start and soon enjoyed a several-seat advantage over the Wisco boys. At the half-mile mark, it looked like the brawny men from the Windy City might have to ease up slightly in a show of sportsmanship. The thought of such charity soon passed from their minds.

As the Chicago oarsmen pulled as hard as they could, they closely watched their foe behind them. What they saw, they didn't like. The young Badgers were slowly closing the gap!

In the final quarter-mile of the three-quarter mile outbound leg, the Wisconsin oarsmen began their ever-so-steady row-through of the Chicago boat.

Nothing more demoralizes a straining crew, at the height of its energies, than to see—watching as if in slow motion—the opposition "walk through" their shell's position on the water. Chicago's stroke, Arthur Dixon from the Catlin Boat Club, first lost sight of the passing Badger bowman, then the 2-seat, the 3-, 4-, 5- . . . and finally the coxswain slid by. The university boys were no longer in the view of any of the Navy's rowers and they didn't like the perspective. Only the anxious eyes of the Chicago Navy coxswain could watch the growing separation, as he pleaded with his crew for more power!

The Badger eight, in this first ever non-intramural crew race, made the awkward turn around the buoy. Their smooth handling of the 180-degree reversal of direction—in a sixty-foot shell that wasn't built for this kind of movement—only added to the margin of their lead, as the Chicago men executed a less proficient turn.

With the first three-quarters of a mile behind them, the university boys, directed by coxswain Henry Morgan, headed toward a small red flag ahead of them on the eastern shoreline. Chicago, to their dismay, having had trouble smoothly rounding the only turn, now began to lose more ground. Their early high spirits were changing to emotions of frustration.

Badger stroke Charles "Jimmy" Case, a letterman in four sports at Wisconsin, set the pace on the home leg. Captain of the best eight oarsmen (the "varsity" at the time) selected from the intramural crews, Case was also the right end on Wisconsin's football team. Three other rowers in the boat were also football lettermen. All four found crew an effective spring outlet for their energies and a great way to remain in shape for the fall football season.

Suddenly, Morgan, the coxswain, realized the point he had picked on the horizon was an extraneous shore flag, not the one marking the finish! Morgan had to quickly, but not too quickly, find and point to a better bearing on the horizon. Nothing annoys an oarsman more than seeing the boat's wake fishtailing down the course as a coxswain steers an inefficient course by wandering down his "lane." The crew could also see the Chicago Navy behind them, halting what had been a widening gap.

The coxswain explained his error through the primitive megaphone strapped to his face. Case, at stroke, raised the rate with a hard "ten" (a series of power strokes meant to cause both a surge forward in one's own boat and to serve as an intimidating discouragement to one's opponents). The Badgers again widened their lead and sped smoothly closer to the finish line.

The Badger rowers were greeted by the cheers of the big crowd watching from the lake's eastern shore as well as from canoes, rowboats, and sailboats along the racecourse. The finish line was just offshore from Commodore Peck's home at 420 Lake Road.

Commodore Peck's Oconomowoc house near start of race against the Chicago Navy, 1892. Source: *The Milwaukee Sentinel.* August 28, 1892.

The *Milwaukee Journal* of the following day described the finish:

The admirers of the crack Chicagoans saw the gig of those college youngsters cut the waters between the finish flags with its sharp prow a full thirty lengths ahead of their brawny opponents, and as the commodore's flag dropped when the winners glided past the stake, a cheer was wafted over the waters from the gay and pretty gathering on shore, and as the students rested on their oars, the sonorous notes of "U-Rah-Rah-Wis-con-sin" chased the dainty cheers into the groves across the lake, propelled by the lusty lungs of the college boys who had seen their crew win the silken trophy from the big city of the Northwest.

Rowing in the *Rheola* in a time of 10:46, the university boys had finished their first extramural competition with a decisive win! The birth of a true varsity men's crew at Wisconsin was recorded as a victory!

As was true with many oarsmen to follow, these nine outstanding university athletes were also outstanding students. The bowman John Freeman, after captaining and playing left tackle on the UW football team, became a surgeon; he died prematurely, fighting an pneumonia outbreak in Topeka, Kansas, in 1919.

J. F. A. Pyre, after several seasons at right tackle, became an English professor at UW and served on its faculty for more than forty years. During one of the periods of lean years for crew at Wisconsin (from 1915 to 1923, when crew was

16   **THE FIRST RACE AS A 'VARSITY'**

W. T. SAUCERMAN.   J. D. FREEMAN.   H. MORGAN, Coxswain.   H. H. JACOBS.   A. E. COE.   C. C. CASE.   O. ROHN.   J. F. A. PYRE.
H. B. BOARDMAN.

banned from the four-mile Poughkeepsie Regatta by the medical and administrative faculty because of perceived health concerns), Pyre provided thoughtful support for the crew. From his position as the Wisconsin faculty representative on the Athletic Council (1912–31), Pyre provided moral encouragement to Coach O'Dea and wrote favorably of the men's crew tradition at Wisconsin, including in his history of the university, *Wisconsin*.

A guard on the football team, 4-seat Herb Jacobs, along with his wife Mary Belle, would later be recognized, as the founders of organized social work (women's and family services) in Wisconsin. Harry Boardman, who held the one-mile record in track at UW for nineteen years, became an advertising executive in Chicago.

Oscar Rohn, 7-seat, became a wealthy mining engineer from investing in Minnesota's Baraboo iron range. He, too, would die prematurely, killed while testing mining equipment of his own design in Butte, Montana, in 1923.

Stroke Charles "Jimmy" Case from Prairie du Chien is listed in UW Athletic

1892 varsity crew (against the Chicago Navy, the first nonintramural opponent). Source: *1894 Badger Yearbook*, p. 133. Courtesy of UW–Madison Archives. Wisconsin's initial varsity victory boating: John D. Freeman (bow), James Francis Augustine Pyre, E. J. Olmstad, Herbert Henry Jacobs, Ray Gilchrist, Harry Bingham Boardman, Oscar Rohn, Captain Charles Chester "Jimmy" Case (stroke), and Henry Hotchkiss Morgan (cox).

THE FIRST RACE AS A 'VARSITY'   17

Department journals as winning letters in crew, football, track, and wrestling (the last perhaps as a result of a special one-time representation of UW, since wrestling as a formal varsity sport had not yet begun). He later became an attorney in Chicago. Coxswain Henry Morgan, born and raised locally, became an attorney in Madison. He served in New York during World War I with the predecessor agency of the Federal Bureau of Investigation and was later a municipal judge in Madison.

✕

On the evening of that first race, a large banquet was held at Oconomowoc's most posh summer resort hotel, Draper Hall, just across the road from Commodore Peck's home and not far from the regatta's start and finish line off the shore of Lac La Belle. The Second Regimental band of Illinois, sent up by train the night before by the Chicago Navy to start the festivities, gave a concert for the evening's celebrants.

To the victorious Badger crew, Chicago Navy Commodore Cregier donated a blue silk banner. Presented to the crew by Wisconsin Governor George W. Peck, it read,

Sixth Annual Regatta
Chicago Navy.
Oconomowoc, Wisconsin
August 27, 1892.
Eight Oared Race
Won by the University of Wisconsin
Presented by D. C. Cregier, Jr.

The banner hung for many years in the trophy case of the Old Red Armory. The last mention of the victory pennant appeared in a Crew Fund capital campaign solicitation brochure of 1979, where the "faded blue ribbon" was described as being in the "UW Athletic Office Trophy Room." The original silken banner cannot be found today.

While racing against clubs from outside the University of Wisconsin soon evolved to racing other college and university crews, varsity crew at Wisconsin began that Saturday afternoon, August 27, 1892, on Lac La Belle in the summer resort town of Oconomowoc, Wisconsin. The victory was a most favorable beginning.

2
UW President Adams Makes Crew a Priority

Following UW's fortuitous invitation to the Chicago Navy's sixth annual regatta in August, Wisconsin's crew fortunes took another serendipitous turn. In the very next month of September 1892, Charles Kendall Adams was named president of the University of Wisconsin. It was he who penned the famous "Magna Carta" of the University of Wisconsin in a report sent to the Board of Regents in 1894. The passage read: "the . . . University of Wisconsin should ever encourage that continual and fearless shifting and winnowing by which alone the truth can be found."

Adams, formerly president of Cornell University in western upstate New York, had seen firsthand how that university's international notoriety had been significantly advanced by the great successes of its rowing program.

Trained under the strong hand of the legendary former sculler Charles E. Courtney, Cornell's crew teams had become almost unbeatable. Following some part-time coaching of the successful Cornell crews from 1883 to 1888, Courtney became the permanent head coach at Cornell in 1889. Between 1884 and 1895, no Cornell varsity crew was defeated. This was in spite of racing against opponents with strong, often older, rowing programs—Harvard, Penn, New York Rowing Club, Yale, and Columbia.

UW President Charles Kendall Adam's appreciation for the sport of crew has already been described. During his prior presidency at Cornell College, which ended in the fall of 1892, Adams was strongly influenced by the successes of that school's legendary crew coach, Charles Courtney.

Charles Edward "Pop" Courtney (1849–1920) was born in Union Springs, New

UW president Charles Kendall Adams, the crew's first supporter. Source: photo of portrait by J. R. Stuart. Courtesy of UW–Madison Archives.

York, on the northeastern shores of Lake Cayuga. There he learned all about boats and rowing. Over his lifetime, Courtney, an amateur and professional rower before turning to coaching, had gone undefeated over eighty-eight amateur races, and won forty-six and lost seven as a professional.[1] His record as the Cornell crew coach was equally impressive.

Cornell crew coach Charles Courtney. Source: *1952 IRA Program.* Courtesy of the IRA Stewards.

To gain an appreciation for Charles Courtney's discipline and leadership style as a coach, a story from 1897 is noting telling here, as recounted by Bob Kane in his history of Cornell athletics, *Good Sports—A History of Cornell Athletics:*

> Courtney was an absolute despot on training discipline. Positively no drinking or smoking in or out of season, walk to and from campus to the boathouse, and follow a strict nutritional diet were among his rules. He learned that five of his varsity . . . yielded to the seduction of strawberry shortcake. He dropped them out of hand, summoned substitutes, and won the Poughkeepsie Regatta two weeks later (twice, in 1897) with what was ever afterward known as "the strawberry shortcake crew."
>
> By contrast, at the Harvard camp, where there was a small "retinue of servants," the men enjoyed a glass of claret at every meal save breakfast and a goblet of champagne after a particularly hard day's work.

President Adams understood the value of publicity, and sports was one way to get it. He was a fan of football and crew, and he did everything he could to promote the two sports. His first opportunity to assist the crew came quickly.

The minutes of meetings in May of 1886 tell of the Wisconsin University Boat Club's formation. One of the club's founders was Professor Edward A. Birge, who later became acting president of the university from 1900 through 1902 and again from 1918 to 1925. During the summer of 1892, the "Boat Club," an aggregation of athlete, student, and faculty supporters, began construction of a boathouse at the university on a site between the Old Red Gym and the shore of Lake Mendota.

In the first of a long series of financial struggles to challenge the success and even the existence of a crew at Wisconsin, boathouse construction stalled in the fall of 1892, as student subscriptions and sponsor funds failed to keep up with construction costs. In December of 1892, President Adams chaired "the largest meeting in the history of the college," which led—after some further negotiation with prior investors—to the formation of the University Boat-House Company.[2] The necessary additional funding ($3,000 on top of the $1,500 already spent) was arranged through the issuance of the Company's shares.

Construction of the boathouse resumed in March of 1893 and was completed by May, two months later. The 72' x 80' building had room, with overhead storage, for eighty small boats and several racing shells.

University Boathouse with the Red Gym behind. Source: c.1904 postcard; image same as Wisconsin State Historical Society Negative # WHI (X3)31488.

ADAMS MAKES CREW A PRIORITY

An interesting sidelight to the boathouse's financing is the story of varsity oarsman W. T. Saucerman, one of the early investors in the building of the boathouse. Though nothing is known of the magnitude of his investment, the sum must have been large for him, as he was later forced to appeal to the university regents, in 1896, to have his law school tuition waived, pleading poverty as a result of his boathouse undertaking. Happily for him, his appeal was successful.

That same spring of 1893 in which the boathouse was completed, a used paper shell, Wisconsin's third boat, was purchased from Harvard University. A fourth shell, a new one from Waters & Sons of Troy, New York, was acquired with funds donated by Captain Frederick Pabst, the former skipper of a Great Lakes steamboat. Pabst, after marrying the daughter of beer entrepreneur Phillip Best (founder, in 1844, of a brewery on Chestnut Hill in Milwaukee, when Wisconsin was still a territory) acquired half of Best's beer business.

In one of the season's few races, Wisconsin faced the Delaware Boat Club, one of the eleven member clubs of the Chicago Navy. The race was a long one—with a two-mile straightaway course agreed upon. The Delawares and Badgers fought it out the entire way, but at the finish, the crew from Chicago won by three feet. After eleven minutes and forty seconds—the Delaware's winning time—the Badgers had been nipped by fractions of a second. Coaching of the crew during that 1892–93 season came from the older rowers, including Jimmy Case, W. T. Saucerman, and Herb Jacobs.

Following the 1893 crew season, and directly encouraged by President and Mrs. Adams, rower J. F. A. Pyre joined the English faculty of the university in 1893 and, after receiving his Ph.D., was named Associate Professor of English at UW in 1909.

Amos T. Marston, Wisconsin's first crew coach (part-time coach in 1894). Source: *The Cornell Navy* by C. V. P. Young, 1907, p. 31.

Wisconsin's First Crew Coach

In the spring of 1894, President Adams continued his active support of the crew's development. Using Cornell as a model, where Charles Courtney had been initially employed as a part-time crew coach (1883–88), Adams arranged similar short-term assistance for Wisconsin's crew.

Adams hired former Cornell rowing captain, Amos T. Marston, who had rowed for four years (1889–1892) under Coach Courtney. Adams had probably gotten to know Marston in 1892, where the two spent their last years at Cornell. Before the Badgers raced the Delawares again and the Minnesota Boat Club later in the summer of 1894, Marston gave the young oarsmen a few weeks of training, their first by a hired coach.

Oscar Rohn, the 7-seat in the first victory against the Chicago Navy in 1892, was the crew captain in 1893–94. The arrival of Wisconsin's first crew coach, a disciple of the master Charles Courtney himself, resulted in a great deal of excitement within Rohn's crew. The possibilities of a higher-profile rowing program at Wisconsin stirred them all.

Marston's short-term coaching assignment helped the young Badgers prepare for their old foes. His direction proved valuable, as Wisconsin came out victorious this time over the Delaware Boat Club of Chicago.

J. F. A. Pyre, in his history of the university, wrote of a five-year racing series between Wisconsin and the Minnesota Boat Club (1894–1898; the 1897 and 1898 results were never found, however). The events were sponsored, as boat races had often been sponsored in the East, by the hotel industry of a lakeside tourist destination. For this series of regattas, the hotels around Lake Minnetonka in Minnesota hosted the crews from Madison and from the Minnesota Boat Club, in an effort to attract visitors to their establishments for a summer weekend.

Competing for the Schlitz Trophy, donated by another major Milwaukee brewery, the Badgers traveled to what is likely to have been their first out-of-state race, a competition against the Minnesota Boat Club in the summer of 1894. The race on Lake Minnetonka was a two-mile straightaway course. As described later in the *Daily Cardinal,* the Badgers "lost a close race principally because of inexperience and a slow boat."

In the fall of 1894, President Adams stepped in again. Now, Wisconsin's crew was to have a full-time professional crew coach.

President Adams lured Andrew M. O'Dea (1868–1936) from the Lurline Boat Club (now named the Minnesota Rowing Club). It is known that O'Dea visited Madison on November 17, 1894, to attend the Minnesota-Wisconsin football game, won 6–0 by Wisconsin. He must have liked what he saw, for he returned to Madison in mid-February of 1895 to take over the crew coaching position at UW.

A professional sculler himself, O'Dea had been a member of many winning boats in the Melbourne, Calea, and Geelong and Barrow regattas, usually as a member of the Yarra Yarra Rowing Club of Melbourne, Victoria, Australia. The rowing club, which exists to this day, is named after the Yarra Yarra River, on which it is located.

Born December 4, 1868, in Kilmore, Victoria, Australia, O'Dea had come to the United States around 1894 as part of the entourage of "Paddy" Slavin, an aspiring Australian boxer hoping to earn a world championship fight with John L. Sullivan. Slavin lost too many matches to accomplish this, so O'Dea returned to coaching in Minneapolis.

O'Dea gave the Wisconsin crew another boost in self-esteem, and with a full-

Andrew M. O'Dea, coach 1894–98 and 1899–1906. Source: *1897 Badger Yearbook,* p. 143. Courtesy of UW–Madison Archives.

time coach the nature of the sport would change dramatically. The oldest sport on campus, crew at Wisconsin had begun as an intramural sport in 1874.[3] Together with football and baseball, crew was one of three sports that enjoyed high visibility on campus. With the addition of a full-time coach, crew would attract even more attention from the alumni, business donors, the press, students, faculty, and, most importantly, other rowing competitors.

The new coach taught them what the press soon labeled "the Kangaroo stroke." To stay in condition over the winter, the training included work on rowing machines in the new boathouse or in the balconies of the Old Red Gym. Other times, O'Dea had the boys push a red boat cart across the ice from the boathouse to the mouth of the Yahara River between Lakes Mendota and Monona, and then unload the shells and row on the open water of the river.

Watching the ice melt off Lake Mendota—on average, the shells got on the lake on April 7 each spring—Wisconsin's rowing coaches would always worry about the boys getting as much "water time" as did the other college crews with milder weather on the East and West Coasts. Before an indoor rowing tank was built, coaches would forever be looking for ways to exercise and to hold the training interest of their athletes over the long Wisconsin winters.

As the 1895 spring crew season began, Wisconsin faced its old foes, the Delawares from Chicago. Incorporating what they had learned from O'Dea, the Badgers again defeated the Chicagoans by two lengths, despite breaking an oar.[4]

Later in the season, the Badgers returned to Lake Minnetonka to race the Minnesota Boat Club. Although recording their fastest two-mile time ever (10:23), Wisconsin was edged out again by one second.

✕

On January 11, 1895, President Adams joined the university presidents of Chicago, Illinois, Michigan, Minnesota, Northwestern, and Purdue to organize and adopt twelve initial rules for a Midwestern Athletic Conference. This organization was later known as the Intercollegiate Conference of Faculty Representatives, then as the Western Conference. We know it today as the Big Ten.

Around this same time, serendipity struck again for Wisconsin athletics. UW President Adam's attention to crew paid off with a surprising benefit in another sport. The positive turn in the prowess of UW athletics would follow crew coach O'Dea's invitation to his younger brother, then living in Australia, to visit him in Madison.

Andrew O'Dea's younger brother, a soccer and rugby player in Australia, came to visit Andrew in Madison in the summer of 1896. A vigorous young athlete, the younger brother soon found a playing field and some students to join him in a game. The kicking skills of the crew coach's brother quickly became the talk of

Wisconsin Crew Out for Row on Yahara River

Yahara River practice.
Courtesy of UW–Madison Archives Negative X252 162.

the student athletes on campus. His kicking distance and accuracy were at a level not seen before in the United States. Word quickly spread to Wisconsin's football coaching staff.

Because field goals were worth five points under the rules of football before the turn of the century, kicking was a highly sought-after skill. It was not long before Coach O'Dea's brother Patrick was persuaded to enroll, as a twenty-four-year old freshman, at Wisconsin and to play varsity football beginning in the fall of 1896. Pat O'Dea's legendary kicking and huge contributions to the success of UW's football team—he once kicked a 110-yard punt against Minnesota in 1897 and a 60-yard-plus dropkick against Minnesota in 1899, the longest successful dropkick in football history—are now part of the permanent sports history at Wisconsin.

President Adams's goal of gaining national fame and recognition for University of Wisconsin through sports had now been accomplished. Pat O'Dea also proved to be a dependable supporter of Wisconsin crew. During the team's West Coast visits to race the University of California at Berkeley in the 1950s, O'Dea regularly greeted the crews at the airport or train station and, along with other UW alumni supporters in the area, hosted the visiting athletes to some sightseeing around the San Francisco Bay area.

Birth of the Intercollegiate Rowing Association

For college crew nationally, as well as at Wisconsin, the year 1895 would be an auspicious one.

Yale, in the 1890s, preferred dual or, at most, three-way meets and sought races on the narrow Thames or Housatonic rivers in Connecticut, while Harvard wanted to prepare for and race only Yale over certain training periods and on certain weekends of the season. This Yale–Harvard rivalry began in 1852 and was the nation's first intercollegiate sporting event. Frustrated with having to work around Yale and Harvard racing season prerequisites, the universities of Columbia, Cornell, and Pennsylvania organized to host their own national regatta.

Malcolm Alama, in his *Mark of the Oarsman*, a history of Syracuse rowing, saw another reason for the three schools to organize: "Rowing offered a splendid opportunity of carving a niche in national collegiate athletics."

After reviewing several venues over the fall and winter of 1894, the three-man committee, one from each of the three founding schools, chose the Hudson River course passing by Poughkeepsie, New York. The first Poughkeepsie Regatta, later known as the IRA, was held in June of 1895.

Only a single varsity eights race was held by the Poughkeepsie Regatta stewards that first year. A freshman eights event would be added in 1896 and a four without coxswain in 1899 (the event was then called the "University Fours" and later, the "straight four," which can be shorthanded as "4." As an historical footnote, a one and one-half-mile single skull event was held in 1901, won by Syracuse). These University Fours races were held from 1899 through 1913 and replaced in 1914 by a junior varsity eight or "second varsity" event (shorthanded as JV8 or 2V8 or simply as jayvee). The straight four event would not return to the IRA regatta's format again until 1974.

The first IRA in 1895 turned out to be an especially memorable race. An estimated 30,000 spectators, arriving mostly by train, crowded into Poughkeepsie on race day Fri-

continued on facing page

day morning. Harvard and Yale—undoubtedly invited—were not in attendance but were instead preparing for their long-standing New London race on the Thames River in Connecticut four days later.

At about the race's scheduled starting time, a tug carrying New York's Governor Levi P. Morton washed the Penn boat into a float (pier) so strongly that the shell was damaged beyond immediate repair. Postponed for one day while Penn made repairs, the races were then postponed a second day because the weather had turned so bad.

Finally getting off the four-mile race on Sunday, the favored Penn boat swamped halfway down the course, as the Columbia and Cornell shells continued racing for the finish. When Cornell also swamped close to the end, Columbia found itself rowing across the finish line uncontested.

Hamilton Fish, Columbia's winning coxswain that day, would be killed in action only three years later, as one of Teddy Roosevelt's Rough Riders in his famous charge up San Juan Hill.

As a result of a bloody fight after their annual football game in the fall of 1894, all Harvard–Yale athletic contests would be suspended for two years, beginning the fall of the 1895. This interruption of the annual Harvard–Yale "Boat Race" allowed Harvard's heavyweight eight to row in the IRAs in 1896 and 1897.

Yale's heavyweight eight, until 2003, would compete in the IRAs only once—in 1897—although Yale would force Cornell to race two separate four-mile Poughkeepsie Regattas one week apart in order to accommodate Yale's demand for a three-way, rather than a four- or five-way, meet.[5] After 1897, neither Harvard nor Yale's heavyweight men's eights would row again in the IRAs for nearly one hundred years. Harvard's eight would finish fourth in 1995, and in 2003 and '04 both schools again came to the IRAs, with Harvard winning the varsity eight race for a first and second time.

But for this early and fleeting interest of a year or two from Harvard and Yale, Wisconsin became the first nonfounding school invited to the IRAs. In 1898 the Badgers raced in the Poughkeepsie Regatta and became the event's longest-attending crew, except for the earlier participation by three years of the three original founders—Columbia, Cornell, and Pennsylvania.

In 1921 both Syracuse University and the U.S. Naval Academy joined the original three founding schools to become the permanent stewards of this annual national college regatta, originally called the Poughkeepsie Regatta and now called the Intercollegiate Rowing Association Championships.

The IRAs continue to this day.

3

The Badgers' First Collegiate Opponent—Yale in 1896

The ice broke early on Lake Mendota in the spring of 1896. On Saturday, April 4, two new shells were delivered to the boathouse, one a coxed pair and the other a straight pair. On Monday, April 6, five men, anxious to try out the newest additions to Wisconsin's fleet, watched the morning storm blow through the noon hour. When the winds paused, the five pushed off in the two boats and headed for Picnic Point northwest of the boathouse—with Coach Andrew O'Dea in the bow of the first shell, L. C. Street ('98) at the stroke in the straight pair. and C. C. McConville ('98) in the bow, sophomore letter-winner John F. Day ('98) at stroke, and Pat O'Dea as the coxswain in the second shell.

Halfway to the Point, the winds returned, swamping both boats and sending all five into the icy, early-spring waters of Lake Mendota. All clung to their capsized shells awaiting help from the distant shore. When rescuers finally arrived, Day had lost his grip on the upside-down shell and disappeared beneath the water. His body was not recovered for several hours.

Wisconsin's first intercollegiate competitor was the Yale freshman crew in 1896. The race was held June 18 on Lake Saltonstall in Connecticut. To travel, the crew needed to raise funds from students, faculty, parents, alums, and local businesses. Interviewed in the *Wisconsin State Journal* of May 6, 1951, Walter Alexander, the crew captain in 1896, recalled the trip preparation:

> Someone . . . I don't remember now who that public-spirited citizen was . . . had given us a new shell. The Badger crew had never gone east before that year; it never was able to raise the price of train tickets or shipping costs. But we went out and raised $600 for the trip. The Madison and Milwaukee businessmen, the professors on the hill, everyone contributed something for that trip. We had to win. And win we did.

This first trip east, and the fund-raising necessary to make it happen, led to increased responsibilities of the "crew commodore." Following the example of many eastern teams, the commodore, usually not a rowing member of the crew, would spend much of his spring each year seeking donations and backers as well as creating fundraising opportunities. Money was solicited on a regular basis from students—sometimes from button sales by fraternities and sororities and sometimes through a club's sharing of concert, theater, or prom revenues. Donors were found among alums, parents, businesses, and other friends of crew. UW's crew commodores routinely raised the funds necessary to defray the train travel, accommodations, food, and the shell-shipping expenses incurred by the Badger crews, who participated in the Poughkeepsie Regatta each year.

Walter Alexander, the 1896 captain, would later be one of three founding members of the Wisconsin Crew Corporation in 1931 (the Corporation's successor is the Wisconsin Rowing Association, or WRA). Alexander was also a regular individual benefactor of men's crew. The Wisconsin Crew Corporation and the WRA, today a registered booster club under the regulations of the NCAA, grew to replace the role of crew commodore and has been a major supporter for more than seventy years. The Wisconsin crews of today, like those in many older college rowing programs, stand on the shoulders of many oarsmen and supporters who came before them.

1896 program cover. Yale freshmen vs. Wisconsin. Courtesy of Brad and Fran Taylor.

Why the Badger varsity raced the Yale freshmen of 1896, and not the Yale varsity, requires some explanation. The well-known rowing historian, Thomas Mendenhall, in his *The Harvard-Yale Boat Race 1852–1924*,[1] describes the first step of this complicated story:

> The Harvard faculty had initiated . . . the suspension of all athletic contests between Harvard and Yale in 1895–96 . . . motivated by the brutality of [their] 1894 football game. All games and races between Harvard and Yale had been indefinitely suspended at the end of the academic year 1894–95.

The interruption in the rivalry lasted only for the year 1895–96. As a result, the annual Harvard-Yale "Boat Race" of the early summer of 1896 was canceled. This crew rivalry, first raced in 1852, had been the first intercollegiate sports contest in the United States. When all competition between the two schools was suspended, the Yale varsity went to England that June to try their luck at the Royal Henley Regatta, leaving their freshmen to face Wisconsin.

Rowing sportswriter Casper Whitney previewed the Yale freshman–Wisconsin varsity race in the *Harper's Weekly* of June 20, 1896:

The Wisconsin Varsity[2] will row Yale Freshman on Lake Saltonstall, New Haven, next Thursday, and has an opportunity of a college lifetime, for the Yale crew is one of the poorest that university has had in many a day. As Wisconsin has no college superior on Western waters, we shall be able to make a very accurate estimate of Western rowing.

Whitney later filed a story of the race results, published July 18:

Wisconsin caught the water first, at a racing stroke of 40, which was lowered by 4 points at the quarter mile, where they had a lead of a half boat-length. Steadily gaining, they were at the mile rowing easily (at 35) and cleanly, while Yale was pulling 38–39, in poor form, and splashing and falling behind. The space between the two boats increased as they neared the two-mile mark, and when Wisconsin finished in 12:06.4, Yale was about ten lengths behind and crossed 34 seconds later.

The Wisconsin varsity eight won so easily their two mile race with the Yale Freshman June 18, on Lake Saltonstall that we feel that we really only half knew the capabilities of the Western crew. But we do know that the blade work and the bodywork of this Wisconsin eight were not very much inferior to the best we saw at Poughkeepsie last week.

They sat up to their work with good backs, caught the water hard and together, left it neatly, and withal had an excellent body swing with a leg drive.

All in all, the crew was somewhat of a revelation to Eastern men of the attainments of Western crews. But in truth this crew may not be taken as criterion of general Western rowing, for it is considerably in advance of its college neighbors. The conditions were unfavorable for fast rowing on the 18th, with a strong head wind and roughish water, and trying, too, to a crew averaging only 152 pounds, as did Wisconsin, against Yale's 164. Moreover, the Westerners lost the toss and the choice of course, and were not in their best condition. So they certainly enjoyed no advantages.

It is true the Yale Freshman crew was one of the poorest, if not the worst, which has come out of New Haven in recent years, but that does not alter the fact that Wisconsin showed decided rowing skill and good stroke.

This Western 'varsity seems too light to stand the work of a four-mile race, but if Wisconsin can turn out a Freshman crew in such good form we should like to see it entered at Poughkeepsie next year.

In January of 1897, an indoor tank was completed alongside the University Boat-House, giving the Badgers for the first time the opportunity to feel the pull on the water on a daily basis throughout the winter.[3]

In the spring of 1897, Wisconsin returned to Lake Saltonstall for a rematch, this time facing a Yale varsity that had just broken its own record for a two-mile course with a time of 10:54. A crowd of 5,000 watched the contest.

"Crack!" reported the starter's pistol, as the two crews jumped off their start.

Spurting ahead from the start, Yale held a forty-per-minute stroke pace for the first quarter-mile.

At the quarter-mile mark, Yale settled to a 32-stroke rate and Wisconsin to a 34. At the mile mark, Yale had an open water lead of one length, where it further lowered its stroke rate to 30. Wisconsin kept its pace up and closed the gap to a half-length of open water but could not gain further ground.

At the finish, Yale crossed first with a half-length of open water victory.

Wisconsin's First Poughkeepsie Regatta

In 1898 Wisconsin attended its first Poughkeepsie Regatta, although the race was held, uncharacteristically, on Lake Saratoga in New York. The move from the Hudson River was made for several reasons. The Spanish-American War had given cause to both the modest threat of the Spanish sending a warship or two up the wide-open and accessible Hudson River and to the war-related curtailment of the availability of the West Shore Railroad's spectator train along the Hudson River racecourse. Perhaps most important, because of the strong sponsorship by the local lake resort industry, the regatta was moved from the Hudson River in Poughkeepsie, New York, to Lake Saratoga.

For the next fourteen years, Wisconsin would be referred to as the "westerners" by the eastern press covering the event. Not until Stanford attended the regatta in 1912 would there truly be a western participant at the Poughkeepsie.

Unable to persuade Harvard and Yale to row at Poughkeepsie, Cornell rowed a four-mile race and beat both Harvard and Yale on June 23 on the Thames River in Connecticut. Just over a week later, a slightly fatigued Cornell lost to Penn on a three-mile course on Lake Saratoga in a race that included Wisconsin and Columbia. Wisconsin showed well in the race, coming in a respectable third place, behind winner Penn and second-place Cornell. Columbia finished fourth.

The Badgers must have looked pretty well coached, because Harvard promptly hired away Andrew O'Dea! His new job was overseeing their University Boathouse crew, one of Harvard's two boathouses. Each of the two crews, and their coaches, fell under the overall supervision of head coach Edward C. "Ned" Storrow. The season O'Dea coached at Harvard was two or three years before Harry Emerson "Dad" Vail, a former Harvard oarsman and crew captain (1893) and future Wisconsin coach, would begin coaching at Harvard in 1902. To replace O'Dea, Wisconsin named Curran C. McConville, captain of the 1897–98 crew, to the head coaching position, effective the fall of 1898.

Once back in the Midwest, the Badgers traveled to Lake Minnetonka for their annual matchup with the Minnesota Boat Club[4] (10:45) and defeated them, in a two-mile race into a headwind, by a quarter-length in a time of 10:42. With the victory, "the massive Schlitz cup of silver and gold reverts to the possession of the Wisconsin crew."[5] The crew also bested the Delawares from Chicago during the same season.

※

On the Badgers' return from New Haven to Madison by train, the *New York Times* reported their brief visit to Poughkeepsie to view the course and the practicing crews,

> The University of Wisconsin crew arrived here to-day at noon in a buffet sleeper over the New-York Central Railroad, and left to-night at 8:05 for Wisconsin. They came on invitation of J. W. McCullough, Commodore of the Cornell navy, and viewed the preliminary work of the crews from the Cornell launch. The rumor that the Westerners would enter the intercollegiate contest was absurd, because they were barred out of it months ago.
>
> Manager Rohn said, "Under no circumstances could his crew enter the race because they had made overtures months ago, but the colleges were unwilling to admit them." Before leaving, the visitors walked over the big railroad bridge over the Hudson.[6]

In the Poughkeepsie Regatta of 1896, the freshman eight two-mile event was added. The frosh finish: Cornell, Harvard, Penn, and Columbia. The order of finish was the same in the four-mile varsity event.

UNIVERSITY OF WISCONSIN CREW

Above: UW crew photo in the 1896 Yale-Wisconsin program. Wisconsin's boating against Yale: William Dietrich (bow), Walter Alexander (Captain), Seymour E. Marshall, Lester F. Street, Harry G. Forrest, Lee Austin, Albert F. Alexander, Curran C. McConville (stroke), and Harry Crandall (cox). Coach Vail is at the center of the back row.

Right: Coach Curran C. McConville, coach 1898–99. Source: *Leslie's Weekly*, July 27, 1899, p. 61.

4
The Berry Crate Crew of 1899

Curran C. McConville (1877–1937) would serve only one year as Wisconsin's head crew coach for the 1898–99 season, but the crew year would become a memorable one! He had, in his college career, won three letters from 1896 through 1898 and was the crew's captain for the 1897–98 season. McConville graduated with a degree in engineering. McConville would also supply the future impetus, over a cup of coffee at the Wisconsin Memorial Union during the fall of 1928, to organize the Wisconsin Crew Corporation, the university's first athletic booster club.

With the help of more fund-raising at Wisconsin in the spring of 1899, the university sent its second crew to Poughkeepsie and thus several more threads were added to the tapestry of the Wisconsin crew tradition. This Badger crew would enter the fable and lore of the university's sports history as the "Berry Crate" crew.

The story is most accurately understood from reading newspaper accounts of the day. One of the best and most thorough accounts appeared on the front page of the June 28, 1899, *New York Times*. The headline and story read:

PENNSYLVANIA WINS
AT POUGHKEEPSIE
Wisconsin, Leading Almost to the Finish, Loses by Bad Steering
PENNSYLVANIA, First; Time, 20:04.
WISCONSIN, Second; Time, 20:05½.
CORNELL, Third; Time, 20:13.
COLUMBIA, Fourth; Time, 20:20.

Poughkeepsie, N.Y., June 27—Pennsylvania's university eight won the intercollegiate boat race here this afternoon, after the finest contest in the history of boat racing. The crew from the University of Wisconsin was second, beaten by a half-length, after the gamest kind of race, and beaten only because her coxswain steered the crew far out of the course in the last mile, and so lost the race that was practically won.

It is estimated that 20,000 persons saw the greatest race ever rowed at the distance of four miles, on any course in America.

[Along the shore] There were forty-eight cars on the train, with a powerful

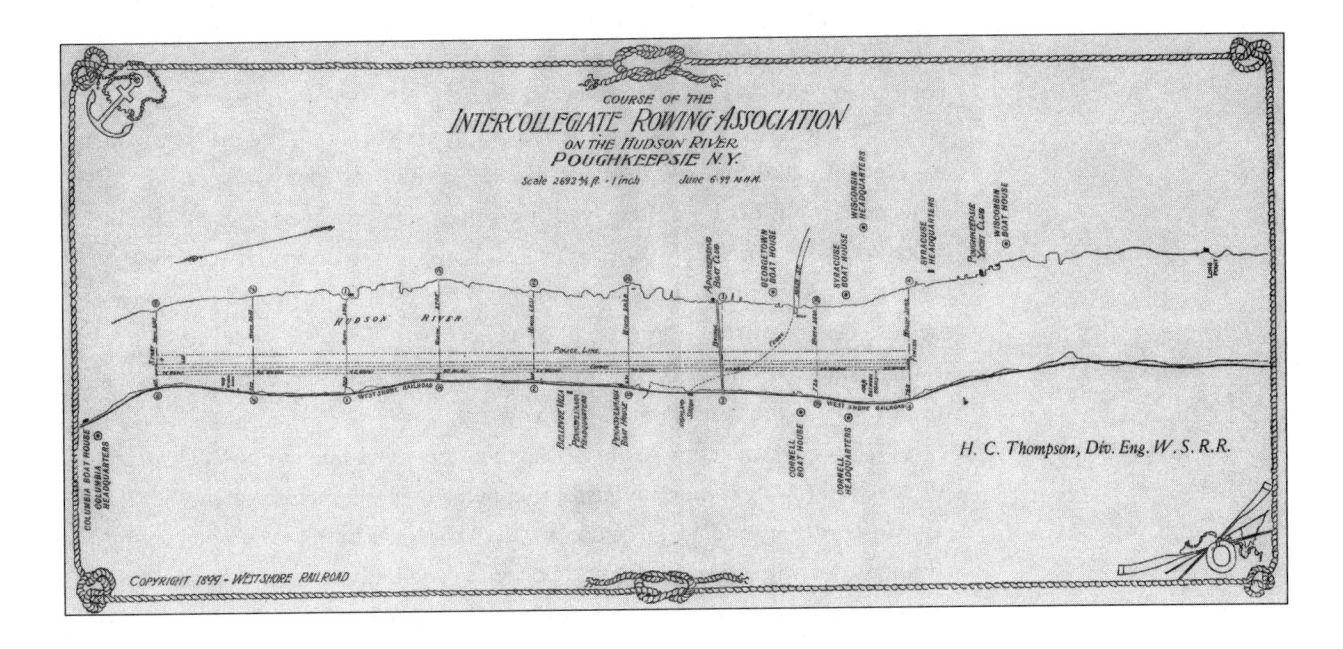

1899 Hudson River course diagram from the Poughkeepsie Regatta program. Courtesy of Brad and Fran Taylor.

locomotive at each end of the moving grandstand. It was a glowing, surging, singing throng, that made merry all afternoon.

Anchored in the river opposite were half a dozen excursion steamers and a score or so of sizable yachts, steam and sailing crafts. Of the lot were the Ballantine yacht *Juanita,* dressed from stem to stern in rainbow fashion, with a couple hundred flags of Cornell, red and white, and one of the prettiest sights on the course.

Pennsylvanians Arrive First

The Pennsylvanian's launch, *Ben Franklin,* with members of the crew, Coach Ward in command, was the first of the contestants to put in an appearance at the start. They reached there at 6:10 [P.M.]. Brown and brawny, most of them were stripped to the waist. They were perfect types of athletes when they threw aside huge bath towels with which their shoulders had been covered on their trip up the river. The new cedar shell was in tow of the launch and was carried up 100 feet above the line where the stakeboats were anchored. There the Quakers awaited the arrival of their rivals.

The Pennsylvania launch circled about near the start for three-quarters of an hour when the lot of starters was increased by the arrival of Columbia at 6:40 o'clock; the boys having rowed up the river in their shell. There was a hot greeting for the Columbia, but hardly a welcome for the Wisconsin boys, who were less than a minute behind the boys from New York. Two minutes later Cornell came down from her quarters to Red Top, a short distance above the start. Her arrival was as notably greeted as any of the others.

THE BERRY CRATE CREW OF 1899

Cheers for Wisconsin

Then there was an almost simultaneous and pretty bit of college sentiment shown by partisans of all the colleges. They saw and pitied Wisconsin's friendless condition and the boys from Columbia, Cornell and Pennsylvania alike all along the length of the train, gave their college cry, followed in each case by thrice repeated shrieks of "Wisconsin, Wisconsin, Wisconsin!" It was all very pretty and gave heart to the gallant lads from the West, who proved themselves the real heroes of the afternoon. The cheers were for plucky strangers in a strange land, and not for men who were unexpectedly to prove themselves heroes worthy of the best foeman's steed or oars.

. . . [I]t was a trifle after 7:30 o'clock when the crews lined up for a fair start. All caught the water when the pistol snapped and all seemed to catch with the same force, deeply and well. For the first dozen strokes there was no perceptible advantage for any one of the eights. Cornell's crew had the outer course, which was to be the most advantageous. Columbia was next to her. Then came the brawny Pennsylvanians, and on the extreme western course were the unknowns from Wisconsin, the crew without friends before the race was rowed, but with as many friends after it was over as had any of the crews.

"If those fellows from Milwaukee can do anything in their position against the fast Cornell boys, with the best place on the course as theirs, then they are simply wonders," remarked a veteran of Pennsylvania who had rowed in the crew in 1895 [the first IRA].

How Wisconsin Lost

Even as the shells of the first two crews reached the very last half-mile mark, the Wisconsins still had a half length the best of it, and but for the erratic course followed by their coxswain would in all probability have taken back with them to Wisconsin the trophy and the honors of beating a splendid lot of oarsmen, probably the very best in the East.

Whistles were screeching, guns booming, and all the noises that man has invented for use on such occasions were making themselves heard as the pair of shells rushed down to where the Judges at the finish were stationed. Perhaps this rattled the Wisconsins. Pennsylvania by holding to its course after the bridge was passed gained an advantage of at least a length.

While the guns were booming and the whistles screeching, Cornell passed through its proper lane three lengths and a half behind Pennsylvania, and, according to the time of the race, nearly three lengths behind Wisconsin (which finished outside the two boats marking the finish line). Columbia, well fagged out, brought up the rear of the procession, a couple of lengths behind Cornell.

An Unsatisfactory Close

Thus the intercollegiate regatta of 1899 was brought to a close that was unsatisfactory as a race to all but the partisans of the University of Pennsylvania, who were rather glad that Wisconsin's unfortunate coxswain made the mistake he did, and so made a doubtful victory for them a certain one.

Oarsmen generally believe here to-night that had Wisconsin been able to keep her boat in the proper course it would have resulted in a victory for her. At all events, up to the point where Wisconsin's shell first got so hopelessly out of her proper course the Wisconsin crew was in the lead. Wisconsin's men were as fresh and apparently rowing with as much power as those of the Pennsylvania crew.

But once the strangers got over among the interfering craft they were attacked with nervousness.

This was shown by the fact that twice between that time and the finish No. 4 of their boat "caught a crab," which, of course, interfered with the impetus of the boat.

These two accidents alone would have accounted for the second and a half time between the finish of Pennsylvania and the Wisconsin crews. However, the steering was where the "crabs" were caught, and so a well-earned victory for Wisconsin was lost.

But Pennsylvania at the same time deserves a lot of credit, for no crew that ever sat in a boat ever rowed a gamer race in a stern chase than did the Quakers.

The Coaches Talk

After the race, Ellis Ward, the coach of the victorious Pennsylvania crew, said "My men rowed exactly as I told them to do. I had no idea that the Wisconsins were the powerful crew that they proved to be. I thought they could beat Columbia without much difficulty, but their form had been so ragged in practice that I did not see how they could beat two crews like Pennsylvania and Cornell. This is one of the cases, however, where splendidly conditioned men, fitted physically for their boat, can often beat crews whose rhythm and form are absolutely perfect. I am perfectly satisfied with the result and management of the race, and glad for the sake of the sport that Wisconsin gave us such a gamy fight."

How Wisconsin Took Defeat

After crossing the line the giants from Wisconsin paused a moment to take in their surroundings and then wormed their way out from among the maze of rowboats and small yachts that lined the course on its shore side. They immediately rowed across the river to their boathouse, which is situated about opposite the finish mark.

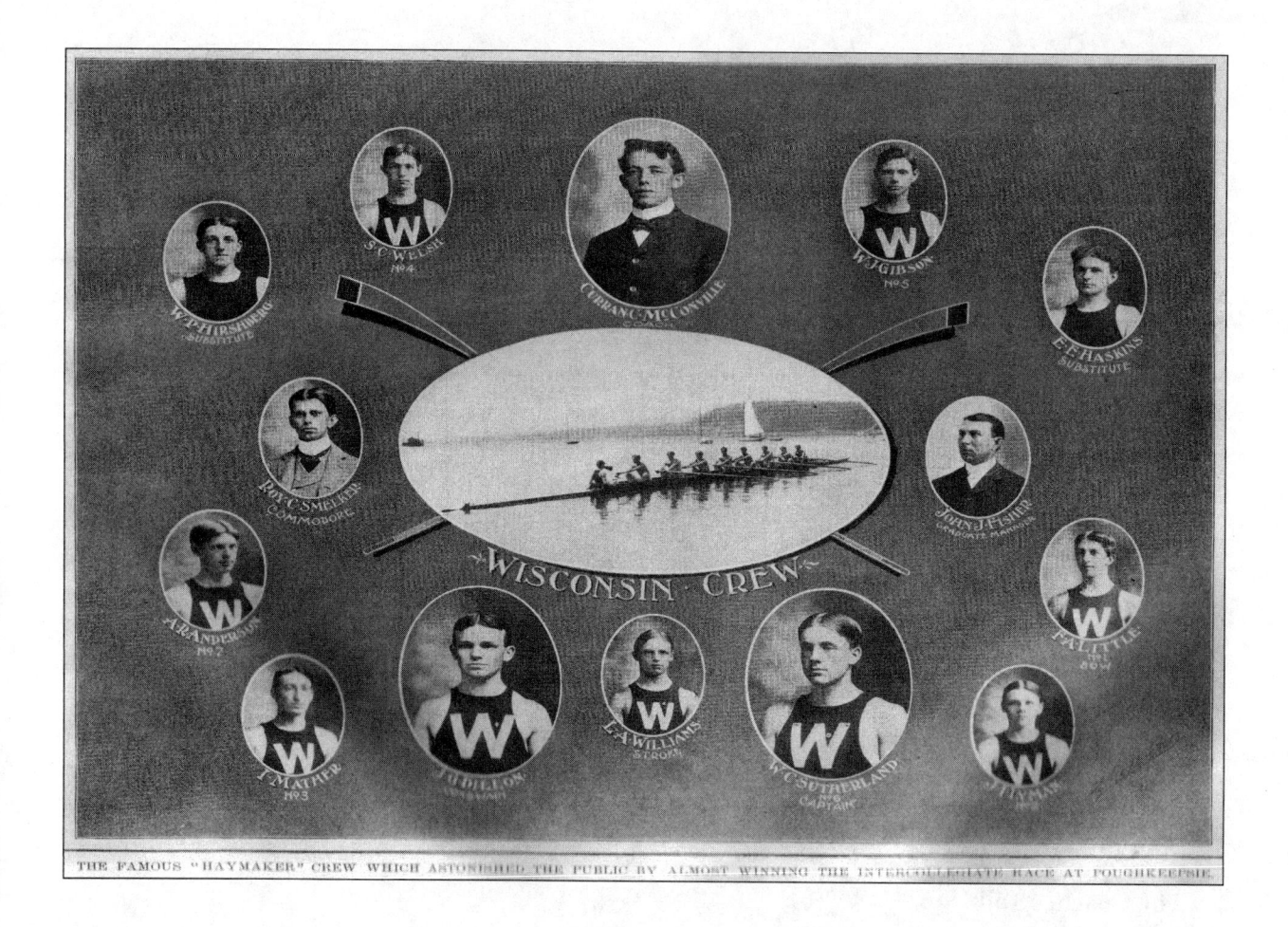

THE FAMOUS "HAYMAKER" CREW WHICH ASTONISHED THE PUBLIC BY ALMOST WINNING THE INTERCOLLEGIATE RACE AT POUGHKEEPSIE.

The Berry Crate crew.
Leslie's Weekly, July 22, 1899, p. 27.

As soon as their boat was housed the Badgers formed a group about Capt. Sutherland and shook his hand, and then they fairly hugged each other. Their enthusiasm was unbounded although they were very much disappointed at not finishing first. The eight were unanimous, however, in relieving their coxswain from all blame for steering them out of their course.

The little steersman himself felt very much depressed over the matter, although he made a good defense for his action.

"Just as we were passing the big bridge," he said, "I noticed a large berry crate floating right ahead of us, hard on our port bow."

"In a few seconds we would have struck it, and in order to escape from a disastrous collision, I veered sharply toward the shore, going so far out of our course that I realized that if I were to attempt to get back again the movement would probably cost us the half length that we were then in the lead of Pennsylvania; and looking down among the small boats inside of the course and seeing what I thought a chance to pass them and reach the finish line, I resolved to keep the shell as she was then headed and take the chance. Of course the manoeuvre cost us the race but I am sure that I did the best that was to be done under the circumstances."

After the coxswain had said this the rest of the crew crowded around him and patted the little fellow on his back.

"You did all right, old man, and we'll stand by you," they exclaimed in a chorus.

The following year, in a postlude to this memorable event, when Wisconsin's crew took its first trial row down the Hudson in 1900, the Penn crew members lined up on their float (or pier), each wearing a strawberry box on his head! The joke was appreciated by all concerned, oarsmen, coaches, and spectators alike, according to an article on the history of UW's crew, titled "Wisconsin—Where They Row," written by Paul O. Eckhardt, Jr., a UW rower from the Class of '33) in *The Wisconsin Alumnus* (June 1948).

5
Wisconsin's First IRA Victory in 1900

Unhappy with his duties at Harvard, Andrew O'Dea returned to Wisconsin in the fall of 1899. Curran McConville, interested in finding a career in which to use his engineering degree, willingly stepped aside from his one-year's coaching duties to make room. McConville would later coach the prep school crew at familiar foe St. John's Military Academy in Delafield, Wisconsin, where future UW crew captain "Will" Gibson first learned to row.

Once again, the regular crew season was modest, with the season's attention falling on the crew's performance at the Poughkeepsie Regatta. D. Hayes Murphy, crew commodore of the 1900 crew, shed interesting light on that spring's season.[1] Responding more than a half century later to a request for support to send a Wisconsin crew to the Royal Henley Regatta, Hayes wrote the following letter to UW crew coach Norm Sonju in 1967:

> As Commodore of the 1900 Wisconsin Crew, it gives me great pleasure to congratulate you heartily upon having a Varsity Crew that meets the standards of the participants in the Royal English Henley Regatta, and you have my best wishes for outstanding success in the coming event.
>
> I am making that wish with the great confidence, based on my experience in 1900 when I was a senior, burdened with the extra curricular responsibility of raising the money to send the Varsity Crew to Poughkeepsie. It looked as though I would make it all right, when the Athletic Board told me that we had such an outstanding Freshman Crew it had been decided to send them to the Poughkeepsie Regatta too and this meant that a redoubling of my efforts would be needed to include them in the party.
>
> I told them it could be done if it were not for the three law examinations coming up on which it would be necessary for me to spend some time studying in order to be sure of passing the final exams and that I could either concern myself with fund-raising—or the law exams—but not both. It was their decision to make. They went to the Faculty and, in due time, I was called to Dean Birge's office for a conference. It was short! He said they had decided that it was more important to send the Freshman Crew to Poughkeepsie than for me to pass my law exams and I could have my diploma on the basis of my class standings.
>
> So . . . I went to work and raised the money for the Freshman Crew to go to

Poughkeepsie too, and they won the race by SIX lengths! The Varsity Crew came in second in a field of five. You can depend upon history repeating itself and I think you can all go to Henley with full confidence of returning to a hearty welcome from all Wisconsin.

My contribution to the cause is enclosed with pleasure and confidence!

Sincerely.
(Signed)
D. Hayes Murphy, Chairman
The Wiremold Company
Hartford, Connecticut

The well-known interest in athletics of UW President and crew supporter Charles Kendall Adams (then away from Madison on a health-related leave of absence), can also be suspected in the Faculty Committee's deliberations of Commodore Murphy's case.

Badger Frosh Come In First!

The freshman victory marked the Badger's first win at the Poughkeepsie Regatta. The gold medal came in only the third year since Wisconsin had first participated in the regatta in 1898 and was achieved in the very first year that Wisconsin's freshmen had raced at Poughkeepsie!

The *New York Times* of July 1, 1900, described the race:

Wisconsin's freshman pulled at a strong 36 strokes after settling out of the start, in front, and Pennsylvania and Columbia were making brilliant efforts for second place. After all settled to an easy stroke, Wisconsin was a length in the lead of Cornell and a quarter of a length ahead of Pennsylvania.

At the half mile Wisconsin and Cornell were pulling thirty-six strokes to the minute, Columbia pulling thirty-five and Penn thirty-six. Cornell and Columbia were side by side at this time and this was the only time that Columbia was in the race. Wisconsin had a three-quarters of a length lead on Pennsylvania, and in short time the Badgers put on another spurt and pulled out of the bunch entirely. They were never headed after leaving the half-mile mark. Cornell came up with Pennsylvania, and Columbia crept along a bad fourth.

At the Pennsylvania boathouse the young Quakers put more power in their boat and again secured a good second position. Cornell was now in third place and Columbia was losing ground. Coming toward the big bridge, the Wisconsin oarsmen had a lead of a full length and open water was beginning to show between the Wisconsin and the Pennsylvania and the Cornell boats. Columbia was over a length behind Cornell.

It was very apparent after passing the mile mark that the Wisconsin junior crew would have an easy time in capturing first place, but there was a spirited contest on between Cornell and Pennsylvania for second position. At the mile and a half mark, the Wisconsin youngsters had gained a lead of a half-length of open water, and Cornell and Pennsylvania were still fighting for second place, Cornell having a slight lead over Pennsylvania's crew of juniors. The Western oarsmen were gaining at every stroke, and, pulling thirty-two to the minute, they had no trouble in holding their lead of a length and a half which they had acquired at this time. Nearing the finish the Wisconsin crew again spurted and increased their lead to over two lengths while Pennsylvania's shell lapped that of the Ithacans.

Wisconsin crossed the finish line a victor by two and a half lengths and Pennsylvania, after a magnificent spurt, managed to forge to second place, their shell being but a fifth of a length ahead of Cornell. Columbia was fourth by several lengths of open water.

In 1901, President Adams stepped down from the Presidency of Wisconsin because of ill health. At the Poughkeepsie Regattas the next three years of 1901, '02, and '03, O'Dea's varsity crews would place third, second, and third, respectively. In 1903 Wisconsin entered its first of three successive years' boats in the University Four event (a four-oared shell without coxswain) and finished third of four, behind Cornell and Penn, and ahead of Columbia.

For the next three years, although the Badgers would compete at Poughkeepsie, they would finish well back each time. Their fund-raising was also lagging. In April of 1906, crew commodore Cudworth Beye raised $1,800 to send the crew to Poughkeepsie. By contrast, Columbia University's commodore had raised $11,000 for the same event, for them, only a few miles up river.

Of historical note, Commodore Beye, a family friend of Frank Lloyd Wright, had several months earlier engaged Mr. Wright to design a second crew boathouse on the newly dredged Yahara River. Although never built, the boathouse drawings formed an important base for the evolution of Mr. Wright's future architectural design philosophies. John O. Holzhueter describes the role of this never-built Yahara River boathouse design in great detail in his article "Cudworth Beye, Frank Lloyd Wright, and the Yahara River Boathouse, 1905."[2]

In another generous attempt to bolster UW's crew and its coach, the wealthy banker/lumberman and U.S. Representative Isaac Stephenson from Marinette, Wisconsin, donated $500 for the purchase of a new motor launch for the coaching staff. Fund-raising continued to generate the money needed to send the varsity and freshman crews to Poughkeepsie. One example, noted from an old program of the day, was the "Crew Benefit Concert" sponsored by the Glee and

1900 freshman 8, winners of Wisconsin's first IRA title. Commodore D. Hayes Murphy is in the center background. Wisconsin's freshmen boating: H. W. Werner (bow), W. K. Murphy, Dwight C. Trevarthen, Robert G. Stevenson, Charles H. Gaffin, Lestor H. Levisee, J. A. Armstrong, Arthur J. Quigley (stroke), and T. F. Sawyer (coxswain). Coach O'Dea is at center. Source: 1902 Badger Yearbook, p. 349. Courtesy of UW–Madison Archives.

Mandolin Clubs of UW. Held at the Fuller Opera house on June 1, 1906, concert proceeds were added to that year's travel funds.

In spite of Stephenson's generous seed money, Wisconsin was still without a coaching launch on the huge Hudson River course for the Poughkeepsie Regatta in 1906. The *New York Times* of June 19, 1906, reported Cornell coach Charles Courtney, noting his crews would be practicing on the same side of the Hudson River as Wisconsin's the morning of June 18, invited UW coach Andrew O'Dea to join him in the Cornell launch. O'Dea coached out of one side of the boat and Courtney out of the other. Behind winner Cornell, the Badgers varsity finished fourth of six and behind Syracuse, the frosh third of five, in the 1906 Poughkeepsie.

Despite the many fund-raising efforts, O'Dea announced his resignation in March, effective the end of the 1906 season, citing frustration with a lack of equipment and facilities. A "shortage of a modicum of on-going financing" was the reason O'Dea gave for his resignation. Some thought his slipping race results might more accurately have signaled a loss of interest in coaching.

Anther reason for O'Dea's departure could be the general "housecleaning" of the Athletic Department in 1906, following the faculty's assumption of responsibilities for intercollegiate athletic activities from the student athletic associations. A similar takeover of athletic responsibilities was happening at other universities in the wake of several betting scandals and recruiting abuses, in the absence heretofore of clear eligibility criteria.

WISCONSIN'S FIRST IRA VICTORY 43

6
Last of the Sculler Coaches— Ten Eyck and Vail

Edward "Ned" Ten Eyck, coach 1906–10. Source: *1912 Badger Yearbook,* p. 282. Courtesy of UW–Madison Archives.

Without a coach in the fall of 1906, the older oarsmen taught the rudiments of rowing to the freshmen. Dr. C. P. Hutchings, formerly Syracuse's football and track coach, had been hired as Wisconsin's Athletic Director "as part of a movement to awaken Wisconsin—the sleeping giant," according to Malcolm Alama.[1] With Jim Ten Eyck, Sr. showing success quickly with crew in his three years at Syracuse, Hutchings was familiar with crew and the Ten Eyck's. The immediate hiring of Jim Ten Eyck's son Edward Hanlan "Ned" Ten Eyck—taking Ten Eyck away from a four year coaching position at the Philadelphia Barge Club—was Hutchings's first step toward an attempted revival of crew at UW.

Ned Ten Eyck was born into a rowing family in Peekskill, New York. Ned moved with his family to Worcester, Massachusetts, at age six. The great-grandfather of Ned was David Ten Eyck, a ferryman between Verplanck's Point and Stony Point shortly after the Revolutionary War and who began rowing as early as 1784. Ned's grandfather, James B. Ten Eyck, affectionately known as "Captain Jim," was the undefeated rowing champion of the Hudson River until the day of his death in Peekskill, New York, on February 21, 1917, at the age of ninety-four.

Ned's father, James A. ("Jim") Ten Eyck, Sr.—for whom the IRA's Ten Eyck team trophy[2] would be named in 1952—had also been a well-known and successful sculler and, at the time of Ned's being named Wisconsin's crew coach, was the head crew coach at Syracuse.

The new Wisconsin coach had been a world-class sculler, going undefeated from 1895 to 1901 (a sculler rows with two oars, in a 1-, 2-, or 4-seat shell). In 1896, at age seventeen, Ned had become the first American to win the Diamond Skulls (the singles skull championship) at the Royal Henley Regatta. By the time he came to Wisconsin, his winning single's skull had been donated to the Smithsonian Institution.

Ned attended the University of Pennsylvania, beginning in 1897. In 1901, following an open challenge to any comers for a final chance to beat him on the Old College Course on Lake Quinsigamond in Worcester, Massachusetts—to which no one replied—Ten Eyck retired from rowing.

Ned's arrival in Madison as the new crew coach was met with a mixture of enthusiasm and resignation. On the one hand, the naming of another full-time crew coach rekindled the pride in rowing and reestablished the importance and visibility of crew on campus. Ned's undefeated record as a single sculler enhanced his image as a coach, as did the reputation of his father Jim at Syracuse.

On the other hand, Ned Ten Eyck may have created a certain tension between the straightforward midwestern personality of his oarsmen and the somewhat professorial, aloof style of this gentleman coach from the East Coast. Indeed, captain Ben Davis, knowing his rowing career would be over by the time the publication of *The Badger of 1909* came out, referred to Ned in his "Review of the 1907 Boating Season" as "the ponderous Ten Eyck."

Jim Ten Eyck, Sr., became the Syracuse coach in 1903 and had already, by 1904, broken Cornell coach Charles Courtney's three-consecutive-year stranglehold on the varsity eight Poughkeepsie title and their two year grip on the freshman eight title. Jim Ten Eyck's fame would only grow.

The three Ten Eycks visiting Madison (left to right): Ned, Jim Sr., and Jim Jr. Source: *Mark of the Oarsmen* by M. R. Alama, 1963, p. 76. Courtesy of the Syracuse Alumni Rowing Association.

Under Ned's badgering, Jim agreed to bring a four-oared and an eight-oared crew to Madison in 1907 from their home campus in upstate New York. The pending Ten Eyck face-off in Madison would go beyond the two coaches; Ned's brother, third-year man Jim Ten Eyck, Jr. was the varsity stroke at Syracuse. Like Ned in 1896, Jim, Jr. had won the Diamond Skulls in 1906.

The Orangemen of Syracuse had never traveled outside the state before coming to Madison (the Poughkeepsie Regatta was in New York). The two races were deemed by some as "The Western Regatta." What a surprise it must have been to the young Badger oarsmen when Coach Ned Ten Eyck announced to his Wisconsin team that his famous father was bringing the strong Syracuse crew to Madison!

The news of Syracuse's crew—and their famous Coach Jim Ten Eyck— coming to Madison caused a stir of excitement to the aspiring Badger athletes. The Orangemen's visit would be the first time an eastern college had ever come to Wisconsin for a crew race!

With Jim Ten Eyck, Jr., a third-year man at Syracuse stroking the Orangemen

LAST OF THE SCULLER COACHES

eight, the stage was set for a wonderful competition in Madison. Syracuse crew historian Malcolm Alama described the two Lake Mendota races between Wisconsin and Syracuse:

> The atmosphere in Madison was one of coolness, father and son standing icily silent, eyes averted at the coin-tossing ceremony. It wasn't improved when the father in winning the toss shrewdly chose courses nearest the shore for both his eight-oared and four-oared crews. Ordinarily, this would be wise, for these were sheltered from extremely rough water and high winds.
>
> The father's face was wreathed with smiles, when the four-oared crew won handily by eight lengths. It darkened, however, and then lengthened during the varsity race.
>
> Stormy conditions postponed that race until early in the evening. At the offset, with a tremendous surge, Syracuse captured the lead and grimly hung on. At half-mile, two smoke bombs wafted skyward from a chemical building, and the spectators were hardly able to see the race for the canopy of darkness; but almost instinctively they knew Syracuse was ahead.
>
> Rowing in a flurry of 40 strokes per minute, Syracuse began to show strain of its unprecedented cadence at the mile mark. It was here that Ned's boat unexpectedly came up and rowed abreast. For the next half mile, both clung together.
>
> Then the early pace began to tell, and Syracuse wilted under the strain.
>
> Oar by oar, Wisconsin inched ahead, until one-fourth mile from the finish, it led by half a boat length. And when the Badgers went over the line, they were a good full boat length ahead.
>
> Wisconsin fans were delirious with joy—shouting, hooting, screaming—from the fervor that came when a hometown victory was snatched at the last moment from ignominious defeat.
>
> The cardinal of the son lowered the orange of the father, true, but in fact it represented a great victory for the Ten Eyck name. Touching was the sight of the father, warmly congratulating an embarrassed son, the prior coolness and misunderstanding washed away and forgotten in the exultant moment.
>
> "A great victory," the proud father admitted without rancor, a twinkle spotting both eyes, "particularly because it's still in the family!"

In addition to all the Ten Eyck's in Madison that day, another noteworthy figure, Syracuse coxswain Frank Eldridge, likely steered the Syracuse varsity eight on Lake Mendota. Eldridge, would later, at the Poughkeepsie Regatta several weeks hence, initiate the tradition of yielding shirts to the winning crew.

In the 1907 Poughkeepsie Regatta, Wisconsin's varsity eight would again beat the Orangemen, finishing fifth to Syracuse's seventh.

Wisconsin's successes continued at the freshman level that year at the Poughkeepsie Regatta on June 26, 1907, when the Badgers dethroned the Syracuse frosh for the title in the yearlings' two-mile race on the Hudson River. Under the headline "Cornell Wins Close (Varsity) Victory . . . Wisconsin Freshman Win," the June 27, 1907, *New York Times* article on page one told the story:

> This [Syracuse's prior victory in the varsity four-oared race] whet Syracuse's appetite, and visions of the return of the 1904 victories began to float before the upstate contingent. They were chipper going by the boat houses to the start of the freshman race and joined Wisconsin in cheering Young Ten Eyck [Ned, the

Sumnicht Iakisch Trane Wilce Druetzer Witte Wirder Dinet Ryan

> new crew coach at Wisconsin] as they passed the Westerners' quarters. The young Diamond Sculls winner stood on the float giving the freshmen their last advice as the train passed. He turned and waved acknowledgment. The crews were not ready at the start, but speedily got into line, Wisconsin joining the other four contenders.
>
> The race was won by Wisconsin from the go. The Western crew, rowing beautifully together, and well within its strength, got away second to Cornell. Its prow showed in front of the other before the quarter mile, and it was never in any danger at any time thereafter. Columbia moved up to second place in the first half mile, and was rowing strongly about a quarter length ahead of Pennsylvania, with Cornell a length behind the Quakers and Syracuse lapping Cornell.
>
> The positions were maintained to the mile, when Cornell began a tremendous spurt, and followed by Syracuse, commenced to move up. Cornell passed Pennsylvania, and then Columbia, but could make no impression on Wisconsin's lead. Syracuse passed Penn, and with her prow almost abreast Columbia, they passed the half-mile.
>
> Then the spurt began to tell on Cornell and she dropped steadily back, but the other three fought it out for second place in a beautiful contest. Just a quarter mile from the finish Pennsylvania moved up to second place, passing Columbia and Syracuse, but Syracuse had more left, and in the last hundred yards won out

Most of the 1907 freshman 8 IRA winning crew. Freshman boating: H. W. Wick in the bow seat, Sam Kerr, H. A. Sumnicht, O. J. Hickcox, P. J. Murphy, Robert Iakisch, Ruben W. Trane, Jack Wilce at the stroke, and Eugene J. Ryan as the cox. Wilce, who also played football for the Badgers, later earned a medical degree from Wisconsin and, changing careers, went on to become a well-known football coach at Ohio State. Source: *1910 Badger Yearbook*, p. 209. Courtesy of UW–Madison Archives.

LAST OF THE SCULLER COACHES 47

second place, less than a quarter length separating the three boats—Syracuse, Penn and Columbia. Cornell was just lapped with Columbia.

After the race it was said that the Columbia shell had sprung a leak and that it was nearly half full of water as she crossed the line. If this were the case she made a mighty plucky effort. These two races were mighty galling to Cornell. Both lost without a contest, second in one (the four-oared race) and last in the other (the freshman race won by Wisconsin), the Ithacans (from Cornell) could not make it out. But they put a bold face on the bad condition.

UW's 1907 IRA winning freshman boating: H. W. Wick in the bow seat, S. Kerr, H. A. Sumnicht, O. J. Hickcox, P. J. Murphy, R. Takisch, R. W. Trane, Jack Wilce at the stroke, and E. J. Ryan as the cox. Wilce, who also played football for the Badgers, later earned a medical degree from Wisconsin and, changing careers, went on to become a well-known football coach at Ohio State.

From the point of view of varsity eight results at Poughkeepsie, the four-year career of Coach Ned Ten Eyck was undistinguished, as the Badger shells finished at or near the bottom of each of the four year's (1907–10) Poughkeepsie Regatta results.

It was in 1908 that Wisconsin, second at the three-and-one-half-mile mark and just under the railroad bridge over the Hudson, fell to last when sophomore and 6-seat Robert Iakisch collapsed, leaving the seven remaining oarsmen to row home without ever finishing the race.

One event that did distinguish 1908 in college rowing history was the challenge offered by Syracuse's coxswain, Frank Eldridge, described by Malcolm Alama as "brash and loud, cocky and aggressive." Eldridge strutted over to the Columbia coxswain before the varsity race and bet his rowing jersey that Syracuse, despite a recent accident damaging their shell, would still win. When Syracuse won and not only the Columbia crew, but all the other losing crews, offered their shirts to their Syracuse counterparts, the "betting of the shirts" tradition had begun. The tradition continues to this day. Having dropped out mid-race with an injury, it is unclear how Wisconsin may have participated in this initial shirt betting day.

Jack Wilce, later head football coach at Ohio State. Source: *1910 Badger Yearbook,* p. 209. Courtesy of UW–Madison Archives.

In 1909 Wisconsin finished fourth of five, beating Penn on the four-mile Poughkeepsie Regatta course.

Three weeks before the Poughkeepsie Regatta of 1910, the Washington "Sun Dodgers" (later renamed the Huskies in 1922) crew, under soon-to-be-famous crew coach Hiram Conibear, came east to race the Badgers (Washington would not attend the Poughkeepsie Regatta until 1913, when they finished what they considered a highly successful third and beating Wisconsin, Columbia, and Penn). On June 4, 1910, on a two-mile Lake Mendota course in a drenching rainstorm, the Badgers (16:06) defeated Washington by three lengths.

Washington's crew coach Hiram Conibear, a former professional bicyclist, had also been a team trainer in professional baseball, a track team trainer at the University of Chicago and man-of-all-trades within the University of Washington's Athletic Department. When Washington decided to add rowing to its intercollegiate sports program in 1904, Conibear was named the head coach—this despite no prior experience in the sport.

One of Conibear's shrewdest decisions in developing his Washington crews was persuading sculler and boat builder George Pocock (and his older brother Dick) to move to Seattle and build shells, and share their rowing knowledge, in October of 1913. While little credit was given, it was the rowing experience of the Pococks that evolved into the "Conibear-(Pocock) Stroke" of 1913.[3]

In the Poughkeepsie Regatta of 1910, Ned Ten Eyck's Badger varsity eight came in fifth of five boats. To add insult to injury, Wisconsin's multi-ton coaching launch—*The Cardinal*, shipped by rail car from Madison to The Highlands on the western shore—was destroyed in a fire at the storehouse of the Central Hudson Steamboat Company on the day after the regatta. Ten Eyck must have decided this was the last straw, and he resigned a few days later.

One of the UW Athletic Department's most mysterious personnel stories followed Ten Eyck's departure. October 13, 1910, brought news in the Madison press of the hiring of Edwin R. Sweetland as UW's new crew coach. A four-letter man in football, baseball, track, and crew, Sweetland (Class of '99) had been a varsity oarsmen (5-seat) for "old man Courtney" at Cornell and was assumed to be a devoted disciple of the successful Cornell rowing style. At the time of Sweetland's hiring, he was the physical education director at the University of Kentucky.

In the fall of 1899, prior to his stint in Kentucky, Sweetland had been Syracuse University's part-time football coach. The same year, he agreed to become Syracuse's first crew coach as well, when the school's first intercollegiate rowers took to the water. (It was also in 1899 that Syracuse changed its colors from pea green and pink to orange, and from then on they became known as the Orangemen.) Sweetland coached crew at Syracuse until 1903, when he resigned and was replaced by James A. Ten Eyck, Sr.

Sweetland came to Madison by January 4, 1911. But on January 17, Sweetland sent a telegram from Chicago to Athletic Director George W. Ehler saying he would be unable to continue his duties. His telegram, giving neither facts as to the nature of his illness, nor the name of the hospital to which he was confined, threw an air of mystery over the entire matter.

"Dad" Vail Begins Coaching at Wisconsin

By March of 1911, Harry Emerson "Dad" Vail had been engaged to replace Sweetland as the new Badger coach, at a salary of $1,500 per year.

Born in Gagetown, New Brunswick, Canada, around 1861, Vail, like Ned Ten Eyck before him, came from a long family line of boatmen. From the early 1800s, the Vail family rowed cargo over the one-mile narrow stretch of Gagetown Creek between the Gagetown wharf and the St. John River.

The rowing career of Harry Vail began with his first race at the age of fifteen, and at thirty-eight, in 1899, his career peaked when he defeated Bedford Brown.

Harry Emerson "Dad" Vail, coach 1910–28. Courtesy UW–Madison Archives Image x25 3478.

The lore in Gagetown was that Vail lost only one race in his lifetime—probably to Jim Ten Eyck, Sr.—and that he avenged that loss. Vail was a long-time acquaintance of both Syracuse head coach Jim Ten Eyck and of Cornell crew coach Charles Courtney, as all three were professional scullers during the 1880s.

Vail had rowed on the Harvard crew from 1891 to 1893 and was captain his senior year (at age thirty-two; college eligibility rules would not begin to be clarified until 1906). Some years later at Harvard, Vail would be an assistant coach for seven years, following coaching positions at the Neptune Rowing Club of St. Johns (Canada), Ariel Boat Club of Baltimore, and Georgetown Prep.

He married Cassie McMulkin in 1899, and the couple never had any children.

By all accounts "Dad" Vail quickly became a popular coach in Madison. The *Wisconsin State Journal* of March 18, 1911, reported, "All of the crew men like the strapping giant, who peals off his citizen clothes and gets into a gym suit to show them how to operate an oar in the shell."

In 1911 the Badgers stayed at "The Elms" in The Highlands, New York. The Highlands, a small village across the Hudson River from Poughkeepsie, seems to have been a resort and The Elms a large boarding house able to house the fifteen to thirty members of the traveling crew team to the Poughkeepsie Regatta. The squad at varying times could include varsity and freshmen eights, a straight four, two or three alternates, a coach and as many as two or three assistant coaches, a medical staff member, a rigger, and perhaps some "stowaways" who came along on the trip unofficially by staying with the shells and the coach's launch in the boxcar on the train ride over and back.

In spite of setting a national four-mile, still-water record (21:20) on Lake Mendota, the Badger experience that year on the Hudson River at Poughkeepsie was a disappointment. Boils, infections, and colds decimated the ranks of the oarsmen. Using a freshman substitute at the 6-seat, because every varsity reserve oarsman was ill, Wisconsin beat Syracuse to finish fourth, only inches behind Penn for third.

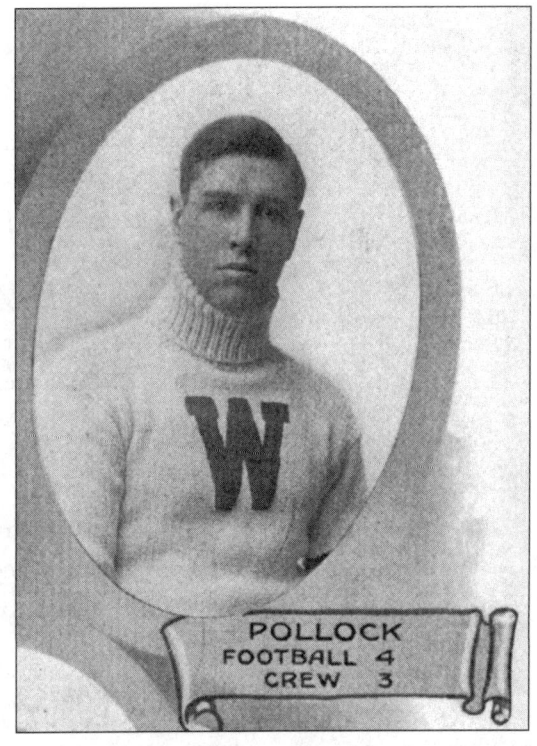

Wisconsin took two boats to the Poughkeepsie Regatta in 1912. Stanford, the first West Coast school to attend the regatta, saw their varsity eight eventually finish sixth of six.

UW crew Captain Charles Pollock, a transfer from Fargo College who had gone out for UW's crew in the spring of 1911, was later a football player at Wisconsin in the fall of 1911, until he broke a leg in the Iowa game. Pollock returned to crew in the spring of 1912, as the team's captain, and led the Badger varsity—described in the local press as "Wisconsin's wonder crew"—to a second place finish at Poughkeepsie. The Badger varsity eight finished second to Cornell by three seconds over the four-mile course, after losing their starting 2-seat oarsman, Ray Cuff, to a hand infection.

1912 captain and stroke Charles Pollock. Source: *1913 Badger Yearbook*, p. 262. Courtesy of UW–Madison Archives.

The *New York Times* of June 30, 1912, described the action in the varsity eight event at Poughkeepsie,

> With a crowd of more than 50,000 people looking on from the river banks, observation trains, hundreds of pleasure boats, the oarsmen of Cornell scored a triple triumph.

LAST OF THE SCULLER COACHES   51

Just above the bridge (and just beyond the two-mile marker), Wisconsin began to attract attention. The Badgers had dropped their stroke and yet they were pulling up steadily on Columbia. Columbia's oarsmen seemed to be all right, but there wasn't the driving power to the pull, which such a high stroke should produce. The hard up-hill fight was telling on Columbia. In front of them was Cornell whom they were trying to catch, and right at their heels was Wisconsin coming on with steady determination. At the bridge Columbia seemed pretty well fagged out. Wisconsin was rowing a gallant uphill race, and had almost caught up with the fast-tiring Columbia eight.

At three and a half miles Cornell was more than two lengths in front. Everybody was sure now that it was Cornell's race, and attention was centered on Columbia's fight with Wisconsin. Columbia could no longer raise her stroke above thirty-five, while Wisconsin, rowing at thirty-six, was gaining fast. A quarter of a mile from the finish Wisconsin was abreast of the Columbia boat, and then slowly forged ahead. Columbia couldn't stand the gaff, that's all there was to it. Occasional splashes and the jerky course of the boat showed that they had about reached the end of their rope.

Cornell was taking things easy with two and a half lengths to her credit, but now Wisconsin, rowing a lively thirty-six, began to edge up a bit on Cornell. That didn't last long, for the Ithacans had plenty of reserve power. Once over the finish line with the tension of the grueling grind over, the big, exhausted athletes of Columbia and Wisconsin let their oars drag listlessly in the water.

The Wisconsin varsity had beaten Ten Eyck's Orangemen but could not ultimately defeat Courtney's rowers from Cornell.

The freshman race of the 1912 Poughkeepsie Regatta was another classic. The *New York Times* of June 30 ran the headline and story:

GREAT FRESHMAN RACE
Cornell Beats Out Wisconsin by a
Length after Desperate Struggle
Special to The New York Times

Poughkeepsie, June 29.—The sturdy freshman crew of Cornell won the second race from Wisconsin by a scant length in one of the greatest races seen on the Hudson. It was a bitter, hard race from the start to the finish, the Badgers fighting it out with Cornell in the gamest struggle which ever marked the freshman event here.

When the Pennsylvania stakeboat got adrift, Pennsylvania had an advantage of more than 15 feet. The lead didn't help any, for Wisconsin shot into the lead by about 10 feet over Columbia, and with Cornell on even terms. Before the mile mark was reached, Cornell, rowing the long steady [Cornell Coach Charles E.] Courtney stroke, slowly nosed ahead of Columbia, while Wisconsin had a quarter of a boat length on the Ithacans. The race developed into a closely fought duel between Wisconsin and Cornell, while Columbia, Pennsylvania and Syracuse were closely bunched behind them.

The great crowds along the river banks and on the excursion steamers and observation train burst into a riot of enthusiasm as Cornell and Wisconsin zigzagged the noses of their shells into the lead only to fall back again on even terms. As the five crews swept down to the bridge, the nose of the Wisconsin boat showed slightly in front of Cornell. As the crews shot past the bridge piers, Cornell and Wisconsin were on even terms and a length behind were Columbia, Pennsylvania and Syracuse, having a fine triangular fight of their own. The closeness of the race aroused the crowds to a high pitch of excitement.

When Cornell's shell showed slightly in the lead, and the Ithacans increased the stroke to 35 in the hope of shaking off Wisconsin, the latter crew fought gamely and refused to be shaken off. Instead little Lewis, the Badger coxswain, called for a spurt, and the shell again shot ahead of the Cornell boat.

Cornell raised the stroke again and nosed ahead, but Wisconsin fought desperately again, and cheer after cheer echoed across the river as Wisconsin pluckily took the lead again.

Enthusiasm ran high as the crews battled toward the finish. Men who have been witnessing boat races for years threw their straw hats in the air at the game struggle which the Wisconsin youngsters were putting up against Courtney's crack freshmen. After Wisconsin had a third time refused to be shaken off, they hit the stroke up to 37, and showed in front again. The pace was killing, and a fourth supreme effort proved their undoing. Cornell was rowing 33, and went to the front. Wisconsin, after falling behind three different times, and fighting ahead of the Cornell boat each time, was finally worn down under the grueling high stroke.

Syracuse in the meantime had shaken off Columbia and was in third place, two lengths behind Wisconsin; the Quakers, with a final spurt, increased their pace and beat Columbia by 10 feet.

In 1913, the freshmen were in another two-mile nail-biter, with the Wisconsin yearlings again coming up three seconds and a boat length short to a Cornell victory. Cornell coach Charles Courtney had struck again, but the Badger frosh had beaten Syracuse coach Jim Ten Eyck's freshman entry for a second year in a row.

Over the spring of 1914, the Badgers saw very little competition before the Poughkeepsie Regatta and it showed. Wisconsin's varsity came in a disappointing sixth of six boats during the summer of 1914. Reflecting the ongoing strain on

Finish of 1913 Poughkeepsie Regatta. Wisconsin, second from left, finished fourth. Source: *Mark of the Oarsmen* by M. R. Alama, 1963, p. 114. Courtesy of Syracuse Alumni Rowing Association and the IRA Stewards.

Badger budgets, the *New York Times* of May 5 1914, (page 9) reported—with a run-on lead sentence:

> The Wisconsin spirit of economy, which has manifested itself in a demand for a non-partisan State convention of anti-high taxers, has struck the athletic department of the State University, and will be in evidence when the Badger crew goes to the Poughkeepsie races in June by sending of the crew to live in tents, instead of in private quarters at Highland, as has been the custom ever since the crew began participating in the races. The crew has been quartered in the Elms in other years, but this time the men will be sent to an open air camp with their own cooks and at a distance from the other athletic teams.

The straight (coxless) four-oared event, a staple at the Poughkeepsie Regatta from 1899 through 1913, was dropped in 1914. Cornell had won the straight four races for ten of the prior fifteen years. Another sixty years would pass before the event would be reintroduced into the IRA regatta's format in 1974. Replacing the four-oared event in 1914, **the junior varsity eight event was initiated**, giving even more college oarsmen an opportunity to "go to Poughkeepsie." Wisconsin would not enter a second varsity eight in this newest Poughkeepsie event until 1947. Similarly, the Badgers had no freshman entry in 1914.

The Near-Terminal Suspension of Intercollegiate Crew

On September 9, 1914, the *Daily Cardinal* reported Wisconsin's medical faculty and athletic council delivered what was almost a deathblow to the UW crew program. In the belief that a four-mile crew race was dangerous to the health of the student athlete, the faculty "voted to discontinue intercollegiate rowing."

Resignations for health reasons of two Badger oarsmen during the spring of 1913—Maurice Sjoblom and Eddie Samp—and a growing crew-health and distance controversy within a few other colleges with crew programs, led to the near fatal decision at Wisconsin.

The department of clinical medicine and the medical faculty concluded that a two-mile race for the freshmen and a four-mile length for the varsity was dangerous to the health of an oarsman. In particular, they concluded this was the case at Wisconsin, where the long winters did not allow enough time for freshmen and varsity rowers to reach the level of conditioning necessary to compete over these distances in early-spring events.

As a result, the medical faculty and athletic council at Wisconsin canceled all further intercollegiate competition in crew, effective the fall of 1914. Not alone in the controversy, other schools, including Navy and Princeton, evaluated the health implications of the sport of crew and their student athletes.

Walter Camp, Stanford's football coach and the founder of football's All-American selections, writing in the July 1915 issue of *Outing Magazine* carefully reviewed the pros and cons of the arguments over conditioning and enlarged hearts. In the end, Camp "encouraged more investigation of the relatively few numbers of athletes rowing to complete the record and place the sport where it belongs at the bar of pubic opinion."

For Coach Vail, the decision was devastating. For the next six years, from the fall of 1914 through the spring of 1920, Vail was relegated to boat repairs, intramural races, an occasional visit from oarsmen of prior years, and probably teaching some classes in physical education. While the annual spectacle of a national rowing competition was suspended for all colleges for three years (1917–1919) because of World War I, the prospects for a renewal of intercollegiate rowing in Madison appeared dark indeed.

The encouraging presence of Professor Pyre—the former 2-seat oarsman in the 1892 victory in Oconomowoc and a member of UW's Athletic Board from 1916 to 1931—gave Vail a flicker of hope that crew could be resurrected at Wisconsin.

Pyre's careful lobbying for the sport of crew can be sensed from a passage from his history of the university:

> Notwithstanding the difficulties, which attended the maintenance of rowing at Wisconsin, only the apparently conclusive proof of its injuriousness to the physical constitution of the participants could have justified the banishment of this otherwise beautiful sport from the realm of intercollegiate competition.

Professor Pyre's additional insights into the plight of rowing at UW before 1900 came out in another passage:

> The most daring undergraduate conceit of those days was the introduction of eight-oared racing. Rowing is the most arduous of college sports and the most difficult to finance.[4]

Intramural rowing grew in popularity during the suspension of intercollegiate rowing from the fall of 1914 to the spring of 1920. Continued student interest in water sports led the university to undertake an extensive remodeling of the University Boat House in 1916, under the supervision of Arthur Peabody.[5]

Interest in intercollegiate rowing would not go away. Some varsity "W"s were awarded in crew in 1915 and 1916 but most likely for varsity competition through the spring of 1914. The flame for rowing continued, not only because of Coach Vail's continuing presence and encouragement but also because of the students' inherent interest in the boathouse and the natural attractions of Lake Mendota.

In 1920 intramural contests were held among several of the separate colleges and class years on campus. The spirit of crew would not die in Madison. In the end, the faculty and medical staff—informed by more and more health studies showing the heart, as a muscle, enlarges with exercise like any other muscle—relented and permitted two-mile intercollegiate races.

The Poughkeepsie Regatta restarted in 1920, after the three-year hiatus for World War I. The race was held on Lake Cayuga, the home waters of Cornell University in upstate New York. All three eight-oared events—varsity, junior varsity, and freshman—were shortened to two miles. Unhappily for Cornell, however, Ten Eyck's Syracuse shell edged out Cornell for the victory in the showcase varsity eight event. As Malcolm Alama described:

> To Courtney, the [varsity] defeat was a heartbreaker. It was disheartening for him to see victory slip away on home water in the final moment. It was also his last race. Courtney died July 17, 1920, after suffering a stroke of apoplexy at his birthplace and now summer cottage on Cayuga Lake.

Courtney's record at the IRAs is likely to never again be equaled! From 1895 to 1920 (keeping in mind three years of the IRAs were canceled during World

J. F. A. Pyre, as a UW oarsman in 1892. Source: *1894 Badger Yearbook*, p. 133. Courtesy of UW–Madison Archives.

War I), Charles Courtney's varsity eights won fifteen of twenty-four races. The junior varsity eights won three of four races from 1914 to 1920. His freshman boats won fifteen of twenty-three events (1896–1920), and Cornell's varsity four-oared shells without coxswains won ten of fifteen races from 1899 through 1913.

One reason—though certainly not the only reason—Cornell became so adept at the four-mile race on the Hudson, from 1895 until the race was shortened in 1920, was the length of their practice course, the finger lake known as Lake Cayuga. The lake is well over ten miles long, north to south. Cornell's crew practices often went a continuous ten miles north, stopped for a short rest, and then rowed ten miles home. No other crew in the country had this much still lake water available to them for daily practice.

> In 1915, rower and footballer Martin T. Kennedy, became the first Big Ten Conference medal winner, given annually thereafter to an individual at each conference school demonstrating "the greatest proficiency in athletics and scholarship."
>
> Longtime sculler and now Syracuse coach Jim Ten Eyck, Sr., celebrating his seventieth birthday in 1920, rowed the Hudson River, from New York City to Albany, a distance of 150 miles.
>
> In this same period, 1919 and 1920, the Green Bay Packer football team was playing its early games with independent opponents and outside any organized league. After joining the American Football League (renamed the National Football League in 1922), the Packers played their first league game on October 23, 1921, winning a 7–6 contest against the Minnesota Marines. Curly Lambeau was both the Packer's quarterback and kicker.

In the early 1920s, crew in Madison gradually crept back into the limelight. The Badgers hosted two interesting races in the spring of 1922. *The Badger 1924,* Wisconsin's annual yearbook, describes the first:

> On May 27, the Wisconsin crew raced against its first international crew when Manitoba's Winnipeg Boat Club came to Madison. The race was hard fought from the start to the very last stroke. Both shells were neck and neck until the half-mile lines were passed when the Badgers began to slowly creep ahead of the visitors. Although the Badgers were three-fourths of a boat length in the lead at the mile line, the Canadians came close to winning as a result of a spurt at the finish.[6]

The second race of note, several days after the close of school in June 1922, came when the University of Washington, on their way to Poughkeepsie (which Wisconsin would not attend), passed through Madison to race the Badgers. The three-mile course proved too much for Wisconsin, which had trained to row only a one-and-one-half-mile course (perhaps still under the watchful eye of the medical faculty). Washington won by fifteen feet. In a May 15, 1985, letter to UW president Irving Shain, the junior captain and stroke for the Washington Huskies, Mike Murphy, described coming in to shore:

> When we came in to the float [dock], Dad Vail came out, met us with a smile on his face and a tear running down his cheek (and) congratulated me and the crew on winning! That was the only time I ever met him in person but I have met that smile and that tear many times since, even to this day at age 87. When things got rough, that smile and tear brought to me again and again the unconquerable spirit of Dad Vail as a wonderful inspiration.

The coach of the Washington crew that visited Madison in 1922 was Ed Leader, a letter-winning Washington rower in 1913 and 1916. Leader had succeeded the famous Hiram Conibear, following the latter's unexpected death after falling out of a plum tree in 1916.

After the 1922 season, Leader would leave Washington to accept the head crew coaching position at Yale, taking Husky junior Mile Murphy as his freshman coach. Leader also took sculler and boatbuilder Dick Pocock, brother of the well-known boatbuilder George Pocock, to New Haven as a shellbuilder and consultant.

Washington junior Mike Murphy, married with one child and needing money to support his family, opted to give up his captain-elect position in his senior year in order to go to work for Leader at Yale. Murphy would later become Wisconsin's head coach in the fall of 1928.

In the spring of 1923, Wisconsin lost to the Duluth Boat Club and to the University of Washington, the latter stopping again in Madison on its way to a Poughkeepsie Regatta. For the ninth straight year, Wisconsin did not attend the Regatta.

The Badgers finally returned to the Poughkeepsie Regatta in the summer of 1924 and once again caused a stir. Only the varsity eight participated in the annual Hudson River crew spectacle. The *New York Times* of June 18, 1924, under the headline "Washington Victor Again on the Hudson . . . 50,000 See Wisconsin Make Sensational Drive and Finish Only Two Lengths Behind," wrote:

> Pennsylvania surprised the 50,000 spectators of the Hudson River regatta in winning the junior varsity and freshman races, but the big upset of the afternoon was provided by Wisconsin.

Wisconsin Springs Surprise

Any small boy in Poughkeepsie could have told you that Washington would win, but not even the experts dreamed that Wisconsin, a green and untried crew, would steal second place from the effete and now chagrined East. Like Stanford in 1915, Wisconsin lost the race but won the moral victory. For one thing, it was the first time since 1914 that a Wisconsin crew had appeared on the Hudson. For several years there was no crew at all at Madison and what material did appear in the last few seasons was raw and inexperienced, lacking the tradition and background that help make a good crew great.

But today, that discounted Wisconsin team sent back to the Hudson with great misgivings on the part of the university, helped Washington make a complete victory for the West. It was a tribute to a beaten but glorious crew that the crowd at the finish line stood and roared their delight as the men of Dad Vail slid out from beneath the railroad bridge (just short of the finish), dug their blades a little harder and deeper into the water and uncorked a tremendous spurt that caught Columbia, caught Pennsylvania, drove Cornell into the rear and made second place safe for the Mid West.

For the fourth straight year, the first two places in the varsity event had gone to outside crews—crews graciously invited to the regatta by the four member universities of the Intercollegiate Rowing Association. Not since 1920, when there were no Washington and Navy and Wisconsin crews to intrude on the happy scene, has Cornell or Columbia or Syracuse or Pennsylvania won the regatta that they established back in 1895. You may call it biting the hand that feeds you: tonight the East is not sure what it should be called, except that they are finding it just a bit monotonous to have the invited guests come to the party and go away with the family plate.

One of the heroes of the day was Wisconsin's magnificent stroke, Howie Johnson, who raised the beat and led the Badger rush to the finish over the final mile of the course.

Wisconsin's race was an exciting return to the national regatta. For Vail, it was the sweetest of experiences. After nine years away from his fellow coaches and the excitement of attending the annual race, Vail had persevered and brought his Badger crew to honor once again at Poughkeepsie. More importantly, his quiet patience had saved men's crew at Wisconsin.

In 1925 the Poughkeepsie course for varsity eights was reestablished at four miles. Wisconsin's varsity eight—unable to replace Howard Johnson, the prior year's stroke—nevertheless staged another startling sprint and passed Penn, Columbia, Cornell, and Syracuse to finish third behind Navy and Washington. The Badger frosh were fifth of five.

Wisconsin's fortunes under "Dad" Vail began to slide in the 1925–26 season. The Washington Huskies again visited Madison on their way to Poughkeepsie. Russell S. "Rusty" Callow, president of his class and captain of the crew at Washington in 1915, had succeeded Ed Leader as the Washington coach in the fall of 1922. Callow's recollections and emotions from that 1926 race against Wisconsin in Madison are recorded on the "Dad" Vail Regatta Web site under "Dad Vail Regatta History":

> I recall once when I was coaching at Washington in '26 or '27 we stopped at Madison to row the Badgers on our way to Poughkeepsie. "Dad" Vail had only a fair crew. He told me that his crew's showing against the Huskies spelled whether or not his Wisconsin crew would go to Poughkeepsie. So I told our coxswain to row around twenty-four and stay beside the Badgers until the last quarter mile, then go and win by a couple of lengths. They did, and right after the race "Dad" came right up to me, stuck out his hand and said with a warm grip, "Thanks Pal." We both went on to the Hudson. Dad did have some very fine crews at Wisconsin, but that was not one of them.

Russell S. "Rusty" Callow as University of Washington coach. Callow initiated the "Dad" Vail Regatta. Curtis Studio photo.

Future Wisconsin coach Norm Sonju was likely rowing 3-seat against Wisconsin that day in Madison in 1926. Washington would win the Poughkeepsie Regatta in 1926, defeating Navy, Syracuse, Penn, Columbia, California, Wisconsin, and Cornell. Sonju rowed 3-seat in the Huskies' victory on the Hudson River.

The Poughkeepsie Regatta, in 1927, would see Wisconsin send only its freshman boat, which finished last of seven. As "Dad" Vail would be quoted decades later in the *UW Centennial Sports Review of 1948*, the varsity crew was "too weak to be a worthy representative of the University of Wisconsin." Future Badger mentor Norm Sonju, now captain of the Washington Huskies, would see his championship-defending eight finished second behind a strong Columbia boat.

Pennsylvania's crew program, seeing its varsity finishing seventh of seven in the Poughkeepsie Regatta, would identify the need for a new coach. Washington alumni and crew coach Russell S. "Rusty" Callow resigned from his head coaching position at Washington (1922–27) and took the same position at Penn, from 1927 to 1950.

In 1934 Callow contributed the first place "Dad" Vail Trophy to a regatta he encouraged for small colleges and new crew programs in Marietta, Ohio. Callow's support and donated trophy evolved into the "Dad" Vail Regatta, now held in Philadelphia in early May. It is the largest college regatta in the nation.

In 1951 Callow succeeded "Buck" Walsh (for whom the annual Wisconsin-

Navy varsity eight race trophy was named) at the U.S. Naval Academy as head coach (1951–59). In 1952, Callow proudly accepted the award of the first Ten Eyck team trophy awarded at the IRA regatta on the new Lake Onondaga venue in Syracuse. Callow and Jim Ten Eyck knew each other well and had competed as head coaches from 1922 until Ten Eyck's death in 1938.

✕

If the 1927 season was bad, the 1928 season was worse! Coach Vail was ill much of the time and unable to direct early training. Vail also classified that year's crew as substandard. The only competition for the team was against the Milwaukee and Minnesota Boat Clubs. Because of weak finances in the athletic department and the modest quality of the team, no boats were sent to Poughkeepsie.

"Dad" Vail's illness worsened and on October 8, 1928, he passed away at age sixty-seven in his hometown of Gagetown, New Brunswick, Canada. Except for Jim Ten Eyck at Syracuse, Vail had been the only former professional sculler in the country still coaching college crews. A deeply religious man, Vail was one of the few coaches taking crews to the Poughkeepsie who refused to do any rowing on Sunday. Gradually, other coaches followed the lead of the Wisconsin mentor and, at the time of his death, it was quite unusual to see an eight swinging down the Hudson on a Sunday.[7]

Coach Vail's eighteen-year coaching career at Wisconsin, from 1910 until his death following the 1928 season, was one of the longest of any head crew coach. Only the head coaching careers of Randy Jablonic (1968–69 through 1995–96) and Norm Sonju (1946–47 through 1967–68) would be longer at Wisconsin. Many Wisconsin oarsmen remember Vail warmly and loyally as a very special man able to easily attract, motivate, and instruct from his own rowing experience.

> It is probably Vail's indomitable spirit that has enabled oarsmen and women at Wisconsin to prevail through periods of adversity and austerity even today.[8]

In another example of student gifting for UW facilities, the Memorial Union, completed in 1928, " Students were extremely active in providing $1.5 million in funding. The building was "Erected and Dedicated to the memory of the men and Women of the University of Wisconsin Who Served in Our Country's Wars." Those memorialized included 218 men and one woman; 179 had died in World War I and 30 in the Civil War.[9]

UW History—1925–1946

UW Enters the Modern Era as the Crew Hangs On

The appointment of Glenn Frank in 1925, the youngest person ever appointed to the university presidency, symbolized the beginnings of the modern era. Wisconsin by now was one of the country's preeminent universities, granting the most PhD's in the nation in 1925. The faculty not only added world-famous scholars but organizationally, the academic staff had coalesced into a tightly knit web of social, political, laboratory, and classroom relationships.

Following Coach Vail's death in 1928 the crew program languished. For the most part, Wisconsin's crew coaches—Mike Murphy, Ralph Hunn, Allen Walz, George Rea, and Curt Drewes—were given meager resources with which to develop the sport and to travel to serious competition. While the promises of larger budgets and more travel had been given to Murphy in his hiring process, the deepening depression and the uneven financial burdens forced on the university's various departments by President Franks kept crew in an ongoing state of malaise and underachievement.

The depression brought major financial pressures to most departments of the university, especially in the Athletic Department, and President Frank brought controversy to himself by continuing to live a grand lifestyle. Crew and much else suffered with the economic times.

By the mid-thirties, economic vitality seemed to be returning to the country. In May of 1936, Harry Stuhldreher, the quarterback in the backfield called the "Four Horsemen of Notre Dame" of 1925, was hired by the Athletic Board to become the Athletic Director and football coach. Doubts about President Frank's administrative abilities, his high-profile persona, and his politics led the Regents in early 1937 to decide not to reappoint Frank in June and to place him on an immediate leave of absence. Rowers of the day say that crew, for one, was better off without him.

Stuhldreher eventually decided he did not want crew coach Ralph Hunn on his staff and, in 1940, forced him out. His choice for a successor was excellent—Allan Walz, an easterner, who was effective with the media, had a great flair for publicity and motivated his young athletes well.

As the Depression waned, the world drifted into another world war. Many of

Bascom Hill c. 1950. Courtesy UW–Madison Archives, Image x252358.

the men enrolled at the university signed up for the service, and life in Madison seemed diminished from 1942 to 1946. Coach Walz himself took leave to serve in the military.

Arthur Hove wrote, "At the beginning of the 1940–41 academic year, 11,376 students were enrolled, 3,720 of that were women. By 1944–45, enrollment had dropped to 6,615, with 4,531 women. The campus resembled a military camp, as it was transformed into a training station for various programs"[1]

Crew kept plugging along—for a year under George Rea and for two more years under rigger Curt Drewes—as a good number of the remaining students, including those slated for later military service after graduation, still found rowing attractive.

7

Never Giving Up—Coaches Murphy to Walz

George W. "Mike" Murphy, coach 1928–34. Source: *1929 Poughkeepsie Regatta Program.* Courtesy of the IRA Stewards.

In the fall of 1928, the Athletic Council at Wisconsin hired Yale's freshman coach of six years, George W. "Mike" Murphy. An interesting figure all his life, Murphy had served in the service in the National Guard on the Mexican border and in World War I as a machine gunner before going to college at the University of Washington. Murphy had rowed for three years at Washington, through the 1922 season, as the stroke and team captain in his junior year.

It was also in 1922, in a February meeting of the University of Washington's own "W" Club, called at the request of the Seattle Chamber of Commerce, that Murphy and a crew teammate had a hand in changing the name of Washington's mascot.

The Chamber had requested the meeting to advise they were very unhappy with the current university's mascot, the "Sun Dodgers." It seemed that "Sun Dodgers" just wasn't selling that well with the city's real estate agents. Murphy, sitting in the meeting next to his 5-seat, Bob Ingram, said, "We have students from Alaska. How about naming us after the Alaskan sled dog the Malamute?" Bob said that was a good idea, but a little long. "How about 'Husky'?" Ingram asked. And so two members of Washington's crew led the change in the mascot name.[1]

During this 1922 season, Murphy visited Madison for a race against the Badgers and met "Dad" Vail for the first and last time.

Upon Murphy's hiring, the Athletic Board announced it would support crew "adequately," so as to send the varsity to Poughkeepsie each year and, as soon as possible, send the freshmen to the same race.

At the time of Murphy's arrival in Madison as the new coach in 1928, a move was afoot among several UW alumni rowers to start an organization that could help raise money to supplement the Athletic Department's support of the crew. *The Wisconsin Crew Corporation Newsletter* of May 30, 1952, quotes a letter from Franklin Orth, stroke and captain of the 1927–28 UW crew, in which he described how he conceived of the idea of the Wisconsin Crew Corporation (WCC) and developed it at the Memorial Union during the fall of 1928. With Orth were other "founding conspirators"—Curran C. McConville, captain of the 1898 crew and coach of the 1899 Berry Crate crew (later WCC's first president); Walter Alexander, captain of the 1896 crew (WCC's first vice president); and Harry Thoma, the class president of 1928 and the editor of *Alumni Magazine* (WCC's first secretary).

The Wisconsin Crew Corporation—reorganized as the Wisconsin Rowing Association (WRA) in 1973—would become a major benefactor to the men's crew program over the years following its formal incorporation November 11, 1931. In ongoing support, the WCC and WRA has contributed money almost annually from 1930 to today to help purchase shells, to underwrite travel expenses, and to build new boathouses (one finished in 1968 and added to in the 1980s as well as a second in late 2004).

In 1971 the WCC had to forcefully intercede with UW's Athletic Department to save crew from being cut. This occurred during a period of poor performance by the football team on the field and a related low attendance at Camp Randall, which resulted in a substantial drop in Athletic Department revenues.

In 2001–2, a $6–6.5 million-plus crew house expansion was on the drawing boards, and again much of the non-university funding was expected to come from a long list of rowing alums and members of the Wisconsin Rowing Association. One can only speculate the fate of men's crew without the ongoing support generated by the ideas launched over a cup of coffee at the Memorial Union that fall of 1928.

In June of 1929, the Washington Husky crew repeated their visit to Madison on their way to Poughkeepsie. This time Wisconsin lost the two-mile match by less than two lengths. Over 20,000 spectators watched from the Madison shore and from power- and rowboats on the water. At the national regatta on the Hudson River, Wisconsin took only its varsity and came in fifth in a field of nine, behind a strong Columbia boat, followed by Washington, Penn, and Navy. MIT, Syracuse, Cal, and Cornell all swamped, in that order!

Around this same time, in 1930, J. Martin "Murph" Wolman—later to become the publisher of the *Wisconsin State Journal*—hung around the Badger boathouse as a newsboy. Wolman, then about ten years old, sold newspapers from a bench in front of the Memorial Union to passersby on their way to the nearby YMCA, student union, the Red Gym, and crew and student boathouse. Coach Murphy would often let him steer the *Dad Vail*—a university rescue boat most of the day and a coach's launch in the afternoons. "So the crew started calling me 'Murph Jr.'" said Wolman. Later the nickname became "Murphy" or just "Murph" and has stuck with the publisher for the rest of his life.

Wolman remembers the crew's budget was very, very lean. Wolman continued:

> Bob Erickson, the owner of the boat rental concession at the boathouse, often donated the gasoline needed by the crew for the coach's launch. Coach Murphy's office was a small cubbyhole on the third floor of the Red Gym. The boathouse

was heated with wood and coal and there being little money, the boathouse was always cold. I don't know how they continued.

The Badgers had only two dual meets during the 1929–30 season, and no new boats were acquired. On May 22, 1930, the University of Pennsylvania visited Madison for a two-mile contest on Lake Monona. Wisconsin lost by half a second before a crowd of 10,000.

On June 17 Washington's three eight-oared crews again visited Madison and swept the Badgers in three separate races. Wisconsin's varsity did attend the Poughkeepsie in 1930, finishing eighth of nine, as Navy swamped one hundred yards short of the finish line.

Adding to the financial constraints on the crew, besides the Depression, was the budget-cutting pressure being applied by the colorful and controversial UW President, Glenn Frank. While constantly squeezing academic salaries and other areas of the university's budget, Frank saw fit to have the university purchase a Lincoln Continental for his own personal use. The Board of Regents later removed Frank from office.[2]

The 1930–31 season was little better, though there were no home races. The fans of rowing, however, remained loyal and supportive toward the sport. When the Athletic Board announced on April 10 that it was sending the Wisconsin varsity to the Poughkeepsie Regatta of 1931, the Wisconsin Alumni Association (WAA), with the strong financial support of former UW crew captain and WAA

UW president Glenn Frank, 1925–37. Source: UW–Madison Archives, Negative #251186.

66 NEVER GIVING UP

board member Walter Alexander, donated a new Pocock Boat Company shell to the crew.

Many Wisconsin students, including most of the fraternities and sororities, raised $1,000 through button sales to other students, parents, and faculty. In April 1931 one of those organizing the sale of buttons on campus to send the crew to Poughkeepsie was Freddy Maytag (UW '33). Fred L. Maytag (1911–1962), the grandson of Maytag founder Fred L. Maytag (1851–1937), became president of the Maytag Company in 1940, at age twenty-nine, upon the deaths of his grandfather and his father, Elmer (1883–1940).

Several hundred students marched to the train station, pulling the crew in the historic "red wagon" (a beautifully maintained large red cart used for transporting shells from the Lake Mendota boathouse to the Yahara River or to Lake Monona practice sites). Amid the cheers of the students, Lieutenant Governor Henry Huber wished the crew athletes success on behalf of all the people of the state. Unfortunately the Badger varsity could manage nothing better than an eighth-place finish in the 1931 Poughkeepsie Regatta, beating only MIT.

In the spring of 1932, at the depths of the depression, Coach Murphy was asked to close down the crew team. He and his athletes worried that if crew were terminated, the team would never start again. After assessing that his savings could keep his family going for some period, Murphy agreed to accept a 70 percent salary reduction, from $5,000 to $1,500, in order to keep crew going at UW.

For the next three years the Poughkeepsie Regatta was financially out of reach for the Badger crews. In the early summer of 1932, the IRA was held, but Wisconsin sent no one. In summer of 1933, the Poughkeepsie Regatta was canceled because so many schools, for similar financial reasons, expressed an inability to attend. By the summer of 1934 the Poughkeepsie Regatta had resumed, but Wisconsin still did not attend. A shortage of financing was the ostensible reason, but some also doubted the will of the university administration to support the sport.

Paul Eckhardt—a crew "W" winner in 1932 and '33 and an early historian of the crew—described the interest in crew of UW President Frank and later university officials:

> President Frank was not a friend of crew. His budget priorities fell unevenly through the university, including indifference as to whether the crew continued its thirty-plus year tradition of attending the Poughkeepsie Regatta. As was typical in those days, including in 1932, the Poughkeepsie Regatta's invitation to Wisconsin's crew to participate in the Regatta was sent to the Athletic Board.

Biography of Paul O. Eckhardt, Jr.

Paul O. Eckhardt, Jr. (UW '33), one of UW rowing's most loyal alumni. Source: *Milwaukee Journal* staff photo, published April 23, 1933.

In the fall of 1931, Paul O. Eckhardt, Jr., transferred from the University of Connecticut in Storrs, Connecticut, to Madison, Wisconsin. Having learned to row in Germany while visiting family during the summer, Paul came to Madison in order to continue rowing at the college level. He would later prove to be one of Wisconsin's most loyal, lifelong supporters.

Paul rowed in the UW varsity eight under coach Mike Murphy for the two Depression-limited seasons of 1931–32 and 1932–33. The Badgers never went to Poughkeepsie while Paul rowed, but his profound affection and energetic loyalty to the program never ended.

In the 1940s, Paul frequently attended Wisconsin's races in the east, in some cases as the Athletic Director's official representative of Wisconsin at the race. A member of the Phi Gamma Delta fraternity in college at Madison, Paul frequently organized dinners for the Badger crews visiting the East Coast in the 1940s and 1950s at the Phi Gam building in New York City.

In the June 1948 issue of *The Wisconsin Alumni*, he wrote a thorough two-page review of Wisconsin's varsity crew history. The Athletic Department used Paul's crew history research in its *Centennial Athletic Review* (1848 to 1948), which issue reviewed the histories of every varsity sport at the school.

In the early 1950s, Paul acted as the secretary of the Wisconsin Crew Corporation. In the course of writing the WCC's newsletter, he would sometimes telephone Coach Norm Sonju two or three times a day to accurately capture the latest news! Paul is remembered as perhaps Wisconsin's most avid fan by rowers and coaches from the 1940s to the 1980s.

In an interview at his Garrison, New York, home in December 2000, tears came to Paul's eyes when this author willingly accepted his heartfelt request to take, safeguard, research from, and ultimately donate his half-century collection of UW regatta programs, news clippings, newsletters, and other memorabilia and photos to the university.

In December 2002 Paul mailed a $10,000 check to Coach Clark for the boathouse campaign. In November 2003 another $10,000 check arrived as a contribution—in honor of his former coach—to the "Mike" Murphy Endowment Fund for Men's Crew at UW. At the end of 2004 Paul Eckhardt, born June 6, 1909, is the oldest living "W" winner in crew. The fire from his interest in UW's crew can still be felt in his voice.

When the request for financial support was run by the university administration, Frank was unsympathetic.

Harry Stuhldreher (the UW Athletic Director from 1936 to 1950) was a strong supporter of the UW crew. Not only was he supportive in Madison, but he also attended the Poughkeepsie Regatta and alumni dinners in New York City as the guest of honor. As an honorary official for the Wisconsin at many of the Regattas, I found Stuhldreher to be encouraging of crew and not just while our seeing one another personally at crew races, but also in all of our correspondence.

In 1934 the first race in what would later formally become the "Dad" Vail Regatta for small college and new program crews was held at Marietta, Ohio. The first place "Dad" Vail Trophy was won by Marietta College. Penn's subvarsity was second (under "Rusty" Callow, who encouraged and co-hosted the regatta and who, as noted earlier, donated the original "Dad" Vail Trophy to the winner), Rutgers came in third (under former Wisconsin coach Ned Ten Eyck), and Manhattan College was fourth (under future Wisconsin coach, Allen "Skip" Walz). Wisconsin, with already a forty-year crew history, did not attend this inaugural race of what would become the "Dad" Vail Regatta.

As Murphy's savings ran out at the end of the 1934 season, the Athletic Department showed its first small surplus. When Murphy's salary was not renewed to its original level, as agreed, he resigned and went to work for the Carnation Company in Wisconsin.

In spite of only modest successes during his tenure—in part the result of the financially difficult period and in part from the administration's ambivalence toward crew—Murphy was very well liked by his oarsmen, many of whom kept in touch with him over the subsequent years.

> *Crew coach Mike Murphy, who had served his country in World War I, would serve on yet another occasion, this time in 1942 in World War II, signing up at age forty-four as a first lieutenant with the Marines. In 1945 now Major Murphy was assigned to counsel and prepare servicemen for battle in the civilian job market. Before a group of kids in San Diego, Murphy and marine flyer and baseball great Ted Williams cooked up a deadpan-serious job-skill inventory during a public interview. Murphy's parting advice to Williams was, "Well, Ted, it seems as if you ought to be able to earn a living if you get back into baseball."*
>
> *Murphy would develop several dozen patents in the early 1950s for the construction of hydraulic loading mechanisms for municipal waste trucks, one or more of which he ultimately sold to the Heil Company in Milwaukee.[3] Badger rower and future UW crew coach George Rea (1942–43) would, in one of history's unusual coincidences, work alongside Murphy at the Heil Company in the 1950s and '60s, before Murphy retired to Arizona in 1964.*

Ralph Hunn, coach 1934–40. Source: *1940 Badger Yearbook*, p. 411. Courtesy of UW–Madison Archives.

Ralph Hunn was named Wisconsin's new head crew coach over the summer of 1934. Hunn, the varsity coxswain and frosh coach and who had been elected captain of the 1934–35 crew, gave up his captaincy and his remaining eligibility to assume the head coaching position. Believed to be from a wealthy Chicago family, the young, new coach was probably hired at Murphy's reduced yearly salary of $1,500.

Hunn worked hard to reinvigorate an interest in crew by the student body. During the spring of 1934, Murphy, Hunn, and hockey coach Art Thomsen encouraged and supported an increased intramural interest in crew, including inviting coeds to row. In the spring of 1935 Hunn also initiated the start of a men's lightweight crew.

The 1934–35 season was not a wildly successful one but was a year of classic college experiences. In May of 1935, Wisconsin did attend the second of the series of races in Marietta where the "Dad" Vail Trophy would again be awarded. Because Wisconsin's program was already a mature one, the Badgers raced as an unofficial entry, invited primarily because of the historical connection to "Dad" Vail.

On the way to Marietta, Wisconsin's shell, the *Dad Vail,* was side-swiped by a farmer's truck and smashed beyond use, forcing the Badger rowers to borrow a shell from Penn. Driving their own cars because of a shortage of funds, the young UW rowers made a stop at Culver Academy in Indiana, where Badger oarsman Howard Heun had gone to school. Commander Fowler was delighted to see them, lent them a shell to practice, and hosted them for dinner and breakfast. At the Marietta Regatta, Wisconsin finished fourth of six in their borrowed shell.

In a wonderful example of the loyalty of UW's rowing alumni, W. K. Murphy, the 2-seat in Wisconsin's IRA-winning freshman boat of 1900 and later a successful insurance businessman, sponsored the Badgers' 1935 crew trip to Long Beach, California, where, on June 28 and 29 of 1935, the second National Intercollegiate Crew Regatta was held at the Long Beach Marine Stadium, site of the 1932 Olympics.

To promote the regatta, organizers had arranged for Hollywood starlets to visit the various crews during practice periods. Future (1935–36) Badger crew captain Howard Heun remembered the trip to California:

> June Knight was the "lucky" lady to come by the Badger workout. Shown the job of coxswain from the back of the boat, the crew proposed she also learn about the tradition of being thrown in the water after winning a race! Jack Cole

grabbed her wrists and Irving Kraemer her ankles. On the count of "three," Cole let go, but Kraemer did not, resulting in Ms. Knight's landing unceremoniously on her behind! The chilling glare she gave the Badger crew is remembered to this day.

Wisconsin's rowers were also invited to work as extras in rowing a becalmed ship in the filming of *Mutiny on the Bounty*. Unfortunately, the filming was deferred two weeks, before which the crews had to return home.

Wisconsin lost to Syracuse and Cal in one of the qualifying heats and to UCLA in the Consolation Final. The future co-captain and 2-seat Robert Heinze (1935–36) remembers Gregory Peck as a Cal rower in 1935. (Wisconsin had already skipped the 1935 Poughkeepsie Regatta by this time.) As for the trip home, Heun, in an undated, unsigned, one-page essay titled "Sea Sick," continued:

On the return home, the Badgers caught a coastal steamer from Los Angeles to Seattle. We had been advised the coastal journey on a small steamer might be somewhat unsettling because we would be riding the landward swells rather than cutting through them. A few of us for some reason made the added mistake of choosing cabins at the stern, just above the propeller.

Fortunately, a railroad rep was on board and, after we inquired, he said those of us who wished to could take the train from San Francisco to Seattle. Coach Hunn and most of the others continued on the journey by sea and two or three took the inland train (before all meeting up again in Seattle).

On the journey back (from Seattle to Chicago), the crew all had steak in the dining car. The menu had a note saying if the passenger especially enjoyed any item, the railroad would be glad to serve you a second portion. When the Badger crew all chose steak, the waiter said "Nossuh!" But the dining car steward, on appeal, said, "That's what the menu says, so we'll have to make good. But no more repeats on the entrees (in the future)." Some in the group felt this helped replace what had been fed to the fishes on the coastal steamer to Seattle.

On August 31, 1936, Australian Andrew O'Dea, Wisconsin's first full-time crew coach and brother of Badger football legend Patrick O'Dea, died in New York City at the age of sixty-seven.

Over the 1935–36 season, the Badgers, in a new Olympic shell, defeated the Detroit Boat Club on Lake Mendota over a rainswept one-and-one-eighth-mile course by three and one-half lengths. An unofficial lightweight Wisco crew dropped their contest against the Milwaukee Boat Club by a length and a half.[4] The lightweight boating: Ebert (bow), Kaiser, Hannahs, Pfannstiehl, Pousseau, Haynie, Kirkland, Paul Waterman (stroke), and LeGrand (cox).

Against Marietta College on June 6, the Badgers won the Col. Charles W.

Dawes Trophy on a two-mile course on the Muskingum River by three-quarters of a length. The second varsity also won their contest. A spectator train followed the action.

On the drive home from Marietta, Howard Heun, then the crew's captain, remembers calling his father to advise he was bringing the crew home to stay overnight. Heun continued: "The following morning, my dad called the Richmond Leland Hotel to advise that a bunch of hungry young lads would be soon stopping by for breakfast and to put the bill on his tab." (These were the days before compliance issues and the fund-raising activities of the UW Foundation, the articles of incorporation for which wouldn't be filed with the Secretary of State until June of 1945.)

> Crew captain Howard Heun, as president of the Student Board, was also a member of the Athletic Board. Heun remembered:
> While on the Athletic Board, we made the decision to hire Harry Stuhldreher in May of 1936 to the position of Wisconsin's Athletic Director and head football coach. Stuhldreher, one of the "Four Horsemen" of Notre Dame as an All-American quarterback in 1925, became a strong friend and supporter of crew at Wisconsin.

Prospects improved during the 1936–37 season, as more men came out for tryouts in the fall. The active intramural program was yielding results. Against Marietta College in Ohio, Wisconsin won by seven lengths over a two-mile course. At the Poughkeepsie Regatta, however, Wisconsin sent only its varsity and came in last, in part due to a crab caught near the end of the four-mile course.

On February 14, 1938, Hunn, taking a page out of Andy O'Dea's coaching book, put his crews back on the Yahara River for some open water winter training. The river, which connects Lake Mendota and Lake Monona, often doesn't freeze in the winter and thus provided a relatively straight stretch of three-quarters of a mile of water on which to practice.

Wisconsin had only one rowing contest during the spring of 1938. Washington, again on their way to the Poughkeepsie Regatta, visited Madison and, against the three Wisconsin's crews, swept all three races.

Wisconsin thus arrived at the 1938 Poughkeepsie with very little racing experience in their boat. Wisconsin's varsity entry rowed ahead of Syracuse and Cornell and placed fifth behind Navy, Cal, Washington, and Columbia. The result was considered a successful effort, given how little competition they had faced over the spring. The Wisconsin Alumni of New York City hosted dinner there for the Badgers before the crew boarded the train back to Madison.

Catching a Crab

"Catching a crab" is getting the stern-facing edge of the oar caught in the water during the recovery phase of the stroke. Usually caused by rolling the wrists too far in the feathering of the oar, the unexpected and sudden sternward thrust of an oar handle, when the blade is unexpectedly "caught" in the water, can throw the oarsman completely out of the boat—a dangerous prospect in the cold waters of early season.

On August 10, 1937, Wisconsin's third crew coach (1898–99), Curran C. McConville, died at the age of sixty in Clintonville, Wisconsin. McConville was captain of the 1897–98 crew, coach of Wisconsin's famous Berry Crate crew at the Poughkeepsie Regatta of 1899, and one of the founders of the Wisconsin Crew Corporation.

On February 11, 1938, famed Syracuse coach Jim Ten Eyck died at eighty-seven. During his thirty-four-year head-coaching career (1903–37), Ten Eyck's Syracuse crews at Poughkeepsie had won five varsity eight, four second varsity eight, and seven freshmen eight titles.

Tributes flowed into Syracuse University from all over the world. Ten Eyck's body was cremated and the ashes strewn that spring in the twilight of an evening on his beloved Hudson River. He had been born in Tompkins Cove near Krum Elbow, the start of the four-mile race in the Poughkeepsie Regatta.

Jim's eldest son, Ned Ten Eyck, former Wisconsin crew coach (1906–1910) succeeded his father as head coach for the Orangemen.

Syracuse crew coach Jim Ten Eyck. Source: *Mark of the Oarsmen* by M. R. Alama, 1963, p. 59. Courtesy of Syracuse Alumni Rowing Association.

The 1938–39 season was another year of limited spring competition for the varsity eight. The freshman eight defeated the Milwaukee Boat Club, St. John's Military Academy, and the Lincoln Park Boat Club. The only frosh loss in a dual meet that year was to Culver Academy in Indiana. The university sent both varsity and freshman boats to Poughkeepsie, and the UW varsity finished fifth of six boats and the freshmen were last in a field of six.

In 1939, Athletic Director Harry Stuhldreher hired Curt Drewes, who had opened a boat shop on Turville's Point on Lake Monona, as a part time boatman or "rigger" (the craftsman responsible for the repair, maintenance, and transportation of all the shells and oars, and who installs and maintains the rigging and seat mechanics). When Drewes took the job, the crew had two boats and one set of oars. Before long, this part-time job grew to sixty hours a week. Curt's second wife and widow, Lyla Drewes, told of his becoming a full-time UW employee:

With that workload, there eventually came a time for Curt to join the university staff on a full time basis. The bureaucratic employment process required Drewes take an entrance exam for the job position. As the job of "rigger" was a new one, neither a position description nor an entrance exam existed for the job. Stuhldreher solved the potential dilemma with common sense. He asked Drewes to first write the position description, then prepare an entrance exam . . . and then to take it! Can you *imagine* how he scored on that exam?

Drewes would continue as the Badger rigger—and act as interim coach at Wisconsin for the two war-restricted 1943–45 seasons—for thirty-seven years.

The 1939–40 season was the last at UW for Ralph Hunn. For reasons that are not entirely clear, Athletic Director Stuhldreher announced the release of Hunn on April 30, 1940. UW attended the Poughkeepsie in the summer of 1940, apparently led by Hunn, pending a summer appeal. Wisconsin's varsity, the only UW entry, finished seventh of eight, defeating only Princeton. Despite later appeals and closed door hearings with the Athletic Counsel, Hunn was never reinstated.

The Coaching Tenure of Allen Walz—A Ray of Light!

In the fall of 1940, Allen W. "Skip" Walz was called to Madison as the head crew coach. Born December 22, 1909, Walz was raised in New York City and remained at heart a New Yorker.

Walz had come to Wisconsin for one semester in the fall of 1929 and played as a tackle on the freshman squad. He returned to New York, however, in the second semester and attended New York University, from which he graduated in 1933.

By the time he returned to Madison in the fall of 1940, Walz had already enjoyed a varied and successful career. In 1933 Walz had been co-captain of his football team at New York University. Along the way, he had won a Golden Gloves boxing tournament in New York. And he had rowed for a total of thirteen years with his prep school and later with the New York Athletic Club. Walz had also been a volunteer head crew coach, replacing his failing father, at Manhattan College for seven years, while working as a speech teacher on the faculty.

Allen W. "Skip" Walz, coach 1940–42 and 1945–46. Source: *1941 Badger Yearbook*, p. 266. Courtesy of UW–Madison Archives.

On October 22, 1939, Walz became the first-ever commentator for a televised pro football game, during the 23–14 victory of the Brooklyn (football) Dodgers over the Philadelphia Eagles at Ebbets Field in Brooklyn. The game was attended by 13,051 fans and reached approximately 500 TV sets over RCA's experimental television station, W2XBS.[5]

During the spring season of 1941, Wisconsin faced, and defeated, Marietta College and the Lincoln Park Boat Club of Chicago. Against Washington, in a one-mile exhibition race in Chicago, the Badgers lost by only a half length.

Coach Walz will be remembered not only as a colorful figure but as an imaginative promoter of the sport. At Poughkeepsie in 1941, Walz's two weeks of practice on the Hudson River had its many moments of color. In the "pickle boat"—the boat generally occupied by the varsity spares brought as backups or reserves to the regatta—the Badger substitute oarsmen occasionally stepped aside for guests of Coach Walz. In one case, it was four sportswriters, including the *New York Times* rowing reporter Allison Danzig, who took Wisconsin's straight four out on the Hudson.

Another friend of Walz was 200-pound boxer Lou Nova, who worked out with the Badger oarsmen at Poughkeepsie. Nova was getting in shape for his scheduled fight for the heavyweight boxing championship with Joe Louis that September (Nova lost in a TKO to Louis in the sixth round at the Polo Grounds).

Another noteworthy sidelight of the regatta, remembered by several Badgers in attendance, was when freshman reserve oarsman Ed Chudik contracted a serious case of poison ivy while painting a "W" high on the rocks of western riverbank of the Hudson River near the town of The Highlands. The painted rocks, which can be seen to this day from Marist College's campus on the banks of the Hudson, face east toward the city of Poughkeepsie and Marist College, on the far shore.

Hudson River observation train on the west side of the Hudson River at the Poughkeepsie Regatta. Source: *1941 Poughkeepsie Regatta Program* cover. Courtesy of the IRA Stewards.

In the Poughkeepsie races, Wisconsin's varsity eight placed sixth, ahead of Rutgers, MIT, and Columbia, but losing to Washington, Cal, Cornell, Syracuse, and Princeton. The frosh, however, pulled a surprise and came in second. The *New York Times* of June 26, 1941, gave a brief description of the two-mile race:

> In the freshman contest, which opened the regatta, Wisconsin put in a real bid and so did Syracuse, but Cornell came from behind in the last quarter mile with a superb bit of rowing and nailed Wisconsin, Syracuse, Princeton, MIT, and Columbia, respectively.

During the 1941–42 season, because of wartime difficulties in transportation, manpower losses, and lack of funds, the varsity competed in only one contest. On

NEVER GIVING UP   75

Biography of Carl A. Holtz

The 1941 stroke of the silver-medal Badger freshman boat was an oarsman from Riverside High School in Milwaukee and new to rowing when he joined the team. Carl Holtz, who'd worked for two years before starting college, initially joined the freshman football squad at Madison. He played opposite All-American end Dave Schreiner, who played on both sides of the ball at Wisconsin.

Holtz remembers, "I wasn't very good since I'd never been out for a sport before. Schreiner was a great guy. After every play, often he'd knocked me down, he'd come over, pick me up and tell me what to do to improve." The football team worked out in the Red Gym. The gym had a balcony circling the court, one floor up. From the balcony one day, crew coach Walz looked down and noticed the tall, slender frame of Carl Holtz and, recalls Holtz, "He sent one of his managers to ask me to come up and pay him a visit." Soon Walz had worked his charm on the young Holtz and had him out for the crew. Holtz joined his friend from scouting and school in Milwaukee, Roy Rom, on the crew team as freshmen. Rom was the backup freshman coxswain.

With World War II causing the suspension of the Poughkeepsie Regatta from 1942 through 1946—and with Holtz's own entry into the service from 1942 to 1945—the biggest race in Holtz's career came in the Eastern Intercollegiate Regatta (later renamed the Eastern Sprints) in 1946, when he stroked Wisconsin to its first national title in the varsity eight. The victory would later land Holtz's varsity crew and coach Walz in the National Rowing Foundation's Hall of Fame and Holtz, individually, in UW's Athletic Hall of Fame.

Carl's senior year would be under new head crew coach Norm Sonju, because Walz had been hired away by Yale University. Following Holtz's graduation in 1947, he joined former UW coaches Waltz and Roy Rom at Yale as the freshman coach. In the spring of 1952, Walz and his wife, Jean, and their growing family returned to Milwaukee and joined the Patrick Cudahy meatpacking company. Five years later, Holtz used his UW agricultural education, in part inspired by one of his instructors, Aldo Leopold, on his 291-acre farm in Mukwonago, Wisconsin.

Holtz, now in his eighties, still carries an infectious twinkle in his eyes while demonstrating a continuing love of and loyalty to his rowing experience at Wisconsin.

Stroke: Carl Holtz, Milwaukee, junior, 6 feet 3, 185 pounds

Carl Holtz, stroke of UW's 1946 Eastern Sprints Winner. Source: *Milwaukee Journal* photo, published June 23, 1946.

May 16, 1942, the Adams Cup Regatta was held on the Charles River in Cambridge. The Wisconsin varsity's second-place showing was described the *New York Times* of May 17, 1942:

> The year's only intersectional rowing race moved over the mile-and-three-quarter course on the Charles River. It was apparent as soon as the crews settled from their racing starts that it was to be a real race. Tech (MIT) led for a while and then Navy, Harvard and Penn, but all five crews were tightly locked.
>
> They all dropped [their stroke rates] to the lower thirties, except Penn, which stayed up to 35 and went into the lead in the first quarter mile. The Quakers had perhaps a deck on Navy, with Harvard and Wisconsin a deck further back and Tech on their flank.
>
> At the three-quarter mark it was impossible to pick a leader from among Wisconsin, Penn and Navy, with the Crimson a few feet back and Tech about ¾ of a length further back in the rear. Then, as they moved under the crowd on the bridge just short of the mile mark, Harvard had begun to move and was a few feet in the lead, with the others just along side.
>
> Here, in the rough water, Phil Childs, the Navy stroke, caught a crab, lost his oar handle and the crew missed two or three strokes, dropping back a length. Navy pulled itself together and rowed very well, but Harvard had taken command. The Crimson had a bit of open water and Darcy Curwen, who is one of the best strokes the Cantabs [a nickname for Harvard] have ever had, moved his boatload along smoothly and well.
>
> Navy came back to challenge Wisconsin while Tech moved up to pass the tiring Penn crew. In the last few hundred yards, Wisconsin and Navy were prow to prow and they slammed over the finish at forty strokes, with only the judges on the finish boat able to pick them apart.
>
> Harvard had gone up to 40 and finished very well, distinctly master of the river for this day. It is unfortunate that Navy had its accident, but the Crimson deserved full credit for their victory. For Wisconsin—denied a chance to race at Poughkeepsie—it finished the only race of the year, and a good one. Wisconsin, with an eight that averaged over 6'4" in height, was very impressive and might well have been a real four-mile crew if the Poughkeepsie regatta had not been called off.
>
> Wisconsin's boating was: Bow [Chester] Knight, 2. [Robert] Jenkins, 3. [George] Rea, 4. [Richard] Mueller, 5. [LeRoy] Jensen, 6. [Hudson] Smythe, 7. [William] Phelan, stroke [Carl] Holtz and coxswain [Robert] Moore.[6]

For his effort in the Adam's Cup, and for being the most inspirational member of the crew, junior George Rea, in the 3-seat, was awarded the George I. Gross

Trophy by Coach Allen Walz later in the summer of 1942. Gross, a Walz friend, had sponsored the trophy.

No IRAs were held the summer of 1942 because of the growing influence of World War II on the nation's priorities. In addition, a large number of student athletes and faculty were joining the armed services. On November 21, 1942, the *Daily Cardinal* noted the impending departure of Coach Walz to the Navy on a leave of absence from the university for the duration of his military service. Walz had been inducted as a PT boat skipper. Roy Rom, a junior coxswain, was named to look after crew affairs during Walz's absence. When Rom himself was called to the service in December, senior George Rea was asked by Stuhldreher to fill the head coach position.

For the 1942–43 season, George Rea—whose uncle, William J. "Will" Gibson, had rowed in prep school at St. John's in Delafield, Wisconsin and in the Berry Crate crew of 1899 and later elected captain of the 1900–01 crew—stepped in as the coach, pending Walz's return. During this period a freshman crew was organized, but a varsity eight never continuously materialized. The frosh rowed against teams in Wisconsin, Illinois, and Indiana, since longer trips were limited by wartime travel restrictions. In the only race the varsity participated in this season, the eight was defeated by the frosh.

When George Rea graduated in June of 1943, the coaching duties were assumed for two seasons by rigger Curt Drewes. The period was almost, but not completely, devoid of competition. The frosh and perhaps a varsity eight were mustered for two or three races, and Wisconsin won them all. For his success during the lean season, Drewes would later become hailed by many as "the only undefeated crew coach in Wisconsin's history!"[7]

In late 1945 Allen Walz returned to coaching at Wisconsin. Arranging an extensive schedule of national competition and using air transportation for the first time to get Wisconsin athletes to their competitions, Walz brought nation-wide publicity to his program. As most of his 1941 and 1942 crew members had returned from the service, Walz soon had a fine team in the making.

The year 1946 turned out to be a watershed year in the history of UW rowing. The crew went undefeated during the regular season and along the way, the varsity won its first major regatta ever! The season's only blemish was a defeat in a postseason regatta in Seattle, their last race of the year.

The biggest race of the year came at Annapolis, Maryland, on the Severn River. Traveling to this regatta, the crew became the first Wisconsin athletic team to use an airplane to attend an event. At the Eastern Intercollegiate Regatta on May 11, 1946, nine varsity eights joined in competition over a one-and three-quarter-mile course. *The Evening Capital* of Annapolis on May 13, 1946, described the event, including coach Walz's distracting claims:

George A. Rea, coach 1942–43. Gift of George Rea family.

The irony of the varsity crew race was that Wisconsin defeated the Navy crew by a length using the midshipman's 1945 shell, while Navy rowed in a 1939 Pennsylvania shell. The nine crews that participated drew for three Navy, three Pennsylvania and three Princeton shells. Wisconsin got the Navy's 1945 "A. B. Yeates" shell while Navy got the "Joseph W. Burke" of Pennsylvania. After the drawing on Thursday, Navy Coach Charles S. ("Buck") Walsh declared that the new shell would give Wisconsin the margin of victory.

Yard patrol boats, motor sailors, yachts, canoes and various other craft lined the Severn, or lay pinched at the varsity finish line when the regatta started behind schedule due to cross winds that prevented the crews from lining up at the stake boats. The bleachers at Severnside were filled.

Fleet Admiral William S. Halsey USN (ret.) and Vice Admiral Jesse B. Olendorf, USN., were the guests of Vice Admiral Aubrey W. Bench, USN, superintendent of the Naval Academy, on the superintendent's yacht, the *Anita Clay*.

In the jayvee race, all nine stake boats were swamped as the crews lined up and the wind swung them at a 45 degree angle with the course. Princeton, Cornell, MIT and Navy was the finish of the JV-8 event. Wisconsin did not have a junior varsity entry.

Colonel Robbins tried to start the nine varsity shells from the stake boats, but he was again forced to use a flying start, sending crews racing down stream at 6:06 P.M. Wisconsin coach Allen Walz, on the press boat, watching the Wisconsin crew moving on the line, declared they were all too heavy and needed more work. He said they averaged 186 pounds in weight and 6 foot 3 inches in height. All afternoon he had been joking about his crew's chances, declaring they were just rowing for the fun of it.

At the start of the varsity race, it appeared that his view might be correct, as Wisconsin fell back of the group of crews that got away in front. After a half-mile of water had been covered, Princeton was leading Navy by a deck, with Wisconsin a deck behind the midshipmen. Columbia, in the outside lane in the middle of the river, was steadily stroking toward the lead and Harvard, which started fast, was beginning to break.

Curt P. Drewes in 1942. Boatman (1938–62) and coach (1943–45). Gift of Curt Drewes family.

Wisconsin Takes Over

Carl Holtz, of Milwaukee, 185 pound, 6 foot 3 inch, Wisconsin stroke, who had piloted [Holtz was actually a navigator] bombers during the war, put on the pressure soon after the start, moving the stroke to a 36. A mile from the finish line, Wisconsin had moved in front of the pack, trailed by Navy, Columbia, Princeton, MIT, Penn with Rutgers, Cornell and Harvard fighting it out in a second group. All nine crews were closely bunched. Princeton had swung into a 36 seeking to keep pace with Wisconsin, but Navy was holding its own at a lower beat.

In the next quarter mile, the leaders, Wisconsin, Navy, Columbia and Princeton were fighting it out with not more than a length and a half covering all four boats. Princeton found the going too tough and began dropping back and Wisconsin swept over the finish line in the unusually fast time of 9:12.8. Navy (9:16.8) came across a length behind, four seconds later, with Columbia (9:18.8) at two seconds, or a half length behind the midshipmen. Rutgers (9:20.8) took fourth, a half-length behind and Cornell (9:22.8), Penn (9:24.8), Princeton (9:24.5), MIT (9:26.5) and Harvard (9:27.5) followed.

The Wisconsin crew consisted of a senior, four juniors, a sophomore and three freshmen. Walz said it was the first varsity intercollegiate boat race Wisconsin had won in 55 years and was the first intercollegiate [title] to go to the Middle West. He said he hoped it would encourage Ohio State, Purdue and Minnesota to take up rowing.

After the varsity race, Walz bewailed the fact he hadn't brought a jayvee eight, declaring this second varsity boat was just as good as his varsity.[8]

For Wisconsin, the win was huge! The victory was the first time the varsity eight had won a major regatta since entering the 1898 Poughkeepsie Regatta al-

UW winning the first Eastern Sprints in 1946. For this inaugural Eastern Sprints regatta, the victorious UW boating: Chester Knight (bow), Paul Klein, Ralph Falconer, Gordon Grimstead, Fred Suchow, Dick Mueller, Dick Tipple, Carl Holtz (stroke), and Carlyle Fay, (coxswain). AP Wirephoto, published May 11, 1946.

This was the moment for which Wisconsin men waited 55 years. It shows the Badger crew slipping over the finish line first in the mile and three-quarter eastern intercollegiate rowing championship on the Severn river at Annapolis Saturday, a half length ahead of Navy. The regatta took the place of the Poughkeepsie race, which will not be resumed until 1947. The Badgers, until Saturday, had never done better than finish second in a race on eastern waters. The seating of the Badger boat (left to right) follows: Carlye Fay of Minneapolis, coxswain; Richard Tipple of Madison, No. 7; Paul Klein of Two Rivers, No. 6; Fred Suchow of Ripon, No. 5; Gordon Grimstead of Madison, No. 4; Ralph Falconer of Brainerd, Minn., No. 3; Tom Blacklock of Greene Point, Mich., No. 2; Chet Knight of Eau Claire, No. 1, and Carl Holtz of Milwaukee, stroke. The Badgers will make their next start against Pennsylvania at Philadephia May 25.

—AP Wirephoto

Wisconsin's Championship Crew pictured with the shirts that they won in the May 11 regatta. Left to right, Navy, Columbia, Rutgers, Cornell, Penn, Princeton, M.I.T., and Harvard.

most fifty years earlier. Yes, the freshmen had already won twice at Poughkeepsie and, yes, the varsity had come in second five times. But this was the first time the varsity itself had won in a major intercollegiate competition, in this case against the best crews of the East.

Later in the spring, Wisconsin attended one of the feature race events in the 1946 American Championships—the Twelfth Annual Scholastic Rowing Regatta in Philadelphia. In the late afternoon varsity eight event, UW (7:11.0) defeated coach Rusty Callow's Penn varsity (7:11.4), jayvee and lightweight eight crews on the Schuylkill River at Philadelphia over a one and one-sixteenth-mile course (the Henley distance). UW's coxswain, Carlyle "Bud" Fay, remembers the Schuylkill, which originates from the mouth of a coal mine, as being "black as coal." Fay had

UW's 1946 crew displaying shirts won at the first Eastern Sprints Regatta. Source: *Wisconsin Crew Corporation News Letter,* June 1946.

found his way onto the Wisconsin crew through his roommate, Ralph Falconer, who himself was discovered by Walz in the registration lines. According to Fay, "anyone Walz had to look up to was invited out for crew."

Wisconsin's crew came close to experiencing another "berry crate" incident during the race on the Schuylkill. A dredge, anchored at the quarter-mile mark forced coxie, Carlyle Fay, to steer the Badger shell around the obstacle in order to find a straight course for the remaining mile. As the shell veered, it collided with the Penn jayvee boat and both crews locked oars for about ten strokes. After getting cleared of this mess, Wisconsin was two lengths behind the Penn varsity. In the UW Office of Sports Publication's *1948 Media Guide*, the race was described in this way:

> A half-mile from the finish, Badger stroke Carl Holtz "caught a crab" and lost his oar behind him for 15 seconds but he raised the beat to 40 against a severe head wind and rough water to send the Badger shell to a deck-length win over the Quaker varsity. A crowd of 5,000 watched. UW rowed in a Penn shell and used Penn's Red and Blue blades, preferring them to their own blades, which they brought.[9]

The Sunday following the Philadelphia event, the UW crew spent the afternoon at Shibe Park watching the Brooklyn Dodger's trim the Philadelphia Athletics in a double header. Between games and after having toured the press box and the broadcasting booths, the Badgers visited the Dodgers in their dressing room. Leo Durocher gave an impromptu comment on what makes athletic winners, and Walz rewarded him with one of Wisconsin's noted products—a brick of Wisconsin cheese. (Walz, originally from New York, probably knew the Brooklyn sports figures from his Brooklyn broadcasting experience in pro football.)

A week later, on June 1, Wisconsin traveled to Ithaca, New York, the home of Cornell's Big Red crew, to face Cornell, Penn, and Princeton. Roy Rom, an assistant coach under Walz, remembers there being gasoline shortages in the East just after the war, so Coach Walz instructed Rom and a student manager to bring a milk can of extra gas for his coach's launch (the gas cans, the launch, and the shells had to be transported on special "end-loading" railroad boxcars, which always had to be reserved well in advance. On more than one occasion, a few extra crew members would also stow away in the boxcars in order to witness the competition).

Bringing the gas-filled milk can into the crew's hotel in Ithaca, the doorman asked the two assistants, "What've you got in the can?" In spite of what must have been a nasty smell, the student manager answered back, "Water. The coach doesn't want his rowers to get sick drinking hotel water." The doorman responded, "Well, take it to the kitchen to store it." Naturally, the two agreed and, once out of sight of the doorman, took a quick turn into their room.

Later on Lake Cayuga, Coach Walz sent the crew home to the boathouse after practice. Soon after restarting their coaching launch to head back to the boathouse themselves, Coach Walz, assistant Roy Rom, and the student manager found that, in spite of their planning, they were now out of gas on the big lake. With only one paddle in the boat, Rom remembers that he and the manager swapped the oar every few minutes, while Coach Walz used his big coach's megaphone as an oar!

The race itself was covered by Coach Walz's old friend from the 1941 Poughkeepsie Regatta, veteran rowing sportswriter Allison Danzig of the *New York Times*, whose article on June 2, 1946, reported:

> The regatta was to have been rowed over a two-mile course on Lake Cayuga. Conditions on the lake, however, made it impossible for the shells to venture forth, and it was necessary to transfer the races to the sheltered inlet and reduce the distance to a mile. Because of the narrowness of the canal, the four competing crews could not become engaged at the same time, and so Referee Ned Ten Eyck of Syracuse held a drawing for two preliminary heats, with the winners meeting in the final
>
> Wisconsin was drawn against Pennsylvania and won its heat by two-thirds of a length in 5:01, to 5:02.4 for the Red and Blue. Cornell led Princeton home in the second heat by almost a full length in 5:03, as against 5:06.5 for the Tigers.
>
> Wisconsin took the lead in the first few strokes of the final and were never headed. They rowed at a much higher beat than the Ithacans, going up as high as forty-two and keeping the stroke around forty most of the way. Penn had rowed at almost the same high stroke in its heat, throwing in one big ten after another, but it could not get the run on the boat that the Badgers did.
>
> Cornell, which had rowed as low as twenty-seven or twenty-eight for the first mile at Annapolis, lifted the stroke higher today, but it was content to go along at thirty-seven or thirty-eight for nearly three-quarters of the race, while Wisconsin was rowing at forty to forty-two and opening up a lead.
>
> At a quarter of a mile, Wisconsin had built up a lead of a half a length. In the next quarter, it did not improve its position by much, but, just before the three-quarter mark, it started to go away rapidly and had a full length. Cornell now made its bid and carried its stroke up to forty. But the increase failed to help. The Badgers, rowing as one, with faultless rhythm and blade work, went steadily ahead, opening up water with each stroke.
>
> The finish: Wisconsin, going away, at a length and a half at 5:08 and Cornell at 5:14. In a row-off for third place, Penn (5:07) defeated Princeton (5:10.6) by the margin of a few feet of open water.

Danzig further summarized:

Wisconsin's oarsmen completed their sweep of the water of the East today and head for the Pacific Coast with high hopes of establishing national collegiate supremacy in the regatta at Seattle June 22.

The heavy, beautifully synchronized crew from the Middle West showed the way to Cornell, Penn and Princeton. Previously, Wisconsin had won the Eastern sprint championship regatta at Annapolis, with nine crews competing, and a week ago defeated Penn on the Schuylkill in Philadelphia.

Whatever the distance has been, the Wisconsin sweep-swingers have measured up to the test, and today they were at their peak, paced by Stroke Carl Holtz, a former Army Air Force bombardier with more than fifty missions in the European theater.

Powerful, smooth and beautifully together, the Badgers were short in the water but they lifted the boat beyond the power of Cornell, with almost faultless blade work. Walz said they rowed their best race of the season today and happily invited everyone to come around to the Ithaca Hotel and have some Wisconsin cheese.[10]

The *Wisconsin Crew Corporation News Letter* of April 1947 reported that UW's crews, as ambassadors of one of the state's leading industries, had distributed over 150 pounds of Wisconsin cheese on their eastern and western trips in 1946!

In a follow-up event at the Northwest Maritime Regatta in Seattle (also known as the Seattle Invitational Sprint Regatta), 150,000 spectators gathered at Lake Washington on June 22, 1946, to watch the climax of the first postwar college crew racing season. *Life* magazine was also there to record the moment. Eight crews were entered in the competition.

The race was covered by *Life* magazine (July 8, 1946) which noted six of eight crews were coached by former Washington rowers and all eight were racing George Pocock shells.

The *Seattle Post-Intelligencer* of June 24, 1946, wrote:

They were hailing Cornell as the sprint champion of American rowing today, as the eight set of oarsmen rested from their strenuous efforts of the previous afternoon. The splendid performance of the Ithacans thrilled the greatest crowd which ever watched a sports event in Northwest history. Coach Allen Walz of favored Wisconsin conceded that the Badgers might have come in better than fourth had the Badgers not become confused 50 feet from the finish line and let up on their oars momentarily. 'But we certainly wouldn't have overhauled Cornell," Walz declared. Many visiting crewmen who were not scheduled to depart until today relaxed yesterday by visiting Mount Rainier or salmon fishing in the Sound.[11]

The slightly less objective UW *Centennial Sports Review of 1948* described the event in this way:

> The '46 Wisconsin varsity crew startled the rowing world, and but for the fact that it encountered delays in air transportation and rough water, which combined to keep the Badgers inactive for five days prior to reaching Seattle for the sprint race, plus the fact that the crew had to race in a borrowed shell and drew an outside lane unprotected from a very strong wind, the Badgers placed fourth in the only race it lost in its greatest season in Wisconsin's rowing history.[12]

At the end of the 1946 season, UW stroke Carl Holtz was selected to the All-American college eight in crew. Years later, Walz would also get the team into the Helm's Hall of Fame, now maintained by the National Rowing Foundation.

Coach Allen Walz, who had also become the voice of the Field House public address system at UW's basketball games, was hired away after the 1946 season to coach at Yale. His assistant coach, Roy Rom, stayed on at Wisconsin until Walz's replacement arrived. Norm Sonju would become one of Wisconsin's longest serving crew coaches starting on December 1, 1946. By prior agreement and after a few months of adjustment by Coach Sonju, Roy Rom left for Yale to act as Walz's assistant.

For Wisconsin's crew, the victory at the Eastern Sprints on May 11, 1946, was the beginning of the modern era of UW's crew's history. Wisconsin's wartime coaching turnover would slow significantly, crew schedules would fill out more consistently each season, and successes in the program at the regional and national level would be more regular. The years of tenacity and never giving up were paying off.

✕

More stories of Allen Walz, after his departure from Madison, tell of the many facets to this interesting man.

One post-Wisconsin anecdote about Coach Walz occurred in the fall of 1949. Wisconsin freshman coach Dick Tipple recalled being in his office when an administrator from Yale poked his head in and asked for the head crew coach (Sonju) at Wisconsin. The Yale man wanted to speak with Coach Sonju about the budget for crew at Wisconsin.

As Sonju was out of the office, the visitor wondered if Tipple could help him with some of his budget questions. "No," Tipple answered, "that's not information I'm privy to." The visitor then explained, "Coach Walz leased a helicopter earlier this summer from which he says he can better observe and coach his crews. As the whole thing is getting pretty expensive, I came to inquire if Wisconsin had ever supported such extravagances."[13]

William N. Wallace, *New York Times* sportswriter for most of the last half of the twentieth century, wrote, "My introduction to intercollegiate rowing came at Yale right after World War II as the undergraduate assistant sports information director. I was close to crew and the coach then. Allen (Skip) Walz, had come to Yale from Wisconsin where he had coached briefly. He was a fascinating man, a New Yorker with ties to football at NYU and also to crew at the New York Athletic Club. What brought him to Wisconsin, I have no idea but his Wisco crew of 1946 won the first EARC (Eastern Sprints) championship."[14]

Wallace told another anecdote about Walz and Bill Stowe, Columbia's crew coach. In 1971, Stowe was trying to bring his team to the World Rowing Championships in St. Catherine's Ontario and sought to find a sponsor. He thought rowing from Columbia, on the Harlem River in Manhattan, to St. Catherine's, Ontario, as a publicity stunt might attract a sponsor. The route would begin on the Harlem River, turn north up the Hudson River, then to the Mohawk River, Erie Canal, Tonawanda Creek, Niagara River, and into Ontario on the Welland Creek and through the Welland Canal into Lake Erie to St. Catherine's, Ontario. Stowe approached Allen Walz, then the VP of Public Relations at Canada Dry, with the concept.

"That's the craziest idea I've ever heard," responded Walz. "But I like it. We [Canada Dry] will sponsor you."[15] The Columbia crew later started its voyage onto the Harlem River and northward for about two miles up the Hudson River, but was called back when the insurance arrangements fell through.

Walz has also appeared in later years in at least two histories of the Central Intelligence Agency (CIA). During his years of coaching at Yale, and later while working in New York, Walz was paid $10,000 a year to provide the CIA with the names (25 per month) of young men who might make good candidates as employees of the agency.

UW History—1946–2004

UW Contributes to Post–World War II Development as Crew Enters Its Modern Era

With the end of World War II, many men came back to the University of Wisconsin to study under the GI Bill. The return of these now more mature students gave the University of Wisconsin a strong shot in the arm. Enrollment more than doubled in 1946–47, reaching 18,598.

With an older, stronger returning varsity, Wisconsin's crew developed a national following during the 1945–46 season. Coach Allen Walz had much to do with this success, with his eye for publicity and a successful coaching method.

By 1950, a major share of the veterans had completed their education and moved on. These graduates entered the economy and brought energy and innovation to an economy badly in need of both. (Tom Brokaw wrote of this historic phenomenon in *The Greatest Generation*.) America and her people, armed not with guns but with the educational tools of a university education, launched one of the longest and deepest economic booms in the world's history.

The outbreak of the Korean War, while the military was still in a state of relative preparedness, led to the continuance of ROTC. Enrollment in ROTC required a two-year stint, and another two years was recommended in order not to have to take one's chances on semester-to-semester draft deferments. Sporadically, students protested the presence of the military on campus, while the public's growing fear of communism was fanned by Wisconsin senator Joe McCarthy.

In 1953 Wisconsin made its first appearance in the Rose Bowl, under coach Ivan Williamson. Camp Randall expanded by 10,000 seats to 63,710 by 1958;

Carillon Tower. Courtesy UW–Madison Archives, Series 9-1b. Photo by Phillip A. Harrington.

enrollment dropped from 18,693 in 1948 to 13,346 in 1954, before rising again to 17,145 in 1959.

Edwin Brown ("E. B.") Fred, named UW president in 1945, oversaw the expansion of residence hall capacity during his tenure. The Fred administration was also the period when the Wisconsin legislature advanced the proposition of integrating all of the state's institutions of higher learning into a single University of Wisconsin system.

Joshua Lederberg, in 1958, received the first Nobel Prize ever granted to a UW faculty member. He later left UW to become head of medical genetics at Stanford University.

Fred served until 1958, when he was replaced by Conrad A. Elvehjem, who saw an academic system facing rising enrollments and the overall challenge of expansion of knowledge, tangibly evident by the day's fast-changing technology.

When Elvehjem died unexpectedly in 1962, Fred Harrington succeeded him and saw enrollment rise from 17,000 in 1959 to 30,000 in 1970. For six years ending in 1965, the Madison campus saw more new construction than in its cumulative history! Protests also increased as students gained an increasing sense of empowerment from protests and media coverage of other campuses.

From the enlarging student body, the registration line's potential universe of walk-on athletes to men's crew grew immensely. In 1972, the UW women began finding athletes who would become world-class rowers.

When Harrington began to lose the confidence of the regents, especially with

Memorial Union Terrace. Courtesy UW–Madison Archives, Series 27-1.

regard to what was felt to be an excessively lenient approach to student discipline, John Weaver was named to head the university in Madison in 1970. Within a matter of months, the state's legislature created a single university system, and the years that followed addressed the organizational meaning of this integration.

In 1988, Donna Shalala became president and recognized very quickly that a losing football team and a well-intended, but severely underfunded McClain Athletic Facility construction project would soon have the Athletic Department drowning in red ink. She took charge by bringing in a former UW multisport athlete and locally popular figure in Madison, Pat Richter, to take the helm of the Athletic Department. Richter soon hired, with Shalala's full support, a nationally recognized football coach, Barry Alvarez, to turn around the football program and with it, the financial fortunes of the entire Athletic Department.

While five sports couldn't last the financial drought and the growing pressures from Title IX gender equity in 1990, the financial condition of the Athletic Department gradually returned to a healthy state. In 2004, Alvarez was named Athletic Director, while retaining the head football coaching position. Shalala left UW's presidency for the Clinton administration in 1993 and was succeeded by David Ward. John D. Wiley assumed the presidency of the University of Wisconsin–Madison on January 1, 2001.

8
Sonju Solidifies the Program

Norman ("Norm") Sonju was born June 6, 1902, in Hudson, Wisconsin. When Norm was five years old, his family moved to Poulsbo, Washington; there Sonju became active in outdoor sports. Always a fisherman, Sonju fished mostly for tuna and salmon, but during his high school years—the same time as World War I—Sonju also fished for shark.

Sonju entered the University of Washington in 1923. After trying several other sports, he joined the Husky crew. The head crew coach, Rusty Callow, was beginning his second year of coaching, having just come back from the school's second visit to the Poughkeepsie Regatta, where Washington had won. Excitement about crew on the Washington campus was pretty high. The varsity eight would win again in 1924.

Rowing in the 3-seat, Sonju captained the Washington varsity eight during the 1926–27 season, which finished second behind a strong Columbia eight on the four-mile course down the Hudson River at the Poughkeepsie Regatta. In three appearances at Poughkeepsie (1925–27), Sonju's varsity eight placed second, first, and second, respectively. One of his teammates at Washington, from the class ahead of Sonju, was R. Harrison "Stork" Sanford, later a fellow coach at Cornell with Sonju.

After college, Sonju worked a year as an assistant coach to Washington's head coach Al Ulbrickson, and then sold real estate in the Seattle area from 1928 to 1932. As the Depression deepened, Sonju moved to Alaska to become a gold miner. Working as a miner at the Stewart Brothers' mining camp in 1934, Sonju lived through the big fire in Nome, Alaska, which burned out most of the town's business center.

Interviewed later, Sonju recalled, "That stay in Alaska was quite an adventure. It's hard to say just what got me interested in going, but I guess the Depression had something to do with it. And the price of gold had gone up from $18 to $35 an ounce."[1]

In the fall of 1936, he accepted "Stork" Sanford's invitation to come to Cornell to "help with the crews." Apparently, no head coach decision had been made. Future Badger assistant Randy Jablonic remembers Sonju tolling him the story sev-

Norm Sonju. coach 1946–68. Photo by and permission from Ed Stein.

eral times that, following Sonju's arrival in Ithaca, Sanford and Sonju flipped a coin to determine who would coach the varsity and who would guide the freshmen. Sanford ended up with the varsity and Sonju with the freshmen. As a result, many would say the two acted as "co-coaches" of the Cornell crew.

Sonju's coaching career at Cornell included two freshman heavyweight eight IRA championships (1940 and '41) and two lightweight championships at the American Henley.

On December 1, 1946—following Allen Walz's departure for Yale—Sonju accepted Wisconsin Athletic Director Harry Stuhldreher's offer to become the next Badger head crew coach. As a man more than twenty years older than most of his oarsman, Sonju could be described as distant and gruff, with a direct, no-nonsense approach. At the same time he projected an enduring love of the sport, a deep respect for his oarsmen, and a dry sense of humor. A good-natured coach, he was perceived by many of his young student-athletes as very much a father figure.

Following the Walz-led Wisconsin crew victory at what would become the inaugural race of the Eastern Sprints, the East Coast college crew coaches began discussions leading to the organization of the Eastern Association of Rowing Colleges (or EARC). Because so many of these coaches had come from the University of Washington rowing program, they all knew Sonju. They liked the Badger coach and thus encouraged Wisconsin's joining the EARC as a founding member, agreeing to calculate travel expenses by the mile and pool travel expenses in order to assist Wisconsin, the most distant participant, in defraying some of the cost of their longer trip to the Sprints.

Then freshman coach Randy Jablonic remembered many of Sonju's coaching techniques, some of which served later in Jabo's own coaching style:

> Norm liked long practices. He also would not frequently change the varsity boating arrangement. Sometimes, he would watch the same guy for two or three days, counting how many bad strokes out of several hundred a rower would make. Five out of 600 was good. Norm liked consistency.

In later years, Sonju, as the last tenured crew coach, would become an associate professor of Physical Education. Coach Sonju never taught class, but for many years, into the late 1960s or early '70s, UW students were required to take physical education. Athletes out for a varsity sport could use their participation as a substitute for taking physical education, in which case the coach was required to render a grade at the end of the semester. (Jablonic remembered a few times when guys who would come out for crew, attend for a few weeks, and then start showing up infrequently. He had no problem giving them an F.)

Sonju loved crew, he said, because it "has most of the virtues of sport with few of the evils that sports are generally accused of." Fairness was a value held dear to Sonju, as his collegiate oarsman and future freshman coach Randy Jablonic would recall learning from his coach. "Treat everybody the same," Sonju would advise. "Even if you don't particularly like a fellow, treat him the same as everyone else."

Despite losing only Chester Knight from the strong varsity eight of the previous season (1946–47), Sonju's first year at Wisconsin—and the second full year of the sport's reactivation at the college level following World War II—was not a great success. While a Badger second varsity boating won a 2½ length margin over Marietta College on the Ohio River, the varsity eight later lost to Cornell, Pennsylvania, Cal, and Washington before ending up seventh among the twelve varsity entries in the 1947 Poughkeepsie Regatta.

A side note here: the Hudson River at Poughkeepsie was wide enough to allow all twelve varsity eight entries to row at once, eliminating the need for heats and repechages, as would become necessary at future venues on narrower courses.

Sonju had ordered two new shells from a University of Washington friend and famous boatbuilder George Pocock, whose boats arrived in early April. Pocock's boat shop was for many years located within the University of Washington campus close to the Husky's boathouse. In mid-June of 1947, Pocock's son, Stan, rowed in the Husky eight, which defeated the Badgers on Lake Monona. In his book, *Way Enough*, Stan Pocock related:

> Most memorable to our stay in Madison were the incredible beefsteaks served to us at the [Memorial] Student Union Building. The chef must have thought that oarsmen had to eat like football players. The steaks were bigger than any sane person would consume at one sitting, and even that was after [Washington Coach Al] Ulbrickson had told the chef to cut them in half.

After the five-year war-related hiatus from 1942 to 1946, the Poughkeepsie Regatta started back up in 1947. Navy won the varsity eight race. After the Poughkeepsie, many teams traveled to the Seattle Invitational Sprint Regatta. Harvard won this 2,000-meter race in a record time (5:49), with the Badgers finishing seventh in a twelve-entry event.

Following the 1947 season, Wisconsin's bowman, Cliff Rathcamp, was named to the All-American crew.

During the summer of 1947, former Wisconsin crew coach (1906–1910) Ned Ten Eyck retired from the head-coaching job at Syracuse. Ned had assumed the position from his father, Jim Ten Eyck, Sr., upon the elder Ten Eyck's death in 1938.

It was that same summer that University of Pennsylvania rower John B. ("Jack") Kelly Jr. (brother of Princess Grace Kelly) won the Diamond Skulls at the Royal Henley Regatta. The victory was considered sweet revenge for his father, legendary Philadelphia sculler, John B. Kelly, Sr., who had been banned from the Henley by the British stewards in 1920 because "he wasn't a gentleman." In those days the English felt it was unfair to the rowing English elite to have to compete against a strong-bodied laborer.

By 1920, Kelly Sr. was a successful businessman and contractor, but he had at one time been a bricklayer. Kelly, Jr. reportedly wore his father's old sculling hat in victory; the elder Kelly later sent the sweaty cap to the king of England. The younger Kelly was the featured speaker at UW's annual crew banquet in March of 1971. Coach Jablonic remembers, "I had asked Kelly to come in order to bring the sport some additional prestige on the UW campus, after Athletic Director Elroy Hirsch almost had the sport shut down that same spring."

It was also in 1946–47 that Mickey's Dairy Bar on Monroe Street, across from

Camp Randall, was founded by Mrs. Mickey Weidman. When the boathouse was built at the end of Babcock Drive in 1968, Mickey's gradually became the primary breakfast venue of choice for Wisconsin's early morning rowers.

During the 1947–48 season, rigger and former Wisconsin crew coach (during the war years 1943–45) Curt Drewes built an eight-oared sweep shell from scratch for the Badgers. Using the same molded materials and glues that went into the Mosquito bomber, a plane made famous in World War II, Drewes incorporated the molding, laminating, and gluing techniques shared with and learned from his part-time work during the war with the U.S. Forest Products Laboratory in Madison.

The new shell saved Wisconsin about $1,200 over an equivalent Pocock shell ($1,600 plus $200 shipping). On April 10 Mrs. Harry Stuhldreher, the Athletic Director's wife, christened the *Mendota*. Among the oarsmen and coaches, however, the shell was known as "Big Red," reflecting its exterior of distinctive cardinal-red stain.

In early May, the Badgers traveled by rail to Syracuse. Rigger and boatbuilder Drewes's handmade *Mendota* did not make the trip; a special end-loaded baggage car would have had to have been arranged with the railroad, for which "privileged service"—a minimum of 35 round-trip tickets—would have had to have been purchased. As the traveling group numbered only 14, a shell had to be borrowed in Syracuse.

Four crews competed on the wind-reduced three-quarter-mile course. As the Lake Onondaga outlet was too narrow for a four-lane race, a run-off format was required. The Badgers knocked off the Orangemen of Syracuse by three-quarters of a length in their qualifier and faced Boston University in the final. BU had defeated Columbia in their earlier qualifier.

Despite being blown dangerously off course in an unfamiliar borrowed shell, the heavier Badger crew prevailed over BU by three lengths in the final. UW's boating: Dick Tipple (bow; Tipple had skipped competing in the previous 1946–47 season), Tom Blacklock, George Crandall, Gordon Grimstead, LeRoy Jensen, Bob Hedges, Cliff Rathcamp, Floyd Nixon (stroke), and Carlyle "Bud" Fay (coxswain).

Wisconsin skipped the Eastern Sprints in 1948 for the second straight year and faced Sonju's old team, Cornell, in Madison in mid-May. The Badgers met the Big Red on a west-to-east Lake Mendota course of 2,000 meters, starting near the current boathouse at the end of Babcock Drive and ending at Frances Street, where the roadway dead-ends into Lake Mendota. Wisconsin got off a fast start and gained a quick lead that was built to a length at the halfway mark. Slugging away at 37 strokes per minute, Cornell's blade work was smoother. The Badgers were throwing a lot of power into their stroke but were showing trouble on the "catch" in the choppy water.

Cornell, which had snapped Harvard's win streak earlier in the year, then lifted its stroke rate to 39 and closed rapidly on the Badgers. The Big Red edged its bow a few feet ahead but couldn't extend their margin as the Badgers closed with a savage rush. At the finish Big Red won by ten feet. Henry McCormick, in sports coverage in the *Wisconsin State Journal* noted quaintly, "Wisconsin lost no caste in being shaded by a Cornell eight that has been rated the finest in the east this year."

In the 2V8 race, where there was never open water between the two shells, Wisco won by a second in time and three-quarters of a boat length. The 2V8 boating (one name missing): Jim Connell (bow), Ralph Falconer, John McBratney, Don Peterson, Bill Sachse, Frank Harris, John Jung (stroke), and Don Linton (coxswain).

Later in May, the Badgers hosted Washington's Huskies, which won by five lengths. Cal repeated the drubbing with a three-length victory on Lake Mendota on June 12. It was Cal that later won the U.S. Olympic trials in Princeton, New Jersey, in July and then went on to a gold in the London Olympics of 1948.

At the Poughkeepsie Regatta, Wisconsin's crew—the last to arrive—shared Columbia's boathouse on the west side of the Hudson River. Washington won the varsity eight contest, followed by Cal, Navy, Cornell, MIT, Princeton, Penn, and Wisconsin in a total field of eleven. Using the Drewes-crafted *Mendota*, the Badgers rowed in the only shell of the eleven varsity boats that was not Pocock-made.

Sonju's 1948–49 crew returned to Yale, the Badger's first collegiate opponent when the two had raced on Lake Saltonstall in 1896. Former Wisconsin coach Allen Walz was now Yale's head crew coach. Before the race he asked former UW rower and crew historian Paul O. Eckhardt, Jr. (Class of '33), "Should I use my lightweight or heavyweight crew? I think I'll use the heavyweight crew." The date was also Derby Day on campus and several of the Elis were celebrating early. Derby Day at Yale, the first Saturday of May, while falling about the same time as the Kentucky Derby, is a combination of Mardi Gras and the English Derby. The Day highlights crew racing in Derby, Connecticut where Yale's first cew house began construction on the Housatonie River in 1923. The First Derby Day was apparently May 5, 1923.

The race down the Housatonic River course in Connecticut was a dandy. Yale's boathouse had been built on the northeastern shore of the river just outside of the small, blue-collar town of Derby and about twelve miles from New Haven. The boathouse itself sits on the finish line of the slightly winding two-mile course down the Housatonic.

Wisconsin jumped to a deck-length lead off a powerful start at a rate of 42. At the quarter-mile mark, Wisconsin held a half-length lead after both crews had to

Yale nosing out UW on the Housatonic River in 1949. Wisconsin's boating for the Yale race: Don Haack (bow), Pete Wachman, Dick Tipple, Bill Sachse, Otto Uher, Gordon Grimstead, Cliff Rothcamp, Earl Lapp (stroke), and Duane Daentl (cox). Source: Photo gift of Paul O. Eckhardt, Jr.

swerve slightly to avoid partying Derby Day boaters and swimmers off both shores of the river.

At the half-mile mark, Yale had closed their trailing pace to ten feet. The Badger lead grew to half a length at the three-quarter-mile mark but by the mile-marker at the halfway point, the shells were gunwale to gunwale.

The lead changed hands a couple of times over the next three-quarters of a mile, where the two crews drew even. The *New Haven Sunday Register* of May 8, 1949, described the finishing stretch:

> Yale, drawing even a quarter mile from home, poured on the juice for a six-foot lead and only gave away two of those important feet in the hectic, soul-searching bolt to the flags. In a bitter, no-quarter dual over the full two miles, Yale's heavyweight varsity crew yesterday afternoon met and mastered the merciless challenge of a giant boatload of oarsmen, powering home for a four-foot victory. A crowd of about 30,000 witnessed the program.[2]

After the race, the UW Alumni of New York, led by Eckhardt, hosted the Badger rowers for dinner at the Phi Gamma Delta Club of New York. De-boarding the train from New Haven to dinner in New York City, Badger coxswain Duane Daentl, a diabetic, recalled feeling the need for an insulin shot as he got off the train. Unable to find a private corner and in urgent need of insulin, the coxswain recalls surrounding himself with his larger teammates in the huge main lobby of Grand Central Terminal and "dropping my drawers and giving myself an insulin injection!"

Two weeks later, following their flight to Oakland, the Badgers rowed against and lost to Cal, the prior summer's Olympic gold medal-winning eight in a three-and-a-half-length defeat.

Against Washington on Lake Mendota June 17, another Yale-like dog-eat-dog race ensued. Over the two-mile course, the shells were never separated by more than half a boat length. At the finish the Huskies won by eight feet. A week before the Poughkeepsie Regatta, the Badgers raced and defeated Columbia and Rutgers on the Harlem River.

While at the 1949 national regatta on the Hudson River at Poughkeepsie, freshman Bob Espeseth recalls the classic open Jeep owned by fellow freshman Delos Barrett. The Jeep had been taken to Poughkeepsie, packed into the end-loaded railcar with the shells, and lent to coach Sonju to make his way up and down both shores of the two- and three-mile courses (the frosh race was two miles and the V8 and 2V8 were both three miles) down the Hudson River.

Freshman rower Bob Espeseth recalls one of those Jeep rides,

> In the evenings, the freshman crew, numbering ten or eleven with spares, often jumped into Barrett's Jeep to head into New York City for a bit of scouting around. Espeseth remembers waiting at one stoplight in Manhattan when a New York City cabbie looked over and noticed both the Wisconsin license plate and the number of boys piled into the Jeep. "My God!" the cabbie shouted over to us, "Don't tell me you drove all the way from Wisconsin like that!"

In this final regatta on the Hudson, Wisconsin's varsity eight placed seventh, behind winner Cal, in a field of twelve. Navy, which finished fourth, had four destroyers on the Hudson watching the race! UW's freshmen, showing signs of future prowess, finished third, six feet behind second place Cornell. The frosh field had nine entries.

The Poughkeepsie Regatta Trophy—the predecessor to the Marietta and Ten Eyck trophies—was awarded to the crew from Washington for its best average finish in the three eight-seat races (second, first, and first, respectively, in the varsity, 2V8, and freshman races).

The Poughkeepsie Regatta ended its fifty-five year run on the Hudson River. Reasons for the move from Poughkeepsie to Marietta were several: decreasing support from the city of Poughkeepsie; dwindling crowds from afar, and a general local apathy; a latent grumbling by coaches that the Hudson River course—because of the current—was not a fair one; and, perhaps most importantly, the Western Shore Railroad decided not to rebuild the observation cars—dismantled for materials during WW II—for this once a year rowing spectacle.

Wisconsin had been coming to the Poughkeepsie Regatta almost continuously for fifty-two of the regatta's fifty-five-year history, longer than any other school except for the three original founders—Columbia, Pennsylvania, and Cornell. What did the Poughkeepsie Regatta mean to the college men whose annual crew seasons peaked for this national regatta? Robert F. Kelley, author of *American Rowing*, sought to describe the significance in his 1941 essay in the Regatta's program:

"That's Poughkeepsie"

What is Poughkeepsie? Well, it's a town hanging to the side of a precipitous hill along one of the most beautiful rivers in the world. The town enjoys several industries and businesses, and some important courts of law. It sent the two most famous bearded portraits the world has ever seen into millions of homes on smallish boxes that contained cough lozenges, the portraits of the brothers Smith. To the fathers of some hundreds—yes thousands—of girls, it has meant a postmark on the outside of those window pane envelopes that harbor bills in their insides, for back of town a piece is Vassar College.

But it isn't for any of these things that men have stuck their heads into radio shacks of Naval patrols on Chinese rivers and asked the radio man if he could get "anything from Poughkeepsie." Nor for any of these that tall men in the forests of Washington would respond if you asked them about Poughkeepsie.

Primarily it is because, in the early part of December in 1895, a tug made a journey from Poughkeepsie upstream for about three miles, with three young men aboard her. With the men was a Judge Hasbrouck of Poughkeepsie. The three visitors were Thomas Reath of Pennsylvania, Charles Treman of Cornell, and Frederick Sill of Columbia. That was a good many years before Father Sill was to wear the white cassock of the head master and founder of Kent School.

The three were looking for a rowing course, now that Yale and Harvard were drawing so definitely together and taking over the New London course. They had looked at other places: Saratoga, Cayuga, Seneca lakes upstate; the Connecticut at Springfield; and the lake at Worcester. They had been down the Hudson at Nyack.

They liked Poughkeepsie. Judge Hasbrouck told them of the old Dutch sailing course, extending from where they stood on the drifting tug at Kromme Elleborg down out of sight. About four miles, they thought. They came back in December, had the course surveyed on the ice—and that June came the first of the Poughkeepsie regattas.

From that day to the present, the word Poughkeepsie has been taking on its meaning for hundreds and thousands of men from all walks of life and all parts of the country. At present, somewhere at sea in the shipping lanes of the Atlantic is Jonas Ingram. He's a captain in the Navy, perhaps an admiral by now. His rowing friends have always called him Jonas. Back in 1907, he sat in the stroke seat of the first Navy shell that ever rowed here. There probably won't be any radio come to him June 25th, wherever he is, but it is highly probable that sometime that day his thoughts will come back here.

A few days before these lines were written, the scrivener was in New London, standing in a hotel lobby, when there appeared a tall, black haired young man in the khaki colored uniform officers are wearing aboard submarines now. He had just come into the Sub Base there with his craft. "Thought you'd be around," he said. "Wondered if you'd been over to Poughkeepsie yet?" He was in a Navy shell there only a few short years ago.

Poughkeepsie, for years now, has meant the Golden Fleece to youngsters rowing at Washington and California. Out in the beautiful water of Mendota at Wisconsin, the fragile prows of shells have been aimed all season at this river town. And each year the delicate tracery of sweep blades writes fresh words in its history.

Poughkeepsie is a tradition now. It is one of the lasting ones of American life. Well, what is tradition? Webster said it is "that which is so handed down; ancient custom." The young men in the boathouses along the river are not alone there any more. There are quite a few ghosts, interesting ones, living there with them.

On the Cornell float, the gray haired figure of Pop Courtney sits, whittling a stick of wood. The hawk eyed, gentle spoken Old Jim Ten Eyck rides the Syracuse launch with his son, "Young Ned," when Syracuse goes out to practice. The side-whiskers of Ellis Ward stick out from under the awning of an old-fashioned naphtha launch to peer at passing crews puzzled not to see Penn among them. [Penn discontinued their Poughkeepsie Regatta participation from 1936 through 1941 at least in part because they felt the four-mile varsity distance was too long. When the IRAs resumed after World War II in 1947, the varsity race was temporarily reduced to three miles, and Penn returned.]

Back on the rocks in the Highlands are old class numerals, peeled and crusted with age. Freshmen have risked their necks to stick them up there and long since ceased to be freshmen. Some of them have had sons go out in the shells.

Ed Leader, dean of the college coaches of today, once rowed at Poughkeepsie with a lumberman's woolen cap on the crown of his head, his twin brother elsewhere in the first Washington shell to come here. Nearly all of the men who coach crews today rowed down the Dutch sailing course that became one of the most famous rowing courses in the world.

Great English coaches have brought their charges here to row. Great American crews have gone from here to win world honors in foreign waters. Yale and Harvard, despite the fact that they are so wedded to their own private party at New London, both have rowed over this course. So have Georgetown and Leland Stanford, both now out of rowing.

Nor has all of the tradition of this event been written in more or less ancient times. There was the great California crew of 1928, stroked by the black headed Peter Donlan, that was to go on to Amsterdam and triumph in the Olympics. And the California crew of 1932 that did the same thing. Washington of 1936.

There was the Washington crew stroked by Al Ulbrickson, present head coach, who finished the final 100 yards in a terrific last minute duel against Navy to win [1926] despite a torn muscle in his shoulder. Ulbrickson is back on the river this year, as is another of the great strokes of the event, Alastair MacBain, assistant at Columbia. MacBain, in 1929, set the beat for one of the best crews the river has seen, one that survived to triumph on a river which saw four crews founder before the race was ended.

It is probably not too much to say that this is the most truly national of our college championships, this despite the fact that Yale and Harvard do not row here. Every other rowing college of real strength is at hand at Poughkeepsie and distance has been no barrier. Each year the men come on from the Pacific Coast.

A tremendous lot of water has rolled under the old railroad bridge since the day that Father Sill and the others laid out the course. For the non-rowing man, it is extremely difficult to see how men can work as long and faithfully as these oarsmen do for a season's climax, which is over in twenty minutes or less in most Poughkeepsie races.

There is great difficulty in explaining rowing to people who have not been close to it. The oarsmen who go away from this regatta will remember the race, of course, but they will remember more vividly the days of practice when the big, handsome river is more or less bare.

Perhaps, even more than the men and the crews of the past, the river itself weaves a lasting enchantment. The memory of long June twilights, with the highlands casting shadows out halfway across the river, and the satisfaction of pulling an oar when you were in great physical shape, the shell coming to life beneath you and the crew fitting in as one man—it is a peculiar and unique sensation not to be described.

And the end of the workout, the coxswain's "let 'er run," and the rippling glide of the shell back to the float, pretty often just as night begins to drop down over the old river. Probably few of them would admit it, especially among the younger ones, but there is a beauty to rowing that is never more thoroughly in evidence than in these June days at Poughkeepsie.

All of these feeble words in an effort to describe *What is Poughkeepsie?* Poughkeepsie is a mood, a memory, an experience, as well as a great sporting event. Year after year, it finds its way into the character of young men from the wide reaches of the country, from Framingham Center, Massachusetts, and to Tujunga, California; from New York City and Seattle.[3]

×

Wisconsin's 1949–50 season began slowly after a late—April 17—start on Lake Mendota. The Badger's first race, against Columbia on Lake Monona, resulted in a one-and-a-half-length loss. Attending the Eastern Sprints for the first time since winning in the regatta's initial year of 1946, Wisconsin's varsity eight finished tenth of twelve entries.

In late May the crew flew to Seattle to face the Washington Huskies. The new Curt Drewes–made shell *Mendota,* arrived by train. As soon as the Wisconsin baggage car was sidetracked near the University of Washington's power plant, the boatbuilding Pococks rushed over to have a look. It wasn't long before they concluded either the glue hadn't stopped shrinking or the pressure mold had been poorly shaped or both! Future builders, despite such interim design issues, would later incorporate many of Drewes's features—diagonal veneers, pressure molding, and modern glues—with their own adaptations.

When the usually heavy winds rose on the course, the Madison-made Badger shell was washed over and eventually sank—in the middle of the race. Local sports writer Royal Brougham, in a typically caustic remark, observed something to the effect that the Badger crew "smelled worse than Wisconsin cheese." It would be another year before the Badgers would make their rebuttal at the IRAs in Marietta, Ohio.

Many in and out of the Badger boat would remember the 1950 IRAs. Badger coxswain Duane Daentl tells the story:

> This was the year Wisconsin jumped the starting gun and was not called back. The entire boat had agreed ahead of time that, because of the distance of their lane from the starting gun, a slight jump could be gotten away with. Because of the churning storm conditions on the Ohio River, Badger cox Duane Daentl also figured there was little chance the judges would want to re-start the race, if a re-start were even possible in the strong down-stream current.
>
> The entire boat's decision to quick-start was taken without the knowledge or consent of Coach Sonju. At the finish, Wisconsin placed third in a field of twelve. Washington swept all three of the eights races.

Stan Pocock, author of *Way Enough,* remembers (incorrectly attributing the jump to the 1951 race) coaches bringing the next day's news photos to Coach

Marietta course on the Ohio River, 1950. Source: Diagram/Card gift of Paul O. Eckhardt, Jr.

Sonju, which Pocock, in an exaggeration, described as "showing other rowers still leaning on their oars at the start."

Badger coxswain Daentl continued,

> Starter Clifford "Tip" Goes was especially "chopped off" at Wisconsin and me. The following year (1951), Goes was especially watching for the Badgers.
>
> On the train back from Cincinnati to Madison in 1950, Coach Sonju was walking down the aisle and, finding a seat next to Daentl, innocently asked, "How *did* you guys catch such a quick start?"[4]

Earlier in the new season—during the fall of 1950—the Badgers decided to destroy their eighteen-year-old training barge, *Old Nero*. Originally built for 16 rowers, the capacity was reduced to 12 when one end gave out prematurely. As someone observed at *Old Nero*'s demise, "Well done—but good riddance, say the thousand men *Old Nero* served. She is mourned by none."

On November 14, the fall windup banquet was held for 60 oarsmen. Attendees included Walter Alexander (captain from 1896), Walter Hirschberger (from the 1899 "Berry Crate" crew), and Joe Steinauer, at the time the Badger swimming coach but a past crew trainer, and before that the manager of the boathouse.

The 1950–51 Badger crew first got onto Lake Mendota on April 11, six days earlier than the prior season, but still five days later than the average opening date of April 6.

In Wisconsin's only home appearance of the season later that spring, the Badgers fell to Yale by two and three-quarter lengths on a wind-swept one and three-quarter-mile course on Lake Monona. The Yale oarsmen had to dip into their own pockets to make the expensive round-trip, but they were housed without charge in the University's new short-course dorms.

On May 12, 1951, against opponents Columbia and Rutgers, Wisconsin rowed in a one and three-quarter-mile contest on the Hudson River. The Badgers, off to a good start, led all the way and defeated Columbia by a half-length. In the jayvee race, Columbia prevailed by one and one-quarter boat lengths. Newly named UW Athletic Director Guy Sundt, the successor to Harry Stuhldreher, attended the races and was the guest of honor of UW's Alumni at the Crew Dinner, which took place that evening at the Phi Gamma Delta Club in New York.

On May 19, Purdue's newly formed intramural crew came to Madison, received some coaching from Norm Sonju, and rowed in a race or two while intermixed with some of Wisconsin's more experienced rowers. The club was the first Big Ten school to initiate an intercollegiate crew effort since Wisconsin's first varsity race in 1892. The lack of Big Ten competition meant the Badgers, for almost sixty years, had had to travel great distances, both east and west, to find collegiate races.

Later in May, the Wisconsin crew took a rail trip to Oakland to race Cal. Heading the UW Alumni welcoming committee in Oakland was Pat O'Dea, the Wisconsin football legend from the 1890s and younger brother of the Badger's first full-time crew coach, Andrew O'Dea (who coached from 1894–1906). Cal defeated UW by a length.

To get to Marietta, Ohio, for the IRAs, UW hired the Chicago, Milwaukee and St. Paul railroad train, including several "horse cars." These were actually boxcars that could load horses from one end—and they worked perfectly for loading Wisco's sixty-foot shells.

Facing another swollen Ohio River, Coach Sonju and coxswain Duane Daentl took the launch out before the race and threw corks into the river in an attempt to discern an advantaged path through the currents.

At the start, referee Goes admonished all boats there would be not extra false starts, "One false start and you're out!" His eyes were now focused on Wisconsin's shell and its coxswain, Duane Daentl. The raging river would probably not allow any restarts. Stan Pocock described the river, "The Ohio was on a rampage, with every piece of flotsam and jetsam from upstate Ohio and beyond in a mad dash for the Gulf of Mexico!"

In a six-mile-an-hour current, the Badgers rowed powerfully the entire course of nearly two miles and defeated the previous year's winner, Washington, by one and one-quarter lengths. Catching the Huskies at the quarter-mile mark, the

UW's 1951 V8 winning finish at Marietta. The boating: Del Barrett (bow), Bob Hood, Jim Schmidt, Vic Steuck, Jim Moran, Bob Espeseth, Jim Healy, Pete Wacikman (stroke), and Duane "Doc" Daentl (captain and coxswain). Source: *1952 IRA Program.* Courtesy of the IRA Stewards.

The University of Wisconsin shell knifes across the finish line in the 1951 varsity race, main event of the Intercollegiate Rowing Association's regatta on the Ohio River at Marietta. Immediately behind the Badgers is Washington's crew. Princeton in left foreground finished third and California was fourth. The Wisconsin shell rowed the two miles in 7 minutes 50.5 seconds.

Badgers were never again behind. In the 54 years since first entering the IRAs in 1898, this was the first victory by Wisconsin's varsity eight! Though it would not be the last varsity victory in IRAs, it could certainly be called one of the proudest.

Roundy, the well-known *Wisconsin State Journal* columnist, may have offered the best salute in an undated newsclip of "Roundy SAYS":

> Man alive, what a victory that was for Wisconsin.
> That's one of the biggest things in the school's history . . .
> Brother that baby echoed around the world. Here's a salute to the Coach,
> the Crew and the Coxswain.
> I'll give them 21 guns, that's the limit.

The 1951–52 season was well chronicled. Varsity coxswain Don Rose, who was also a varsity gymnast, wrote a regular sports column for the *Daily Cardinal* and made sure crew received a fair share, if not a disproportionate share, of the newspaper's attention.

In April of 1952, just after the ice had come off Lake Mendota, sophomore coxswain Duane Hopp was practicing a sprint against the varsity as both shells rowed past the Memorial Union. Hopp remembered, "All of a sudden, I saw Bob Hood come flying my way from out of the varsity eight. He'd just caught a big crab and had launched in my direction. When our second varsity finished ahead of the varsity, my crew suggested throwing me, as the coxswain, into the lake." To that idea, Coach Sonju barked, "Not today, boys! We've already nearly frozen one of you, let's not go for two."

On May 3—the same day on which Navy overcame UW's varsity and 2V8 were

104   SONJU SOLIDIFIES THE PROGRAM

at Annapolis—the UW frosh became the first Badger crew to compete against and defeat a foe from the Big Ten—the Purdue Rowing Club. MIT then came to Madison on May 10 and was defeated by the varsity by four and a half lengths.

At the 1952 Eastern Sprints in Princeton, Wisconsin lost again to Navy but finished second, ahead of Harvard and Cornell. The following month Cal, winner over Stanford in the West Coast Sprint Championship Regatta, came to Madison for a one and seven-eighths-mile race. With a fast start and a strong and steady race, the Badgers defeated the Golden Bears by a two-length margin. The UW boating was Delos Barrett (bow), Robert Hood, James Schmidt, Victor Steuck, James Moran, Robert Espeseth, James Lorenzen, Robert Nelson (stroke), and Don Rose (cox). Rusty Callow, now the crew coach at the Naval Academy, later thanked Rose for beating Cal, as it proved to his Navy crew that Cal could be beaten.

At the IRA regatta's new venue on Lake Onondaga in Syracuse, Callow's crew then did prove Cal's crew could be beaten, winning the varsity eight three-mile event. In fact, Navy swept all three events and won the first Jim Ten Eyck Memorial Trophy, sponsored by the Syracuse Alumni Rowing Association and named after their beloved coach, who'd passed away in 1938. This team trophy, previously named the Poughkeepsie Regatta Trophy (through 1949) and the Marietta Trophy (in 1950 and 1951), was awarded, using a weighting formula, to the school scoring the highest finish in the three eights events. With tears in his eyes, Callow accepted the Ten Eyck award, saying, "I think old Jim would appreciate my winning. Jim was an old friend of mine, a great teacher and once a Navy coach [in 1898]."

Badger junior, 4-seat, and future captain, Vic Steuck was named an All-American in May of 1952. Coach Sonju raved, "He pulls more water than any other oarsman in the country."

Winter training for the 1952–53 season—the first of what is a today a winter routine of finding open water and warm weather in the south for training over the semester break—was held at Rollins College in Florida. U. T. Bradley, crew coach at Rollins, was an old friend of Norm Sonju's. Coach Bradley, who was also active in the "Dad" Vail Regatta and wrote the monograph titled "The 'Dad' Vail Story," was very generous to Wisconsin. He arranged for the Badger crew to stay without charge at the Langford Hotel and eat at the Rollins College cafeteria for free. Wisconsin's only cost was gasoline to and from Madison.

Later in the spring, on April Fool's Day, the *Daily Cardinal* covered "Crew Cut Day" at the Armory (Red Gym) when the crew was "encouraged" by Coach Sonju to set the tone for a hard spring's competition by getting a short haircut. Free haircuts were also offered to any other interested students.

When two new Pocock 60-foot shells, costing $2,000 each and weighing 300 pounds apiece, arrived in Madison, varsity coxswain and senior Don Rose, still writing sports columns in UW's daily college newspaper, described the boats, "Within this 300 pounds, each 5/32 of an inch of cedar had a coat on which the varnish weighs 2 pounds and nails account for 20 pounds. Twelve different wood types are included in the construction with western cedar the most important."

In early May, a rowing exhibition was held at the Wisconsin Dells. In the first male-against-female race in UW history, two boats of four women each (from Rockford College in Illinois) were given a half-mile head start in a one-mile race. Both Rockford entries finished well ahead of the red-faced Badger eight!

After the race, a reporter wanted to know whether starter and head coach Norm Sonju had underestimated the girls or overestimated his varsity. Wisely, Sonju demurred from answering. UW's apparent boating: Jim Healy (bow), Virgil Trummer, Bob Roehrs, Al Wheeler, Jim Moran, Harry Miller, Jim Lorenzen, Vic Steuck (stroke), and Don Rose (cox).

The May 16, 1952, finals of the Eastern Sprints on the Potomac River in Washington, D.C., were scheduled to be televised on WTMJ-TV, based in Milwaukee. The announcer was to be Allen "Skip" Walz, former crew coach at UW and later Yale. Wisconsin managed to "nip" Cornell for third, behind Navy and Harvard.

On the Oakland estuary on May 30, Wisconsin again prevailed over Cal in a three-mile course—the margin being 15 seconds, or 4 lengths!

In the IRAs that year in Syracuse, Wisconsin varsity finished fourth among eleven entries.

> **What is the difference between a Sculler and a Sweepswinger?**
>
> A sculler rows with two oars, whereas a sweeps rower pulls only one.

The 1953–54 season reflected a common pattern for Wisconsin's rowing season. With ice on Lake Mendota until early April, the Badgers were typically one of the last crews to get on the water each rowing season. As a result, the Badgers often showed poorly in the early races of their schedule, only to climb up the rankings over the spring.

Such was the case in the spring of 1954. Finishing third in a five-entry race in Syracuse on May 1; sixth in the Eastern Sprints on May 18 in Washington, D.C.; and second with a deck-length loss to first-time Lake Mendota visitor Harvard on May 22, Wisconsin finally found victory with a defeat of Cal on Lake Mendota on June 12 (setting a one-and-three-quarter-mile course record of 8:52.0).

The national regatta on Lake Onondaga was marred by the determination—some days after the races—that the Navy coxswain, William Arthur Kennington, was ineligible. He had completed a BA degree at Vanderbilt before entering the Naval Academy. Though never an athlete at Vanderbilt, the rules stipulate that eligibility expires five years after one's first matriculation at any college. Thus, Navy is listed as the winner in the official records, but with an asterisk.

Wisconsin wound up an amended third in a field of eleven at the June 19th

IRAs in Syracuse. Wisconsin's boating: William Mueller (bow), James Williams, James Lorenzen, Lou Uehling, Jerry Fink, Foster Smith, John Severance, William Schneider (stroke), and James Winslow (cox).

In early December of the 1954–55 season, the New York Times's *Allison Danzig reported that Norm Sonju had been reelected president of the Rowing Coaches Organization of America.*

Over a late winter break of the 1954–55 season, the Badgers practiced again in Florida and defeated Florida Southern College and Rollins College in two early season races at the beginning of February.

While defeating Cal a fourth consecutive time in their tenth dual meet against the Golden Bears on the Oakland Estuary, the Wisconsin varsity failed to qualify for the Eastern Sprints finals and finished ninth in the Syracuse IRAs.

X

The Badgers fared better in their 1955–56 season. Again, Wisconsin started slowly, not qualifying for the finals of the Eastern Sprints in Washington, D.C., on May 12.

On May 25 on Lake Mendota, the Badgers met the Midshipmen of the U.S. Naval Academy. Navy jumped off to an early lead. Halfway through the race, the shells evened up and rowed bow to bow for another quarter mile. From this point, Wisconsin pushed to a one-length lead. At the finish, the UW sweepswingers crossed three-quarters of a length ahead in the one and three-quarter-mile competition. UW boating was: Richard Smith (bow), Foster Smith, Robert Graves, Lou Uehling, John Morgen, John Shaw, Joseph Irwin, Dean Walker (stroke), and Eugene Huske (cox).

At the Syracuse IRAs, Navy avenged their earlier season loss to the Badgers and snatched second place from Wisconsin with a rush at the finish the three mile race. Rowing five seat for Wisconsin was senior Bob Graves, a Korean War veteran who had been awarded the Silver Star. In the grandstand, watching her dad row, was three-year-old Carie Graves.[5]

At the Olympic Trials, eleven days later, the Badgers finished fifth by two lengths, or seven seconds behind winner Yale.

UW rower and captain (1956–57) Dean Walker was selected as an alternate (Yale's varsity was not deep) for the Olympic squad and practiced for two weeks with the national team. Sadly, Walker then learned his father had Lou Gehrig's disease. In one of the most difficult decisions of his life, Walker elected to resign from the U.S. crew to finish school on time in order to take over his father's farm.

Yale went on to win the Melbourne Olympics in November. It was the eighth consecutive eight-oared gold medal for the United States.

After finishing exams of the first semester, rower Randy Jablonic remembers departing Madison on Thursday evening/Friday morning for semester-break training in Florida. Arriving Saturday, the team immediately began rowing. On Friday, the Badgers rowed to a quarter-length loss to Rollins College.

The next day, UW raced Tampa College. Jablonic recalls being so worried about losing his 6-seat he never rowed a harder race in his life. Although they defeated Tampa by a quarter length, the two close races signaled a rough-water season for the Badger crew in 1956–57.

On the way home, Rollins coach U.T. Bradley invited the Badgers to stop by one of the orchards owned by the college and to fill up their cars with oranges. "Fill" was taken literally, with oranges stuffed into the car until the windows had to be rolled up. Jablonic remembers hearing of Sonju's finding oranges rolling around in his 1952 Dodge for months thereafter.

After winning five straight contests against Cal over the prior 20 years, the Badgers, in a three-way race, faced Cal and UCLA on the Oakland estuary. Cal jumped off to an early lead in the three-mile event. At the halfway point, Cal was three and one-half lengths ahead. Before the finish, the Badgers managed to close the margin to two and one-half lengths but lost in the end by that margin.

Randy Jablonic remembers the Oakland trip well and the squad being met by famous UW footballer Pat O'Dea and other Wisconsin alumni. The athletes were taken on a tour of Oakland and San Francisco, including a memorable visit to Chinatown.

In the only home event of the season, Wisconsin edged out Stanford on a one and three-quarter-mile Lake Mendota course. There was never open water between the two shells, and the outcome was in doubt to the finish until Wisconsin edged ahead by two seconds. UW's boating: Brian Bagley (bow), Robert Schmidt, Randy Jablonic, Terry Rose, John Morgen, Dean Walker, Joe Irwin, Herb Degner (stroke) and Eugene Huske (cox).

In the IRAs, Wisconsin finished a distant ninth in a contest won by Cornell.

The 1957–58 season of dual meet competition began again, for the sixth consecutive year, with preseason winter practice on the campus of Rollins College in Winter Park, Florida.

The best race of the 1957–58 season took place on May 10 on a one and three-quarter-mile course on the Charles River in Boston. Against crews from MIT,

> **Origins of the Four-Oared Race without Coxswain**
>
> In the March 1957 *Wisconsin Rowing News*, Coach Sonju told of the origins of the four-oared race without coxswains. It seems the late W. B. Wordgate, when competing in this event in the Brasenose Four in 1868 arranged that on the word "Go!" from the starter, the coxswain should jump overboard. Lightened by the ejection of this passenger and, aided by a Wordgate-designed foot-based steering mechanism, the Brasenose Four went on to win, only to be disqualified. The next year presentation prizes were offered for a four-oared race without coxswain, and thus this four-oared race came into being.

Boston University, and Columbia (the latter coached by former UW coxswain and *Daily Cardinal* sports reporter, Don Rose), the Badgers managed to defeat all three.

While winning three straight early season triumphs, the UW crew was unable to win again. Against Cal on Lake Mendota June 7, the Badgers were edged out by six feet. Their eighth place finishes in the Eastern Sprints and the IRAs belied their potential in the following season. UW's IRA boating: Charles B. Pope (bow), Robert Schmidt, William Erhke, Dale Sharpee, Richard Ahner, James Bowen, Joe Irwin, William Brauer (stroke) and Alan Clark (cox).

In 1958, former Badger crew coach (1906–10) and the first American to win the Diamond (single) Sculls title in 1896, Edward Hanlan "Ned" Ten Eyck was inducted into Helms (now the National Rowing Foundation) Hall of Fame.

During the 1958–59 season, Coach Sonju returned to open-water practice on the half-mile stretch of the Yahara River, which was often free of ice for most of the winter. In a *Milwaukee Journal* article, Coach Sonju described how the crew "carted the huge shells down to the Yahara" to catch the open water. In the same 1959 article, he mused, half to himself, "It could be a pretty good year."

When the crews practiced on weekends, before classes, or in the mornings before the lake winds picked up and made difficult the rowing on Lake Mendota, the often stoic but usually good-natured Sonju would often get the boys started off from the docks with, "Let's go over and wake up the governor!" (whose mansion sits about two miles from the boathouse on the southeastern shore of Lake Mendota. An American flag typically flies on a lakeside pole on the lawn of the mansion). Sonju is remembered for other "starting instructions" when heading for Picnic Point as the first leg of a morning's exercise, not all of which can be mentioned here.

In one of the first attention-getting incidents, which seemed to later surround UW's future crew coach, 3-seat Randy Jablonic, discovered that his own clothing had wrapped together with a sweat shirt he'd curled around the oar handle. The resulting intertwining grip of fabric led to his oar's crabbing and Jablonic's (also known as "Jabo"—pronounced *Jah'bo*) flipping into the frigid April waters of Lake Mendota.

Jablonic remembered attempting to swim back to the shell only to find he was fast becoming too numb to even be able to move his arms at all in the water. Coach Sonju, who'd immediately taken the helm of his motorized launch upon seeing the accident, drove the boat quickly toward the struggling oarsman. The coach then wrenched Jablonic into the motor boat and wrapped him up in blankets.

> ## The Pickle Boat and UW's Pickle Boat Captain
>
> The "pickle boat" is an expression long used by college crews. The exact origin of the expression is unknown. Oarsmen in the pickle boat were spares or alternates brought to major regattas to step in and replace a varsity rower in the event of an injury. The pickle boat rowers—usually one each on the port and starboard sides—stood ready to stand in for an injured varsity rower from either side of the boat. Such rowers were usually the ninth and tenth best rowers on the squad, just shy of making the varsity boat (or the seventeenth and eighteenth best rowers, if a 2V8 boat were also in the regatta). The fact that a crew's reserves, or spares, were usually held on standby, (or "preserved") for potential duty, may be the origin of the phrase.
>
> During the period of the Poughkeepsie Regatta (1895–1949), with only three eights races and often two weeks of prerace training on the Hudson, races were almost always staged among pickle boats, each of which would be made up from a mix of self-selected boatings from the reserves of all the participating schools at the Regatta. The practice seems to have disappeared with the advent of the Open 4+ event in the 1984 IRA Regatta, which gave up to three varsity and at least one freshman a chance to row in a regular event.
>
> At the University of Wisconsin varsity crew program, a pickle boat captain has been elected at the end of each season since at least Randy Jablonic became head coach. Only those who'd rowed in the third or fourth eight were eligible for election and only those who had ever rowed in the third or fourth eight, in at least one practice, were eligible to vote.
>
> The honorific election identifies that rower who was either a lower
>
> *continued on facing page*

In early May of 1959, the Badger crew flew west for competition. As he had on the crew's earlier trips west to race Cal-Berkeley, UW footballer Patrick O'Dea—brother of the turn-of-the-century UW crew coach Andrew O'Dea—met the team at the airport, along with other Bay Area Badger alums, and showed the boys around San Francisco.

Against the Golden Bears on the Oakland Estuary on May 2, the two crews—in their fourteenth meeting since 1937—finished in an unprecedented tie over the two-mile course. Both boats were timed at 9:53.3. Jablonic remembers the judges were watching the finish from a bridge that wasn't quite lined up with the finish classman on his way to one of the higher boats later in his college career, or a senior not quite able to make either the varsity or second varsity eight shell. In either case the chosen captain was someone who demonstrated an unrelenting determination in his athletic work ethic and therefore put fear into the hearts of those ahead of him that their position was never quite secure.

It was the constant pursuit by these pickle boat oarsmen that forced those in the first two boats to work harder to maintain their seats. Each individual pickle boat rower also served as an example to the aspiring freshmen as well as to the oarsmen in the smaller boats of the IRA Regatta.

Indeed, to pursue the team Ten Eyck Trophy, once smaller boat competition was introduced into the scoring, such a motivating oarsman kept the competition stronger through the entire squad, up and down the rowing rankings. Smaller boat performance became especially important, beginning in 1975, when the Ten Eyck award formula first incorporated the results of the smaller boat events in the weightings of the national IRA regatta's team award calculation.

line, so they could not confidently name the winner—and neither of the coxswains could tell. As a result, both coxswains were thrown into the water and both teams exchanged shirts.

Back in Madison on May 9, the Badgers managed to eke out a victory in a four-way race against MIT, Columbia, and Wayne State (Michigan). It was Wayne State's debut in big-college racing. The win in Madison, however, did not help the Badgers the following weekend where they finished tenth in the Eastern Sprints on Lake Carnegie in Princeton.

Randy Jablonic remembers the pre-IRA race against Navy in Annapolis as an important race for 1959 varsity. Both crews got off to roughly equal starts and were 500 meters into their race when a fisherman and his outboard crossed into the racing lanes just under the bridge over the Severn River course. The angler turned down the course toward the race and passed between the two varsity shells! Rather than be distracted, however, the Badger shell "powered away from Navy and, by winning, found themselves going into the IRAs with a newfound confidence," recalled Jablonic.

One month later, the Badger rowers demonstrated again how they often experienced a slow start to their season, only to gain relative speed on their opponents as their experience and training accumulate. Wisconsin's long winters and the re-

1959 UW V8, IRA winners. Front (left to right): Phillip Mork, Charles Pope (bow), Palmer Taylor (cox), Ernest Smith, and Dale Sharpee. Back: Herb Degner (stroke), Courtney Freeman (7-seat), Captain Jim Bowen (6), Graham Hoffman (5), Dick Ahner (4), Randy Jablonic (3), Bill Braver (2), and Jim Hanke. Photo courtesy of UW Athletic Communications.

sultant late melting of their home course (the average opening of the ice on Lake Mendota is around April 6 or 7) generally mean the Badger crews' times drop faster in the ten to twelve weeks leading up to the IRAs than the time improvements of most of the other teams in the country. The mystery question early in the season was always, "How fast will these times drop?" In 1959, the answer for the Badgers was, "A whole lot!"

At the 1959 IRAs in Syracuse the races were still limited to varsity, junior varsity, and freshmen eight events. As a result, each crew had two to six spares, who, but for injuries, would otherwise seldom be moved into the first-string boats at the regatta. Staging pickle boat races (combining spares from several schools to compete against each other) solved this lack of competition. The pickle boat competition pitted five eight-oared boats against one another in a one-mile contest. At the finish, the Washington Husky-Princeton-Badger combo, at 5:21, won by a quarter length over the Cornell-Navy-MIT blend of oarsmen (5:22). The traditional award, a jar of pickles, was awarded the winners.

The varsity race was an exciting one! Malcolm Alama described why each of Cal, Navy, Washington and Syracuse all wanted victory so badly:

> Cal wanted to win for its Crew Coach Ky Ebright of 35 years and who was retiring after rescuing the Golden Bears from rowing extinction. Navy wanted the victory to honor their famous coach, Rusty Callow, who was ill and retiring.

Washington was emotionally high after release from a two year IRA suspension imposed by the NCAA and their coach, too, Al Ulbrickson was also retiring. Lastly, Syracuse wanted victory as the host and favored crew, having only lost to Harvard at the Eastern Sprints by two feet.

The varsity race, as predicted, was one of high drama and fury. Off to a bunched start, the crews frantically fought for positions. First Cornell grabbed the lead. Soon Syracuse snatched it from her. Meanwhile, Wisconsin replaced the fading Cornell boat in second place. Advancing from fifth, then to fourth, Washington came up strong and drew abreast of both the Big Red of Cornell and Navy at the mile.

While this trio fought for third, the Badgers, with their strong sweeps, passed the [coach] Schoel men of Syracuse. And at the two-mile point, Syracuse was a quarter of a length behind. A few minutes later, the smooth-rowing Badgers swept out to a full-length lead.

Once before triumphant in IRA competition, Wisconsin, half a mile from glory, lengthened out its lead. Desperately, Syracuse increased its stroke—29 to 30, to 31, to 32, and to 33, then to 34, to 35, and finally to 36!

Unmindful of those valid reasons why California, Navy, Washington and Syracuse all desired victory, Wisconsin administered the coup de grace to the threatening Orangemen by increasing its stroke to 40. The Badgers smelled victory, and later they won it by sweeping across the line, stroking a lowered 33 strokes per minute.

While Wisconsin poured it on, things were happening other places on the course. Navy, after fighting off Cornell and Washington, began to move up on Syracuse. And for the second time in the championship race, the Syracuse men were forced to row a killing pace in order to salvage second place. Right down to the final stroke the two battled, but the Orange took second by one and one-tenth second.[6]

Wisconsin's finish showed again how a slow start in the Eastern Sprints could often be turned around by the time of the IRAs. The UW boating: Charles Pope (bow), William Brauer, Randy Jablonic, Richard Ahner, Graham Hoffman, James Bowen, Courtney Freeman, Herbert Degner (stroke), and Palmer Taylor (cox).

The early years of the 1960s did not start off well for the Badgers. In the spring season of 1960, Wisconsin failed to qualify for the Eastern Sprints finals on Lake Quinsigamond in Worcester, Massachusetts. In the IRAs the UW oarsmen, winners the year before, finished a disappointing eleventh, beating only Columbia.

The 1960–61 season was not much better. The Purdue Boat Club (5:06) beat UW's varsity (5:07.2) for the first time ever. The race was lost by ten feet on a one-mile course on Lake Mendota. UW Coach Norm Sonju had been encouraging

> **Seat Numbering**
>
> Oarsmen refer to their seat-number in the shell—whether the boat's an eight- or a four-seat boat—starting from the bow in the front and numbering back to the stern. The 1-seat is always referred to as the "bow" seat and the stern-most rower as the "stroke," with the numbers 2 and 3 (in a four-oared boat) or 2 through 7 (in an eight-oared boat) in between.

other Big Ten schools into the sport of crew. He helped by Purdue by offering some coaching, the bargain purchase of a couple of old shells, and the mixing of Badger and Boilermaker oarsmen in an exhibition race in the spring of 1951. The following spring (of 1952), the Badger frosh raced the Purdue Boat Club, Wisconsin's first Big Ten crew opponent.

For the teacher to lose to the student nine years later caused mixed feelings in Coach Sonju—glad the sport had taken root at Purdue, but more than a bit sorry to see the fall of his own crew from being IRA champions two years earlier to second in the Midwest.

On May 13, 1961, the first Cochrane Cup race was held. The competition among Dartmouth, MIT, and Wisconsin had been initiated when Mrs. Edward Cochrane placed a cup in competition to honor her husband, Edward L. Cochrane, a former admiral and director of the Navy's Bureau of Ships and more recently the president of MIT. The venue for the annual Cochrane cup series rotated from Madison to Hanover, New Hampshire to Boston, Massachusetts.

Wisconsin (9:14) lost this first year of competition for the Cochrane on a one and three-quarter-mile course on Lake Mendota by one and one-half lengths to MIT (9:03.7) and Dartmouth (9:10.4).

Jablonic, who had been named the freshman coach for the 1960–61 season, found Sonju conservative when it came to traveling with the freshmen squad. While Coach Sonju hadn't brought the frosh to the IRAs in two years, Jablonic thought is was important to give them a taste of the big end-of-season race—and said so.

From Rail to Truck-Trailers

In the late winter of the following season, the January 1962 *Wisconsin Crew Letter* announced that UW crews would henceforth use truck-trailers for transporting shells around the country to their various regatta venues. Use of the railroads for this purpose ended following the June 1961 IRAs in Syracuse.

For the previous sixty-five years, Wisconsin's shells had traveled by rail to the Poughkeepsie Regatta and elsewhere. Coaches had often sneaked a few extra participants along on the trips by allowing the stowaways to hide in the railcars for the two to three day trips. Coach Walz, in the early 1940s, even loaded extra milk cans of gasoline for his launch into the end-loading boxcars in order not to run short at several east coast races, amid the war-rationing of gasoline.

As a result of the switching from railcars to trucks, the newsletter proclaimed, "Three dirty, old mattresses and a five gallon milk can were available for sale at the boathouse!"

"The frosh can go if they finish within a boat length of the varsity," challenged Sonju. While training a few days later, the varsity eight started a three-mile timed run, with the freshmen to join them at the one-mile mark. Initially, the frosh pulled ahead, being fresh, but then fell behind, eventually by open water. As the end neared, however, the frosh recovered and overlapped the varsity at the finish. Jablonic didn't look up for some time, but finally he stole a glance at Sonju. "Well, I guess the freshmen can go," Sonju grumbled. At the IRAs in Syracuse, Wisconsin's varsity eight finished eighth of thirteen, while the frosh ended ninth of twelve.

On April 4, 1962, UW and the crew team lost a great friend of crew, a host and supporter during their West Coast trips, when Wisconsin's biggest football legend, Patrick O'Dea, died in San Francisco at the age of ninety.

In May, another Big Ten boat club, this one from Minnesota, came to Madison to work out against the Badgers. At the Eastern Sprints on May 19, Wisconsin failed to make the finals, but in another example of rapid improvement over a short rowing season, the oarsmen garnered a fourth place in the IRAs the following month. The UW varsity had been eleventh of thirteen with a mile and a quarter to go in the three-mile Lake Onondaga course at Syracuse. For the first time since 1948, UW had entered boats in all three races. The 2V8 finished fifth of eleven and the frosh eight was seventh of twelve entries.

UW's boating in the victory against Navy a week earlier is believed to have been the same as at the IRAs in Syracuse: John Albright (bow), Vic Johnson, Charles Kemp, Tom Kronke, Ben Logertman, Bernie Losching, Doug Reiner, John Shaffer (stroke), and Larry Hurwitz (cox).

The 1962–63 season saw UW place well, with a fourth in the Eastern Sprints (excluding the guest crew from the Ratzeburg rowing club of Germany under well-known coach Karl Adams. This German crew had for ten years demonstrated the benefits of hard basic exercise and physiological development in their athletic training. Adams, a physicist, also added innovations in his mathematical measurements of the best rowing leverage angles and boat styles, among other things).[7]

Jablonic and others remember Ratzeburg probably didn't really qualify for the finals out of their first heat, losing to Wisconsin. As the big-name guest boat, however, the officials wanted them in the finals. They found their cameras had (allegedly) broken and, ultimately, decided Ratzeburg finished where needed to get

> **Port and Starboard-Rigged Shells**
>
> The "normal" eight-oared shells are rigged for a port-rowing stroke oarsman. This typically results in all the even-numbered seats being port-rowing oarsmen and all odd-numbered seats being starboard-rowing oarsmen. When the stroke of a shell is a starboard-rowing oarsmen, the shell is then "starboard-rigged." Occasionally, the rigging for the rowers is not alternating but has two oars consecutively rigged on the same side; this configuration is called "bucket-rigged."

into the finals. Amid the heavy water in the finals, the Germans rowed into and out of the windless bays along lane six and eventually won the Sprints.

The Badgers also logged a victory over Navy by two and one-half lengths on the Severn River and a fifth in a field of fifteen at the Syracuse IRAs. UW's stroke, Bernie Losching, had had a wisdom tooth extracted on the Tuesday before the IRA finals. When the stitches broke in the finals on Saturday, he crossed the finish line with blood running down his cheeks. Since then, Coach Jablonic made sure everyone has his teeth checked in February or March.

The boating against Navy (and probably at the IRAs): Tom Willett (bow), Vic Johnson, Marv Utech, Al Heggblom, Ben Logterman, Tom Kroncke, Doug Reiner, Bernie Losching (stroke), and Larry Hurwitz (cox).

Harry Emerson "Dad" Vail was posthumously elected to the Helms Sports Foundation Hall of Fame (for Rowing) in 1963.

1964 UW freshman 8, IRA winners. Source: *1965 IRA Program.* Courtesy of the IRA Stewards.

In 1963–64, Wisconsin's freshman eight stole the season's limelight. In spite of a three-quarter length loss to Marietta College on May 2, the frosh from UW came roaring back six weeks later.

In the first UW frosh victory in the IRAs since 1907, the Badgers chased the Washington Huskies, the early pace setters, for two-thirds of the course. Arnie Burdick, longtime sportswriter and rowing enthusiast from the *Syracuse Herald-American*, described the race:

> After a ding-dong fight for the first 1,200 meters, Wisconsin's brilliant freshman oarsmen rowed away with the championship. The young Badgers, stroked by 19-year-old Neil Halleen from Sheboygan, Wis., wrestled the lead from Washing-

ton, the early pace-setter, with only about 800 meters to go, and drew away, winning pretty much as they pleased.[8]

As the Badgers crossed the finish, Washington had faded to fourth, behind Brown and Columbia. UW's freshman boating: David Quam (bow), Harold Thomas, John Halleran, Thomas Sy, John Norsetter, Don Lange, Bill Clapp, Neil Halleen (stroke), and James Rowen (cox). With his hair cut in an unusual Mohawk style, 7-seat, Bill Clapp, would later use the same look to motivate himself and his crew.

> *During the summer of 1964, the first All-Star Camp to select U.S. Olympic rowers was held in Laconia, New Hampshire, with MIT coach Jack Fraley as the head and Norm Sonju as his assistant. In the 1964 summer Olympics in Tokyo, Coach Sonju served as co-manager of the U.S. team, and the American eight won the gold!*

The 1964–65 season was not memorable. UW's varsity lost the Cochrane Cup to MIT, placed ninth in the Eastern Sprints at Worcester, and finished sixth at the IRAs in Syracuse.

Navy swept all three IRA eights events, while the Badger eight suffered such injuries as a foot infection (stroke, Tom Sy), a rib cage muscle pull (6-seat, Tom Mitchell), and a bad cold (4-seat, Roger Seeman). Wisconsin's varsity eight (17:11.4) finished sixth in the IRA's premier three-mile event, five lengths behind winner to Navy (16:51.3) over a three-mile course.

The Badger 2V8 (17:13.4) garnered second place, behind Navy (17.07.5). UW's silver medalists: Donald Mowry (bow), Steven Bergum, Robert Boettcher, William Blakely, David Quam, Dave Storm, Tom Haworth, Neil Halleen (stroke), and Dan Schwoerer (cox).

The 1965–66 season showed substantial improvement. In the fall of 1965, the first Head of the Charles races—now the most prestigious head race in the United States—were held in Cambridge, Massachusetts, on the Charles River. UW did not attend, waiting to see how the event developed and to avoid budget battles for another East Coast trip. Two women's crews from Philadelphia Girls Rowing Club were invited to compete against each other, although there were no women's events until 1969.[9]

Around February, 1966, the UW Campus Planning Commission, the Board of Regents, and the State Building Commission approved a new boathouse at the north end of Babcock Drive, after the proposed Willow Beach site 750 meters to the west drew strong protest from Madison's west side residents. Ground was later broken on the $250,000 facility in October of 1966.

By the middle of May, after a ninth place finish at the Eastern Sprints, Wisco's rowers showed modest improvement, with various victories over smaller crew programs at Wayne State and Kansas State. In a one and three-quarter-mile race on Lake Mendota against Navy on June 11, the Badgers were unable to jump ahead on their closing sprint and were defeated by three-quarters of a length by last year's IRA champion. Wisconsin would have its chance for revenge a week later in Syracuse. On June 18, 1966, the Badgers again showed big improvement over their short season.

Allison Danzig's June 19th *New York Times* account on page one of the Sports Section, read:

Wisconsin First in Rowing Upset

Wisconsin, Pennsylvania, and Dartmouth rowed to unaccustomed glory in the 64th regatta of the IRA on Onondaga Lake. Norman Sonju's Wisconsin Badgers won the varsity race for the first time since 1959, defeating Navy's defending champions by half a boat length and rowing the three miles in almost dead calm water against a five-mile head wind in 16:03.4.

Wisconsin's victory in the varsity championship, its third in history, was as confounding as Navy's here a year ago. The Badgers had failed to qualify for the Eastern Sprint finals in May and had been beaten a week ago by Navy at Madison, WI by a boat length. Sonju had picked Navy to win here, despite the fact that the victory at Madison was the Middies only one of the season. It followed that the Wisconsin coach must have thought highly of his own crew in giving Navy a close race, but he expressed no opinion about it, limiting himself to extolling the strength of the Badger freshman.

There was no indication of the surprise that Wisconsin was to furnish until after the first mile had been rowed. Rutgers, Dartmouth and California had gone out in front at the start and waged a close fight for three-quarters of a mile. Brown now came into the picture and went by Dartmouth and California and challenged Rutgers, which had definitely taken over the lead at the low stroke of 29. Then, past the mile mark, Wisconsin, which had been in fifth place, put on a drive and took second place.

From now until the last half-mile of the race, Brown and Wisconsin waged a tough fight in which the lead fluctuated. Wisconsin definitely was in the front a mile from home, rowing at 32, a shade under the Bruins. It seemed Brown was still in the fight as they entered the last half-mile. But now Navy, which had been well back for the first half of the race and moved ahead of Cornell into third place at a mile and three-quarters, came on. At the same time, Princeton and Penn, which were far on the outside with Navy, made their move, too, from well back.

UNIVERSITY OF WISCONSIN VARSITY—1966 I.R.A. CHAMPIONS
Jim Decker (left), Chairman of the I.R.A. Board of Stewards, presents the Varsity Challenge Cup—Cox Willard Witte, Coach Norm Sonju, Stroke Tom Sy, Jim Tonn, Don Lange, John Norsetter, Tom Mitchell, Greg Farnham, Roger Seeman, Bow Bill Clapp.

Photo—Syracuse Herald American

1966 UW V8, IRA winners. Photo by and permission granted by *The Post-Standard*.

With 15,000 spectators on the shore in a high state of excitement as the crews neared the finish line, Navy and Wisconsin slugged it out in the high 30s. The Middies went all the way to 41, but Wisconsin, at 38½, just managed to win in the last 10 strokes by half a length. Princeton, with a superlative effort, snatched third place from Brown by a second. Joe Burk's Pennsylvanians, with their electronic device, the Wizard, in the boat, followed Brown by three-quarters of a length and Cornell was next, less than half a length behind Penn.

Wisconsin, in addition to winning the big race, placed third in freshman and seventh in the junior varsity race and was runner-up to Pennsylvania (first time winner with 15) for [Ten Eyck] point honors with 12.[10]

As in 1964, Bill Clapp had again found good fortune by cutting his hair in a Mohawk style. In an interview with *Sports Illustrated* writer Paul Stewart, Clapp—despite a recent boat-length loss to Navy on Lake Mendota—dreamed of avenging this loss and defeating all comers in the IRA's annual collegiate championships. Knowing a dream alone wouldn't get the job done, Clapp described his strategy to Stewart, who would later write, in his June 27, 1966, *Sports Illustrated* article, under the headline:

Putting on the Old Indian Sign

"When I was a freshman," [Clapp] explained at Syracuse last week, "I did this Mohawk Indian bit and guess what? We went out and beat all the other freshmen in the IRA." Figuring that what made powerful medicine once might well do it again, Bill persuaded his crew mate, No. 4 Oar Tom Mitchell, to shave his [Bill's] head in Mohawk style one hour before the race started. Result: contrary to the predictions of every expert in the business, the Badgers won the IRA, beating defending Navy by half a length and the highly touted University of Washington Huskies by 11.

In what would be the only University of Wisconsin athletics' title in 1966—at the Big Ten, regional or national level—the varsity eight crew had defeated fourteen other crews on the three-mile IRA course at Syracuse for the national title in the men's eight event.

UW's boating: Bill Clapp (bow), Roger Seeman, Greg Farnham, Tom Mitchell, John Norsetter, Don Lange, James Tonn, Tom Sy (stroke), and Willard Witte (cox and Captain).

In a sad historical footnote to the beginning 1966–67 season, freshman Leo Burt from Havertown, Pennsylvania, joined the Badger's novice crew in the fall of 1966. Four years later, September 4, 1970, Burt would be added to the FBI's "Ten Most Wanted" list "in connection with the destruction by explosives of the United States Army Mathematics Research Center located on the University of Wisconsin campus in which one person was killed and several injured." As of this writing, Burt is still at large.

Novice teammate Ron Kuehn noted, "The Vietnam war made a lot of people crazy during this period in our history. Leo was liked by his teammates, had been a schoolboy oarsman in Philadelphia and had a great family. This was a tragedy for everyone involved, including Leo. His teammates know that the Leo they used to know was not the Leo who committed this crime. The war changed him tragically."

Wisconsin started the 1966–67 season in grand style. On October 30, attending the second annual Head of the Charles for the first time, the Badgers won their eight-oared event by twelve seconds over Northeastern, which was rowing on their Charles River home course. Harvard, also on their home course, rowed with a coxswain weighing only 56 pounds!

UW's Head of the Charles boating: Bill Clapp (bow and Co-captain), Al Horner, John Norsetter, Neil Halleen, Greg Farnham, Don Lange, Doug Sahs, Tom Sy (stroke), and Arnold Polk (cox).

Over the Thanksgiving vacation, however, the crew's celebratory spirit changed when assistant crew coach, Tom Chapman, died in a private plane crash while leaving Madison for the holiday in New York. Chapman had rowed in college at UCLA. Chapman's parents donated the UW boathouse trophy case, which rigger Curt Drewes built from materials donated by the family, in Tom's honor. Coach Jablonic also renamed the varsity launch the *Chapman.*

In the second ever race against a Big Ten opponent (the first being Purdue on May 3, 1952), Wisconsin freshmen raced against the University of Minnesota Boat Club on the Mississippi River. In an October race with 15 mph winds, snow, and temperatures in the high thirties, the UW eight won handily.

UW's first official crew banquet in the modern era was held March 11, 1967, at Welch's Embers Steakhouse on East Washington, where the red interior remains a vivid memory to Badger oarsman Ron Kuehn and the rest of his novice team of 1967.[11] The oldest alumnus attending, from UW's 1903 crew, was Dr. Verl A. Ruth from Des Moines, Iowa.

In the May 6, 1967, Cochrane Cup competition, first raced in 1961, Wisconsin hosted MIT and Dartmouth on a 2,000-meter course on Lake Mendota. The Badgers broke ahead first and held a lead of a couple of seats for 750 meters. At that point, MIT took a slight lead and Dartmouth fell far behind. The Badgers regained the lead by a half length at the 1,300-meter mark and stretched to a one-length lead with 500 meters to go. The Badgers (6:40.3), winning by about a length over the tiring Engineers (6:49.2) and a trailing Dartmouth (7:03.6), were greeted by fans crowded at both the Memorial Union and at the Boathouse.

Eighth overall at the Eastern Sprints, the Badger eight again found itself in need of a fast finish to its rowing year. In the inaugural varsity-eight Buck Walsh Cup race, Wisconsin faced Washington and Navy. Fred Emerson, from the Class of '32, had donated the trophy in honor of the former Navy rower and coach, Charles S. "Buck" Walsh. Emerson was a former UW rower and a major contributor to Wisconsin rowing, as well as to many other crew programs around the country. In a heavy wind, strong tide and rough water, the Badgers edged out Washington by half a length and Navy by nearly two.

At the Syracuse IRAs of 1967, Wisconsin again was close to victory in the varsity eight contest. The race was delayed one hour by a storm that caught the crews on the water at the exposed end of Lake Onondaga. Facing what was described as the best Penn crew in generations, the race saw Wisconsin, Navy, and Penn challenging one another. By the mile mark, Penn had pulled in front, Wisconsin was giving chase, and Navy had dropped behind. At the two-mile buoy, Penn was in a three-quarter-length lead over Wisconsin.

At the finish, 1967's varsity-eight winner Wisconsin was unable to close the gap, and Penn crossed two lengths ahead—their first IRA varsity victory since 1900! History had dealt Wisconsin a continuing ironic twist. Of the Penn varsity eight's last three IRA victories, 1899 (the year of Wisconsin's "Berry Crate" crew), 1900, and now in 1967, the Badgers had been a close second in all three.

In the postseason summer of 1967, Wisconsin made its first trip to the Royal Henley Regatta where it was defeated by Oxford University in the Grand Challenge Cup competition. A powerful East German team from Leipzig eventually won the trophy. Also in 1967, UW crew Coach Sonju was inducted into the Helms Athletic Foundation Hall of Fame (now administered by the National Rowing Foundation).

The 1967–68 season was a transition year for the Badger crews. As the oarsmen moved into a new $330,000 boathouse, completed in mid-November of 1967, the UW Board of Regents, on January 12, 1968, approved demolition of the balance of the old boathouse. The season was also Norm Sonju's last year—he would turn 66 on June 6 of 1968.

The U.S. Olympic Committee exerted its influence on college crew in several ways in 1968. Madison was designated as the Midwest Rowing Center, one of nine around the United States to train future national team members. Incoming UW crew coach Randy Jablonic would oversee the Center during the summer training leading up to the 1968 summer Olympics. Such training centers were part of the transition from selecting the fastest college eight as America's entry in the Olympic eight-oared event. Now rowers would be selected individually into the eight-oared national team entry.

The Olympic Committee also persuaded the stewards of the IRA to shorten race distances and add several small boat events. In 1967 both the IRA's varsity and second varsity eights had been three-mile events, while the freshman eight distance was two miles. Now the standard distance would be 2,000 meters. In addition, the Committee asked, and the IRA agreed, that smaller boat events be introduced into the IRA Regatta in order to further introduce Olympic events into college rowing. In June of 1968, the IRA stewards thus introduced the first small-boat event at the regatta since 1913—the varsity four plus coxswain.

During Wisconsin's 1968 spring season, the Badger varsity lost the Cochrane Cup to Dartmouth on the Charles River, placed fifth in the Eastern Sprints, and lost by a deck length to Washington in a race on Lake Mendota.

At Coach Sonju's retirement party at the Park Motor Inn in Madison on May 30, guests included Madison Mayor Otto Festge, UW Vice Chancellor James Cleary, Athletic Director Ivy Williamson, and Clifford ("Tip") Goes, the Syracuse coxswain in 1910 and an IRA official for many years. Goes was the referee who watched the Wisconsin eight jump his gun start in the storm-ravaged waters of the Ohio River during the 1950 IRAs at Marietta, Ohio.

In the IRAs of 1968, UW could manage only an eighth place in the varsity eight event. Cornell won the newly initiated coxed-four event.

UW crew coach Norm Sonju retired with three IRA titles by his varsity eight (1951, '59, and '66) and one by his freshman eight in 1964.

Following the regular 1967–68 college season, UW coxswain Stewart MacDonald became the first member of a Badger crew to participate in the Olympics, placing fifth in the coxed pair event at the Mexico City Olympics. MacDonald would repeat his Olympic team participation in 1972, and other Badger oarsmen would follow, putting Wisconsin rowers in ten of the next ten Olympics (1968 through 2004).

9
"Jabo" Takes Over

Coach Randall ("Jabo") Jablonic, Norm Sonju's freshman and assistant coach (1960–1968), was named to succeed Sonju as Wisconsin's head coach beginning in the fall of 1968. Jabo had been in the 3-seat on the Badgers' second varsity eight to win a gold medal at the IRAs in 1959. His frosh eight had won the IRAs in 1964, the third novice eight winner for UW since 1900.

Jablonic, like Sonju before him, loved the out-of-doors. The two also had similar charismatic, down-to-earth coaching styles. Both coaches also encouraged strong academic performances by their athletes and, whether such motivation was causal or not, Badger rowers regularly ranked among the top student-athletes, as measured by GPA results, of any of UW's teams.

Over the next twenty-eight years as head coach, Jablonic would develop his own unique style for motivating his rowers over the long Wisconsin winters, using a mixture of humor, intimidation, challenge, respect, creative workouts, fair treatment, gratitude for hard work, and a personal brand of charisma that touched almost all of his young oarsmen.

Randy "Jabo" Jablonic, head coach 1968–96. Source: UW Athletic Communications. Photo by Duane Hopp.

Coach Jablonic had what some would call old-fashioned qualities to his style, but no one would say Jabo's personality and charisma weren't completely memorable. From the research undertaken by this writer, Jablonic's multifaceted character—his skill at balancing sometimes dicey relationships with the parents of his athletes; his drive to fund-raise when fund-raising was critical; his ability at keeping administrative budget pressures out of the boathouse; his energy, fix-it-yourself and entrepreneurial skills at property management—make him stand out as a unique personality among the thirteen interesting crew coaches Wisconsin has had over its history of coaches beginning in 1894.

Jablonic would also face the near-elimination of men's crew in the spring of 1971 and again during the spring of 1991, following, in both cases, the declining gate and television revenues, which followed seven consecutive and six consecutive losing seasons, respectively, by UW's football teams. In spite of these "off-the-water" external threats, Jabo's record of success on the water would only grow.

Coaching crew at Wisconsin was a mix of many challenges. Long winters kept the athletes off the water for long periods, forcing Jablonic to constantly work at keeping his squad enthusiastic about their training. From rope pulls to stadiums to running long distances through the snow, Jabo saw the winter off the water as an opportunity to push individual athletes harder than they might push themselves in a group rowing together.

While the crews had a rowing tank for indoor training, the erg machines of the day were quite primitive. With only six Gaumet rowing machines, not many men could ever be erging at one time. The Gaumet was not only heavy—it usually took two or more people to move it—they were also difficult to maintain, with riggers constantly engaged in their upkeep.

On the water, one of Jabo's techniques was using the megaphone to block and isolate his view of a part of a rower's stroke or body in order to focus on its fluidity and movement and not be hypnotized by the athlete's overall motion.

Jablonic would later support the introduction of women's openweight crew, first as a club sport in 1972, then as a varsity sport in 1974. The UW inventory records of the day also show many of the boat gifts, solicited by Jabo during the economic stresses on the men's crews in the 1970's would be shared or given to the developing women's openweight crew.

Asked to address what, as an athlete (not as a coach), was the allure of rowing, Jabo replied:

> One of the basic attractions to me is the inherent allure of the water. What kid doesn't like water? Most people like being around water and playing in it, one way or another.
>
> More specific to the sport of rowing, it is the challenge of reaching perfection. I remember rowing in an eight when it was going well and thinking "Wow" can it get any better than this . . . the connection, the feel of the lock-up of the blade to the water at the catch . . . the lock-up of your heart and soul. The feel of the boat lift off the water, leaping ahead.
>
> At a certain moment, when all the rowers are in that special sync, the feeling is heavenly, almost like you're flying . . . soaring. Then fatigue begins and you might lose it. You try to get it back . . . you seek to get it back. It may be several months from one of those special moments to the next. The sense is one of "wonderfulness . . . of effortless motion."

In his first year as head coach, beginning the fall of 1968, the team showed improvement over the prior season. Jabo's first victory came against Purdue on

April 26—Wisconsin's first, last, and only home appearance that season. (The absence of home appearances by Wisconsin's crew would soon become one of the reasons men's crew would be characterized as "expendable" by some in the Athletic Department.)

In Hanover, New Hampshire, Jablonic faced his first serious opponent as a new varsity crew coach. The race was against Dartmouth and MIT and their two well-known coaches, Pete Gardner and Pete Holland, respectively—Gardner in particular had been an idol of Jablonic's as Jabo grew in the freshmen coaching ranks.

When Wisconsin knocked off Dartmouth and MIT for the Cochrane Cup on the Connecticut River in Hanover, New Hampshire, Jablonic remembers feeling "bad" as he glanced over at Gardner and saw a tear in his eye. Jabo suspected the Dartmouth coach must have felt this way, with some justification, after losing to "this new upstart coach." Jabo vividly recalls how "guilty" he felt from this victory, which, in retrospect, he now feels may be part of any young coach's first victory. After attending many camps over the years, Jabo says "I got hardened later."

The Badger four also defeated their two opponents Darthmouth and MIT.

At the Eastern Sprints, Harvard (6:05.6) led the pack with Wisconsin (6:08.3) finishing not far back in fourth.

Harvard's Cincinnati Alumni Club—celebrating a centennial weekend—sponsored the Brown, Wisconsin, and Harvard eights to a rematch of the Sprints on the Ohio River on May 17. Harvard and Brown boosters each watched from their separately chartered paddle wheelers.

Wisconsin jumped off to a two or three seat lead at the 500-meter mark, but the stroke-rate was higher than Coach Jablonic had planned for in his prerace strategy. Averaging 212 pounds, this was Wisconsin's biggest crew ever, and Jablonic had wanted to settle at a rate below 40. Harvard pulled ahead and won at 5:05.6, with Wisconsin (5:09.7) second by a length. Brown, the Purdue Boat Club, Marietta College, and Notre Dame followed in order.

Against Navy, a week before the IRAs, Wisconsin's varsity eight prevailed by two lengths of open water over Georgetown and Navy on the windy and tidal Severn River in Annapolis, Maryland. Wisconsin's varsity boating: Tom Hertzberg (bow), Mike Lohuis, Richard Zondag (or Richard Purinton), Doug Sahs, Phil Resch, Guy Iverson, Tim Mickelson, Gary Jacobson (stroke), and Stewart MacDonald (coxswain).

In the preliminary varsity heats of the 1969 IRAs, 2-seat Mike Lohuis's oar broke (and a spare oar at that) and he was flipped into the water 200-meters from the finish—his boat still placed second in the heat. In the end, Penn swept all three eight-oared events, with Wisconsin fourth in the varsity eight race. Wisco's 2V8 was second in the finals, the frosh eight finished in eighth, and the coxed four was fourth.

In April of 1969, former UW stroke and crew captain (1927–28), Franklin Orth, a sixty-one-year-old attorney, was named president of the U.S. Olympic Committee. In addition to initiating, and being an active member of, the Wisconsin Crew Corporation's board in the late 1920s and 1930s, Orth also had had a rugged military background.

As reported in the New York Times *of April 20, 1969, Orth, in World War II, volunteered to serve in Merrill's Marauders on long-range penetration operations behind Japanese lines in Burma. Later, he commanded a regimental combat team in guerilla-type operations in the jungles. He left the service with the rank of colonel.*

Orth later served as deputy assistant secretary of the Army, an executive of the National Rifle Association, and a member of the executive committee of the International Shooting Union, the governing body for international and Olympic shooting.

For the eight-oared entry, the selection process—over the summer of 1969—for representing the United States on a national level evolved from a process of selecting a "set crew" from one college or club to a process of selecting individual rowers. Badger Dean Walker ('57) was the first Badger rower to attend a U.S. Olympic training camp in 1956, and Stewart MacDonald ('72) was the first Badger to row for the United States in the Olympics.

For the Worlds of 1969 in Klagenfurt, Austria, three Badgers were chosen to row for the United States, including Guy Iverson (rowing stroke in the coxed pair which finished seventh) and, in the ninth-finishing eight-oared entry, Jay Mimier (3-seat) and Tim Mickelson (4-seat).[1]

In the 1969–70 season, led by a 1968 Olympic coxswain, Stewart MacDonald, and a future Olympic silver medalist, Tim Mickelson, the varsity eight started their short season of open-water training in the usual way—slowly, but with rapid improvement.

At about the same time the ice melted off Lake Mendota on April 8, newly named UW Athletic Director Elroy Hirsch was quoted in the *Daily Cardinal* saying, "We should support all our Big Ten Sports. But crew and fencing are not Big Ten Sports." Notwithstanding these occasional public manifestations of budget challenges and of threats to the continuance of crew, Stewart MacDonald noted, "Credit to Jabo, the pressure from the AD's office was something he kept out of the boathouse."

On May 2, Dartmouth (6:09.9) took the Cochrane cup from Wisconsin (6:11.5), with MIT (6:32) third. At the Eastern Sprints, UW finished seventh, with Harvard winning its seventh consecutive contest at the Worchester event.

Sometime in mid-spring, Jay Mimier (senior oarsman, U.S. National Team rower the previous summer, and future UW head coach of the women's openweight crew) remembers that an unusually high number of oars were being broken by the Badgers. For a few weeks, young men were beginning to feel they must have really been developing into something special until Coach Jablonic brought the matter up with George Pocock, the supplier of shells and oars to UW. After doing some research, Pocock found that the wood for all the oars had been harvested from a recent forest fire. While most wood recovered from a forest fire remains usable if left standing for up to a year or two, this wood had obviously been weakened beyond recovery.

The Pocock Boat Company willingly sent new replacement oars to Wisconsin, and Jablonic, true to his legendarily parsimonious form, either auctioned or sold the unusable oars at the next crew banquet to raise money for the tightly budgeted crew program.

The largest entourage of outboards and cruisers in several seasons was out to view the race against Navy on Lake Mendota on June 6. After an equal start, Wisconsin stroke Tom Flammang lost his slide and missed a stroke. Navy moved up. After recovering Wisco's position over the next several strokes, Flammang lost his slide again and a crabbed oar clubbed him across the chest. The race was stopped when team physician, Dr. Allan Ryan, riding in one of the nearby launches, came over for a look.

Once Flammang was judged okay, the race started again by realigning the boats in roughly the same positions they were in when the race was stopped. In this unusual restart procedure, the boats were told to row at half-speed until they heard the command of "One more stroke!" Wisco went on to lose by a length.

Some revenge came to the Badgers in the IRAs as they again showed rapid improvement. The Badger varsity eight finished second, behind Washington, but ahead of the crews they'd lost to earlier in the season—Dartmouth and Navy.

The stewards of the 1970 IRA, having introduced the varsity coxed four event in 1968, introduced a second small boat—the freshman coxed four as the "fifth" men's heavyweight event. The victory in this year's Novice 4+ competition went to Cornell. Wisconsin's 2V8 ended in sixth and the frosh eight finished seventh.

Rowing 7-seat in Wisconsin's freshman eight at the 1970 IRAs was the future Luke Duke of The Dukes of Hazard *television series, Tom Wopat. He would return to Madison many times in the future, at the invitation of UW band conductor Michael Leckrone to join the UW band in concert presentations.*

In the 1970–71 crew season, budgetary pressures to eliminate rowing as an official sport at Wisconsin grew to a head—despite its nearly 100-year existence since appearing in intramural contests in Madison in 1874. With the big money generator, football, in a seven-season losing streak, attendance and media revenues were in a tailspin.

Within the Athletic Department, crew was deemed an expendable sport, based on several arguments: rowing was not a Big Ten sport (only Purdue and Minnesota rowed and these were club sports), rowing was rarely held on Madison's home waters, travel expenses (to either the East or West coasts) were high, and equipment was costly. The crew budget for 1970–71 was $33,700.

On March 11 Wisconsin Crew Corporation president, Dick Mueller, sent an all-members letter advising that Athletic Director Elroy Hirsch had recommended crew be discontinued. Names of people to contact were part of the message in his letter.

On March 22 Professor Aaron J. Ihde, a UW chemistry professor and former Badger rower (Class of 1931) wrote a carefully argued one-and-a-half page letter to Hirsch. Ihde received a four-and-a-half-page response.

The *Wisconsin State Journal* reported on April 3, 1971, of the meeting the previous Friday of the Athletic Board, the "W" Club, and the Wisconsin Crew Corporation. The room was packed. The Athletic Department reiterated its arguments, "a poor spectator sport, not a Wisconsin high school sport, not a Big Ten sport and too costly."

Professor Ihde's response was equally pithy and ultimately persuasive, "Aren't all sports intended for participants rather than spectators and is high school training necessary when crew has won five national championships in 24 years with students, 99 percent of whom have never rowed and 80 percent of whom are from Wisconsin?"

Ihde continued, "Before you ask if crew is expensive, ask what you are getting for your money. Nothing is spent on scholarships; one-seventh of Wisconsin's student-athletes are on crew and compete with 2 to 3 percent of the Athletic Department's budget. The University receives national prestige from its annual competition and the program trains young men for possible Olympic competition."

The sentiment in the room began to build behind a continued crew program. Gus Bostad, stroke on UW's 1913 crew added, "Any outsider would wonder how a dropping of crew could come about with our facilities and lake locations and our record. They would doubt our judgment and our common sense."

When Hirsch shifted the discussion from "WHY have crew?" to "HOW to have crew?" the battle lines surprisingly fell a bit more. A proposal by George Rea—the 3-seat on the 1941–42 varsity, the UW head crew coach in 1942–43, and nephew of 1901 crew captain, "Will" Gibson—asked, "If a small group of crew alumni can support the crew program when threatened, why can't the National 'W' Club of all of Wisconsin's letter-winners get together when the whole Athletic Department is threatened?"

Rea's question about why crew was singled out when the problem was an across-the-athletic-department problem became the cornerstone for further discussion. Wisconsin Alumni Association director Arlie Mucks later commented, "We can raise the money nationally if we exert the energy we've seen today from the Wisconsin Crew Corporation. . . . We'll give full cooperation."[2] The Wisconsin Crew Corporation had been initiated during the fall of 1928 and incorporated in 1931. Today known as the Wisconsin Rowing Association, the WCC was UW's first booster club for any sport.

The Athletic Department's budget tensions of the spring of 1971 were eased a few days later in an unusual way. The UW Field House won out over the Dane County Coliseum as the venue for up to five basketball play-off games of the Milwaukee Bucks. At a rental rate of $9,000 per game, plus a percentage of the gate and concession incomes, the newly found revenue put the Athletic Department's budget back in the black.

On the Charles River in early May, Wisconsin regained the Cochrane Cup and the next day defeated Boston University by two lengths. A week later at the Eastern Sprints in Worchester, the Badger varsity eight finished fifth. On June 12 in Annapolis, UW's varsity defeated Georgetown. As Navy's varsity eight was on an all-expenses-paid invitational to race in Germany, they did not boat a varsity eight entry that same day against the Badgers.

In the 1971 IRAs, the varsity straight pair event (another Olympic event) was introduced into the competition as the third small boat event and the sixth men's heavyweight event. Cal won this first straight pair event. UW's varsity eight finished thirteenth.

On June 26, a week after the IRAs, a Wisconsin straight four (7:10.5) lost to the Vesper Boat Club (7:03.4) in the Pan American Games trials on a 2,000-meter course on Lake Onondaga.

The crew's prospects showed signs of a turnaround as the 1971–72 season began. In spite of losing a rudder midway through the curving three-mile course up the Charles River, Wisconsin placed seventh in the growingly popular Head of the Charles race in October of 1971.

Former 1940s coach Allen Walz, one of UW's most colorful coaches and the man who led Wisconsin's varsity eight to its first major regatta title at the initial Eastern Sprints race in 1946 (the war had halted the IRAs from 1942 through 1946, so the Eastern Sprints were the closest substitute), was the featured speaker at the crew's annual banquet in March of 1972.

In the spring of 1972 a women's openweight crew program was started at Wisconsin, initially as a club sport. By sheer coincidence, Title IX gender-equity legislation was then under active discussion in the U.S. Congress.

On May 6 MIT won the Cochrane Cup on the Charles River. The *Wisconsin State Journal*, incorrectly informed, reported two erroneous news items—Ken Nelson had separated his shoulder during the race and that "this was the first reported injury in Wisconsin rowing history." In fact, Nelson had stretched a shoulder tendon during horseplay in Boston while waiting a week for the Eastern Sprints and, secondly, Wisconsin indeed had had many previous rowing injuries, the earliest known was a fatality on April 6, 1896, when John Day drowned in a coxed pair that flipped in the cold early spring waters and high winds on Lake Mendota. C. C. McConville had been in the bow and recently arrived footballer Patrick O'Dea was the coxswain.

At the 1972 Eastern Sprints, the varsity eight ended sixth. The 2V8 finished third, and the frosh eight, after qualifying in an earlier heat with the fastest time of the day (6:18), was unable to follow up and rowed to a fifth in the finals.

In 1972, Navy decided it did not want to come all the way to Wisconsin the week before the national regatta, so, like the previous year, the Walsh Cup race was again put off. For a series of reasons thereafter, the Walsh and Fisher Cup competitions—the former for the varsity eight winner and the latter awarded to the combined-events winner, together a great tuning-up practice for both schools before the following week's eight-event IRAs—were not competed for again until 1981.

In the last race of the season in Madison, the UW varsity eight edged out the U.S. Coast Guard Academy—winner by open water of the "Dad" Vail Regatta—by 0.5 seconds on a 2,000-meter course. Coach Jablonic described how Coast Guard coach Bill Stowe had gotten his crew—and their shells—to Madison, "Defined as an exercise to measure the loading and unloading of cargo and men, Stowe arranged for a Coast Guard cargo plane to be assigned the task of loading and unloading shells, and transporting strapped-in rowers to and from Madison, Wisconsin."

The 1972 IRAs were exciting for the Badgers. Penn won the varsity eight event, followed by Brown, Wisconsin, and Washington.

The competition for the 2V8 gold medal turned out to be the most exciting of the regatta's fifteen races. Washington gained an early lead and led the entire way, with Wisconsin closing so fast a video tape of the finish had to be consulted. The officials' preliminary call was Washington first by 0.2 seconds. The videotape took thirty minutes to be delivered to the judges stand for review, by which time at least two rowers from Wisconsin's 2V8—sophomores, Ken Nelson and Bill Klinger—had made their way to the judges stand.

Both Badger sophomores insist they heard one of the judges say, "Wisconsin won, but we can't change our call because they've already traded shirts." The photo of the finish in the following year's IRA program shows how close a call it

The UW 2V8's second place finish in the 1972 IRAs, with Wisconsin in the foreground. UW's boating: Jim Ricksecker (bow), Robert Koca, John Osborn, Bill Klinger, Ken Nelson, Bruce Neidermeier, Mike Gross, Jim Swanson (stroke), and Mark Malak (coxswain). Source: *1973 IRA Program.* Courtesy of the IRA Stewards.

1972 UW freshman 8 IRA winners. UW's boating (right to left): Robert Espeseth, Jr. (bow), Gary Melis, Lou Schueller, Jr., Ted Blodgett, Dale Schultz, Jim Dyreby, Jr., Jim Kirsch, Doug Trosper (stroke), and Dan Kammer (coxswain). Photo courtesy of UW Athletic Communications.

was. Jabo recalls the issue seemed to revolve around which boat might have "touched" the finish line against which one "penetrated" the line.

It was the UW freshmen that clearly won their event by an indisputable margin! Taking the lead at the 900-meter mark, the Badger frosh defeated Cornell by a boat length. Three of those Wisconsin freshman rowers would ultimately collect four gold medals each at the IRAs in four years of rowing in the freshman and varsity eights. Those Badger oarsmen were Jim Dyreby, Jr., Robert Espeseth, Jr., and Lou Schueller, Jr. Another member of the freshman eight—Dale Schultz—would go on to become a Wisconsin state senator from the seventeenth district around Richland Center.

Wisconsin's third-, second-, and first-place finishes in the varsity, junior varsity, and freshman eights, respectively, gave Wisconsin its first Jim Ten Eyck Trophy (all of UW's boatings in Ten Eyck–winning years appear in the appendix). The Ten Eyck scoring—based on the results of the three eights races—showed Wisconsin

132   'JABO' TAKES OVER

Pictured above is Tim Mickelson, Deerfield, Wisconsin, showing the silver medal he won as a member of the United States eight-oared crew that placed second in the recently completed Olympic Games in Munich, Germany. Left to right: Coach Randy Jablonic, Mickelson, Norm Sonju, Scott Springman, Madison, the 1973 captain-elect, and Curt Drewes.

Above: Tim Mickelson, the Badgers first Olympic medallist, 1972.

Left: The Jim Ten Eyck Trophy. Source: Photo by Brad Taylor.

with seventeen points, ahead of Washington's thirteen, and Cornell and Penn with eleven points each.

> On June 23, 1972, Congress enacted Title IX, the gender-equality amendment to the Education Act. The act would eventually have a major impact on increasing women's participation in college sports, including, significantly, in women's lightweight and openweight crew. It would also open opportunities for women in many sports at the high school level and generate a multitude of coaching and administrative opportunities for women in sports at all levels.
>
> On the controversial side, Title IX led directly to the elimination of many men's sports—some estimates suggest 300 to 500 or more teams—at the nation's colleges and universities. For men's crew at Wisconsin, the regulations and interpretations would eventually inhibit scholarships and "profile" the sport into early roster headcount dates and tight annual budgets, often requiring contributions from alumni or others to cover such expenses as winter training.
>
> In the summer 1972 Munich Olympics, UW crew coach Randy Jablonic served as one of the manager-coaches, and Curt Drewes served as the rigger, for the U.S. squad. For the German-born Drewes, it was an exciting return home.
>
> For UW rowers Stewart MacDonald (fifth in the four-plus-coxswain) and Tim Mickelson, it was good to have a familiar coach and their own rigger with the team.

'JABO' TAKES OVER   133

The 1972–73 college season would turn out to be an even bigger year for the men's crew at Wisconsin. Responding to the public display of financial pressures on the Wisconsin men's crew program, loyal alumni rower Fred Emerson (Class of '32) donated three new shells to the men's program in September of 1972. Emerson's generosity emanated from his long-term loyalty to Wisconsin and UW rowing. His deep love of rowing in general had led Emerson to support crew, or initiate rowing clubs, around the United States.

In the October Head of the Charles, Wisconsin's varsity eight won their event, defeating the prior year's U.S. entry and silver medalist in the Munich Olympics, as well as the Huskies of Northeastern, who had dedicated themselves to winning the race on their Charles River home course. The Boston Globe Trophy for winning the Head of the Charles came to Madison for the second time (the first was in 1966) since the event began in 1965.

On April 7, 1973, the inaugural races of the San Diego Classic were held before a crowd of 10,000. No money was offered to participants to defray travel expenses, and since the UW coaching staff was organizing its own initial Midwest Rowing Championships in Madison, Wisconsin did not attend this first Classic.

At the inaugural Midwest Rowing Championship on Lake Wingra in Madison in 1973—a regatta organized to encourage and publicize men's and women's crew around the Midwest—UW's varsity and second varsity eights swept their way to victories in their respective races by six lengths in each of the two races.

In the twice-started Cochrane Cup, held on a 2,000-meter Lake Mendota course, Wisconsin again prevailed, defeating MIT by over 11 seconds and Dartmouth by almost 14 seconds.

Avenging their disappointment at losing the Head of the Charles to Wisconsin, Northeastern outbattled the Badgers by 2.3 seconds in the Eastern Sprints. Wisconsin was also second in the second varsity eight, 0.6 seconds behind Harvard, while the Wisco frosh dragged in tenth overall, with a fourth in the Petit Final. But in the IRAs, Wisconsin's season came together!

"Wisc . . . Wisc . . . Wisc" read the *Syracuse Herald-Standard*'s lead paragraph, as Wisconsin swept all three men's heavyweight eights events on June 2, 1973!

Wisconsin's run-of-the-table in the eights began with the freshman event, where MIT's crack frosh crew and Dartmouth's novices, winners of their Eastern Sprints event, jumped out to an early lead. The Badger frosh seemed to get out of the gate slowly. But halfway through the race, Wisconsin moved into third and then wrested second from the Dartmouth Green.

As the two leaders—MIT and Wisconsin—approached the finish line, the young Badgers began cutting into the fading Tech's lead with every stroke. At the wire, Wisconsin nipped MIT to win by two feet. It was the first "Wisc" of the Wisconsin broom!

For Wisconsin's freshmen, this was their fourth IRA title, the first in 1900 during the sixth year of the Poughkeepsie Regatta. UW's 1973 frosh boating: Ross Graves (bow), John Storck, Reinhardt Rose, Karl Neuman, John Mercier, Larry Trotter, Joe Knight, John Bauch (stroke), and Arno Weiner (cox).

The Washington Huskies, always strong at the IRAs, would miss that year, although the Badgers would defeat Washington twice in Nottingham, England, later in June to become the U.S. entry in the Guinness Cup competition. For 1973 and the next twenty-one years of the IRA (1973–1994), the Huskies would not attend the IRAs, due in part to scheduling conflicts with regatta dates and the end of their academic year.

The Badger Jayvees, stroked by sophomore, Doug Trosper, had an easier time. Wisconsin gave up a fast start to Penn, but by the 500-meter mark, the Badgers were back in control for the rest of the way, winning by one and one-quarter lengths.

In the varsity eight contest, the weather was sunny, with only a slight headwind. Wisconsin was determined for revenge on an unbeaten Northeastern, which had edged them out two weeks earlier at the Eastern Sprints. While Penn again got off to the fastest start, it was no contest. After only 400 meters, the Badgers fought their way past Penn. By 850 meters, there was open water on both Penn and Northeastern. A portion of the cheering crowd of 15,000 greeted the triumphant Badger boat at the finish. Many broke into "On Wisconsin."

1973 UW 2V8, IRA winners. The boating: Jim Kirsh (bow), Jim McNett, Eric Aserlind, Ted Blodgett, Gary Weyers, Bill Klinger, John Osborne, Doug Trosper (stroke), and Mike Malak (cox). Photo courtesy of UW Athletic Communications.

'JABO' TAKES OVER 135

1973 UW V8, IRA winners. The varsity boating: (left to right): John Bosio (cox), Jim Dyreby, Jr. (stroke), Lou Schueller, Jr., Robert Espeseth, Jr., Jerry Phelan, Loren Bartz, Jim Ricksecker, Jim Swanson, and Bob Eloranta (bow and Co-captain). Photo courtesy of UW Athletic Communications.

"We rowed our race here," smiled a happy Coach Jablonic. "We're just coming on, you know. We're peaking." With a perfect score of 20, Wisconsin took home the Ten Eyck Trophy for a second time.

To this day, Coach Jablonic remembers seeing all three of the prized IRA eights trophies on his mantle at one point and saying to himself, "That really is an amazing sight!"

In the postseason, all three of UW's boats went the Royal Henley Regatta, thanks to a major ten-day fund drive by parents and alumni. Generous UW rowing alums—in an energetic statewide campaign led by UW rower Robert Graves (captain and 3-seat in the Class of '56) and in a Neenah-Waupaca area campaign led by James Dyreby, Sr.—funded the trip. Following the appearance of a photo in the *Milwaukee Journal* showing one or more Badgers celebrating with a can of Schlitz in their hands, Schlitz too made a small contribution.

One of the donations that most stands out in Coach Jablonic's memory was that from a UW professor who stopped as he was jogging past the boathouse. "I understand you guys are raising money to go to Henley and I'd like to help." When he reached into his jogging pants, the professor found he had no wallet or checkbook, only some spare change. He handed it over to Jablonic and ran off. "Seventy-six cents is what he gave me!" chuckles Jablonic. The donations, which reached $36,000, included a gift from the 1900 crew commodore D. Hayes Murphy, whose brother, W. K. Murphy, rowed 2-seat in Wisconsin's first IRA championship crew of 1900—a Badger frosh eight.

Each of the three UW entries made it to the Henley semifinals where they were eventually eliminated—the varsity lost to Northeastern by a length, the 2V8 to Harvard by a half-length, and the frosh to England's Thames Tradesmen. Along the way, the UW varsity and freshmen shells each set course records (Henley started keeping records in 1922). Evidence of these two fastest times appeared thereafter in the *Guinness Book of World Records,* according to a 1997 film put together by freshman 6-seat Larry Trotter for a crew reunion that same year. Trotter donated a copy of the film, titled *1973—The Most Victorious Year of Wisconsin Rowing,* to UW's Steenbock Library in 2002.

On October 5, 1974, the Wisconsin Rowing Association (WRA), now an officially tax-exempt entity, became the successor to the Wisconsin Crew Corporation as the primary crew alumni fund-raising organization.

The WRA, for example, funded many crew expenses, including the men's and women's participation at the Head of the Charles from 1966 to at least the late 1980s.

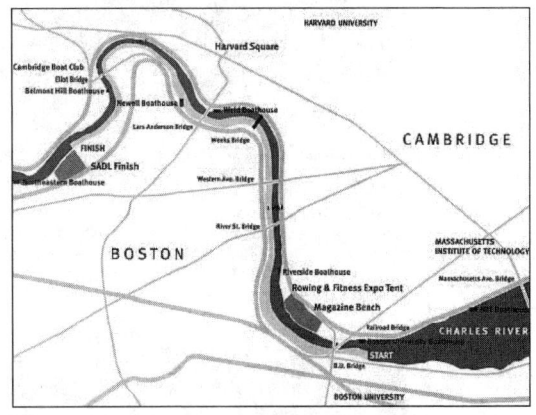

Badger expectations were high for the 1973–74 season, after having swept the three eights events at the IRAs the prior season. Awarded the Boston Globe Trophy as the 1973 winner of the fall's Head of the Charles Regatta for the second year in a row, Wisconsin's aspirations were affirmed. The Wisconsin 2V8 entry finished fifth in the same event.

Head of the Charles course diagram. Courtesy of Head of the Charles® regatta.

Junior stroke Jim Dyreby remembers that after the Head of the Charles (or possibly after the Cochrane Cup the following spring), Coach Jablonic instructed each of the boys to take their oars to Logan Airport by way of Boston's MTA. The MTA, an above and underground commuter train, made stops on the Boston University campus across from the Charles River's launching site. From there, the rail connection made its way through downtown Boston and on to the airport. Dyreby still remembers the bemused look of the rest of the passengers as a group of eighteen rowers—6'3" or taller—came on the train, each carrying an 11', red-bladed oar.

For the second San Diego Classic, the sponsors offered to pay 100 percent of some of the participant's travel costs, including Wisconsin's. Coach Jablonic remembers learning that the team had a large credit for food at their hotel, so the crews completely used it up on room service. Earlier that day, the Badgers (6:11) finished second to Washington (6:09.5).

In the Eastern Sprints, one of the best Harvard eights ever whipped a strong Wisconsin varsity by one and one-half boat lengths. Over the years, a Badger varsity victory in the Eastern Sprints seemed more difficult to achieve than a victory in the eights at the IRAs. Once again, the long winters and short crew season forced the Badgers to look for their peak later in the spring.

Wisconsin's 1974 Varsity Crew picture above — KNEELING — John Bosio, Merrill. **STANDING**, left to right, Jim Dyreby, Waupaca; Jim Ricksbecker, Beloit; Bob Espeseth, Champaign, Ill.; Lou Schueller, Milwaukee; Loren Bartz, Suring; Karl Newman, Middleton; Captain Jim Swanson, Wisconsin Rapids; and Eric Aserlind, Madison.

Wisconsin's 1974 NIRC Championship Junior Varsity Crew pictured above, KNEELING — Mike Malak, Milwaukee. **STANDING**, left to right, Doug Trosper, Ronan, Montana; John Storck, Mayville; John Mercier, Madison; Ken Nelson, Kenosha; Ross Graves, Spring Green; John Bauch, Watertown; Joe Knight, Madison; Jim Kirsh, Beaver Dam.

Top: 1974 UW V8, IRA winners.

Bottom: 1974 UW 2V8, IRA winners.

Harvard repeated a victory over Wisconsin by about a half-length in the 2V8 event. The Badger frosh finished fourth behind winner Cornell.

In the IRAs, the Badgers resumed their winning ways, even though a second sweep was not in the cards in 1974. Wisconsin won the varsity and second varsity events, but the frosh were nipped by a strong Cornell boat—the same Big Red Cubs that had prevented a Harvard sweep of the Eastern Sprints a month earlier at Worcester.

138 'JABO' TAKES OVER

Also in 1974, the IRA Stewards added the coxed pair event (also an Olympic event at the time) and a varsity straight four race, bringing to eight the number of heavyweight men's events.

The Ten Eyck Trophy—for the first time weighted to include all eight of the men's heavyweight events—went to Wisconsin for the third consecutive year.

With neither the University of Washington nor Harvard at the IRAs, Washington proposed an invitational "national championship" race. As William N. Wallace, sports and rowing reporter at the *New York Times*, speculated in the *Official 1974 Program of the IRA*:

> What Washington is doing this year is cutting the IRA regatta off at the knees. Harvard, the wealthiest college in the land and a non-participant in the IRAs since 1897, can go to Seattle comfortably without any torn loyalties to the IRA. But what about Wisconsin, the likely IRA winner? If invited it would be very hard for the Badgers to refuse on some tenuous grounds of loyalty.
>
> However, who would pay their way to Seattle and back? In the beginning Washington was to pay travel expenses for all invited crews. That changed. The invitees have to get it up. Should Wisconsin be invited, it is important to remember that Elroy (Crazylegs) Hirsch, the athletic director at Madison, was about to do away with crew four years ago because it was so expensive to maintain. Who's going to ask Elroy to fork up the money to send the crew out to Seattle for an "invitational national championship?" Not me.

As foreseen by Wallace, the proposed Washington–Seattle trip became a noteworthy episode in the saga of UW's crew history. When Wisconsin's Athletic Department told Coach Jablonic his varsity had to defeat Harvard in one of the two contests in Wisconsin before traveling to Seattle, Harvard kindly agreed to a stopover in Wisconsin for the qualifying race series imposed on the Badger crew (Harvard was going to Seattle anyway, whatever the outcome of the races in Wisconsin).

In Milwaukee, the competition was billed as "The Race of the Century" and staged as part of the Wisconsin crew's centennial regatta (since the first intramural races in Madison in 1874). The *Milwaukee Sentinel* had agreed to award the Milwaukee Sentinel Cup. The start was to be from Bay View Park—the first-ever crew competition held inside the breakwater on Lake Michigan—and conclude in the vicinity of the South Shore Yacht Club.

The two varsity crews flipped a coin to select shells; the agreement was that the two schools would switch boats for the second race on Lake Mendota in Madison. If a third race were needed, there would be another flip of the coin. Harvard won the coin toss and selected Wisco's newest and lightest fiberglass Schoenbrod. Wisconsin got an older, heavier Schoenbrod.

The race was twice postponed because of rough water. So as not to disappoint the estimated 5,000 Milwaukee spectators who had waited over six hours, the race was shortened to 1,500-meters and rowed at dusk, around 9:00 P.M. The race did not match its billing. When the boats finally reached the starting line, the water, which earlier had calmed, was again rough.

Harvard, after a favorable starting alignment, gained a length lead at the start and held that margin for the first 500 meters. Wisconsin, which settled at 37 strokes per minute, to Harvard's 35, slowly inched up on the Crimson. Both crews were chopping through the rough water, shipping splash with each stroke.

Harvard, in the outside lane and with 500-meters to go, then dropped to 32 in an effort to handle the choppy water but found its lead slipping and picked up its beat back up to 37. Wisconsin, with 250 meters remaining, was gaining momentum and beginning to pass when sophomore 3-seat Karl Newman "caught a pretty good crab," and Wisco lost its inertia.

Harvard emerged victorious, timed in 5 minutes 29.2 seconds, beating Wisconsin by a boat length and 1.2 seconds. *New York Times* rowing reporter Norman Hildes-Heim later wrote, "the badly lined start gave Harvard the edge it finished with."

When the time came to switch boats in Madison, Harvard coach Harry Parker refused the change—arguing that his boys weren't "used to" the other boat—and threatened to simply leave for the University of Washington. Hampered by the Athletic Department's travel ground rules, which Parker knew of in coming to Wisconsin, Jablonic was unable to call what might have been Parker's bluff.

The second race was to be held on Lake Monona in front of the Civic Center, rowing west to east. Because of heavy winds, the second race was also postponed to later in the day. As none of the rowers had yet had breakfast, Coach Jablonic called the owner of Mickey's Dairy Bar, Norm Bass, to arrange breakfast for the two crews.

Bass advised that most of his staff had gone home already, but if the two teams would pitch in to serve breakfast, Bass would cook. Coaches Parker and Jablonic each worked tirelessly bringing plates to the rowers. During much of the time, Jablonic was making malted milks with real ice cream, all the while keeping a rough tab for Norm Bass for his "super malts."

The Lake Monona course had neither buoys nor finish line, so the two crews agreed to row "for six minutes" and whoever was ahead at that point was declared the winner. The coxswains were kept informed by the coaches as they went with announcements like, "one and one-half minutes gone!" Coach Jablonic remembers it as being, "a fabulous race. Harvard roared out of the start and gained a small lead. With 500 meters to go, Wisconsin started to slowly reduce the margin. Having no goal to row for was hard on everyone. I think we lost by one-and-a-half seats, but had there been another 100 meters," Jablonic figures, "I believe we would have caught them."

Jablonic recalls Harvard coach Harry Parker leaning over to him after the race and saying, "Jabo, we've just watched two of the finest crews in the U.S. We've seen a phenomenal performance." Because Harvard won that second race, Wisconsin stayed home from the Seattle regatta.

In late June, Wisconsin's coxed four of Lou Schueller (bow), James Ricksecker, Loren Bartz, Jim Dyreby (stroke), and John Bosio (cox) finished third behind Russia and East Germany at the Nottingham International Regatta.

✕

If rowing has some sort of snob appeal, it wears off once you start pulling.—Harry Parker, Harvard head crew coach

In 1974–75, Wisconsin's varsity had their familiar early season troubles with a third in the Eastern Sprints on Lake Carnegie in Princeton. But by the IRAs, Wisco's top eight was humming again.

1975 UW V8, IRA winners. The boating (left to right): Jim Dyreby, Jr., Fred Robertson, Robert Espeseth, Jr., Lou Schueller, Jr., John Mercier, Jim Kirsch, Tom Schuchardt, and Eric Aserlind (bow); kneeling, Greg Atkins, (cox). Photo Courtesy of UW Athletic Communications.

Arnie Burdick, writing in the *Syracuse Herald-American*, described the day:

Stung in the frosh and jayvee races by slow starts, the Wisconsin varsity took advantage of the calmer starting conditions at 5:00 P.M. and got away well this trip. First was Coast Guard [Academy], on the inside, with Cornell chasing. MIT and Northeastern, the two other favorites along with the Badgers, took off slowly.

After about 500 meters, the Badgers took over the lead, with high-stroking Cornell still second, as Coast Guard dropped back to third. At the halfway mark the Badgers had open water on Cornell, but MIT was moving up into the pack.

Going down the stretch, the Badgers were beating it out at 37, as MIT and Northeastern moved into the fight for second. The Badgers (6:08.2) held them off comfortably and the Engineers (6:11.5), with a tremendous finishing kick, managed to just get up for second over Northeastern (6:13.2). Cornell (6:13.9), Rutgers (6:17.6) and Coast Guard (6:17.8) flashed over the line in that order. A crowd of 15,000 to 20,000 watched the action.[3]

UW stroke and four-time 8s gold medalist at the IRAs, Jim Dyreby, Jr. Photo courtesy of UW Athletic Communications.

Biography of Jim Dyreby

Jim Dyreby, along with Carl Holtz, must be considered one of the best two strokes in the Badgers' long rowing history.

The Holtz history as a stroke includes leading his freshman eight to a second-place finish in the national collegiate rowing regatta at Poughkeepsie in 1941 and, following World War II, to first place in the 1946 Eastern Sprints—a Wisconsin varsity eight's first victory at the national level and the beginning of a new era of Badger success in national college rowing.

Dyreby's achievements were spread over four years of college rowing. With a nearly unheard of series of four gold medals at the IRAs—first in the freshman eight (rowing 6-seat) in 1972 and then three consecutive gold medals stroking the varsity eight in 1973–75, Dyreby is one of only sixteen college rowers since 1895 to have ever won four golds in the eights at the IRAs! Two gold medals for winning in the eights at Boston's Head of the Charles in 1972 and 1973 add to his place in Badger history.

Jim Dyreby (born April 10, 1953, in Neenah, Wisconsin) attended Neenah High School, graduating in 1971. He became an avid sailor from his summers at the Long Lake Yacht Club, and he also loved swimming and racquetball. Two influences led to Dyreby's coming out for crew—meeting Coach Jablonic in the Physical Education line and the encouragement of Rick Whitman and others, rowers in Jim's fraternity, Theta Chi.

Besides the competition of college rowing, Dyreby rowed internationally with several of his UW teammates in Moscow in 1973 (following UW's invitation to and participation in the Royal Henley Regatta) and in Nottingham in 1974.

With his excellent grades, Dyreby was accepted into a combined and accelerated undergraduate and medical school program after his junior year. Unsure how much time his medical school studies would take in his

continued on facing page

UW's varsity boating was Eric Aserlind (bow), Tom Schuchardt, Jim Kirsch, John Mercier, Lou Schueller, Jr., Robert Espeseth, Jr., Fred Robertson, Jim Dyreby, Jr. (stroke), and Greg Atkins (cox).

Another gold medal Wisco boat at the IRAs in 1975 was the straight four of Jim Sullivan (bow), Dave Eloranta, Jim Freeman, and Joe Knight (stroke) and Wisconsin carried away the Ten Eyck for the fourth consecutive year.

Badgers Jim Dyreby, Jr., Robert Espeseth, Jr. and Lou Schueller, Jr. would enter an elite club of only sixteen rowers (through 2004)—from a universe of 10,000 or fourth year, Dyreby informed Coach Jablonic that he would have to drop out of crew. Luckily the academic load was manageable, and Jim came out for crew again in the spring of his fourth year.

His undergraduate degree was in Medical Science. The medical degree was awarded in 1978, after which Jim spent five years in Madison rotating through four local hospitals—UW Hospital, St. Mary's, Methodist, and Madison General.

He then moved to Rhinelander, where he is currently a principal in Northland Orthopedics, practicing orthopedic surgery. He married the former Katy Corr, who was one year behind him at Neenah High School, and the couple has three children, Sarah, John (also a rower at UW), and Mikhail.

Asked what was the attraction of rowing for him, Jim thought a while and replied, "Rowing's initial allure was the physical challenge. I soon found I was extremely fortunate to be rowing with many talented and committed athletes and to have Randy Jablonic as a coach. While athletics had always been a big part of my life, crew gave me the privilege of participating in a sport where the whole was so much greater than the individuals involved. The lessons and values learned have proven to be among the most valuable parts of my college experience."

Four-time IRA 8s gold medalist Lou Schueller, Jr. Photo courtesy of UW Athletic Communications.

more college oarsmen at the Poughkeepsie and IRA regattas since 1895—to win four golds in the frosh and varsity eights. (The thirteen others are from the crews of Brown [1992–95]; Cal [1998–01 (02)]; Cornell [1908–11; 1909–12; 1954–57, and 1955–58] and Penn [1966–69].)

Dyreby, demonstrating "proficiency in scholarship and athletics" would also be awarded the Conference Medal of Honor (formerly the Big Ten Conference Medal and before that the Western Conference Medal). Crew winners before him included Martin T. Kennedy (in the inaugural year of 1915), Howard J. Bentson ('24), Jefferson T. Burrus ('27), Louis E. Oberdeck ('31), Howard T. Heun ('36), Carlyle W. Fay, Jr. ('48), Don Peterson ('49), and James "Jim" T. Moran ('53).

Robert Espeseth, Jr. would go on to become a member of four U.S. Olympic teams and row in numerous other international rowing events over a thirteen year postcollege rowing period. In September of 2003, Espeseth was also inducted into the UW Athletic Hall of Fame.

Carl Sweetwater Reed ('05), a donor estimated to have contributed over $50,000 to UW for equipment and boathouse projects, died October 24, 1975. Reed rowed stroke for coach Andrew O'Dea's 1902 freshman eight which finished second to Cornell at the Poughkeepsie Regatta. When thanked for his generosity, Reed

UW four-time Olympian and UW Athletic Hall of Fame member Robert Espeseth, Jr. Photo courtesy of UW Athletic Communications.

would invariably say, simply, "I am just giving back what the crew gave to me." A plaque in the boathouse memorializes Reed's lifelong contributions to Wisconsin rowing.

The following season (1975–76), Coach Jablonic, knowing it was hard to stay on top, started "looking for another Jim Dyreby," according to rowers of the day.

At the three-mile Head of the Charles in the fall of 1975, UW's varsity eight (15:38.1) finished a close second to Princeton (15:36.6) in the college category. In the Eastern Sprints, Wisco led to the 1,200-meter mark, when Harvard pulled by and finished 3.7 seconds ahead of the silver-medalist Badgers, with Penn third and Princeton fourth. UW's boating: Fred Robertson (bow), John Mercier, Karl Newman, Tom Schuchardt, John Bauch, Ed Jackson, John Storck, Pat Litscher (stroke), and Greg Askins (cox).

The three Wisconsin entries at the Head of the Charles—two men's eights and one women's eight—were entirely funded with $4,000 donated by the WRA, as the event was not supported by the Athletic Department. The WRA, in the same year, also funded the purchase of a $5,700 new eight for the varsity men.

The IRA results of UW's favored varsity eight in 1976 were disappointing to the boat, though the crew did make it to the awards dock. The Badgers took home a bronze, behind Cal and Princeton, in a race where all six finalists finished within a margin of two boat lengths. The second varsity was sixth, and the frosh eight powered to a second-place silver.

The straight four from Wisconsin won a second consecutive IRA title in 1976. UW's boating: Jim Sullivan (bow), Dave Moecher, Jim Freeman, and Joe Knight (stroke). Penn broke Wisconsin's four-year string and went away with the Ten Eyck.

Curt Drewes, both a boatman and a coach throughout his thirty-seven years at Wisconsin, retired following the IRAs in 1976.

In the 1976 Montreal Olympics, Neil Halleen and Robert Espeseth were both members of the American squad, with Halleen finishing fifth in the quad (4-man sculling entry).

In January 1977, the members of the 1946 varsity eight, who had won the Eastern Sprints with their coach Allen Walz, were inducted into the Helms Hall of Fame (the rowing section of which was later assumed by the National Rowing Foundation).

The season of 1976–77 would be have to be described as "average," with a fourth-place San Diego Classic finish and an Eastern Sprints and IRA finish of sixth in both. The varsity finished first in the Midwest Championships and the Cochrane Cup race.

In the beginning of the 1977–78 season, Wisconsin finished second to Harvard at the Head of the Charles. The varsity UW boating: Dan Wilms (bow), Jay Starr, Mike Gasper, Mike Gitter, Christopher Landry, David Zweig, Doug Verhaalen, David Moecher (stroke), and Paul Smith (cox).

Over the spring break of 1978, the Badgers went—for the first time—to Edgerton, Wisconsin, to get on the open (though icy cold) waters of the Rock River. Bill Ehrke, a teammate of Jabo's, was a dairy farmer in Fort. Atkinson. Erke regularly crossed over the Rock River on a bridge in Edgerton and thought it would be a good place to practice. He then called his friend and fellow UW rower, Edgerton lumberyard owner R. Y. Nelson, and the two of them took another look at the Rock River together. They then called Jabo for a visit.

From 1978 until his passing in 1993, R. Y. Nelson and his wife, Judy, were tireless supporters and hosts to Wisconsin's crew during this spring break training. R. Y. (stroke in the Class of '53) donated lumber for boat docks and boat racks along the Rock River; Judy made many a meal for the tired Badger rowers and put together at least two scrapbooks of newspaper clippings from the 1930s and earlier to the mid-1970s.

At the 1978 IRAs, the varsity eight managed an eighth place.

Dave Krmpotich added interesting facets to UW's rowing history in 1978. A basketball letter-winner at the University of Minnesota–Duluth for four years, Krmpotich used his remaining one year of eligibility in an unusual way. He enrolled at UW–Madison in the spring of 1978 and used his fifth year of eligibility (if used in a sport other than basketball) to row. Krmpotich went on to become an international oarsman for U.S. national team squads over a period of thirteen years, including winning a silver medal in the straight four at the Seoul Olympics in 1988.

The IRAs of 1979 were an exciting regatta for all concerned, with eight different schools winning each of the eight heavyweight events! The Badger freshman eight, coached by one-year frosh coach Neil Halleen, was Wisco's winner, beating Syracuse by seven feet (half a second) in the last two strokes. The Orangemen's Cubs had led from the stake boat to the last couple of strokes.

Halleen had worked the freshmen hard. More than once, while leading the freshmen crew out to practice on fog-covered mornings in early spring, the freshman eight had driven their cedar shells up onto the ice drifts still floating in Lake Mendota. Straddling the boat with each foot, the forward rowers would have to walk the shell backward off the ice and into open water before continuing.

Jabo complimented his frosh coach : "Halleen got everything out of every kid. There was nothing more to get out of them when they got to the varsity."

Paul Jirak described the freshman race in May/June 1979 *The Oarsman:*

1979 UW freshman 8, IRA winners. The boating (left to right): Doug Berninger (bow), Brian Steinbrecher, Charles Williams, Aaron Jacobs, Steve Shenkenberg, John Streur, Dan Royal, Bill Supernaw (stroke), and Steve Manicor (cox). Photo courtesy of UW Athletic Communications.

Northeastern was favored going into the IRAs. They were 1.5 seconds behind Yale at the Eastern Sprints and Yale was not in the regatta. But Wisconsin also had to be considered a top contender. Third in the Sprints, 1.2 seconds behind Northeastern, they are traditionally a late-blooming team. Due to frigid weather in the Mid-West, they rarely, if ever, have as much water time as their eastern rivals: a factor, which may have proved beneficial in the long run. AND then there was Syracuse. They usually have a lackluster match race season and peak for the IRAs, achieving a great deal of success with that plan of attack. They have won the last three freshman eight titles, were second the previous year and third the year before that. They followed that pattern perfectly again this year. While they failed to qualify for this year's Sprints grand final, they won the Petite finals handily. So it appeared that the home course advantage, which in this case means knowing that the bells and fog horns let loose in the last 500 meters are in your honor, Syracuse seemed to have the makings of another title winner.

Wisconsin and Northeastern both qualified for the finals on the first day. Syracuse and Brown were first and second, respectively, in the first repechage. On their way to qualifying, Cornell broke the freshman course record. Thursday's times were consistently fast as a tail wind blew all day, but Cornell was the only crew to beat any course record.

On Saturday, Cornell proved it was fast without a following wind. They blasted out of the start with Syracuse. Those two and Wisconsin and Northeastern all mixed it up for 1,000 meters at which point Syracuse must have figured it was time to go. They began to move away from the hitherto pesky Cornell, lengthening their lead gradually during the third 500. Just as Syracuse moved, so did Wisconsin and they passed Cornell too. But it seemed the Syracuse boat smelled blood and were set for the kill. They were one length up on Wisconsin and as the Syracuse shell approached the 1,500-meter mark, the horns and bells began to resound.

Wisconsin looked just about out of it. But according to the coxswain, Steven Manicor, they were sticking to their race plan. Even though Wisconsin was afraid that Syracuse had an insurmountable lead, said Manicor, Wisconsin had confidence in their closing sprint. As it turned out, bells and horns were no match for a crew's confidence in themselves. Translated, that means Wisconsin ate up Syracuse's one length lead in the last 500 and began sticking its bow in the lead every few strokes. At the finish, Syracuse fans were cringing and counting on "the angle" to pull the team through for victory number four. Most spectators, and even the oarsmen it seemed, were in the dark as to the winner. When a sudden outburst of cheers erupted from an until-then exhausted and silent Wisconsin shell, no announcement was needed.

1983 UW freshman 8, IRA winners. Wisconsin's boating (right to left): John Hallett (bow), Norm Steiner, Tim Ritzenthaler, Mike Risse, Mark Berkner, Hans Borcherding, Tom Tryon, Dave Evenson (stroke), and Michael New (cox). Photo courtesy of UW Athletic Communications.

'JABO' TAKES OVER 147

Jirak's account of the jayvee race was just as graphic:

Yale was a conspicuous entrant in this event. Their presence was explained after a careful perusal of the program. It turned out that they were all lightweights and, in fact, they were the lightweight varsity Eastern Sprints champions. But in competing against heavyweights, they admitted their handicap and entered the second varsity level race.

The lightweights showed their talents on the first day as they qualified with a 4.3 second margin over the second place boat. In the other heat, heavyweight sprints runner-up Northeastern won by 5.6 seconds over the second place crew. Friday's tail wind brought the winning times in the repechages to six minutes flat as Syracuse won their repechage in 6:00.5 and Wisconsin theirs in 6:00.0. Cornell and Dartmouth were the second place teams in the two repechages.

Saturday's conditions turned against Yale as their hopes for victory decreased with each increasingly stronger gust of wind. The start of the second varsity final was delayed 20 minutes after the Syracuse four man broke his oar (of fiberglass construction) during the warm-up. The oar was replaced expeditiously but the bent top back brace required lengthier repair. The disruption apparently had little effect on Syracuse. After the start, they jumped to a lead over Wisconsin, with Northeastern and Dartmouth close behind. Wisconsin went by Syracuse at the 500 as Northeastern stuck to Syracuse's side, a few seats down. By the 1,000, Northeastern had passed and gone ½ length up on Syracuse. Wisconsin had only a few feet on Northeastern.

Yale had as tough a time with the wind as with the competition. They were fifth most of the race and occasionally challenged Cornell for fourth, but they never got anywhere. Back at the lead, Northeastern was still ½ length down on Wisconsin going into the last 500 meters. Unfortunately, Wisconsin's second varsity could not duplicate their freshmen's sprint. Northeastern was the team that followed that example as they moved steadily past Wisconsin. Northeastern moved from ½ length down to almost ½ length up in the 500 meters. They finished an even second ahead of Wisconsin. It was nip and tuck for third as Syracuse nipped at the right time and Cornell tucked at the wrong time with the result being a 0.3 second advantage for Syracuse at the finish line.

Jirak also described the varsity race:

Dartmouth, third in the Sprints, behind Harvard and Yale, looked to be the favorite in the final event. Besides their physical advantage, they had a bed-ridden coach to motivate them psychologically. Pete Gardner, Dartmouth's varsity coach, was hospitalized before the regatta with an inflammation around the heart. Dartmouth predictably displayed a "win it for the Gipper" mentality. The Syracuse press loved it.

Sick coach or no, Dartmouth came to Syracuse to race and they proved it by winning their heat. In Friday's races, Syracuse and Northeastern qualified from the first repechage. The closest race of the regatta by far was the second repechage. Only 0.4 seconds separated the first three crews. Brown was eventually declared the winner with Cornell and MIT, second and third, respectively. The times were 5:53.3, 5:53.6 and 5.53.7!

A clear sky and a disappearing haze accompanied the grand final on Saturday. After a clean start, the crews took 500 meters to sort themselves out. By that time, Wisconsin had moved into the lead and had ¾ to a length on Dartmouth. The boats stayed that way for most of the second 500, with Brown following Dartmouth and then Syracuse, Cornell and Northeastern bringing up the rear. Brown began at the 1,000 what Northeastern and Wisconsin in the previous races had waited till the last 500 to do. Nothing Wisconsin could do countered Brown's steady march through them. Some Brown oarsmen were to say later that they were a headwind crew and when they felt the wind on their backs as they progressed, they knew it was theirs. Judging from the way they moved, no one was in a position to argue.

In the last 500 it came down to how far away Brown could get from Wisconsin. It turned out by almost ½ of a length. Wisconsin meanwhile had their hands full with Syracuse and Dartmouth, who were fighting for the second place spot together. Wisconsin eventually held those two crews off for second place as no more than the width of a blade separated third place Syracuse from fourth place Dartmouth. Cornell, who was in the chase for third till the last 250 meters fell 1.9 seconds off the pace and wound up fifth, way ahead of fading Northeastern.[4]

Crew sportswriter William Wallace would note in the *New York Times* of June 3, 1979 that this was a historical first IRA victory in the eights for Brown, which sport was elevated from a club sport status in 1962.

Al Erickson, 7-seat, and Coach Jablonic both retain a lingering frustration that no one in his boat saw Brown coming up so strongly in lane 5.

With a first and two seconds in the eights, Wisconsin took home its fifth team Ten Eyck Trophy.

✕

October's Head of the Charles in Boston kicked off the 1979–80 season. Starting in the number four position, Wisconsin (15:31.3), passed Dartmouth on the long straightaway and finished a close second to Princeton (15:28.3), which had passed Brown within their first 30 strokes. The Badger boating: Curt Jelinek (bow), John

Jablonic, Dan Royal, Jim Seefeldt, Paul Lambert, Aaron Jacob, Ken Lawrence, Al Erickson (stroke), and Tom Kirk (cox).

In the 1980 IRA regatta on the first of June, Coach Jablonic split his second varsity eight into two entries—a straight four and a coxed four (the latter an eventual gold medal winner)—and did not enter the second varsity event. The move was not to take advantage of the relative Ten Eyck weightings of the three events but to give the boys in his second varsity eight a chance to earn a major "W" with an IRA win. Forced to choose, scoring higher in the two four-oared events (and skipping the 2V8 event) did yield more Ten Eyck points than entering and even winning the 2V8 event (and skipping both the fours events).

Wisconsin's first-place coxed four boating: Brian Steinbrecher (bow), Dan Royal, Ned Kline, Ken Lawrence (stroke), and Matthew Franke (cox).

With the straight pair also winning gold (Franklin Remington in the bow and Curt Jelinek at stroke)—the only school winning two golds—Wisconsin came away with their sixth Ten Eyck.

Worth noting is that in 1986, the IRA Stewards changed the Ten Eyck event weighting system by increasing the relative value of all three eight-oared events.

Badger Robert Espeseth, Jr. saw the United States boycott the 1980 Olympics in Moscow; he would likely have rowed in the straight pair.

The 1980–81 and 1981–82 seasons were building years with Wisconsin's varsity out of the IRA finals in both years. For the first time since the Midwest Championships began, Wisconsin lost—in both 1981 and 1982—the varsity eight event. In 1982 Coach Jablonic, while giving a coaching clinic in Nebraska, saw a large "Remember Wisconsin" poster on their boathouse wall, as encouragement to Nebraska rowers that Wisconsin could be beaten by midwestern crews.

UW's 1981 "pairs without" entry of Tom "Nezi" Neczypor (bow) and Zoran Karakajic (stroke) won their IRA event. Bill Baker (bow) and John Heinrich (stroke) repeated the straight pair victory in 1982. The varsity 4+ also won gold in 1982. Their boating: Paul Egelhoff (bow), Greg Gaskill, Mark Hallett, Val Runge (stroke), and Mark Rowell (cox).

✕

In the summer of 1982, the first Cincinnati Collegiate Invitational Championship Eights Race was held. Perhaps the same Harvard alumni who sponsored the Wisco-Brown-Harvard regatta in Cincinnati in 1969 picked up on Washington's 1946 and 1974 attempts to create a "national regatta." Because academic scheduling conflicts kept Washington from attending the IRAs (from 1973 to 1994) and Harvard skipped the IRA for its annual four-mile race against Yale (and usually peaked for regular trips to the Royal Henley Regatta), the IRA was not always a determining race for the fastest college boat in the country.

Men's crew is not sanctioned (i.e., regulated) by the NCAA, and thus the college sport has a bit of the Wild West to its unregulated structure. Financial resources—including endowments, scholarships, and financial aid—at many rowing schools are raised to whatever level the alums and sport's administrators of that school want to support. Perhaps it was this absence of consistent, inclusive competition and to-each-his-own crew strategies that created the void for the Cincinnati sponsors to jump into. The first Cincinnati Regatta was won by Harvard.

Coach Jablonic coached the American team eight in 1981 at the Worlds in Munich, Germany, where they placed third. Again in 1982, Jablonic coached the eight, which placed fourth in Lucerne, Switzerland.

✕

The 1982–83 season does not stand out for the either varsity or second varsity eights. At the Head of the Charles, UW managed an eighth. The Badgers did not attend the San Diego Classic. The annual crew banquet was March 19 and its sponsor, the Wisconsin Rowing Association, raised $60,000 for the boathouse addition, Phase 1 of which, the $154,000 shell storage addition, broke ground two and one-half years later.

The frosh eight won the bronze medal at the 1983 Eastern Sprints, behind Harvard and Brown. And in the IRAs, the Wisco frosh eight (6:55.1) came back with a gold, followed, in order, by Penn (6:58.4), Brown, UCLA, Northeastern, and Navy. Stroke Dave Evenson remembers the day:

> There was a strong headwind and it was really choppy. We had a poor start (like we usually did), and we caught a crab in the first 500 meters. Amazingly, I never doubted we would win the race, even at that point. We were still third or fourth with 500 meters to go. The last 500 was amazing. It felt like the most powerful and fastest 500 of the race! Watching the other lanes fall back as quickly as they did was a LOT of fun.
>
> Our crew was rough, but had incredible strength. Even the varsity boats that I rowed in didn't get up speed as quickly as that crew could. It was great! And a tremendous group of guys to be around.

Also in the IRAs, Wisconsin's coxed four of Rich Hallet (bow), Mark Hallett, Tom Martell, Brian Christensen (stroke), and Jeffrey Grady (cox), and the straight four of John Turgai (bow), William Meyer, Christopher Schulte, and Stuart Krause (stroke) also won gold. In spite of these small boat victories, UW's varsity finished twelfth and Navy won the Ten Eyck Trophy. A record 30 schools, 87 crews and 600 oarsmen competed in the 1983 IRAs.

1985 UW freshman 8, IRA winners. The boating (left to right): John Tucker (bow), Pat McDonough, Dan Gehn, Pat Duray, Jim Periard, Bryan Griesbach, Sam Huntington, and Dan Hilliker (stroke); kneeling, Ray Mejia (cox). Photo courtesy of UW Athletic Communications.

Badger John Jablonic rowed to a bronze in the straight pair at the Pan Am Games in Caracas, Venezuela. Future UW crew coach Chris Clark rowed to a silver medal in the coxed pair while representing the United States at these games.

The 1983–84 season was even less successful than the previous season, although the Wisco straight pair won the IRAs with John Hallett in the bow and Scott Gabelli at stroke. The Badger varsity eight finished ninth. Also in the IRAs, the Open 4+ event replaced the coxed pair as a small boat event.[5] With the advent of this event, which required at least one freshmen and one varsity rower to compete, the "pickle boat" event, which allowed spares (or alternates) to stay in shape and race, was discontinued at the IRAs.

Robert Espeseth, Jr. (Class of '75) rowed to a bronze in the coxed pair in the 1984 Los Angeles Olympics. On June 6, 1984, UW coach Harry Emerson "Dad" Vail was posthumously inducted into the Madison Sports Hall of Fame (administered by the Madison Sports Hall of Fame Club, formerly known as the Pen & Mike Club).[6]

In the fall of 1984, two new shells—the *John and Ellen Morgen* and the *David C. Falk*—were dedicated at midfield on November 10, before 70,000 fans at the halftime of the Purdue-Wisconsin football game in Camp Randall Stadium. The two

152 'JABO' TAKES OVER

shells took up forty yards of the football field! As Purdue was only the second Big Ten school, after Wisconsin, to take up crew, the choice of football opponents was perfect. And the Badgers won 30–14!

The balance of the 1984–85 season was almost uneventful. The year was made exceptional when the frosh eight, having finished eighth at the Eastern Sprints, defeated all comers at the IRAs and took the gold.

Freshman (7-seat) and future captain (1987–88) Pat McDonough, in a December 15, 2002, e-mail, described some of their season:

> Our performances up to IRAs were pretty inconsistent and not very noteworthy. We drew #1 ranked Harvard in the heats at the Eastern Sprints, panicked, blew up and ended up in the Petite Final. I think we were second in the Petites. Harvard beat Yale by a couple of seats and Navy was ¾ or so down, finishing third in the Grand Final.
>
> We made several lineup changes and finally learned how to take advantage of some of the power we had in the boat in the weeks between Sprints and IRAs. As continues to be the schedule, we raced Navy [at Annapolis] the week prior to IRAs. [Freshman coach Dave] Kucik motivated us to grab the lead early, and make certain we were up on them by the mid-point bridge. We were, and we beat them by a bit of open water, I believe.
>
> We had a best 2 of 3 over 1,000-meter brush with Syracuse [frosh] in the canal the next day. We pounded them easily in the first two, building even more confidence for the coming weekend.
>
> That left California as the only crew we had not seen before IRAs. We drew them in the heat, and where we responded properly to Kucik's motivation on Navy the week before, we were pretty freaked about his warnings about Cal (I think they won Pac 10's). The wind, as usual at Syracuse, was blowing like mad, and after delaying the start of the regatta, the regatta committee finally moved the heats over to the alternate course. I don't trust my memory on this one, but it seems to me that it was damn near dark when we finally raced our heat.
>
> The water on the other side of the lake was rowable, but the tailwind made it pretty frustrating for a novice crew to figure out how to row hard. We were spooked by Cal taking the lead early and not falling apart as we attempted to surge. The details are fuzzy now, but we did pass them in the closing strokes to win the heat. What I remember better was how John Tucker (stroke, I was 7) turned around after the race and yelled to everyone behind him in the boat, "You guys suck!" Pat Duran (5-seat), who had a short fuse under normal situations, responded by climbing up on the gunnels to go beat the snot out of Tucker who was 3–4 inches shorter and probably 50 pounds lighter. Duran was restrained by Gehn in the six seat and Kucik's shouts from shore to bring the boat in.

The heat victory sent us straight to the Saturday finals with an off day used for reps. Saturday's conditions were rougher than Thursday's. They may have gotten some finals done on Saturday, but ours was moved to Sunday at around 6:00 A.M. (which explains why you didn't find anything in the paper).

After all this build-up, I really can't remember the final very well. I know Navy took the lead from the start. We had our worst start since Eastern's, but everyone stayed calm over the fact that we were down a bunch (nearly a boat length) over the middle of the course. We settled down in the third 500 and got within half a length. I remember Mejia [the coxswain] calling for the last 30, saying we were 2 seats down, and all we needed was another 30 strokes to be IRA champs. We blew through them and won by nearly half a length.

Yale beat Harvard at the H-Y race that weekend, and they were anxious to establish themselves at the true national Frosh champs, so they contacted Kucik to see if he wanted to race at the Cincinnati regatta, home of the varsity national championship two weeks later. I think Kucik knew his chances of keeping this funky crew focused for another two weeks were slim, so he declined the offer. We called ourselves national champs regardless. I've since gotten to know two guys who were on the Yale frosh, and they told me they called themselves the champs. With four different Frosh winners at the majors: Pac 10s, Sprints, IRAs, Harvard–Yale, I bet there were a lot of Frosh thinking they were national champs in '85.

The boating was John Tucker (bow), Pat McDonough, Dan Gehn, Pat Duray, Jim Periard, Bryan Griesbach, Sam Huntington, Dan Hilliker (stroke), and Ray Mejia (cox).

At the fourth annual National Intercollegiate Varsity Eight Rowing Championship on the Ohio River in Cincinnati in June of 1985, the Badgers finished fifth. Harvard won the Invitational's Herschede Cup.

In another typical year with a slow start and a fast finish, the Badgers began the 1985–86 season with a collision. At the Head of the Charles, the Princeton varsity ran into Wisconsin's eight, causing the Badgers an eighteenth-place finish in a forty-boat event. The *Row Wisco* newsletter of December 1985, described the follow-up: "In a classy act, the Badgers received a letter of apology from Princeton signed by every member of the team."

Wisconsin's record improved from there. In the IRAs, the Badgers grabbed their seventh Ten Eyck trophy with the help of golds in the second varsity eight and the Open 4+ events. The Badgers second varsity defeated Brown, two Princeton eights, Cornell, and Navy. Had Wisco and Brown reversed their finishes, Brown would have walked away with the Ten Eyck. The Open 4+ boating: John

Righini (bow), Scott Lynch, Chris Johnson, Chris Farmer (stroke), and Mike Farrar (cox). Also rowing the 2V8, Farrar may be the only Badger to win two golds medals at the same IRA! The varsity, with a bronze, missed silver by one-tenth of a second with "too late an effort" to sprint, according to Coach Jablonic. Wisconsin took silver in the straight four, the frosh four with and the straight pair.

But the best was yet to come in June 1986. The fifth postseason Cincinnati Invitational Intercollegiate Championship Regatta was held to determine the men's national championships. The women's openweight national championship was also held at the same venue.

The men's eight-oared event was a five-way affair—with everyone but Wisconsin having a shot. For winning major races earlier in the season, four schools received automatic bids and had all their expenses paid—Brown (for winning the IRAs), Penn (Eastern Sprints), Harvard (the winner of the annual Harvard-Yale four-miler), Yale (raced well in the Harvard-Yale boat race . . . and Harvard/Yale alums may have been big sponsors in Cincinnati) and Cal (the Pacific Championships). Wisconsin's varsity eight, on the strength of its third-place finishes in the Sprints and the IRAs (and perhaps its victory in the Midwest Championships), was sent an invitation but was left to pay its own expenses.

Norman Hildes-Heim reported the race for the June 15, 1986, *New York Times*:

1986 UW 2V8, IRA winners. The winning boating (right to left): John Tucker (bow), Brian Griesbach, Tom Tryon, Jonathan Murer, Mike Risse, Patrick McDonough, Thomas Thornton, Joe Cincotta (stroke), and Mike Farrar (cox). Coach Jablonic is at lower left. Photo courtesy of UW Athletic Communications.

> It was Wisconsin all the way today as both its men's and women's varsity eight-oared crews captured national rowing titles in the Cincinnati Intercollegiate Rowing Championship Regatta. The Cincinnati regatta was established five years ago to provide a venue for the winners of the major regional regattas to have a race-off for a national title. Penn, winner of the Eastern Sprint Championships; California–Berkeley, the Pacific-10 champion; Brown, last week's IRA victor; and Harvard, which defeated Yale in their annual four-mile duel last Saturday, all qualified for invitations to today's race.
>
> Yale, which a week ago raced well against Harvard for two and one-half miles, came to Cincinnati to have another go at Harvard over the shorter 2,000-meter distance. And Wisconsin, which has been narrowing its losing margin against its Eastern rivals all season, entered this event "to get back in the winner's circle," as Randy Jablonic, the Badgers' coach, said.

'JABO' TAKES OVER 155

1986 UW V8, national champions. The boating (left to right): Kevin McAleese (stroke), Bryan Hanson, Duncan Kennedy, Dan Gehn, Mark Berkner, Christopher Schulte, Dave Evenson, Eric Moeller (bow); kneeling, Ray Mejia (cox). Photo courtesy of UW Athletic Communications.

Today, the Wisconsin men's eight did just that, surprising almost everyone but its staunchest supporters by pulling off the biggest upset in the five-year history of this regatta.

The early stages of the race went according to form. Penn took the lead at the start, and at 500 meters was two seats out on Brown, with Cal-Berkeley in third position. Brown, rowing in lane two, close to the shore and somewhat sheltered from the moderate headwind blowing obliquely down the course, coupled its strong 37-cadence stroke and flattened water to move into the lead at 750 meters. Brown capitalized on its momentum, and increased its lead to a length over Penn by 1,000 meters, while Wisconsin, in the outside lane six, started to move. In the final 500 meters, as all the crews raised their racing cadences, Wisconsin just lifted its boat and closed in on the Bruins.

Wisconsin caught Brown with 100 meters to go, and powered its shell to a 2.1-second, or half-length, victory over Brown. Penn finished nine-tenths of a second astern of Brown for the bronze medal, followed by Harvard, Cal-Berkeley and Yale. "It took us two big races, the Sprints and the I.R.A to do it, but we knew if we were in touch with the leader with 500 meters to go, we'd win," said Duncan Kennedy of New York City, Wisconsin's sixth man.[7]

Badger women completed the sweep! In both the varsity and second varsity openweight eight events, the Wisconsin women—favored to dethrone five-time

Wisconsin's men's and women's varsity eight crews celebrate winning both the men's and women's collegiate rowing national titles at Cincinnati in 1986. The Badger men went on to compete in the Royal Henley Regatta that year.

1986 UW varsity men and openweight women celebrate their national championships in Cincinnati. Wisconsin's men's boating: Eric Moeller (bow), David Evenson, Christopher Schulte, Mark Berkner, Dan Gehn, Duncan Kennedy, Bryan Hanson, Kevin McAleese (stroke), and Ray Mejia (cox). The women's boating: Kathy Haberman (bow), Laura Graf, Mary Beth Blanding, Katy Drissel, Carol Feeney, Carolyn Potter, Cindy Eckert, Sarah Gengler (stroke), and Amy Krohn (cox). Photo courtesy of UW Athletic Communications.

reigning champion Washington—did just that! The openweight varsity eight boating: Kathy Haberman (bow), Laura Graf, Mary Beth Blanding, Katy Drissel, Carol Feeney, Carolyn Potter, Cindy Eckert, Sarah Gengler (stroke), and Amy Krohn (coxswain).

The Badger men went on to Royal Henley Regatta for the third time. In the semifinals, the Badgers lost to the British national eight, which went on to narrowly defeat Penn for the Grand Challenge Cup.

On August 9, 1986, long-time Badger coach Norm Sonju died in Poulsbo, Washington, at the age of 84.

✕

Participation in the Henley Regatta leaves its character on an oarsman like an indelible dye on a piece of cloth. To have rowed at Henley is to realize that not to have rowed at Henley is like not having rowed at all. It is the fulfillment of recognition, of applause, of win or lose in the absolute sense.—Randy Jablonic, Row Wisco newsletter, October 1, 1986

Over the 1986–87 season's winter break, the crew trained for the first time at the Hills Athletic Club on Town Lake in Austin, Texas.

At the Eastern Sprints, Wisconsin had a great showing with a second, first, and third in the varsity, second varsity, and freshman eight events, respectively. Unfor-

1987 UW 2V8, Eastern Sprints record setters. The boating (right to left): Eric Moeller (bow), James Anderson, Robert Knickerehm, Frank Raia, Todd Williams, Scott Paulman, Thomas Thornton, Joseph Cincotta (stroke), and David Rugolo (cox). Photo courtesy of UW Athletic Communications.

tunately, Brown finished first, second, and second in the same events and won the Rowe Cup by one point over Wisconsin.

In winning the Eastern Sprints in a record-setting time of 5:44.5, Wisconsin's 2V8 smashed Navy's earlier record time of 5:50.3, set in 1982. The victory set an Eastern Sprints record, which would hold until 2001 when the Badger second varsity again won the gold and established a new mark.

In the IRAs, all three of Wisconsin's eights finished second! Wisconsin's varsity eight (6:07.4) finished behind a very strong Brown eight (6:02.9). With a gold in the coxed four, silvers in the varsity, second varsity, and freshmen eights, bronzes in the open 4+, the straight four, and the frosh 4+, the Badgers came away with their eighth Ten Eyck.

Wisco's winning varsity 4+ boating: Paul Stevens (bow), Kurt Borcherding, Greg Werner, Tim Wike (stroke), and Michael Lindsay (cox). The silver-medalist V8 boating: John Tucker (bow), Patrick McDonough, Mike Risse, David Evenson, Dan Gehn, Duncan Kennedy, Bryan Hanson, Kevin McAleese (stroke), and Ray Mejia (cox). The 2V8 boating was the same as for the Eastern Sprints. The silver-medalist frosh eight boating: Bill Shenkenberg (bow), Fitz Dunne, Shawn Kriewaldt, Bill Bakken, Phil Hoffman, Jerry Meissner, Todd Hinrichs, Pat Wolf (stroke), and Chris Bull (cox).

Besides Wisconsin's three second-place eights, the 1987 IRA was unusual in several other ways. Brown's Bruins became the first varsity eight to win both the Eastern Sprints and IRA titles in the same year, since Cornell accomplished the same feat in 1963. Also, Harvard won its first gold in the IRAs when its straight four defeated Princeton, Wisconsin, Georgetown, Orange Coast, and Navy. And Dartmouth was banned from the Syracuse IRAs by New York State Health Department when measles broke out on their Hanover, New Hampshire, campus.

At Cincinnati's sixth Invitational National Regatta, Harvard defeated Brown, Wisconsin, UCLA, and Temple.

The summer of 1987 would be the last time UW's crew coaches would be able to recruit freshman candidates for the team in a single on-campus registration line outside the Red Gym. Computerized registration was planned for the following summer.

As often happened in Madison, the 1987–88 season began slowly. At the Eastern Sprints, Wisco showed only fairly well, winning the Petite Finals for seventh overall. In the IRAs, the Badgers' final finishes improved, with a varsity eight bronze, a second varsity silver, and a frosh eight bronze. The Badgers' straight pair—Tim Gregor (bow) and Brandon Foss (stroke)—was the squad's only gold medal winner of the day, helping to give UW its ninth Ten Eyck.

In June, Wisconsin again participated in the Cincinnati Invitational Regatta and finished fifth.

In the 1988 Olympics in Seoul, Korea, Robert Espeseth, Jr. finished eleventh in the coxed pair, and Dave Krmpotich won a silver medal in the straight four.

Another crew season, 1988–89, began slowly and sprinted to a fast finish. Wisco ended in sixth at the April San Diego Classic. At the Midwest Championship in Madison, nine of the Big Ten universities were represented in the men's events. Wisco (5:18.4) won the varsity eight event, defeating Purdue (5:30.0) and the Milwaukee Rowing Club, among others.

At the Eastern Sprints, Wisconsin's varsity performed well, as described by William Wallace in the May 14, 1989, *New York Times*:

Harvard's varsity eight crew came from behind with a strong effort over the last 500 meters of the 2,000-meter course to win the championship on Lake Quinsigamond before a crowd of 11,000. Penn held the lead today for three-fourths of the distance. But it was a small margin: two seats, the distance taken up by two oarsmen in the 58-foot shells, was the difference between the first four boats.

Near the end, Penn could not hold off the Crimson sprint and dropped back to third place behind Wisconsin. Then came Syracuse, a surprise finalist that had been seeded 10th, Northeastern, the only crew to beat Harvard this spring, and

Navy. The winning time was 5 minutes 58.3 seconds; UW's runner-up time 6:00. The margin of victory was about a half a boat length. Penn's time was 6:01.8. Wisconsin, seeded fourth, among the heavyweight varsities, did a commendable job, moving up to pass Penn in the final 400 meters.

This regatta, an annual springtime rite of rowing that involves 639 athletes in 71 eight-oared crews, dates back to 1946.[8]

Coach Jablonic recalled that Wisconsin finished only 1.7 seconds behind the winner, and that UW's coxswain, was watching the winning Harvard crew so hard that he allowed the shell to drift off a straight course into Navy's lane (although Navy, finishing sixth, was too far behind to claim any interference). There is room for some speculation whether a straighter course might have led to a UW victory.

In any case, the Badgers rowed right through the finish line without slowing the beat. Stroking hard to the far shore, Kurt Borcherding jumped from the shell and dove into the back seat of the waiting car driven by Coach Jablonic. In the back seat, Borcherding stripped from his crew uniform and pulled on his civilian clothes. He had to catch the last flight from Boston to Madison, which departed sixty minutes after the race's scheduled finish, in order to attend a test in Madison, which exam his professor would not agree to reschedule.

Back at the awards pier, the judges handing out the second-place medals wondered how Wisconsin had managed to place so well with only seven oarsmen in the boat!

The Wisco-Penn order of finish in the Sprints reversed in the IRAs. The Badgers, with a one-length lead with 200 meters to go, saw Penn row through to win by two feet! The *New York Times* headline over William Wallace's June 4, 1989, account of the race read, "Sprint Past Wisconsin Gives Penn IRA Title."

On January 16, 1990, colorful UW crew coach Allen Walz died in Rancho Mirage, California, at age 81.

The 1989–90 season began at the Head of the Charles regatta on October 22, 1989. Wisconsin finished fourth among the college crews, a category in which Penn finished first.

In the Eastern Sprints regatta, Harvard charged into the second 500 meters and cruised to victory. Wisco then nipped Penn by seven-tenths of a second for the silver medal.

One of Jablonic's traditions, as each senior was getting settled into his seat for the rower's last race for Wisconsin at the IRAs, was to walk out to the launching dock and speak personally to each senior, thanking him for his commitment to UW crew for the past four years and wishing him "Good luck!" in this last race. Often, Jablonic would then turn to the undergraduates in the same boat and say,

"This is Steve's last race as a Wisconsin rower. You younger guys have a responsibility to give this senior the best ride of his career." (In at least one case, in 1980, Jabo walked out into the water to shake hands with two of his seniors in a boat that had already left the dock and, because of other boat launching traffic, could not easily come back to the launching area. One of those seniors, Ken Lawrence, in an eventually gold medal winning effort stroking the V4+, came back to shore and told Jabo and his teammates, "I was so choked up by the coach's effort to wish us well before the race, I just wouldn't let us lose after that.")

At the IRAs, Scott Conroe, a local Syracuse sports reporter, undertook an unusual project—he wrote his own private six-page account of the race, titled "Rivals," and then sold it, with the photos he had taken incorporated into the piece, to the race participants.

With permission, here is Steve Conroe's account of the varsity eight contest.

Jabo wishing senior Steve Hatton well before the race. Scott Conroe photo.

The first [varsity eight] heat brought disappointment for Syracuse, as Brown won by four-tenths of a second. Now the Orange would have to qualify for the final through repechage [a second round of qualifying heats among the non-winners from the first round of qualifying heats. The repechage regatta format—especially when there may be no "seeding" in the initial heat—gives a crew a second chance for getting into the championship finals].

Penn easily outdistanced Boston University and Navy in the second heat. Wisconsin cruised to a six-second victory over Rutgers in the final heat. Cornell's varsity eight not only lost, but was swamped in the process.

Friday was a day of relaxing and practicing for Brown, Penn and Wisconsin. It was a day of anxiety for the other varsity eights, who faced must-win situations that morning. Syracuse coach Bill Sanford joked about the pressure, saying, "We have a heck of a hometown advantage—one title in 70 years."

Penn senior stroke Chris Boland knew all too well the pressures of the IRA. After winning IRA championships as a freshman and junior, he wanted to be a champion one last time. That evening's *Syracuse Herald-Journal* raised the Wisconsin rower's hackles, for it contained Boland's comments about a new rivalry between Wisco and Penn. The reporter, Jeff Alessio, had asked Boland, among others, about the rivalry Thursday. Boland's quote said Penn knew it was the fastest boat, and its rivals could "bring it on" and try to beat the Quakers. Alessio was astonished by the blunt words. Boland later said he'd been quoted out of context, that he was referring to racing in any water conditions. He also admitted he was tired from that afternoon's race and wasn't thinking clearly. But the damage was done. The Wisco rowers were angry. The Wisco rowers, some of them already feeling they weren't respected in the East—a feeling encouraged by their coach, Randy Jablonic—used the quotes to feed their will to win.

Saturday's weather was typical for the Syracuse region—it changed a little every few minutes. Midway through the regatta, after a feeling of impending thunderstorms filled the air over Onondaga Lake, the varsity eight championship was postponed for an hour. Cornell's boat, in another casualty, had collided with a buoy and broken three riggers. The Syracuse varsity eight fled its boathouse and the hubbub that swirled around it. The rowers gathered at six-man Chris Ludden's house nearby and watched a movie. Their choice was unfortunate: *Casualties of War*, a Vietnam film.

The delay calmed Wisco No. 5 seat Jim Almquist's jitters but irritated some of his fellow Badgers until Jablonic reached into his store of tricks. "We were upset to come back, but Coach made us laugh," said senior Fitz Dunn (stroke). "He put tons and tons of tape on our boat, which we thought was funny."

The race finally began at 6 P.M. The water conditions were the best of the day. Syracuse jumped into the lead, surging to almost a length ahead of the other five boats. The Orange was in Lane Five. Wisco was in Lane Four. The Quakers, to their dismay, were in Lane Six for the second straight year. "No Man's Land," said Boland. Penn had come to the starting line feeling sluggish from the delay. And the Quaker's start was slower than normal.

Syracuse led by three seats at the 500-meter mark. They waited for Wisco and Penn to make their moves. They didn't have to wait long. At about 750 meters, the Badgers and Quakers turned up the power for their famous row-through moves. By now the rowers were pouring everything into their bodies, focusing on the commands of their coxswains, but still managing to sneak looks out to the side.

"Give me everything! Now!" John Parella, junior cox, shouted to the Orange. "Don't let 'em walk!"

He could see Wisco and Penn gather steam, their backs shining with water and straining against their oars. Syracuse held them off at first. Wisco No. 3 Dean Olson knew at the 1,000-meter mark that Wisco was moving but Syracuse was too. They were all past rational thought. Their long shells looked like eight-legged insects skimming across the water.

Finally, there were only the last 500 meters, when the mind tries to stifle the body's cries for rest. Now it was between Penn and Wisco. On the rocky shore next to the trophy dock, about 30 Penn rowers gathered to wait for the finish. But this was one time when the Quakers wouldn't be able to come back from their slower start to win. Wisco rowers were thinking too much of their narrow loss to Penn in the year before. And Wisco cox Mark Sniderman, looking for words to drive his rowers, knew it.

"No way, not again!" shouted Sniderman with 30 strokes to go. "We're not going to let it happen again!"

"That really got us going," said Olson. Wisco edged Penn by three quarters of a length, 5:55 to 5:57.6. Syracuse followed in 5:59.1. Navy was fourth. Cornell was fifth and Brown last.

Floating on the murky water, the oarsmen gasped and felt the burning ache of their muscles. Penn stroke Chris Boland looked over at Wisco stroke Fitz Dunn, who mockingly called out, "Bring it on, Penn. Bring it to us!"

The Badgers second gold of the day came in the coxed four event. The boating: Geoffrey Cann (bow), William Shenkenberg, Aari Roberts, Steve Hatton (stroke), and Dennis Schrag (cox). The Ten Eyck went to Navy.

On June 25, 1990, at the ninth Cincinnati Invitational, Michael Jaffe's article in *Sports Illustrated*, covered the varsity eight race and wrote:

Rude Red Crushes Crimson
Wisconsin Used a Power 20 to Beat Harvard

Wisconsin coxswain Mark Sniderman stood outside a room at the Holiday Inn-Eastgate in Cincinnati last Thursday waiting to have his picture taken for an ID card for the Men's Collegiate Nationals, known as the Cincinnati Regatta. Sniderman scanned the walls and noticed the regatta's promotional poster, a sculler finishing his stroke. Sniderman didn't like it. The rower had a large crimson H across his chest.

"Can you believe that?" he said.

Never mind that Harvard had won the heavyweight eight title at the previous three Cincinnati regattas and five of eight national championships since its inception in 1982.

The 1990 Wisconsin collegiate championship varsity eight crew—(L-R) Fitz Dunne, Todd Heinrichs, Pat Wolf, James Almquist, Matt Dahl, Dean Olson, Paul Stevens, Nick Donovan, coxswain Mark Sniderman.

1990 UW V8—IRA winners. The winning boating in the eights (right to left): Nick Donovan (bow), Paul Stevens, Dean Olson, Matt Dahl, Jim Almquist, Pat Wolf, Todd Hinrichs, Fitz Dunn (stroke), and Mark Sniderman (cox). Photo courtesy of UW Athletic Communications.

"Maybe they won't win this year," said Sniderman. "Maybe we will."

Two days later, Wisconsin did just that. The Badger eight won its second national championship the first time in 1986, making it the only crew other than you-know-who to win more than one national title in the eight years since the championship became official.

Last Saturday afternoon, as the temperature pushed 90°, Wisconsin coach Randy Jablonic paced the shore of Harsha Lake. Giving race prophecy to anyone who cared to listen. "If we're near the action at 1,000 meters, we've got a shot," he said.

Traditionally a slow-starting crew, Wisconsin came off the line quickly this time, and at the 1,000 mark, halfway through the race, the Badgers weren't just near the action, they were ahead of it.

"At the 600 meters all the crews were together, so I called for a Rude Red 20 (20 all-out power strokes)," said UW coxswain Mark Sniderman. "After that, we caught the lead and kept moving."

The Badgers finished 4.3 seconds ahead of second-place Harvard, which in crewspeak is like being in another zip code. But what was even more remarkable than Harvard's losing was Wisconsin's winning—in fact, Wisconsin having the gall to be competitive at all. People expect the Badgers to be good in hockey (they are national champs this year), cross-country skiing and the cheddar cheese toss. But crew? How do you row on ice?

"We don't get nearly the amount of water time that the East and West Coast schools get," says freshman coach Dan Gehn. "We're usually off the water for five months. This year, the ice broke early." Early in Madison is the last week in March. "I don't know how they do it," says University of Washington No. 5 seat senior Gordon Gruendell. "We're only off the water for about three weeks, during Christmas break."

Wisconsin pounds through the long winter training schedule devised by Coach Jablonic. "I like to change the program around so that it's interesting," says Jabo. "Every year I pull something new." Jabo knows winter training. His "something new" has included: rope runs, with the entire team (about 50 people) hanging onto a rope and trudging across frozen Lake Mendota, often in waist-high snow; the Hour of Power, 60 minutes of running up and down the steep steps of Camp Randall Stadium while Jabo plays polkas on his boom box; deer tails, where as part of a weight training circuit, a sock attached to a rope hangs from the boathouse ceiling, nine feet off the floor, and for one to three minutes at a stretch the oarsmen have to jump high enough to touch it.

"We go out and run when it's 40 degrees below zero," says captain Todd (Moose) Hinrichs, whose nickname comes from Moose in the *Archie* comics—

not that someone who's 6'8" and 220 pounds needs another reason to be nicknamed moose. "The first time we were pretty apprehensive. But Jabo just told us that as long as we dressed for it, we'd be O.K. He also said that if we were worried about frostbite on a certain part of our anatomy, we should stuff newspaper down our pants," says stroke Fitz Dunn.

Sometimes training gets interesting for spectators as well. A few weeks ago, just before the team left Madison for the IRAs in Syracuse, the Badgers celebrated with a ceremony they call the Grand Row. In it the crews, (in a range of dress and undress), row past the boathouse while Jabo stands on the bow of his launch, a John Philip Sousa march rumbling from the boom box, and a man playing bagpipes stands on the dock as fireworks go off overhead.

"In his Wisconsin country-boy style, he'll get you to dream about things," says former Badger oarsman Earl Anderson. "He can get you to do things you didn't think you could do. It builds a relaxed confidence."

It is Jablonic's intention to let that relaxed attitude carry over into other aspects of his athlete's lives. Last week, when Hindrichs suffered an upset stomach after eating at a Mexican restaurant in Cincinnati, he received some Jabo Medicine: a box of toasted oats, a bag of puffed rice, several apples and a bottle of Kaopectate. Jabo knows his first aid.

"It worked," says Hindrichs, "although I'm not sure which part did the trick."

A self-proclaimed jack of all trades, Jablonic is a brilliant salesman. He has worked at everything from bee-keeping ("selling honey from eight-once jars and 55 gallon drums") to real estate to negotiating for the Badgers' racing jerseys (99¢ apiece at Champion outlet store). The side jobs have allowed him to coach.

"Coaching is one of the few things I thought I could be a pro at and be good," says Jabo.

"Wisco [Wisconsin] was just too fast," says UCLA's Brad Marquardt, after the Badgers had beaten not just Harvard but also UCLA, Syracuse and Washington, who finished in that order.

Most of the prerace talk concerned the animosity that exists between Harvard and Washington. At an April regatta the Huskies had won the race, then lost it to Harvard after a protest led to a re-row, then won it back when the decision to re-row reversed.

"At least we beat Washington," said Harvard's George Henry.

After the race, Jabo wandered by as the Wisconsin boat was being loaded onto a trailer and whispered to Sniderman: "It was all those Mary Lou Retton's." For the uninitiated, a Mary Lou Retton 10 is 10 strokes with perfect form. Jabo knows rowing.[9]

Wisconsin's coxed four, in a largely different boating than at the IRAs, also won at Cincinnati, out-racing Washington, Cal, Toulon and Cincinnati. The boating in the 4+ in Cincinnati: Jim Howery (bow), Brian Folz, Matt Imes, Tim Gregor (stroke) and Dennis Shrag (cox).

Having won both the IRAs and the Cincinnati Invitational, the Badgers ventured off to their fourth Royal Henley Regatta since 1969. The Crimson of Harvard—very familiar with the course and the surroundings since 1914—outdueled the Badgers by 8 seconds in the semifinals and eventually won the second-level Ladies Plate event.

The spring of 1991 proved to be another dangerous period for the continuance of men's crew at Wisconsin. The Badger football team, with six straight losing seasons, was seeing a loss of interest (and revenues) at both the gate and from the television sports networks.

Together with the resulting decline in sports revenues, the intensifying pressure from Title IX legislation to add new and larger teams in addition to more scholarships to the women's programs, and the financial burden of an unfunded McClain Athletic Facility under construction led the Athletic Department to identify six sports for likely elimination—the men's sports of crew, baseball, gymnastics, and fencing, and the women's teams in gymnastics and fencing.

Of the six sports identified to go, only men's crew survived. An unspent boathouse capital fund of $250,000 probably helped, as did the alumni's history of providing financial support. Winning the varsity eight contest at IRAs the prior spring may have also added to the equation. The budget for men's crew was capped at $180,000 per annum, beginning the fall of 1991 and would remain capped at the same level for the next ten years. The budget for women's crew was capped at $150,000, although Title IX pressures relaxed this constraint within a few years. Any shortfalls were to be the responsibility of the rowing alums of UW or the athletes themselves.

On the water, the 1990–91 season was uneventful. The Wisconsin varsity won the Midwest Regatta and the Cochrane Cup against Dartmouth and MIT. The Badger varsity eight finished eighth at the Sprints and ninth in the IRAs.

On June 6, 1991, Coach Randy Jablonic was inducted into the Madison Sports Hall of Fame.

The 1991–92 season was noteworthy as Dartmouth surprised the Badgers at the Cochrane Cup by using new "hatchet" oars—a square-ended oar that resulted in less drag at the recovery point of the stroke cycle. Winning by over 13 seconds, Dartmouth broke Wisco's eight-year winning streak in the series.

By the Syracuse IRAs, most schools had acquired hatchet blades and seven of eight records were broken. The Ten Eyck scoring was also noteworthy: Wisconsin won the straight four with senior Paul Savell in the boat. Savell had rowed for some part of the fall semester at Navy and then resigned from the Naval Academy. He later enrolled at Wisconsin and apparently skipped a semester of fall rowing to reconcile any eligibility issues; then he joined the Badger crew.

It is clear prior discussion did take place at the IRAs among and between UW, the stewards, and Navy to find a compromise for Savell's foggy eligibility status and to determine which boat Savell might be allowed to row in—and the straight four was then apparently "unofficially" agreed upon by all parties.

Late in the day of the IRA finals, Dartmouth and Navy seemed to be in a photo finish in the last race of the day—the varsity eight-oared event. Penn, not too far from the leaders, filed a protest saying an official's boat had washed their shell and impeded their progress. While the officials sought to determine from photos who won the varsity race, they were similarly concerned with what to do about Penn's protest.

As time continued to pass without a resolution to the protest, several schools departed to get their athletes back to their respective campuses, as many colleges were still in their final exam periods.

Officials finally broke the logjam with a compromise—given the race could no longer be rerun. The IRA stewards from the Eastern Association of Rowing Colleges (or EARC, the "league" or conference in which the Badger men's crew competes) declared a first place tie among all three schools in question—Navy and Dartmouth, from their photo finish, and Penn for their protest!

The highly unusual equal-sharing of the total points from the first three finishing places rendered a bizarre result to Wisconsin—a Ten Eyck victory, though fleeting, by about a point over Navy.

Then, a few days later, the eligibility of Paul Savell came quietly back to the attention and scrutiny of the IRA stewards. Ultimately, the stewards reversed their earlier, unofficial position and ruled Savell ineligible. The elimination of Wisco's straight four win from the Ten Eyck calculation gave Navy the Ten Eyck trophy in 1992. The shirts given Wisco's straight four, the related medals, and the Ten Eyck Trophy were thus returned to the EARC and redistributed to the respective second-place finishers—Georgetown in the case of the varsity straight four, and Navy in the case of the Ten Eyck.

In the 1992 Olympics in Barcelona, Spain, Badger Mark Berkner was a member of the American squad. Mark had earlier rowed with the U.S. national teams on its World's crews of 1987 and 1991.

The following four spring seasons ending in the years 1993–96 may have been some of the most recently disappointing. At the 1993 IRAs, Badger boats managed no better than fifth—by the frosh coxed four and the straight four. The national college rowing regatta was held in Camden, New Jersey, because of flooding at the traditional venue in Syracuse.

Reasons for Wisconsin's poorer varsity eight results beginning in 1993 are not entirely clear. One factor may have been an underactive (or simply less lucky) recruiting effort in the summer registration lines. Another factor was a steady but unrelenting growth in men's crew scholarships (or growth in "financial aid" at the Ivy League schools, which give nothing in the name of athletic scholarships) and the related talent improvement at Wisconsin's major competitors. Men's crew at UW continues to this day as the only sport without scholarships. In addition, one of these scholarship-strengthened crew powerhouses—the University of Washington Huskies—returned to the IRAs in 1995, after a twenty-two-year absence!

Until an exceptional class or two of student-athletes were discovered and/or recruited, Wisconsin's strategy in men's crew would be to attract, coach, and hold a large group of talented, if not superstar, athletes and compete regularly for the Ten Eyck team trophy and smaller boat medals and—only opportunistically—for medals in the larger boat events. With such an approach, a breadth of talent and a deep bench could win team championships, even if the American and international "horses" were attracted to the varsity eights of those programs with larger financial resources.

Absent scholarships and support in finding experienced U.S. and international rowers, Wisconsin's recruiting would have to further intensify within the Wisconsin-Minnesota pool of outstanding high school athletes and among those club and prep school athletes coming to the University of Wisconsin for a high-quality, reasonably priced education, and a greater opportunity to row.

In the fall of 1993, long-time UW rigger and coach (1943–45), Curt Drewes died at the age of 83.

Wisconsin rowing also lost one of its most steadfast alumni and supporters when R. Y. Nelson (Class of '53) passed away.

Owner of a lumberyard in Edgerton, Wisconsin, R. Y. and UW rower Bill Ehrke ('58) suggested spring-break rowing on the Rock River in Edgerton. Over time, R. Y. and his wife, Judy, made Edgerton a more and more pleasant place to practice, overcoming the icy cold waters, winter weather, and the oarsmen's annual loss of another spring break to athletics.

The Nelsons not only donated lumber and helped build docks and boat racks for the crew but also opened their homes to the rowers for eating and resting between practices.

As with the prior crew year, the 1993–94 season was uneventful.
Small bright spots included placing fifth at the San Diego Classic after having

had only two weeks of open water practice on Lake Mendota before the race and defeating Boston University at the Midwest Championships on May 1, 1994.

Wisconsin lost the Cochrane Cup to Dartmouth by six seconds and finished ninth overall in the Eastern Sprints. Third places in two of eight events were the Badgers' highest finishes in the last of the Syracuse IRAs in 1994.

> *The reduced winds and the more central location of Camden, New Jersey, led the stewards to make the long-term decision of moving the IRA regatta from Syracuse to Camden. After a test of the Camden venue in 1993 and a return to Syracuse in 1994, the IRA stewards elected to move more permanently to Camden in 1995.*

Initially penalized one minute at the Head of the Charles in October of 1994, Wisconsin's varsity would have ranked thirty-seventh of forty entries in their category. The penalty was later rescinded, putting the Badgers in eleventh.

In the 1995 IRAs in Camden, Wisconsin managed two bronze medals—in the freshman 4+ and in the frosh eight.

Brown won the prestigious varsity eights event for the third straight year, while Washington—back for the first time in twenty-two years—finished second to Brown. Harvard's eight, back to the IRAs for the first time since 1897, finished fourth.

> *Aaron Berger, a future UW crew captain, was named to the first team of USRowing's 1995 Collegiate All-American crew.*

With a gold in the freshman 4+ and a silver medal in the second varsity eight at the 1996 IRAs, the Badgers' 1995–96 season began to show signs of revival. The frosh 4+ boating: Hickory Foudray (bow), Pat Woerner, Peter Dietric, Paul Tegan (stroke), and Kristian Knutsen (cox).

After twenty-eight years as head coach and eight years before that as the freshman coach at Wisconsin, Randy Jablonic became coach, for one year, of the varsity squad, as his "transition to retirement."

When asked to describe what made a one athlete a varsity rower and why not everyone made it, Coach Jablonic answered:

> A varsity rower must have the physiological package—that is, a great cardiovascular capacity . . . a strong heart and lungs. But an excellent physiology is not sufficient. Many athletes have such capacities. He or she must also have the mental capacity. Some people are inconsistent; others have different priorities and interests . . . a desire for a lot of socializing—beer on Friday nights with their friends, or girls or any other interests. And that's okay. I respect that.
>
> A strong mental capacity has a lot to do with attitude. It takes an "eliteness," a pride at wanting to be the best varsity rower in the country or as close to that

as you can be. An athlete may have to recognize honorable defeat at the varsity level and accept doing his best at the JV level.

Something else that separates a varsity rower from others is how he or she makes the boat go. Some people are excellent on the ergs. But ergs are mechanical. They don't require perfect coordination. One can have a strong erg score and still be a boat killer.

The differences between boat killers and those that make a boat go involve athleticism, coordination . . . a sense of feel. A perfect ratio[10] . . . an elegance. Boat killers hang on the drive, they don't explode.

An example might be two pianists . . . same music, say the *Warsaw Concerto*. The pianos are the same, the rhythm, their motion, their hand and finger dexterity and speed are the same. Volume . . . the same. But one plays a symphony and the other plays notes.

In the 1996 Atlanta Olympics, UW rower Eric Mueller won a silver medal in the quad (an eight-oared, four-rower sculling event).

In January 1997, Robert Espeseth, Jr. was inducted into the USRowing Hall of Fame. Among Espeseth's many achievements were four golds in the eights at the IRAs, from 1972 (in the freshman eight) through 1975 (over three years in the varsity eight) and his U.S. Olympic team membership four times from 1976 through 1988.

10
Chris Clark Assumes the Helm

Christopher H. Clark was named head coach in the fall of 1996, after two years as the freshman coach at Wisconsin and two earlier years as freshman and then assistant head coach at the U.S. Naval Academy in Annapolis, Maryland.

Born September 18, 1959, in Fullerton, California, Clark attended and graduated from Sunny Hills High School. Frank Clark, Chris's father, who still actively follows the sport at UW, was an instructor at the Orange Coast Community College.

Clark's crew background, including rowing at the international level, is impressive. In addition to winning a silver medal in the coxed pair at the 1983 Pan American Games in Caracas, Venezuela, and representing the United States at the Worlds in 1985, Clark rowed for Oxford College in the Oxford-Cambridge race of 1986, an event dating back to 1839 and which inaugurated intercollegiate athletics throughout in the world. Clark's international experience created a renewed emphasis on the developmental benefits of such summer training and racing abroad to still-eligible college rowers.

Chris Clark, head coach 1996 to present. Photo by Brad Taylor.

Clark would also coach the U.S. national teams from 1997 through 1999 and the "Under-23" squad (formerly the Nation's Cup) in 2002, when his eight-oared entry of three Badgers and four Huskies won the gold. With a coaching style both impatient and encouraging, Clark has managed to motivate his rowers with a dramatic blend of humor, intimidation, fear, the cold truth, and a sense of the unexpected.

It is the combination of the sense of mystery from his days at Oxford and his obvious-to-everyone record of success at coaching individuals and crews in many different situations that distinguishes Clark's coaching style.

Clark's major-event debut as Wisconsin's head coach was at the Head of the Charles on October 20, 1996. For the first time in its thirty-two-year history, the regatta was cancelled because of gale-force winds and the threat of flood conditions. The Badgers arrived in Boston, only to have to turn around and go home.

While winning the Midwest Championship, the Cochrane Cup, and the Walsh Cup over the 1996–97 season, the Badger varsity eight took fifth at the Eastern Sprints.

In the 1997 IRAs, Wisco took the Ten Eyck Trophy without winning a single race among the eight heavyweight men's events—a feat accomplished by managing a large and talented squad, rowing in all eight of the heavyweight men's events with credible boatings and then finishing high in the finals of all the eights.

The frosh eight and frosh 4+ won silver, while the second varsity and the straight pairs took home bronze and the varsity eight finished fourth.

The end of the 1997 spring crew season is remembered nostalgically by many UW rowers and supporters because of the retirement of their beloved coach, Randy Jablonic, after thirty-seven years as freshman, varsity, and head coach. His varsity eight crews won four Challenge Cups at the IRAs (and another six second places), a total of eight 2V8 titles and six freshman eight titles (including one as the freshman coach). In 1973, Jabo's crews swept all three eights events at the IRAs!

Wisconsin won its first nine Ten Eyck Trophies under Jablonic, including twenty-eight gold medals in the IRAs. In the Olympics, Badger rowers would be on nine straight U.S. teams (through 2000), and Randy Jablonic coached all of them!

Jablonic's contribution to Wisconsin's proud rowing history of success cannot be over-estimated. The "on the water" legacy of success of Badger rowers at the national and international level is unequaled at Wisconsin. He was also an early supporter of women's crew at UW in the 1970s.

Jabo's interest in off-the-water matters was also significant, including twice saving men's crew during budget and regulatory challenges. His final legacy, through Jabo's ongoing effort to bring permanent men's rowing endowments to Wisconsin, continues to this day.

The 1997–98 season was a building year of ups and downs for the Badgers. In an example of the "ups," junior Jeff Maples crabbed out of his 4-seat and into the river after passing under the Elliot Bridge at the Head of the Charles. Demonstrating another classy act within the rowing fraternity, the Navy eight, next in line behind the Badgers in the head race, sacrificed their position in the competition and pulled the struggling Maples from further danger. It is in appreciation, as well as for a general respect and affection, that the Badgers frequently root for Navy if there's no Wisconsin entry in a race.

Navy is also remembered for their unique handling of the tradition of the "betting of the shirts." When UW oarsmen are fortunate enough to prevail over Navy in a race, the Midshipmen inevitably present their shirts in a tightly folded bundle to each of their same-seat counterparts in the winning boat.

At the San Diego Classic, Wisconsin dropped to fourth after a photo-review of a three-way, dead-heat finish for second put Cal second (6:13.73), Penn third (6:14.16), and Wisco fourth (6:14.36).

For the first time ever at the Naval Academy, Wisconsin beat Navy in Annapolis in all eight of the IRA-preparatory men's heavyweight events raced on the Severn River. Both the Walsh Cup (for supremacy in the eights) and the Fisher Cup (awarded for a school's weighted results in all eight events) went to the Badgers. At the IRAs, the varsity was eighth, and the second varsity finished second to Princeton.

While Wisconsin won gold medals in three small-boat events, the Ten Eyck Trophy went to Princeton in 1998. The straight four Badger winning boating: Justin Bauman (bow), Ira Simpson, John Cummings, and Tom Flint (stroke). In the freshmen four gold medal finish, the UW boating: John Remington (bow), Ed Golding, Nate Altfeather, Chuck Roman (stroke), and Zach Gutt (cox). The pair's gold medal boating for Wisconsin: Nic Shilling (bow) and Pat Woerner (stroke).

In 1998, men's crew at Wisconsin lost another key supporter. Dr. Donald R. Peterson, 7-seat on the 1949 crew and a crew longtime supporter, had served on the UW faculty as an Extension agronomist. Peterson provided advice and counsel to coaches Sonju and Jablonic for many years. Don's father, Ralph, lettered on the crew in 1913 (awarded in 1915).

In the 1998–99 season, Wisco's varsity eight finished fourth in the Eastern Sprints and fifth at the IRAs. The 2V8 finished second, 0.86 seconds behind Princeton, at the Sprints and fifth at the IRAs. The frosh eight pulled to just out of the medals, at fourth, in the Sprints and, with the addition of Cal and Washington, slipped to sixth at the IRAs. The deep Badger squad won four IRA golds in the smaller boat events, including the straight four, the coxed four, the open 4+, and the frosh 4+. The result was another Ten Eyck team trophy, Wisconsin's eleventh.

In July 1999, the WRA's fund balances were $65,000, much of which would be later donated to the new boathouse reconstruction campaign. In late summer of 1999, Badger stroke and captain Carl Holtz was inducted into the UW Athletics Hall of Fame.

In 1999–2000, the coaches' recruiting in the Summer Orientation and Registration (SOAR) lines bore major fruit. A strong freshman crew with a few experienced rowers tried out for the squad in September. The many strong prospects, including novice Beau Hoopman from Plymouth, Wisconsin, brought new hope to the Badgers' future.

In Madison on May 6, all three Wisconsin eights defeated Dartmouth and MIT in the Cochrane Cup. The next day, Wisconsin's varsity (5:49.71) set a course record defeating Boston University (6:03.39). Coach Clark surprised former coach Randy Jablonic who was in attendance, by awarding the first Jablonic Cup to the winner of the varsity race between the two schools.

UW's frosh eight won the 2000 Eastern Sprints for the first time ever in an impressive open water victory over Princeton. One spectator watching the powerful Badger finish exclaimed, "I think I saw Ron Dayne in that boat!" (Dayne, Wiscon-

2000 UW freshmen 8, Eastern Sprints champions. The boating: Top (left to right) Dan Harrison (5-seat), Dan Mueller (4), Joe Peplin (7), Pete Nagle (stroke). Bottom (left to right) Beau Hoopman (2), Ian Welsh (bow), Adam Franklin (cox), Pete Giese (6), and Paul Daniels (3). Photo courtesy of UW Athletic Communications.

sin's premier football running back from 1997 to 2000, had just been named a candidate for, and would later win, the Heisman Trophy.)

Not only did Wisco's second novice eight (2F8) also win their event, but so did the Badger 3V8 in its category—by the margin of a bow ball! With the 3V8 victory by 1/100ths of a second, the Badgers took home the first gold medals ever offered in the event (the first year 3V8s were raced was in 1994, but no medals had been awarded until 2000, and only golds at that).

The first frosh, second frosh, and third varsity eights' wins were the first UW victories in the eight-oared events at the Eastern Sprints since 1987, when the Badger second varsity eight, powered by senior stroke Joe Cincotta, set the course record in the event!

174 CHRIS CLARK ASSUMES THE HELM

The freshman eight gold medal Sprints boating: Ian Welsh (bow), Beau Hoopman, Paul Daniels, Dan Mueller, Dan Harrison, Pete Giese, Joe Peplin, Pete Nagle (stroke), and Adam Franklin (coxswain).

This successful depth, demonstrated at the Sprints, projected a powerful presence at the upcoming IRAs. In Camden, Wisconsin, again won four of the five small-boat IRA golds on their way to their second consecutive and twelfth overall Ten Eyck Trophy. The straight four, the coxed four, the open 4+, and the frosh 4+ all achieved first-place finishes! In the eights events, the varsity finished eighth, the 2V8 was fifth, and the frosh were third.

In summer of 2000, future UW freshman coach (2004–5) Eric Mueller, who placed fifth in the straight four, and Kurt Borcherding represented the United States (and Wisconsin) in the Sydney Olympics. It would be the ninth consecutive Olympics in which Badger rowers were selected to represent the United States squad.

Late in 2000, after a one-year "quiet campaign," the Athletic Department and UW Foundation announced their public capital campaign of fund-raising to help finance the expansion and modernization of the boathouse in order to better accommodate their three crews—men's heavyweight, women's openweight, and women's lightweight. The current boathouse, completed in 1968, had been built for only one crew. Of the then $6.6 million estimated construction cost, the Athletic Department projected to contribute two-thirds of the total and to seek the balance of $2.2 million from the alumni and supporters of crew at UW.

In order to simplify their appeal to the men's rowing alumni over the public period of the $2.2 capital campaign, the Athletic Department elected, during the early months of 2001, to drop the $180,000 cap on the men's crew budget, effective the following August 1. The cap had been maintained since the 1991–92 budgeting period.

Without such an elimination of the budget cap, the men's alumni, with a finite amount of funds, would have been unsure whether to fund the larger boathouse or to "save their powder" to underwrite and protect the men's crew's very existence by supporting the annual budget shortfalls faced by a men's crew under a decade-long budget cap.

In a year similar to their previous season, Wisconsin's 2000–2001 crews enjoyed some notable early season success. The varsity eight finished second among all college crews (behind Northeastern and 8/100ths of a second ahead of Harvard—both rowing on their home courses) at the 3.3 mile Head of the Charles regatta in October.

While on the cold April waters of the Rock River during a week's workout over spring break, Badger Mike Seelen crabbed and flew out of the boat amid a fleet of eights storming down the river. Seelen later commented with great emotion at the crew banquet in May of how cold to the bone he was after thirty seconds in the dangerous waters, and how much he appreciated how quickly his teammates were to pull off their shirts and sweats and offer them to him for warmth and comfort. The special fraternity of rowing is formed by many and varied threads; the connection is strong and lasts a lifetime.

At the 2001 Eastern Sprints, Wisconsin's eights again grabbed two more golds. The 2V8 of Wisconsin broke the course record of 5:44.6 previously set by the 1987 Badgers in the same event. UW's 1987 stroke in that event, Joe Cincotta, was on hand to watch and was one of the new record-setters biggest supporters. Wisco's 3V8 also stretched their winning string—and winning margin (to more than a bow ball)—as they won for the second consecutive year.

The winning UW 3V8 boating: Dan Chin (bow), Eric Knecht, Mike Seelen, Mike Niemczyk, Aric Montanye, Ben Kaker, Ross Hart, John Remington (stroke), and David Kaplan (cox).

Winning small boat golds in the straight four and the open 4+ helped the Badgers win a third straight Ten Eyck at the IRAs. The varsity eight finished a disappointing eighth, while the 2V8 won bronze behind Cal and Washington. The frosh worked hard and delivered a much-needed fifth-place finish. The Ten Eyck scoring that year was so tight that, for example, had there been nineteen entries instead of eighteen in the 2V8 event, the additional hypothetical entry—wherever it had finished—would have changed the relative Ten Eyck scoring differences (between place-finishes in the 2V8 event) such that Princeton would have won.

In the summer 2001 postseason, UW's senior-to-be coxswain, John Taylor, picked up valuable experience at the U.S. national training camp in Princeton and finished sixth in the coxed four at the Worlds in Lucerne, Switzerland.

Other Badger rowers also benefited from summer development camp training as juniors-to-be Beau Hoopman won a silver in the eight and Pete Giese finished fifth in the coxed pair at the Nation's Cup in Linz, Austria. The Nation's Cup was, later that year, renamed more appropriately as the "Under-23 World Championships."

The 2001–2 season was expected to be one of the Wisconsin crew's best years. Riding the strength of the Class of 2003, Coach Clark saw great potential if the right development, enthusiasm, and motivation could be brought together to ignite the varsity eight.

Men's rowing—and especially the men's crew coaching staff—lost a wonderful young man in the prime of his life when former Badger rower and current assistant coach, Dylan Cappel (UW '00), passed away on January 23, 2002, after a long bout with colon cancer. Dylan was 23 years old.

A decent start to the 2001–2 season began with Wisconsin's varsity eight fin-

2001 2V8, another record-setting Eastern Sprints winner, celebrating their victory. From left to right: Nate Altfeather, Dan Mueller, Ken Price, Sam McLennan, Nick Kitowski (bow), Scott Alwin, Paul Daniels, (in the air) Zach Gutt (cox), Reed Kuehn (stroke). Photo by Brad Taylor.

ishing third among the college crews at the Head of the Charles. The Badgers were beaten by both Harvard and Northeastern, which finished one and two among the college boats. Both opponents know the water well; they row on the Charles River's winding course every day.

Harvard likes the Empacher shell on a straight course, but for the Head of the Charles, the Resolute is the Crimson's favorite, because the shell is shorter, quicker turning, and leaves more of a wake for the trailing opponents to deal with on their Charles River home course! Other tips for a curve-filled head race include using a longer rudder for better control and sharper turns and, at the Charles, keeping a shorter line by staying on the outside of the final turn to the finish.

At twenty-one days, the ice on Lake Mendota for the 2001–2002 crew season was the shortest-lived freeze-over of any winter on record since 1855–56! The Badgers skipped the San Diego Classic in the spring of 2002 in order to conserve traveling expenses and avoid traveling on four consecutive weekends. Instead, Coach Clark combined a Saturday April 20, dual meet against the University of Washington in Seattle, with two dual meets the next day at Redwood Shores, just south of San Francisco, California. The Badgers—who once again, for the tenth consecutive "random" draw got the less attractive middle lane through the Montlake Cut—lost by seven seats to the Huskies.

The next day, the Badgers lost to Cal by open water. Two hours after racing Cal, the Badgers triumphed by nearly eleven seconds over the rapidly improving Stanford Cardinals. While Cal was formidable, Wisconsin's narrow loss to Washington came about in part because of a ragged early 500 meters. The experience,

CHRIS CLARK ASSUMES THE HELM 177

2002 UW V8, Eastern Sprints champions. The boating: Top (left to right); Micah Boyd (5), Dan Mueller (6), Beau Hoopman (7 and Captain), Paul Daniels (stroke) and Coach Chris Clark. Middle; John Taylor (cox). Bottom (left to right); Pete Nagle (bow), Sam McLennan (2-seat), Brian McDonough (3), and Pete Giese (4). Photo by Brad Taylor.

however, gave the Badgers the quiet confidence that they were one of the best college crews in the country.

Victories seemed to come easily in the following Cochrane and Wisconsin–BU competitions. After trouncing Dartmouth and MIT on a Saturday in Hanover, the Badgers drove to Boston for the Jablonic Cup against the Boston University Terriers. The race was given a mid-Sunday morning slot on the busy Charles River rowing course from a start nearer downtown Boston to a finish in front of the Cambridge Hyatt Hotel—just short of the BU boathouse.

From the shore of the Charles, Harvard rowers, waiting for the Radcliffe women's race that followed, watched Wisconsin impressively defeat Boston University Terriers by ten seconds. One of the Harvard varsity rowers asked, "Why don't you guys race stronger crews so we can all judge your relative strength?"

"But we have!" answered this writer. "We just raced Washington and Cal two weeks ago."

"Oh, yeah. That's right," rejoined the oarsman, perhaps wondering whether the question should have been asked of his crew rather than of Wisconsin's.

The Badgers defeated the Terriers with the year's fastest time posted on the Charles River by a collegiate crew.

Then came the Eastern Sprints. Undefeated Harvard, with strong freshmen, second varsity, and varsity eights this year, was planning to peak for the Royal Henley Regatta in early July. The Sprints and their annual four-mile Yale-Harvard boat race were viewed as just warm-ups along the way. The Crimson expected a sweep by all three of the major eights races at the Sprints.

The Harvard frosh and second varsity eights did their jobs and teed-up the sweep for their varsity. When Harvard, Northeastern, and Wisconsin each won their qualifying heats, the crowd of 10,000 expected the finish would be in that order. But, not this day! Wisconsin's varsity coxswain John Taylor recalled the race:

> While we had a good, clean start, after 10 strokes we were 4 seats up on Northeastern and a half-seat down on Harvard. Around 1:10 into the race (about the 500-meter mark), Harvard was a half to one full seat up on us. At the 500, I called a "15" (fifteen power strokes) and we went up by two and a half seats.

Harvard's senior Hugo Mallinson (7-seat) was later quoted on the *Harvard Crimson* Web site, "Wisco had four seats on us from the 500 to the 1000. They took a big move at the 1,000."

At about the 900-meter mark, Taylor recalled:

> We hit a "10 by 2 by 10" [a power 10 followed by 2 more normal strokes followed by another power 10] and went up another seat. I remember looking across at Harvard's 6 seat, whom we all knew from last summer's rowing camps, and then I tried to "jack my boat" by telling my guys who I was looking across at and what seat that was.
>
> At the 1,250, I asked our guys to "put in 10 of your strongest. This one's for Dylan Cappel!" (Wisconsin's assistant crew coach, lost to cancer in January, four months earlier). After that point, I was on their 3- or 4-seat and I knew the race was ours.
>
> We didn't stop rowing until we were 3 or 4 strokes past the finish line, as I didn't want to take the chance of misjudging where we were!

The Badger varsity eight (5:36.6) won by 4 or 5 seats over Harvard (5:38.08) for Wisconsin's first varsity eight victory at the Eastern Sprints since Badger Captain Carl Holtz stroked the varsity to a win at the inaugural Sprints race in 1946. The UW shell in 2002 was named, aptly, the *Carl Holtz*! Princeton finished third (5:42.26), followed by Northeastern (5:43.09), Cornell (5:46.26), and Penn (5:49.59).

Wisconsin's winning 2002 Eastern Sprints varsity eight boating: Pete Nagle (bow), Sam McLennan, Brian McDonough, Pete Giese, Micah Boyd, Dan Mueller, Beau Hoopman, Paul Daniels (stroke), and John Taylor (cox).

While Wisco's 2V8 finished third and the frosh eight twelfth, the 3V8 won a Sprint's title for a third consecutive year! The 3V8 boating: Peter Turney (bow), Kyle Schaible, Erik Knecht, Dan Chin, Mike Anderson, Ross Hart, Jason Devlin, Aric Montanye (stroke), and Jaron Berman (cox).

2002 Ten Eyck Trophy winners, UW's fourth consecutive and fourteenth win overall. Coach Clark is at the back left with Beau Hoopman to his right. John Taylor is kneeling at center front, to the right of the Ten Eyck Trophy. Photo by Brad Taylor.

This was at least two out of five golds in the annual Eastern Sprints events for each of the last three years (in 2000, the second novice eight also won gold)! Wisconsin's varsity crew was on another upswing, and strength in the 3V8 gave the squad the depth for another strong shot at the Ten Eyck team trophy at the IRAs.

When the IRAs came around three weeks later, Wisconsin's prospects were clouded in several ways. A relatively weak freshman class meant that meaningful Ten Eyck points in the two freshman events would be hard to come by. At the varsity eight level, the usual combatants—Cal and Washington—stood in the way of a gold.

By the final day of the IRAs of 2002, Wisco's varsity eight had lost twice that season to Washington's Huskies—once in the dual contest in Seattle, and once in the semifinals of the IRA.

When Wisco's freshman coxed-four were second in their Petite Final flight (eighth overall), Wisconsin's hopes for a fourth-straight Ten Eyck picked up. Even the freshmen eights' thirteenth place overall finish, with a first place in the third flight final, brought essential points to the team trophy-scoring count. Literally every finish under the Ten Eyck's weighted scoring system over eight heavyweight men's events is important!

For the fifth straight year, Wisconsin won the IRA gold medal in the straight four event! The Badger tradition in the event was so strong, they also won the silver medal, even though only a team's highest placing boat is awarded Ten Eyck points. But Wisco's straight four rowers in this event stood on the dock together—one set of rowers receiving silver and another receiving gold! (In the Ten Eyck

180 CHRIS CLARK ASSUMES THE HELM

weighting formula, the boats of other schools move up in their rank of finish to calculate the balance of the scoring in any event where a school(s) enters two or more boats.)

The 2V8 finished just out of the medals, at fourth, when the first five finishers crossed the line within the margin of one boat-length.

The stage was set for the varsity eight finale at the end of the day. The Badger eight and their coxswain—with eyes fixed in a faraway game-face stare as they mentally prepared for the competition ahead—rowed smoothly past the energized Wisconsin spectators in the crowd of several thousand. Coach Clark had worked hard for the previous two weeks in putting their Sprint's victory out of their minds. "That victory will be an annuity you can draw from over the next five years or more. But until the IRAs are over, forget about it," was his advice. Wisconsin's season peaks at the IRAs, so that was what he wanted the varsity to focus on.

From out on the water, the report came from the ship-to-shore announcer at the start that the race was underway! Cal was reportedly off to its usual fast start, its seven international oarsmen (six of eight were past Olympians) experienced from years of top-level competition. Washington and Wisconsin battled for 1,250-meters, with neither boat giving any quarter.

At the 1,500-meter mark, Badger coxswain Taylor took a power 10 and decided to shift up the pace to the finish—a full 150 meters earlier than usual. The modest tailwind meant the race would be over sooner than usual, and he believed his oarsmen would therefore have the extra margin of energy necessary for the somewhat longer sprint range to the finish.

Wisconsin began to open its margin over Washington and close the margin on leader Cal. Taylor then heard the Husky coxswain disparaging Wisconsin in the final 500, while trying to urge on his own rowers, "We're the fastest final 500 in the country! No one's going to row through us, certainly not Wisconsin!"

When Taylor passed word of this insult over his coxswain's speaker and through the boat, Wisconsin's 6-seat Dan Mueller took personal offense. Wisconsin captain and 7-seat Beau Hoopman said later, after the race, "That comment drove Mueller berserk!"

Cal finished first by a diminishing margin of 4 to 5 seats and 1.5 seconds over the Badgers—who in turn defeated Washington by 6 or 7 seats and nearly 2 seconds. With Princeton squeezed back to fifth by Oregon State, the Ten Eyck Trophy again passed to Wisconsin by the smallest of margins.

For Wisconsin, the season was one of the best ever. No, they had not swept the IRAs, as had the Badger crews of 1973. And no, they had not made Wisconsin history by winning both the Eastern Sprints and the IRA in the same year, nor would the Badgers get to try their hand at the Henley Regatta this year (where Harvard's varsity eight would win the second level Ladies Challenge Plate).

But for a crew with no scholarships and mostly walk-on, instate, never-before rowers who'd been found in the summer's freshmen orientation lines, the results for the 2001–2 season had been exceptional! The Badgers had tamed two of the nation's strongest crews—Harvard and Washington—and almost slayed a third—Cal.

With a bounty of men's crew scholarships and substantial financial aid at each of these three competitor schools (a total of twelve of twenty-four of whose varsity eight rowers were international oarsmen with national team experience in each of their home countries), Wisconsin could be justly proud of its year's accomplishments.

Recruiting may need intensifying and scholarships might help level the playing field, but for this year, life was good!

Having studied the history of Wisconsin's successes at the IRAs, Clark noticed a seemingly natural and random cycle of nationally competitive Badger crews roughly every seven years—until the 1990s. Today that cycle seems to have lengthened toward twelve years, and Clark still wonders the reasons. The intensified introduction of international rowers into the college ranks, supported by a growing pool of endowment resources at a half-dozen or more universities, could well be a major influence in lengthening any kind of natural cycle at Wisconsin.

A shift from the current process of recruiting almost exclusively from the registration lines, and a deepening of the endowment and scholarship resources supporting men's crew at Wisconsin seem necessary steps toward the right strategic horizon.

> During the summer of 2002, Coach Clark opted not to take his Sprints-winning, second-in-the-IRAs varsity eight to the Royal Henley Regatta in the U.K. Such a trip, he reasoned, would make his continuing rowers feel as if one season just rolled into the next, with the risk of creating a stale 2002–3 season. Clark viewed Henley as an appropriate "reward" for a boat made up of mostly seniors whose college careers were over. Harvard—so often at Henley they keep at least one shell there—would go on to win the Ladies Challenge Plate at the Henley Royal Regatta in 2002.
>
> Also that summer, Clark coached the Under-23 Worlds team for the U.S. in Madison. The eight-oared U.S. entry, of three Badgers—including Beau Hoopman, Pete Giese and Paul Daniels—and four Washington Huskies won the gold medal in Genoa, Italy.
>
> Senior oarsman Nick Kitowski was named the Remington Scholar, following the 2002 season, as the student-athlete with the highest GPA.
>
> On August 29, recent graduate and former captain Alan Geweke (UW '02) died unexpectedly, the second loss (Dylan Cappel in January) of a young alumnus from UW's rowing community in barely seven months.

The 2002–3 season began with high expectations. Six of the previous year's juniors in the varsity eight, who'd won the Eastern Sprints as freshman in 1999, were returning in the fall.

At the Head of the Charles in the fall, the Wisconsin varsity eight finished first among the college crews, again out-racing home-course favorites Northeastern and Harvard.

At the EARC coaches' meeting following the Head of the Charles, Coach Clark was named the Men's Heavyweight College Crew Coach of the Year and the Badger varsity eight of 2001–2 was named the recipient of the Rusty Callow award for "the crew that prevailed in spite of adversity." In December of 2002, *Rowing News* named Clark their "Men's College Coach of the Year" and UW's varsity eight of 2001–2 as the "College Crew of the Year."

In the Windermere Collegiate Crew Classic in Redwood Shores, California, on March 29 and 30, 2003, Wisconsin lost to a perennially powerful Cal Bears eight by a mere 0.05 seconds. In other races, the Badgers prevailed over Stanford, Sacramento State, and Princeton.

In an unusual streak of five straight home appearances, Wisconsin won all five contests. The first of these Badger victories (6:35.6)—in a stiff cross-wind on Lake Mendota—was against Oregon State (6:59.2) and Michigan (7:04.1).

Against the always difficult University of Washington, the Badgers (6:09.1) jumped on the Husky varsity (6:12.0) over a 2,000-meter Lake Mendota course on April 19 and won the W Cup by just under a boat length for the first time in eleven years. Jim Almquist's e-mail broadcast to UW rowing alumni described the race,

> Washington had a little better start than Wisco, but only by a seat or two. After the settle, Wisconsin pulled back even and then took about a 3 seat lead at the 500. They continued to open up to 8 seats at the 1,000, until within 5 feet of getting open water. Heading into the last 500, Washington started to pull back a little, getting within 7 seats. In the last 200, Wisco moved back out to the final margin of [the equivalent of] 10 seats.
>
> Wisconsin had an excellent race, especially considering they have had [only] 8 practices on [Lake] Mendota thus far. Washington will improve too, if they can harness their power. [Coach Clark] calls them the largest-ever collegiate crew. The boat average is around 215 lbs, with the two Serbs in the stern pair around 230. [The Badgers] average about 195 with the biggest guy about 205.

In the Midwest Rowing Championships April 26th, the varsity eight set a course record of 5:14.40 on the 1,850-meter Lake Wingra course, beating the 1996 mark by 0.20 seconds.

In the Cochrane Cup May 3rd on a Governor's-Mansion-to-Tenney Park course on Lake Mendota, the Badger varsity eight (6:01.48) defeated Dartmouth (6:06.31) and MIT (6:55.94). In the Second Varsity Eight race, the order of finish was the UW 2V8 (6:04.35), UW 3V8 (6:06.83), Dartmouth 2V8 (6:17.02), and UW 4V8 (6:24.75).

May 4 was the Jablonic Cup on Lake Mendota, where the UW eight (6:11.9) defeated Boston University (6:29.9), with former Wisconsin coach Randy Jablonic, for whom the cup is named, in attendance. In the 2V8 race, Wisconsin's second, third, and fourth eights (6:21.1; 6:29.6 and 6:36.8, respectively) outraced BU's 2V8 (6:44.9).

Following the Jablonic Cup races, the UW Athletic Department organized a Crew House Farwell ceremony at the old boathouse to commemorate the last time the structure, completed in 1967–68, was be used in hosting a home race on Lake Mendota.

At the Eastern Sprints May 11 on Lake Quinsigamond in Worcester, Massachusetts, UW made its presence felt when all five of its entries made the Grand Finals in their events, giving Badger fans much to cheer about. In the varsity eight races, the match was expected to be between Harvard and Wisconsin, in a field of sixteen. The finish in the Grand Final was Harvard first and Wisconsin second.

Wisconsin's 2V8 (in a field of 14) and the frosh 8 (in a field of 16) both won bronze medals for third. The 2F8 was fourth in their final's contest. For the fourth consecutive year, the Badger 3V8, against a field of seven others, came away with a fourth consecutive gold medal in their event. UW's 3V8 boating comprised Ryan Kipp (bow), Tyler Resch, Eric Knecht, David Farnia, Mike Anderson, Ed Burnett, Joe Peplin, Ross Hart (stroke) and Garrett Meader (coxswain).

The Walsh Cup against Navy in Annapolis, Maryland, was cancelled because of rain, fog and an apparently reluctant opponent.

At the 2003 IRA championships on the Cooper River in Camden, New Jersey (across the road from Cherry Hill, New Jersey), the event saw two entrants who'd rarely participated. Yale's varsity eight—which since 1852 had traditionally prepared for their four-mile dual race against Harvard on this weekend of the annual calendar—had attended the IRA and its predecessor a grand total of four times in over one hundred years. Only for the four-mile Poughkeepsie Regatta on the Hudson River race in 1897 and the IRAs of 1975 through 1977 had Yale sent their eight. But this year, Yale again chose to participate in the IRA college championships. Harvard's eight—which had only participated in the Poughkeepsie Regatta in 1896 and 1897 and in the IRAs in 1995—opted to join Yale and attend the contest. Harvard had chosen not to attend in 2002, partly from tradition and partly because their varsity eight had been so entirely shocked at losing to the Badger varsity in that season's Eastern Sprints.

Notwithstanding high hopes for another upset, the Crimson Sprints' championship eight prevailed easily over the Cal, Washington, and Wisconsin challengers in the event, with the finish in that order. Despite a strong boat of six seniors, four years of high finishes at major college rowing events and some impressive individual participation internationally over past summers, Wisconsin was disappointed to finish out of the medals. UW's varsity boating team included Pete Nagle (bow), Alex Cockerill, Mike Niemczyk, Pete Giese, Micah Boyd (captain), Dan Mueller, Paul Daniels, Beau Hoopman (stroke), and Mike Lucey (coxswain).

UW's 2V8 finished fifth. Mike Triebwasser (bow), Chris Podbregar, John Dyreby, Ryan Schwend, Kyle Schaible, Jason Devlin, Anders Boyd, Pete Turney (stroke), and David Shore made up that boating. The Badger freshmen were sixth overall, with the boating of Mike Webb (bow), Mike Miller, Sam Austin, Larry Lawrence, Jim Murphy, Mark Sievert, Mike Tupek, Tom Velarde (stroke), and Dana Nadler (coxswain).

Wisconsin did take home its share of gold, however. The varsity straight four (without coxswain)—Ryan Kipp (bow), Tyler Resch, Ed Burnett, and Ross Hart (stroke)—won a fifth consecutive gold. With this gold, Hart, over his UW career, had won an incredible three gold medals at the IRAs and four in the Eastern Sprints! And in the pair's event—starting with a large field of eighteen—Wisconsin pair's boating of Nate Kelp-Lenane (bow) and Shawn Wanta (stroke) led their Grand Final field to the finish line, winning the gold medal by over four seconds. The official record: Wisco (7:08.56), Princeton (7:12.72), Cornell "A" (7:14.23), R Stockton, St. Mary's, and Loyola.

The varsity coxed four, placing fifth, boated Anders Pesavento (bow), Joe Peplin, Mike Kuklinski, Eric Knecht (stroke), and Garrett Meader (coxswain).

Two Wisconsin open 4+ entries made the finals, with the two boats finishing third and fourth (only the highest finisher counting toward the Ten Eyck). The bronze medal boating of Matthias Kuhn (bow), Ben Lawrence, Kyle Bunnow, Scott Hardenbergh (stroke), and Jeff Egley (coxswain) and the fourth place boating: Joe Waggstaffe (bow), Don Schneider, Mike Anderson, Dave Farnia (stroke), and John Costello (coxswain).

The frosh 4+ boating finished ninth and comprised Greg Orciuch (bow), Ryan Larson, Matt Helmrich, Chris Anspach (stroke) and Matt Neis (coxswain).

With a strong and deep squad, Harvard also captured the Ten Eyck team trophy for the first time ever. The final Ten Eyck scoring was Harvard (355.33), Wisconsin (340.47), Cal (309.56), and Cornell (299.90). It was Wisco's first loss in five years.

After the IRAs, the recently established tradition of an end-of-season parent cocktail was held at the Cherry Hill Hilton. Asked by Coach Clark what were his plans following his four years of rowing at UW, senior Beau Hoopman responded, "I'm going to the national training camp in Princeton to try to make the U.S. Olympic team."

The 2003 Remington Scholarship to the UW male (and female) student-athlete "who graduates with the highest grade-point average" was awarded to Ryan Kipp, a Badger rower majoring in kinetics and entering the UW Medical School in the fall. This was the second consecutive year a men's rower won the award and the third in five years.

At the Pan Am Games in Rincon, Dominican Republic, former Badgers Paul Daniels and Beau Hoopman were busy. In the straight four, the U.S. entry won the silver, with Daniels in the 2-seat and Hoopman at stroke. In the eights, the United States won the gold, with Daniels in the 4-seat and Hoopman again at stroke.

In the Worlds in Milan, Italy, former Badgers Ryan Torgerson (bow-seat) won a silver in the eights race and Brian McDonough (bow-seat) won a gold in the 4+.

With the loss of six seniors from the varsity eight, Wisconsin faced what is frequently called a building year in the 2003–4 season. The squad was also without a boathouse. When demolition of the old 15,000-square-foot boathouse began in September of 2003 to make way for the new Wisconsin crew house, all three men's and women's crews moved to temporary quarters under a large tent nearby Willow Beach. The facility was affectionately dubbed "The Big Top!"

At the Head of the Charles, Wisconsin's eight finished tenth overall of the forty-one entries and fourth among the college crews. In the "championship four" entry, UW placed ninth overall, which was fifth among the college entrants. The coxed four boating comprised John Dyreby (bow), Mike Kuklinski, Anders Boyd, Jason Devlin (stroke), and Garrett Meader (coxswain).

Against thirteenth-ranked Michigan on Lake Mendota April 10, Wisconsin took advantage of some errant steering by the Michigan cox and defeated the Wolverines by over 9 seconds. The races then shifted to Governor Nelson State Park because of northeast winds, where Michigan's second freshmen eight defeated Wisconsin before the Badgers came back and won with their 2V8, novice eight, novice four, and varsity fours.

For the W Cup on April 17, only the varsity eight traveled to the University of Washington. The Badgers (5:55.0) surprised the Huskies (5:57.5), ranked second in the country in the preseason, for a second consecutive Wisconsin victory. The win was Wisco's first win in Seattle since the W Cup was initiated 12 years earlier. The Badger varsity eight boating were Kyle Schaible (bow), Shawn Wanta, Anders Boyd, Jason Devlin, Micah Boyd, Mike Tupek, Tyler Resch, Alex Cockerill (stroke and captain), and Mike Lucey (coxswain).

On May 1, on the Charles River between Boston and Cambridge, Wisconsin took the Cochrane Cup from Dartmouth and MIT (Boston University joined in as an unofficial participant to get some more racing experience early in the season). The Badgers swept all three eights events from the three opponents. The next day, all three UW eights again out-raced Boston University—the varsity race for the Jablonic Cup.

At the Eastern Sprints on May 16, however, the reality of the "building season" became more obvious, as only one of UW's six entries in this all eight-oared format made it to the medals dock: the 2V8 (6:27.9) picked up the bronze, behind Harvard (6:22.4) and Princeton (6:26.5). Kyle Bunnow (bow), Mike Kuklinski, Chris Podbregar, Ryan Schwend, Sam Austin, Jim Murphy, Tom Velarde, Rex "Mike" Miller (stroke), and Garrett Meader (coxswain) made up Wisco's 2V8 boating.

In the Walsh Cup on the Severn River at Annapolis, Maryland, on the morning of May 21, Navy's varsity eight (5:49.6) triumphed over Wisco's varsity (5:53.3) for the first time since 1996, though the 2V8 (6:02.3 vs. 6:02.85) and novice eight (6:05.18 vs. 6:09.70) both won their races. The UW freshmen eight boating included Alex Evans (bow), Mike Quakenboss, Hans Wildebush (replaced by Nate

Temporary "Big Top" crew quarters at Willow Beach, from September 2003 to December 2004. Photo by Brad Taylor.

Millin at the IRAs), Ben Szymanski, Max Vice-Reshel, Andy Kaufman, Matt Donaghue, Scott Wallen (stroke), and James Sands (coxswain).

In Annapolis, only three of the usual eight pre-IRA warm-up events were actually held, again apparently because of a reluctant Navy opponent. The result of this was that at least twenty-one athletes made the long and expensive trip by van from Madison to Annapolis and back without having a race.

Over June 3 to 5, 2004, the IRAs were held on the Cooper River in Camden, New Jersey. For the second straight year, Harvard and Yale attended.

The wheels came off the cart for Wisconsin at the regatta, however, with only one of eight entries making it to the grand finals (versus seven of eight in 2003). That Grand Final entry—the straight pair of Tom Webb (bow) and Chris Anspach (stroke)—finished fifth.

The varsity eight finished twelfth (sixth in the Petite Final). Harvard (5:53.18) ran away from the field for the Varsity Challenge Cup—its second in a row. Following the Crimson were Washington (5:58.03), Cal, Navy, Princeton, and Dartmouth.

The 2V8 finished ninth. The novice eight failed to qualify for the Third Level Final so they did not race on the last day. The straight four (V4-) finished seventh with the boating of Nate Kelp-Lenane (bow), Scott Hardenbergh, Mike Treibwasser, and Anders Pesavento (stroke). The F4+ was tenth, with the boating of Steve Voss, (bow), Tyler Dunn, Tim Wenzel, Collin Payne (stroke), and Chase Phillips (coxswain). The open 4+ "A" entry finished eleventh with John Estes (bow), Andy Henn, Ryan Larson, Tim Cose (stroke), and Jeff Egley (coxswain), followed by the "B" entry at thirteenth, Matt Hemke (bow), Ben Kiel, Ari Metzger, Dan Rice (stroke), and Simon Lu (coxswain).

The V4+ was twelfth, with the boating of Greg Orciuch (bow), Matt Helmrich, Lawrence Stuart, Dan Schneider (stroke), and Dana Nadler (cox). In the Ten Eyck scoring, Harvard (359.91) again won the trophy, followed by Washington (268.63), Princeton (257.86), Cornell, Cal, Yale, and Navy. Wisconsin, which over the five previous years had finished first for four years and second the previous year, ended in eighth with 181.87 points, less than 1.5 points ahead of ninth place Brown.

Several individual efforts for the season were recognized: Andy Kaufman and Tyler Dunn were jointly awarded the Jablonic Award for "the most valuable freshman rower"; Micah Boyd received the Norman R. Sonju Award and Ryan Schwend was elected captain for 2004–5.

The 2003–4 season was then followed by some extraordinary postscripts.

For the fourth time in the previous five years (Borcherding and Torgerson in 2000; Taylor in 2001; and McDonough in 2003), a Badger rower was named to the U.S.

coxed four entry in the Worlds. Paul Daniels rowed 2-seat in Seville, Spain, and won a bronze at the 2004 World Rowing Championship.

At the Bearing Point World Cup in Lucerne Switzerland on June 20, 2004, the United States faced especially strong opposition in the straight four event, with famous UK Olympians James Cracknell and Matthew Pinset in the British entry and another favorite team from Canada. In a shocking display of strength and speed, the United States (6:02.21) knocked off both the second-finishing Canadians (6:04.17) and the third-finishing Englanders (6:05.01).

Former UW rower Beau Hoopman in the 3-seat (along with Jason Read [bow], Dan Berry, and Bryan Wolpenhein [stroke]) were in the gold medal boating. The victory landed all four rowers in the U.S. eight-oared entry for the Olympics in Athens.

For the first time in forty years, the U.S. men won the gold medal in the premier eight-oared event at the 2004 Athens Olympics. Beau Hoopman became the first ever Badger oarsman to win a gold medal in the Olympics (Carie Graves and Kris Thorsness won gold for the women in 1984). Another Badger rower, Matt Smith (bow-seat), finished ninth in the lightweight straight four.

On September 3, 2004, former UW crew Coach Randy Jablonic was inducted into the UW Athletic Hall of Fame for his successes as a Badger rower (winning an IRA gold in the eight in 1959) and as a Wisconsin coach for thirty-eight years. At a dinner the following evening honoring coach Jablonic, the $125,000 Jablonic Boat Fund—intended to purchase a racing eight-oared shell every five years—was announced as fully subscribed.

Beau Hoopman holding his gold medal from the eight-oared event at the 2004 Athens Olympics. Photo by Roger Waterman.

Men's crew at Wisconsin celebrated its 113th year of competition against college and club crews with its 2003–4 season. The program has been a success for many reason—undeniable water resources all-around, wonderful walk-on Wisconsin athletes and experienced out-of-state rowers rowing for the joy of it, a strong history of supportive alumni and a world-renowned university beckoning serious scholar-athletes.

Many challenges remain, including a competitor field which is already fully international. But with a long and proud rowing history; several rowing venues on Madison's surrounding lakes and rivers calling out to potential oarsmen; and a constant quest for intercollegiate excellence among its undergraduate student-athletes, the Badgers should continue to do well as that late-peaking, underdog crew from . . . Wisconsin where they row.

11
The Pioneer Years of Badger Women's Crew

There must be pioneers in every movement and usually the pioneers' lot is not one of the happiest.—Andrew M. O'Dea, "Coach O'Dea Writes," Daily Cardinal, May 3, 1901, 1.

Interest by University of Wisconsin women in the sport of rowing was first evidenced in 1896. Anticipating the fifth annual spring regatta of the naval department, scheduled for Saturday morning May 30, 1896, the *Daily Cardinal*, in an article dated April 30, 1896, reported,

> Last evening, the young ladies of the university held a meeting at Ladies' Hall to consider the advisability of forming a boat crew. Representatives of the naval management, Captain (Walter) Alexander and Vice-Commodore (Fred) Peterson, were present and agreed to do all in their power to aid this innovation. There is abundant material among the girls to put out a first class crew. There will be several boats at the boathouse at the disposal of the girls and Mr. O'Dea has kindly consented to coach them.

The *Daily Cardinal* later described an enthusiastic group of thirty "girls" who turned out at half past six on the evening of Monday, May 4, to begin to learn more about the sport. A large and extremely appreciative audience also attended.

Head crew coach Andrew O'Dea gave coaching advice from the coxswain's seat to the first group of eight lady rowers. The gig *Nysea* had been especially fitted up for their use. The sliding seats were locked, "as it was thought that the fair oarsmen would have sufficient trouble to keep their balance on firm seats. The girls were dressed in street costume."[1] Reportedly, members of the men's crew rowed out in several pairs to offer advice.

The first eight boated that night included: Ms. James (a freshman, in the Class of '99 in the bow), James ('96), Hughes ('99), Bowen ('99), Adams ('99), Copp ('98), Nash ('97), and Dopp ('99 at stroke), with Coach O'Dea as the evening's coxswain. Another boating of interested women was planned for the following day.

An even larger crowd witnessed the follow-up crew the next evening, with "Coach O'Dea . . . a very imposing figure standing in the stern of the boat. The

Early UW women rowers, 1896. Source: UW Athletic Communications.

boating: Emma Bibbs ('99, in the bow), Lucile Schreiber ('97), Helen G. Verplanck ('99), Anna L. Mashek ('98), Laura A. Sceets ('99), Helen Dorset ('99), Ella Smith ('98), and Jennie C. Evans ('99 at stroke)."[2] The rowers were reported to have shown great improvement over the previous night's eight in handling the oars.

A third crew practiced on Lake Mendota soon after, including: Clara Stedman ('97), Anna ("Nan") Mashek ('98), Rose O'Brien ('97), Grace Howe ('97), Helen Copp ('98), Myrtle C. Hughes ('99), Adda J. Westerhaver ('99), and Augusta Miller ('98).[3] The May 13, 1896, *Daily Cardinal* described the formation of the "U.W. Girls Boating Association" of thirty-two members. Officers included: Grace Merrill ('98), president; Clara Stedman, vice president; Ella Smith, secretary; Jennie Evans, treasurer; and Trustees—Nan Marshek, Helen Dorset, and Emma Bibbs.

The day before the big spring class regatta, the May 29 *Daily Cardinal* anticipated the ladies exhibition in gig rowing, advising as how one of the crews would be dressed in dark skirts and shirt waists and the other in duck skirts and shirt waists. Unfortunately, the next day's *Daily Cardinal*, its last edition of the academic school year (and perhaps only one page long), did not report the final results of the race. The Badger Yearbook of 1898, writing of Class Day crew races of May 30, 1896, was equally silent as to any women's class races.

While it is believed a race was held in 1896, interest in women's rowing seems to have disappeared until 1901, when the *Daily Cardinal* reported that sixty women had joined the rowing clubs and now were seeking boats and coaches.[4] Two class boats from the freshman and sophomore classes were expected. The *Daily Cardinal* went on to report, "(Women's) Rowing has been adopted with great success at several of the eastern schools, notably at Vassar and Wellesley. Milwaukee Downer College also has a crew."

In the *Cardinal* of May 3, 1901, Coach O'Dea wrote,

There is a great deal of talk, and no little interest manifested in the revival of a girls' crew. It will be remembered that in '96 the girls inaugurated rowing as a branch of their athletics, and the energy displayed at that time deserved better results.

There is no doubt of the benefit derived from rowing and there is no reason why rowing should not be a popular and beneficent undertaking for the girls.

There are oarsmen in college who will when called upon, undoubtedly donate their services in the capacity of coaches. One of the old gigs has been found to be practically useless, the other, with some repairing, will undoubtedly serve to float the girls in their new enterprise. If there be sufficient determination to make the venture a success, outside of the novelty of the undertaking, then there is no reason why in time Wisconsin girls should not have a boat house of their own, and be as well equipped as Wellesley or Vassar. There must be pioneers in every movement and usually the pioneers' lot is not one of the happiest.

The women had their first workouts of 1901 on the morning of May 18, "under the direction of Miss Harris and Assistant Coach Stillman."[5] Successive articles reported the following boatings: for the junior class—Lelia Bascom, Charlotte Fischer, Leora Klahr, Ida Brewster, Lorine Knauf, Bessie Cottell, and Bessie Kratz;[6] the sophomore class—Marshall (bow), Case, Osborne, Stokes, Bennet, Storm, Harris, and Martin (stroke)—no coxswain was named; the two freshman class boats—in the first crew: Kelly (bow), Stewart, Case, Dodge, Schmidtman, Redfield, Harris, and Darrow (stroke), the second crew: Bowl (bow), Eastman, Adams, McCollins, Mutchler, Baker, Harris, and Smith (stroke).[7]

Unfortunately, there again seems to have been no report in the *Daily Cardinal* (and there was none in *The Badger of 1903*) of there ever being a women's race among class crews. Women's interest in boating was mentioned again in a supportive Cardinal editorial dated May 25, 1902. No subsequent articles were found that spring, although Lucie Case ('04), believed to be one of those listed in the sophomore class boating of 1901, was a reporter—and the only woman listed—on the flag of that 1902 issue of the *Daily Cardinal*.[8]

In 1933 and 1934, men's head coach Mike Murphy remembered that Miss Blanche M. Trilling prevailed upon coach Murphy to initiate an interest in crew by the university's women.

Ms. Trilling, a strong believer in an inclusive form of intramural women's athletics, rather than the more elite, and thus less participatory, format of intercollegiate athletics, was by then a national figure in women's athletics. Trilling's philosophy was summarized, "a team for every girl and every girl on a team."[9]

From Women's Athletic Associations on many campuses, Trilling, in 1917, had spearheaded the development of a national organization of such associations into the Athletic Conference of American College Women (ACACW), the name later changed to the Athletic and Recreation Federation of College Women (ARFCW).

Several UW rowers agreed to assist in organizing the effort, including UW rower and future benefactor Fred Emerson, (he later donated at least six shells to Wisconsin rowing). Coach Murphy put up an oar as the prize.[10]

Two sororities—the Alpha Gamma Delta and the Kappa Kappa Gamma—later challenged each other in two successive annual rowing contests. In the first contest, the Alpha Gams "walked off with the title by sliding in ahead of the Kappas by a good sized margin."[11] In the second year, the Kappas evened the record.

The series was not continued, and so the Kappas kept the prize oar for many years. The trophy oar, which used to hang in the Kappa's "smoking room," is now held in the boathouse by the women's rowing program.

Almost forty years later, women's crew at Wisconsin began in earnest in the winter of 1972. Kathy Wutke, a New Berlin, Wisconsin, native, can be considered the "founder" of varsity women's rowing at UW for her work organizing the first continuing women's crew effort.[12] While Kathy's father, Robert W. Wutke, had rowed with the war-interrupted crews at UW in 1942–43 under coach George Rea, her interest in crew came, at least in part, on a dare.

A freshman at Wisconsin living in the Showerman House of the Kronshage dormitory complex, Wutke was an early-morning swimmer on the swimming team. Walking the one long block back from the natatorium to her dorm in Kronshage in the fall of 1971, she began to notice the men's crews rowing silently along the borders of Lake Mendota, the coach's megaphone echoing instructions back to shore.

Also a member of the UW band, Wutke had begun chatting with fellow band member Bruce Niedermeier, himself a Badger rower. Soon, she was visiting the boathouse only a few blocks east of her dorm.

Wutke remembers talking with Niedermeier and eventually bantering about rowing, and at one point, Wutke remembering his saying something like, "Rowing? Women never do it."[13] For a woman of Wutke's single-mindedness, such an apparent summary dismissal of women's athletic potential became the basis of a special challenge! In subsequent days she began to seriously probe the interest in rowing among her friends.

Sensing the group's coalescing interest, Wutke approached men's crew head

Top: Two sorority crews, 1934. Source: UW Athletic Communications.

Bottom: Kathy Wutke in 1972. Original organizer of modern women's crew at UW. Photo provided by Sue Ela.

THE PIONEER YEARS OF BADGER WOMEN'S CREW   193

coach Randy Jablonic to tell of her interest, and that of several other women, in learning more about the sport of crew. Jablonic remembers Kathy's visit and, while perhaps skeptical of how enduring would be their enthusiasm, was encouraging of Kathy's and the other's interest. After advising of the physical limitations of the boathouse facility and the need to work around the varsity's scheduled use of the facility and boats for their practices, he offered them the use of the boathouse and any equipment they needed.

For insurance and liability reasons, all parties agreed that organizing the group into a formal "club sport" was important. Jablonic remembers giving a heads-up to Milt Bruhn, the former Badger football coach and then Director of Club Sports, since that entity's formation in 1970.

Kit Saunders, Advisor/Director of the Women's Recreational Association (the Association), was the first stop in organizing a new women's club sport. The Association, by 1967, had helped to organize twelve women's sports, which competed with other colleges and universities within the state and in some unofficial Big Ten championships. The Women's Intramural Directors of the Big Ten schools had been meeting for many years and were at this time discussing the possibility of a more formal "intercollegiate" competition.[14]

Saunders, in her 1977 thesis "The Governance of Intercollegiate Athletics," described the next step, "The need for a more structured governing organization which would provide leadership and initiate and maintain standards of excellence was soon apparent. The Association for Intercollegiate Athletics for Women ("AIAW") was formed in 1971 to meet this need."[15]

Having met with Saunders, Kathy Wutke and fellow pioneers Sue Ela and Cindy Holden then visited Bruhn to further the case for supporting this club sport. The Club Sports entity was responsible for approving intramural clubs as well as to schedule UW athletic facilities, vans, equipment, and playing fields. Coaches were "recruited" by the clubs themselves.

Bruhn in turn asked for input from Dr. Allan J. Ryan, a professor of physical medicine at UW and national authority on the pros and cons of rugged physical activity. Ryan welcomed the idea and recommended it.[16] Eventually, the other steps in the bureaucratic labyrinth were completed and the new club emerged.

Having negotiated support of the Women's Recreational Association and Club Sports, the women's crew club then had to go to the Intramural Recreation Board, headed by Professor Jim Bower, where intramural financial resources were allocated to individual clubs. It is fair to say the creation of additional clubs—one more mouth at a finite trough—was not always encouraged at this stop.[17]

As all campus clubs need an advisor, Wutke had to find such a sponsor. Fellow swim team friend Bob Romanelli suggested his English teacher, Sister Marjorie Smelstor. Around Thanksgiving, Sister Smelstor agreed to fill that role. She had come from a family of athletes. Her father was an all-around athlete from NYU and a scout for the Boston Red Sox. Her mother had trained as a candidate for the 1948 U.S. Olympic swimming team.

By Christmas of 1971, the club became one of twenty official clubs on campus. The recognition also brought $100 of support to get started!

Other support came from Kit Saunders, in her role as Advisor to the Women's Recreational Association to extramural sports, which was housed within the Department of Physical Education and Dance. Most club "coaches" were on the staff of the Physical Education Department or were graduate assistants there.[18]

While men's crew had been given some hand-me-down practice and racing clothing, many other teams, including women's crew, often ended up having to "check out" some of the older basketball uniforms from Ms. Saunders's office in order to appear in common gear on the day of competition. Boat rigger Curt Drewes also lent a hand over the spring by adjusting and maintaining the barges and boats used by the club.

Wutke began putting up notices around the dorms on the west end of campus, inviting women interested in rowing to come to a meeting to discuss how to move the idea forward. The club's first formal meeting to solicit additional membership was held at 1:30 P.M. on January 25, 1972, in the den of Showerman House, where ten to fifteen women attended. At least one other meeting was organized, this time by both Wutke and Ela, and on March 15 at 7:00 P.M. in Chadbourne Hall's Main Lounge, the group of interested athletes eventually grew to thirty-eight.

At the start of the second semester, the club began a grueling three months of winter training in the rowing tank (beginning at 1:20 P.M., so as not to disrupt the varsity men's schedule). Training also included weight lifting, running the nearby paths and hills of Madison, and several elements of the Royal Canadian Air Force Aerobic Program (at the time, known as the "5BX" exercise program).

The Women's Rowing Club, eventually forty members, elected Kathy Wutke as president and Sue Ela as secretary-treasurer. They assessed themselves eight dollars apiece in order to build a fund for expenses, including a token amount for a future coaching stipend.[19]

The local press picked up on the story in a number of articles, including this one:

Kathy Wutke and Sue Ela were impressed last fall by the beautiful synchrony of the men's rowing team. But they were depressed by its male exclusiveness. Why shouldn't women have the same opportunity to participate as men? So they went to the men's full-time rowing coach, Randall Jablonic.

"He was marvelous," they recounted. "He gave us inspiration and hope, and best of all, he volunteered his own time and that of his assistant, Doug Neil, to help us coach."

"This is a pilot project," Jablonic explained. "If the girls can prove their dedication and capability, then hopefully we'll be able to drum up funds for establishing them as a recognized sport."

As soon as Lake Mendota thaws, the here-to-fore all male crew will begin to see women manning the 60-foot shells. It will be rough work: rowing indoors all winter is no substitute for the real thing. Yet this feminine crew will be in top physical shape, thanks to a sympathetic coach and his invaluable donated time. And if determination and enthusiasm have anything to do with it, then these dynamic young women may well have launched one of the most successful and worthwhile new programs in women's athletics.[20]

Ela remembers Jablonic providing instruction early on with the basics, coaching the women in the rowing tank every day for the first week. Doug Neil, the highly regarded coach of the Wisconsin men's freshmen crew, soon took over the coaching of the women. Wutke remembers Neil as a quiet, reserved person, and also as someone initially not quite sure what should be the training routine for this group of hopeful women rowers.

Kathy especially remembers one day when Coach Neil's discomfort with the particularities of coaching women emerged. Out on Lake Mendota, one of the starboard rowers was having trouble with the shell's rigging of the oar on her side.

Doug Neil (left), women's crew coach 1972–73, rigger Curt Drewes, and coach Randy Jablonic. Duane Hopp photo.

196 THE PIONEER YEARS OF BADGER WOMEN'S CREW

The oar kept hitting her in the chest. "She tried to relay this message to coach Neil, but to no avail. Finally she screamed out, 'The oar keeps hitting me in the boobs!'" Wutke continued. "After watching Doug turn a bright shade of red, I thought for sure he was going to fall out of his launch."

The group boated their first shell in late April of 1972. Three weeks later, on an approximately 1,000-meter course on Lake Mendota on May 20, two Badger eights faced two visiting crews from Minnesota. Kathy Wutke, rowing in the 4-seat, remembers that on this day, the Badgers didn't borrow uniforms from the inventory of hand-me-downs at the Sports Club. The oarswomen had all purchased matching ribbed, cream-colored tank tops with red trim and WISCONSIN in red from the Lakeshore Store.

Wisconsin's two newest eights finished in front of two crews from the University of Minnesota and the Minnesota Boat Club. The winning time was 3:42, and the winning margin was sixteen lengths ahead of the opponent's first shell!

In spite of rowing in an eight-oared barge,[21] the win was—unofficially—four seconds faster than the national 3:46 record for women's crews on a 1,000-meter course. The new Badger women's crew was, justifiably, thrilled!

The winning boating: Jessica Bulgrin (bow), Carol Milner, Liesel Geyer, Kathy Wutke, Debbie Crozier, Sue Ela, Kathy Galles, Donell Rogness (stroke), and Allison Snyder (coxswain). The second-place 2V8 boating: Ruth McGraw (bow), Mary Schuette, Liza Hubbard, Mary Mattias, Chris Anderson, Nancy Heck, Linda Canarie, Barb Schaefer (stroke), and Chris Mahoney (coxswain).[22] Several in the varsity boat also rowed in a later four-oared event and won. That four's boating: Kathy Galles (bow), Sue Ela, Cindy Holden, Donell Rogness (stroke), and Allison Snyder (coxswain).

The women's soon-to-be-varsity crew at Wisconsin had begun its own history with a good omen—an initial victory! The latest chapter in Wisconsin's already eighty-year-old varsity rowing history—this one of the women rowers—had begun to be written.

The importance of this first day of successes cannot be underestimated. Sue Ela, looking back, felt the victory achieved many positive results. The momentum generated with the taste of first victory gave significant impetus and energy to fund raising the entire following fall. The confidence gained and the credibility created among the important alumni and athletic department supporters of the program laid the foundation for growth in the development of the program in the future. As inevitably occurs, winning by itself unleashed many forces in support of the new program.

In some part because Liesel Geyer needed to complete a summer civil engineering course and in larger part for lack of funds, the UW women did not attend the 1972 NWRA national regatta in Seattle.

With one very successful and highly satisfying race under their belts, the new athletes went off for their summer vacations, dreaming of all the things needed to be done in the fall semester to restart the program and also to build some operating funds with which to travel. Interestingly, the new women's rowing program at Princeton was only a year ahead of Wisconsin's in its own organizing effort—and this only one year after women were first admitted to that school.

Over the summer of 1972, influences favoring women's crew were percolating elsewhere. In July, following passage of Title IX of the Educational Amendments Act by the U.S. Congress, UW chancellor Edwin Young appointed a committee to study women's athletics. The university's interest and involvement in women's athletics was beginning to build.

Also in 1972, the International Olympic Committee decided to add women's rowing to its competitive format for the 1976 Montreal Olympics.

12

Mimier Named Women's Crew Coach

To raise funds to defray the sport's training and travel expenses, the women's rowing club worked tirelessly earning money in a variety of ways. Activities included running concession stand "C" at Camp Randall in the northwest section of the football stadium, sock hops, and Friday night outings at the Pine Room in Carson Gulley Commons. The work at the football concession, run by Sue Ela for two years, is remembered in several ways: very hot or very cold, early arrivals and late cleanups, missing the football games, and sending 10 percent of their sales to the club's treasury.

Sometime in the fall of 1972, the club gave checks of $500 each to coach Doug Neil and rigger Curt Drewes for all their help.

At the eight-year-old Head of the Charles, the regatta's first openweight eight event was held, competing for the Governor's Cup. Wisconsin's women traveled east, but without Coach Neil. Rather, men's coach Randy Jablonic gave them some

Top college crew at the Head of the Charles, 1972 Wisconsin's V8. The winning UW women's boating for the race: Liesel Geyer (bow), Kathy Wutke, Kathy Galles, Sue Ela, Cindy Holden, Carol Milner, Janet Blackstad, Donell Rogness (stroke) and Mary Schuette (coxswain). Photo by Carmie Thompson of the *Capital Times*.

thoughts for the course. The rowers themselves paid most of their travel and meal expenses, with some help from the Club Sports organization. With the assistance of Coach Jablonic—whose varsity rowers often stayed at the old policemen's barracks on MIT's campus, now converted to visiting athlete dorms—the women stayed in dorms on the MIT campus.

In this first major competition against other collegiate opponents, the women's eight did well. In spite of two very confident crews from Brown and Radcliffe (Sue Ela recalls the Harvard oarsmen, taking early note of the many tall, blonde, women from Wisconsin, were especially encouraging in wishing the Badgers well in beating Radcliffe), the UW women—one of twelve entries in the championship women's eight event—finished as the top college crew at the 1972 Head of the Charles, losing outright first place (UW finished second) to the Vesper Rowing Club of Philadelphia! (Initiated in 1965, the Head of the Charles regatta was first attended by the Wisconsin men's varsity in 1966, when they were the outright winner.)

The second-place UW women's boating: Liesel Geyer (bow), Kathy Wutke, Kathy Galles, Sue Ela, Cindy Holden, Carol Milner, Janet Blackstad, Donell Rogness (stroke) and Mary Schuette (coxswain).[1]

Jay Mimier, left, women's coach 1973–79, and Yale coach Nat Case. Photo by Sue Ela.

Doug Neil, whose Wisconsin novice men had just won the IRAs the previous spring, was beginning to find his time stretched beyond what he could handle. Jablonic and Neil again approached Milt Bruhn and a little money was found to hire a women's openweight coach. The workouts, under Neil, continued throughout the winter, including the group's rowing twice a day during spring break.

In the spring of 1973, Jay Mimier succeeded Doug Neil. Mimier was a former Badger letter-winning varsity rower (1968–70) and UW law student. He assumed the coaching position for women's crew on a part-time paid basis paying $500 per year (the good-natured Mimier joked, "It sounds like good beer money").[2] The women's coaching role would continue to be a part-time position until the fall of 1979.

Mimier, born September 5, 1948, in Milwaukee, also rowed on the U.S. national team as the 3-seat in the eight, which finished ninth at the 1969 Worlds in Klagenfurt, Austria (fellow Badger Tim Mickelson rowed in the 4-seat). The national team coaches were two well-known Harvard rowing mentors—heavyweight men's coach Harry Parker, and lightweight men's coach Steve Gladstone, the latter now Cal's head crew coach and one-time Athletic Director.

Mimier had been attending UW's law school from the fall of 1971 until being named coach in the spring of 1973. After graduating from law school December of 1974—and following his five-and-a-half-year tenure ending in the spring of 1979 as UW's head coach of the women's crew—Mimier joined the Dane County District Attorney's office, where he is now an Assistant District Attorney.

The new coach of the women's crew at UW was proud of the long tradition of men's crew at the school, and he wanted to use their successes to build from with the women. As time passed and the women's program notched so many of their own successes, he was hopeful—during times when the men's crews were in need of successes to build on—the reverse would also come true.

As the spring break of 1973 approached, Kathy Wutke, who had been rowing for about a year, finished a particularly strenuous effort on a Friday erg test. With one of the top results in the boathouse, Wutke was particularly pleased as she began her weekend. Two days later in church, she collapsed. The diagnosis was a bad case of mononucleosis. She never fully recovered and had to drop out of college rowing. To this day she is unable to row without quickly tiring, but the UW women's program she initiated with her passionate interest and superb organizing skills only continued to strengthen.

Kathy Wutke (her married name is Smith) graduated from UW in 1976 with a degree in education. Since then, she has taught at both the high school and college levels and is, at this writing, teaching special education students at Batavia High School in Illinois.

After Coach Jablonic made a bid for a competition in the Midwest, the Midwest Rowing Championship was initiated in Madison, on Lake Wingra on April 28, 1973. Former UW rower Allan Anderson ('71) and many others helped organize this first regatta and also supported the event by collecting entry fees.[3]

UW rower Bruce Niedermeier ('74), a member of the Reserve Officer Training Corps (ROTC) on campus, remembers arranging for the ship-to-shore audio equipment, which allowed a commentator from a launch alongside the competitors to broadcast a race description back to a speaker and spectators along the race course. Using ROTC backpack radios, shore-based audio receivers, and pole-mounted speakers found at Radio Shack, the crowd was able to follow the race for its entire 1,850-meter distance, even if unable to clearly see the shells themselves until the final 500 meters or less.[4]

In early spring of 1973, the annual men's crew banquet was held. Sue Ela remembers the rowing club was not invited this year—unless they happened to be going as the date of one of the men (the banquet included both crews in 1974).

The openweight eights—two equally balanced boatings—placed first and second at the 1,850-meter Midwest Championships, with the B boat (6:47.30) winning out over the Wisconsin boat (6:53.9) designated as the A. Women's entries from other schools and clubs included the University of Minnesota (7:34.5), two entries of the Minnesota Rowing Club (A's time was 7:13.8 and B's time was 7:57.8), and Nebraska (8:13.3).[5]

The openweight crew, for lack of a sufficient travel budget, did not attend the 1973 Eastern Sprints sponsored by the EAWRC. Unlike the men's-equivalent EARC, which for decades has helped subsidize founding member Wisconsin's travel expenses (as the member-competitor with the longest distance to travel), the EAWRC did not agree to such a cost-sharing system with the Wisconsin women's varsity. While Wisconsin was, like the UW men, a charter member of the EAWRC, and the openweight programs of many eastern schools were financially more robust than Wisconsin's, there was no money left over to subsidize the travel budgets of other members, according to Sue Ela.[6]

The women attended their first National Women's Rowing Association (the NWRA)[7] regatta in the spring of 1973 in Philadelphia, again paying their own way. Photos show the Badger eight garnered a very respectable fourth, but the official records show Wisconsin sixth. The finish line officials used "UW" for both Washington and Wisconsin, but those publishing the final results assumed Washington had been fourth.

Notwithstanding, the newly minted club sport from Wisconsin had done well!

At the 1973 Worlds in Moscow, Joan Lind, rowing in the single scull event, became the first American woman to medal at this level of competition when she won a silver.[8]

The 1973–74 season appeared to start inauspiciously, although a 6'1" sophomore Carie Graves showed up at the boathouse that fall to look for a spot on the novice squad. She'd never rowed before.

Under coach Mimier, the squad attended the Head of the Willows in Madison, where all of Wisconsin's boats came in ahead of crews from St. Thomas (Minnesota), Nebraska, and Notre Dame. The Wisconsin B boat was the winner in the eights event, followed by Wisconsin A, Nebraska, and Notre Dame A. In the four, the shell order across the line was Wisconsin, Notre Dame, and St. Thomas.

For budget reasons, in spite of finishing as the top college crew the previous year, the Badger women could not afford to attend the 1973 Head of the Charles.

All fall and winter, the crew worked on a daily training regimen, led by Coach Mimier in a "winter of discovery." His approach, especially with the novice rowers, ranged from the literal discovery of the beauty of the landscape the oarswomen were training on (the long runs to Topping Drive initially included

Biography of Carie Graves

Although Carie Graves would eventually become a world-renowned international rower and later a member of both the National Rowing Foundation and UW Athletic Halls of Fame, she'd never rowed before the fall of 1973. Her reasons for coming to the initial rowing tryouts were complex.

When I came to UW as a freshman in the fall of 1971, there was no women's rowing. After the spring semester of 1972, I dropped out of school and spent a year hitchhiking around Europe, in large part to try to find about more about who I was as a person.

About the time I had made a decision to return to UW, my father mentioned the start of a rowing club for the women at Wisconsin. I'd been familiar with rowing all of my life, as my father rowed at UW (Robert Graves lettered in 1955 and '56). As a result, I'd been to several crew picnics and even a few races as a young child, so I was already a fan of the sport.

Because there were few, if any, athletic opportunities for women in high school—and women were then discouraged by the connotation of being "jocks"—athleticism wasn't something young women talked about. In the 1970s, some women were afraid to tap into things like the aggressiveness it takes to realize one's athleticism.

For these reasons, I had no athletic background. On top of that, I was not fit. At a conscious level, I knew I wanted something to do, to be active. Internally, as a maturing woman still finding myself, also knew I wanted to work out some of my youthful anger. For these reasons, I committed in my own mind to be part of the new rowing program.

I would later learn that rowing was a sport where I often did not feel good. Being out of shape, and at the time smoking a pack of cigarettes a day, the daily workouts soon became terribly painful. What I came to love about rowing was the challenge of pushing myself.

I loved the process. After all, we only raced twice that year before going to the nationals, so the daily regimen of practicing . . . the process . . . was attractive to me. It was a great way to channel energy and passion. I also came to love the group I was with. Feeling part of something was very satisfying. All I felt I had to do . . . or anyone else on the team had to do to be successful . . . was to try hard. Try hard and you were part of the group. It was safe.

Born June 27, 1953, Graves later

continued on following page

Biography of Carie Graves
continued from preceding page

attended River Valley High School in Spring Green, Wisconsin. She had majored in English while a student at the University of Wisconsin through the spring of 1976, after which she immediately began training for the Olympics. A member of the U.S. rowing team for the 1976, '80, and '84 Olympics, Graves won a gold medal in the eight-oared event in the 1984 Olympics (along with fellow Badger Kris Thorsness).

Graves took her unique experience in rowing to coaching at the college level. She began coaching women's crew at Harvard/Radcliffe (1978–83). In 1985 Graves completed her master's degree at Harvard University, receiving a M.Ed. in administration, planning, and social policy.

Later at Northeastern University (1988–98), Graves orchestrated the move of women's crew from a club status to a varsity status in 1990. In 1997 she led her varsity eight to an invitation to the NCAA's first-ever crew championships. The invitation to the championships was repeated in 1998, where her varsity eight finished fourth. For her success, Graves was named the 1997–98 Coach of the Year by the Eastern Association of Women's Rowing Colleges (EAWRC).

In the summer of 1998, Graves was hired away from Northeastern by the University of Texas in Austin as the head coach of their openweight women's crew. She lives in Austin today with her son Benjamin, born in 1990.

In the new millennium, UW listed Graves as No. 16 on its "Top 100 Athletes of the Century."

Badger Carie Graves, three-time Olympian. © Arthur Grace, photographer.

3" x 5" index cards with sights to notice and enjoy along the way) to the more philosophical discussions of how much could be accomplished if an athlete focused intensely on their training.

The team continued to work on many fund-raising activities. Staffing a "W"

Club concession stand for football games at Camp Randall, according to the March 1974 *WRA Newsletter,* was again a source of funds for the crew. At about the time of the Newsletter's publication, the UW Athletic Board telegraphed its desire to upgrade the club's activities to a formal intercollegiate sport by suggesting a roughly $100,000 budget behind the program for the coming season.

At the second annual Midwest regatta on April 27, 1974, again using Lake Wingra's 1,000-meter course, UW's varsity openweight eight A entry (3:50.7) defeated its B entry (4:01.9); they were followed by Nebraska (4:11.2), Washburn University (4:13.7), Notre Dame Rowing Club (4:23.7), and the University of Minnesota, in a six-participant event. The winning boating: Kathy Galles (bow), Barb Schaefer, Mary Connell, Carie Graves, Kathy Plager, Sue Ela, Karen Ela, Carol Milner (stroke), and Chris Kunz (coxswain).[9]

Reporting on the second Midwest Sprints on April 28, 1974, the *Wisconsin State Journal* quoted seventy-four-year-old spectator Edison Lerch from Delafield, "Ah, this is great! Some people call horse racing the sport of kings. Well, rowing is the king of sports." Wisconsin again won the varsity eight contest.

Budgetary constraints prevented the crew from attending the Eastern Sprints in 1974 for a second time. Later in the spring, the Badgers traveled to St. Paul to row against Minnesota on Lake Elmo. Amid thunderstorms, and with Carie Graves rowing 4-seat in the varsity eight (there were too few novice rowers on the squad at this point to fill a boat), the Badgers (5:11) defeated the Gophers by a substantial margin in a 1,500-meter sprint race.[10]

As the season wore on, many on the UW crew became increasingly tired—not from all the hours of practice—but from all of the time spent, in addition to practice, raising money to travel. Reporter Ann Beckman wrote:

> There's something about skimming across the top of the waters of Lake Mendota that totally captivates a group of University of Wisconsin women. Given the incredible obstacles they face, women on the UW crew show an amazing commitment to rowing. It's almost an addiction. The 22-member women's rowing squad is getting a bit weary, however. Weary not from the six days a week devoted to practice but from the energies they have to muster to keep their team financially above the tide.
>
> In addition to rigorous training, the team has raked an enormous number of lawns, sold T-shirts, sponsored a dance, run a concession stand at UW football games, and, in the end, raised $2,500. Their immediate goal is to drum up more than $5,200 to get 12 oarspersons, a coxswain, coach and shell to the Women's Nationals in Oakland, California.
>
> The campus club sports program has come up with $1,000 and the Men's Athletic Department another $850. But that still leaves the team almost $1,000 short.

"We're relying on service clubs and individuals to come through with that $1,000 to get the team to the nationals," said newly appointed director of intercollegiate athletics for women, Kit Saunders.

(Carie) Graves stressed the need for the team to bring its own shell. If not, "we'll have to draw for one and take what we get. It could be a real tub—which would make all the difference." Team member Laura Dykstal (after mentioning the varsity eight placed sixth [(sic), fourth] at last year's Nationals) noted, "We don't have a chance to show anybody how good we are because we can't get there to compete."[11]

The 1974 NWRA national open regatta was held from June 14 to 16 on Lake Merritt in Oakland, California. In the early events, Wisconsin's four finished third in their heat and did not make the finals.

The Badger eight, participating in a regatta with neither a true seeding methodology nor a system of repechage, drew the two toughest contenders in their qualifying heat—College Boat Club of Philadelphia (a national team development camp, most members already out of college) and Radcliffe.

As Graves had speculated in the *Capital Times* interview, when Wisconsin couldn't raise the money to take their own boat to Oakland, they were lent a shell—it weighed fifty pounds more than Radcliffe's. Reporter William B. Blankenburg described the final 250 meters,

> Wisconsin was closing on (leader) Radcliffe. No open water remained between the shells, and the only other threat was from the third power in the heat, College Boat Club, which, like Wisconsin, had been trailing. All hands remembered that second place in the heat was as good as a victory, because the first two boats would advance to the finals Sunday.
>
> Suddenly College began the most remarkable performance of the entire meet. Spectators who had focused on Radcliffe and Wisconsin became aware of an undulation of red and blue from deep in the pack, bending and pulling, gaining with every stroke.
>
> Then it was over.
>
> They slumped over their oars, coughing, their throats dry, their lungs desperate.
>
> Someone gasped, "What is it? How did we do?"
>
> "Third," Beth (Traut, the coxswain) said. "We came in third."
>
> College Boat Club finished in 3:51.4, four-tenths of a second ahead of Radcliffe and three and one-half seconds ahead of Wisconsin.[12]

The UW boating: Kathy Galles (bow), Judy Marohl, Mary Connell, Sue Ela, Debbie Oetzel, Carie Graves, Kathy Plager, Carol Milner (stroke), and Beth Traut (coxswain). Marohl, Connell, and Oetzel were all freshmen, and Graves was a novice sophomore.[13]

In an historical footnote, Badger coxswain Chris Kunz was loaned to Minnesota's coxed four entry and became the only Wisconsin athlete in the 1974 finals of the NWRA!

In May of 1974, the UW Athletic Board voted to add an eleven-sport women's intercollegiate program, which included badminton, basketball, fencing, field hockey, golf, gymnastics, ice hockey, rowing, swimming and diving, tennis, and track and field. On July 1, 1974, the university formed the Women's Athletic Department, naming Kit Saunders as the department's first Director.[14]

Women's openweight crew had just become a varsity sport!

> *The University of Wisconsin women athletes became eligible to receive a major "letter"—the block "W," a symbol of varsity athletic achievement—over the 1974–75 season. In May of 1977, after a year of debate, the board of directors of the National "W" Club voted to extend membership to female varsity letter winners. The first woman athlete to purchase a lifetime membership in the National "W" Club was rower Barbara Schaefer (Class of '75).[15]*
>
> *Membership had been, to that point, only male letter-winners since its formation in 1948. This made Wisconsin one of the first universities to integrate their letter clubs in this way.[16]*

As the 1974–75 season began and the women's club crew transitioned to an "official" varsity crew, budget allocation pressures at the administrative level (as well as the tensions related to squeezing two crews into a boathouse built for only one crew) began to emerge. At the coaches' level, offices, locker rooms, showers, toilets, boat racks, shells, rigger's time, trucks, and many other elements of the expanded crew program now had to be shared among two crews. To describe one program as over eighty years old and the other as a few months old hints at where each was coming from. Human nature couldn't be overlooked.

On the rowing alumnus level—a generous group of donors, all men for the moment—were now being approached to contribute shells and funds to both programs. The appeals came in spite of the fact that the men's program, now highly dependent upon donor gifts, had faced near-cancellation only a few years earlier, in the spring of 1971.

At the athlete level, however, a relationship of growing respect was apparent, and many friendships developed between the squads. Inevitably, evidence of an increasing number of romantic interests between the crews began to emerge. The future would show many marriages among the athletes.

With eleven new varsity women's sports and budgetary constraints so significant, the Badger women again skipped the 1974 Head of the Charles, the major fall regatta, in spite of having been so successful in 1972.

The Badger women first participated, as a varsity, in the third annual Midwest Championships held on the 1,000-meter course on Lake Wingra, on Saturday, April 26, 1975. UW (3:53.9) won their first in what would become an unbroken string of twenty-five consecutive victories as a varsity eight.[17] Following UW were Minnesota (3:57.0), Wisconsin B, Nebraska, and Kansas State. The varsity boating: Mary Connell, Barb Schaefer, Karen Ela, Sue Ela, Debbie Oetzel, Carol Milner, Elizabeth Zanichkowsky, Carie Graves (stroke), and Beth Traut (coxswain).

On the water, Coach Mimier gave serious attention to safety—always a concern, especially in the cold lake waters of early spring. He would charge his managers in the launch with being very watchful for any rowers who might end up in the water. Crabbing was the most common reason for an oarsman or woman to unwittingly end up in the water. To drill his managers, Mimier would suddenly throw a cushion or empty gallon water jug into the water and time his managers until they recovered the object.

The season saw the first eight-oared shell purchased for the women's program. The boat was delivered, unrigged, for use at the spring's Eastern Sprints on Beseck Lake near Middlefield, Connecticut on May 10 and 11.[18] It was the Badger women's first time at the Sprints and their first big race as a varsity.

Daniel J. Boyne, in his *The Red Rose Crew*, has written a wonderful story of the 1975 U.S. national team summer selection camp process and the international competition of the U.S. women's openweight eight entry at the 1975 World Rowing Championships in Nottingham, England. Boyne leads into his summer selection camp focus by describing the background of most of the ten women ultimately selected to the summer's U.S. national team. His study of Badger Carie Graves included a description of the May 11, 1975, varsity eight Eastern Sprints race of college women's crews:

> Radcliffe coasted through an easy heat in the morning, rowing virtually unchallenged (in their qualifying heat). In the other heat, Wisconsin had battled fiercely with Yale and Princeton to make it through to the final. Part of the problem for Wisco was that they were getting used to a new racing shell, which had just been delivered, unrigged, to the race site in Middletown, Connecticut. To change boats just before a race was to invite disaster—especially a rounder, tippier one like the Schoenbrod they had ordered.
>
> Boatbuilder Helmut Schoenbrod made a different boat than the Seattle-built shells of English expatriate George Pocock. The Pocock shells were made from traditional wooden materials, had relatively flat hulls, and "fixed" riggers. They were a no-fuss, easy-to-balance boat. For years, Pocock, whose advertising slo-

gan was "Building Boats to Help Build Manhood," had served American crews well. But Schoenbrod had different ideas. His hull was to be the first successful American boat made out of glass fiber, making it a little lighter than the wood counterpart but just as strong. It had a rounder bottom, too, which would yield more speed for a technically adept crew, and the riggers could be adjusted to achieve the right amount of "load" the crew had to bear on each stroke.

The lighter hull and adjustable riggers would prove a boon to women's crews, which had generally been handling oversized hand-me-downs from the men's crews. Unfortunately, Wisconsin coach Jay Mimier didn't have the first idea about how to rig the newfangled fiberglass boat. With the old Pococks, all he had to do was bolt the metal riggers on the wooden hull, an operation similar in ease to taking the wheels on and off a bicycle. The fully adjustable riggers of the new boat were a mystery to him—what were the proper dimensions for a women's crew? Finally, he asked the Yale coach, Nat Case, if he could run a tape measure over his Schoenbrod, an identical boat, and copy the various settings of the oarlocks. Graciously, the Yale coach agreed.

What Case couldn't provide was the time necessary for the rowers to adjust to the lighter, tippier boat. The Wisconsin crew was a young crew, and not so technically adept that they could make such adjustment with ease. They slogged through their heat, wasting a lot of energy to hold off Princeton and Yale. For the afternoon final, they were too tired to take on Radcliffe, a crew they might have beaten easily in their old boat (and Wisco finished second).

1975 novice 8—Eastern Sprints winner. The boating: Lois Harrison (bow), Sue Hutkowski, Peggy McCarthy, Mary Van Der Loop, Carolyn Hegge, Jackie Zoch, Jean Loeffler, Mary Grace Knight (stroke), and Beth Brenzel (coxswain). Photo provided by Carolyn Hegge.

Case and Mimier, who had not known each other before, later became good friends, another example of the kind of special fraternity (or sorority) that inevitably develops among rowers and coaches in the sport.

The Badger novice eight was even more successful, winning the gold in their event. Boyne wrote of the freshman race:

While Carie Graves and the varsity were struggling with their new boat and their East Coast rivals, the Wisco freshmen won their race easily by two lengths of open water—an enormous margin that got Mimier thinking. After the race, he decided to take three of these freshmen rowers—Peggy MacCarthy [sic], Mary Grace Knight, and Jackie Zoch—and promote them into the varsity eight. Equipment issues aside, the varsity should not have lost to Radcliffe. Perhaps the three novices would lend some speed to the boat.

Sue Ela remembers the novice eight victory at the 1975 Eastern Sprints as one of the major milestones in the early development of women's crew at Wisconsin. By the novices' beating all the other older, financially healthier rowing programs in the east—together with the varsity's valiant second in their unfamiliar shell—Wisconsin had proven to itself they could compete with anyone at the national level. Good things for Wisconsin rowing could now be seen more clearly by the coaches and athletes. Within the recently minted Women's Intercollegiate Athletic Department at UW, the new varsity sport was beginning to attract attention.

Leading up to the 1975 women's NWRA nationals and the first-ever summer selection camp for choosing U.S. national team members for that year's Worlds (and, over the following summer, selecting athletes to represent the U.S. at the 1976 Olympics), a drama was building. Daniel Boyne set the stage:

> Vesper Boat Club was a stronghold of club racing, one of the old Philadelphia clubs that lined the Schuylkill River and made up the alliance known as the Schuylkill Navy. Vesper had complained about the new camp idea for women, arguing that a group of diverse individuals who spend eight weeks together were no match for a set crew that worked together for several seasons. They had even contested the camp system in court and won a temporary injunction that allowed them to challenge the new selection process—if they won the 1975 Women's Nationals in May.[19]

One might ask whether Wisconsin's "set" college crew, if they were to win the upcoming nationals, might also have made the same argument to the court? As it turned out, this was never an issue for several reasons. Mimier knew that neither the Wisconsin nor the Vesper set crews would have made it to the finals of the Worlds. He was also personally familiar with the camp selection process—having been through a camp and chosen to represent the U.S. in the eight in 1969—and he was a strong believer that such a process would yield the best result.

At the 1975 NWRA's Nationals on Lake Carnegie in Princeton on June 16, Wisconsin (3:34.5) qualified third in the faster heat, behind winner Vesper (3:30.7) and the Eastern Development Camp from Boston (3:32.0). Coach Mimier had looked into his strong novice lineup and brought three of the oarswomen—Peggy McCarthy, Jackie Zoch, and Mary Grace Knight—into the varsity boat. It would prove to be a successful move.

Yale, Princeton, and Cal qualified in the slower heat. Vesper, a proud club, was coached by Gus Constant, also proud, whose wife, Karin, was rowing in the eight as well as in the lightweight singles race.

On the 1,000-meter course, Boyne, while developing his profile of Graves, described the finals:

> Carie came off the line at full tilt, never really settling into a rational race pace. When the other crews settled, she just kept sprinting—exactly what he (Mimier) had cautioned against. What he did see was a rough-looking but very determined Badger boat, barreling down the racecourse at thirty-nine strokes a minute, ahead of all other crews. Carie was stroking three or four beats higher than the rest of the field, pulling another kamikaze maneuver. In the tail wind, however, she was getting away with it—if the rest of the crew could stay with her. Vesper was closing now for the sprint, closing the gap with every stroke they took. As the crews crossed the finish line, Wisconsin fell apart, the port side crabbing their oars in the water.
>
> The (Wisconsin) boat came to a sudden, ungraceful stop—but they had beaten Vesper by 3.3 seconds.
>
> The . . . Olympic Committee officials who had come to the regatta and nervously watched the race, were secretly rooting for Wisconsin. By defeating Vesper, the Badgers had saved the whole selection camp—and provided every woman there with a chance to make the U.S. team. Theoretically, if they had wanted to, Wisconsin could have seized the victor's right to row at the Worlds—something no Wisconsin team had ever done. Humbly, they declined. Most of the women in the boat had done better than they had ever dreamed possible.

The order of finish, after Wisconsin (3:07.3), was the Vesper Boat Club (3:10.6), Eastern Development Camp (3:15.2), Yale (3:24.4), Princeton (3:24.8), and Cal (3:26.1). Carie Graves would later say "winning the nationals in 1975 was my greatest experience in rowing while at UW." Graves's gold medal is now displayed in the UW Kohl Center's historic sports exhibit in the east hallway of that basketball and hockey venue's first floor.

No betting shirts were exchanged, as was the custom among men's teams (Coach Mimier explained there were two reasons for this: it wouldn't have been the shirt they were wearing, and the tradition had been the men's for a long time and didn't seem easily assumed by the newer women's sport).

The coxed four faced a large field and was beaten in their first heat and then nipped in their repechage. That boating: Carolyn Hegge (bow), Carol Milner, Gail Sauter, Elizabeth Zanichkowsky (stroke) and Beth Brenzel (coxswain).

Coach Mimier observed, "Wisconsin's program really got going on the strength of two of the most fortunate classes of novices imaginable, which included Carie Graves, Deb Oetzel, Karen Ela, and Mary Connell in 1974, and Peggy McCarthy, Mary Grace Knight, Carolyn Hegge, and Jackie Zoch in 1975."

Kit Saunders, Director of Women's Intercollegiate Athletics at UW wrote to

1975 V8—National Women's Rowing Association "Open" champions. The boating: Karen Ela (bow), Mary Grace Knight, Peggy McCarthy, Jackie Zoch, Debbie Oetzel, Sue Ela, Mary Connell, Carie Graves (stroke), and Beth Traut (coxswain). Photo provided by Sue Ela and Barbara Schaefer.

each rower to congratulate them as UW's "very first National Championship Women's Team."[20] Of the eleven women's varsity sports initiated during the fall of 1974, women's crew had been the fastest sport to come from out of the gate to national success!

Carie Graves remembers winning the 1975 women's open national rowing championship as her most exciting experience while rowing at Wisconsin:

> Winning in 1975 was unbelievably satisfying, mostly because we weren't supposed to win. After all, we'd rowed only three or four times that year. Several of the women's college crews were good, as were several club crews, including Vesper and the national team development camp boat.
>
> I remember speaking over the season at several women's clubs, trying to raise money for our own shell. I can clearly recall saying, "We need this new shell to compete effectively at the nationals. And we're going to win the national championship." The amazing part about thinking back on that year was how somewhat matter-of-factly we described our goals and how sure of ourselves we were about the outcome. And the best part after that was that it actually worked out the way it was supposed to.

During the summer of 1975, the first selection camp was organized by the women's Olympic Rowing Committee and funded by the U.S. Olympic Committee. The camp's objective was to identify women to represent the U.S. at the World Rowing Championships being held in Nottingham, England. Badgers Carie Graves and Jackie Zoch were selected as candidates. "Coached by Harvard's Harry Parker, Graves rowed stroke-seat in the eight, finishing second by 1.6 seconds to the East Germans."[21]

At start of the 1975–76 fall season, coach Mimier saw about 100 women (including returnees) attend the early practices, including many he had found in the summer registration lines (5'9" or taller was his standard). Men's crew coach Randy Jablonic also helped Mimier find women rowers in the registrations line, as Sue Bott recalled, "He (Jablonic) scared the heck out of me. I said to myself: 'My God, what have I done' when he came up to me and demanded my name."[22] New recruits are essential to the renewal of the program each year. By the spring, only twenty-seven would remain.[23]

The coaching of two crews side by side—one men's and one women's—gave coaches some opportunity for creating challenges between the two. Jablonic and Mimier occasionally conspired together. At times Jablonic would boat his top varsity rowers against a mixed boat of graduate men and women. Mimier recalls Jablonic driving his launch alongside the varsity and yelling, "Are you going to let that boat half full of women beat you to the (Picnic) Point?" After harassing them for a few more minutes, Jablonic would then circle back to the mixed eight and provocatively shout, "Are you going to let my varsity beat this boat? Pull harder!"

Assistant coach Bob Eloranta and Mimier would similarly challenge some women to beat the erg scores of some of the second varsity men's and freshmen's scores. Later, Mimier would use future Olympian Carie Graves's erg scores to reverse the challenge and taunt the men. Other times, Jablonic and Mimier would initiate "hat races," creating mixed boats of men and women (pulling names out of hats) and challenging the shells up and down the length of Lake Mendota or in the tank.

The Wisconsin Crew Corporation (which later became the Wisconsin Rowing Association) had financially supported the Wisconsin men since 1931 and helped the varsity get to the Head of the Charles since 1966. They now assisted both crews with expenses, contributing $4,000 to send two men's eight-oared crews and one women's eight-oared crew in the fall.

At the 1975 Head of the Charles, the women's eight—which hadn't been able to afford attending the race since 1972—was seeded twenty-fifth in a field of forty. UW's participation was also the team's first attendance as a varsity; their first entry, in 1972, was as a club crew.

The Badger eight (17:59.2) did well, with a third place (and, as in 1972, the first among the college crews) on the cool and windy Charles River course, behind winner Vesper Boat Club (17:29.1) and College Boat Club of Philadelphia, a national development camp in Philadelphia (17:32.8).[24] UW's boating: Karen Ela (bow), Debbie Sonnenberg, Peggy McCarthy, Mary Grace Knight, Debbie Oetzel, Jackie Zoch, Elizabeth Zanichkowsky, Carie Graves (stroke) and Beth Brenzel (coxswain).

At about this period in the season, the Wisconsin oarswomen attracted national attention from young aspirants when *Weekly Reader,* a middle school oriented newspaper published across the country, featured the 6'1" and 170-pound Carie Graves in their "Eye on Sports" column. Graves was also the subject of an article in the October 27 *People Magazine,* the "focal point" of a PBS movie, and the feature of an article in *Time Magazine.*[25]

At the Eastern Sprints in Worcester, Massachusetts, the varsity eight won its first gold at this regatta by 7/10ths of a second over Yale. The order of finish: Wisconsin (5:46.0), Yale (5:46.7), Radcliffe (5:50.7), Dartmouth (5:59.4), Princeton (5:59.5), and Cornell (6:03.3).

In the 2V8 race, Wisco was second to Radcliffe but the novice eight, in their event, won by seven seconds over number two Dartmouth! The novice boating: Beth Worley (bow), Barb Bradley, Kathy Lunda, Margie Steuck, Karen Winnemann, Kristi Aserlind, Debbie Kelly, Mary Holtz (stroke) and Chris Cruz (coxswain).

Daily Cardinal reporter Judith Burns described the program in her May 20, 1976 article: "The women's crew accurately characterizes the situation of women's ath-

1976 V8—Eastern Sprints winner. The boating, which line-up coach Mimier juggled at the last minute to substitute nervous junior Sue Bott into the 4-seat: Karen Ela (bow), Mary Grace Knight, Mary Connell, Sue Bott, Peggy McCarthy, Carolyn Hegge, Deb Oetzel, Jackie Zoch (stroke), and Beth Traut (coxswain). Graves was out with an injured rib. Photo possibly from the *Wisconsin State Journal*.

letics. Both are fairly new and unestablished, both have managed to quickly chalk up an impressive record, and both expect to see progress and increasing quality ahead."

At the regional NWRA regatta held in Minneapolis on May 22, 1976, the varsity race was cancelled because of thunderstorms, after the smaller boats had completed their competition. The Badger four and pairs entries each won.

The NWRA's nationals, on a 1,000-meter course, were in Long Beach from June 17 to 20, 1976. Before the regatta, four Wisconsin rowers and a coxswain were selected to try out at the Olympic selection camp, held simultaneously in Massachusetts, and therefore did not participate in the NWRAs.[26]

Coach Mimier took the Olympic candidates to Boston, and the men's assistant coach, Bob Eloranta, accompanied the Badger squad to Long Beach. Without these strong individuals and rowing in lane six—the toughest lane—UW's eight (3:25.1) lost the lead with 200-meters to go and finished second, behind Philadelphia's College Boat Club (3:23.4). Cal was third at 3:26.29.

UW's boating at the 1976 nationals: Karen Ela (bow), Barb Bradley, Carolyn Hegge, Kristi Aserlind, Elizabeth Zanichkowsky, Sue Bott, Mary Connell, Mary Grace Knight (stroke), and Chris Cruz (coxswain).

The Badger four plus coxswain (3:51.4), competing with two rowers from their eights entry, finished in second, nine seconds behind College Boat Club (3:42.4). UW's boating: Lois Harrison (bow), Lisa Danielson, Kristi Aserlind, Mary Grace Knight (stroke), and Chris Cruz (coxswain).

The college rowing career of Carie Graves ended in the spring of 1976, after serving as president of the UW club sport in 1974–75 and as captain of the varsity sport in 1975–76. As a later coach, Graves talked of what separated a varsity eight rower from those who might not make the varsity:

> A varsity rower has several attributes. One of these is genetics. A VO2 measure—an athlete's ability to process oxygen. One must have the physiological tools to be a varsity rower . . . and some athletes squander it.
>
> Another required attribute is aggressiveness. Everyone is born with it, to one degree or another. Not everyone knows they have it, but it is totally possible to bring out aggressiveness, once discovered, and to develop it. It's so clear, as a coach, to see who wants it and who doesn't. On an erg test, aggressiveness is very easy to see, though it is less easy to see on the water. For example, with novices beginning in the fall of their second year, even though some may not be in shape, you can easily tell who rows like they care about winning.
>
> Others are boat-killers. They just can't feel how their body makes a boat respond. Some can't really ever get it . . . how the body is a lever . . . how their body can pry the boat past the water.

Three Badger rowers—Carie Graves (third from left), Peggy McCarthy (fourth from right), and Jackie Zoch (far left, receiving her bronze medal)—were selected to the 8 for the 1976 Olympics in Montreal. Photo courtesy of UW Athletic Communications.

UW coach Jay Mimier was invited as an assistant coach to the women's 1976 Olympic selection camp in Boston, led by Harvard coach Harry Parker. It would be the first time women's rowing was made an Olympic event.

Three Badger rowers, Carie Graves, Peggy McCarthy and Jackie Zoch, were selected to the eight for the 1976 Olympics in Montreal. With McCarthy rowing 3-seat, Graves at 6-seat and Zoch as stroke, the eight drew lane 7, which was plagued with a head wind and choppy water. The order of finish on the 1,000-meter course was East Germany (3:33.32), Russia (3:36.17), and the U.S. (3:38.68).

Early in the summer, before the 1976–77 season, former Badger letter-winner and aspiring national team rower Sue Ela made a phone call to Kit Saunders to say hello. From Saunders, Ela learned there might be a coaching opening at Wisconsin for the women's novice squad. The contact, Saunders advised, was head coach Jay Mimier.

From Mimier, Ela learned that an offer was outstanding, but it was uncertain whether it would be accepted. A few weeks passed and Mimier shifted his employment offer to Ela. A Rochester, Wisconsin, native and a UW rower, Ela had graduated from UW–Madison in 1975 with a degree in horticulture.

Since there had been no predecessor, Ela justifiably felt somewhat overwhelmed with the open-ended nature of the job, as she began the work in the fall of 1976. Recruiting posters had to be made, registration line schedules had to be coordinated, meetings organized, and daily practice routines thought through.

UW's women rowers, which as a club had, in the spring of 1972, squeezed into a boathouse built for one men's crew of sixty, began to speak more assertively about the need for larger, more complete quarters. In a precursor of things to come, the *WRA Newsletter* of October 1976 described the similar locker-and-shower-challenged Yale women's crew of a year earlier, which had appeared unannounced in their Athletic Department Director's office completely sans vêtements.[27]

At the 1976 Head of the Charles, Wisconsin's eight started in the second spot, behind 1975 winner Vesper Boat Club, which now had six rowers from the prior summer's Olympic team. The race was not decided until the final few feet (although times and order of finish took about an hour to post), when Vesper finished with a course record 17:26.5, followed by Wisconsin at 17:26.6. Dartmouth crossed a distant third at 18:15.9. Although second by so little after three miles, the Badgers were still the top college finisher in the race!

Before the final times were posted and the Badger crew knew their order finish, Coach Mimier began preparing his rowers at the dock: "Did you have a good race?" When most seemed to answer, "Yes," he would encourage them. "Even if we lose this one by a close margin, it's early in the season and an experience we can build on." For those who may not have felt they had done their best, Mimier would encourage them, "Take the boat's good result as a starting point . . . we can build from this race."

In this manner, Mimier allowed his athletes, as he would say, to "put this race behind them, to 'be done' and still feel good." He worked on building each rower from there, over the balance of the season. The varsity boating: Mary Connell (bow), Barb Bradley, Karen Ela, Carolyn Hegge, Debbie Oetzel, Kristi Aserlind, Peggy McCarthy, Mary Beth Knight (stroke), and Beth Bosio (coxswain).

The varsity had a more difficult time, as the defending champions, at the 1977 Eastern Sprints on May 15 on Lake Quinsigamond in Worcester, Massachusetts, finishing fourth (4:53.8) to Yale (4:50.3), Radcliffe (4:51.7), and Princeton (4:52.7). The crew would regain its prowess over the balance of the season.

In Ela's first year as the novice coach, the yearling eight won their third consecutive Eastern Sprints race. The order of finish: Wisconsin (5:17.3), MIT "A" (5:23.4), Rutgers (5:25.9), Holyoke (5:29.4), Brown (5:49.9), and Syracuse (5:57.4). The novice boating: Betsie Aaron (bow), Beth Ebert, Meg Galloway, Barb Hasz, Jane Ludwig, Kris Mesman, Janet Halvorson, Cindy Walters (stroke), and Colleen Mellen (coxswain).[28]

On June 4, in a dual meet against the Vesper Boat Club of Philadelphia (3:15.0) on Lake Mendota, the Badger (3:18.4) eight—seeing Vesper with its five Olympians take a slight lead at the start and gradually open the lead through the race—lost by 3.4 seconds. Former Badger Jackie Zoch was rowing with the Vesper eight. The eights then split into two boats each of coxed fours. In two qualifying heats, the Badger four won the first heat by three-fourths of a length and Vesper the second, by a similar margin. In the row-off of heat winners, the Wisconsin four prevailed.

The 1977 NWRA nationals, a 1,000-meter event again open to collegiate and senior club entries, was held in Philadelphia June 16 to 19. The varsity race was described in an undated summer of 1977 *WRA Newsletter*,

> In the varsity event, Yale took the early lead and held it for the first 250 meters until Vespers pulled by them. Wisconsin, in the pack from the start, was third at the 250, with Cal close to the Badgers.
>
> The Badgers began moving on Yale at the 500 mark and went by at the 750, while College Boat Club of Philadelphia came from sixth to also challenge Yale. With a furious sprint, the Badgers made a move on Vesper but couldn't pass.

Vesper (3:15.8) won by six seats, with Wisconsin (3:17.2) second, followed by Yale (3:19.0), College Boat Club (3:19.6), Lake Washington and Cal.

The Badger silver medalist boating: Lois Harrison (bow), Barb Bradley, Mary Connell, Carolyn Hegge, Deb Oetzel, Mary Grace Knight, Peggy McCarthy, Sue Bott (stroke), and Chris Cruz (coxswain).

UW's novice four plus coxswain entry in the varsity four event of twenty-five entries finished fifth against several strong, upperclassmen-filled competitors, several of which boats had one or more Olympians.

UW coach Mimier was again selected to coach at the national selection camp over the summer. The Women's Olympic Rowing Committee selected Mimier as the Women's National Rowing Team Coach to work with the eight-oared entry. The 1977 Worlds were held August 22–28 in Amsterdam, the Netherlands. In the eight, which finished seventh, were Badger rowers Carolyn Hegge (2-seat), Peggy McCarthy (3-seat) and Debbie Oetzel (5-seat).

In July 1977, Badger Carie Graves was named Radcliffe/Harvard's women's crew coach and became the first full-time women's head coach in the country.

During the 1977–78 season, Coach Mimier again took his varsity eight to the 1977 Head of the Charles and came back with its first outright win in the event! The Wisconsin women (18:06.2) outrowed Vesper B.C. (18:09.2), St. Catharine's of Canada (18:59.2), and MIT (19:11.6).

The boating of the women's winning eight: Lois Harrison (bow), Barb Bradley, Amy Luchsinger, Sue Bott, Debbie Kelly, Carolyn Hegge, Peggy McCarthy, Margie Steuck (stroke), and Chris Cruz (coxswain). With the UW men placing second (16:12.4, behind Harvard at 15:51.2), Wisconsin fared the best of all the college entries.

The Eastern Sprints were cancelled in the spring of 1978 because of inclement weather and high winds. For Wisconsin, the expensive trip was nearly a disappointment, but Yale coach Nat Case—whose crews may have been the ones to beat that season—kindly agreed to stay another day and race the Badgers on Onota Lake outside Pittsfield in western Massachusetts. Three events were held, with each race lasting five and one-half minutes. The leader at the 5:30 mark was determined to be the winner. The Wisconsin varsity lost to Yale by one and three-quarters lengths, while the 2V8 defeated Yale by one length and the novice eight won by two lengths. [29]

Wisconsin and Yale had a gusty rematch on Lake Mendota on June 10, where Wisconsin's varsity (3:17.2, a 1.6 second victory) and the Badger 2V8 (3:26.9 vs. 3:31.9) both defeated Yale entries.

In the June 15–17 NWRA open nationals in Seattle, the *Wisconsin State Journal* of June 18, 1978, described the 1,000-meter race: "For a while, it looked like the Badgers would finish fourth. With just 250 meters to go on the 1,000-meter Green Lake course, the Wisconsin crew finally made its move and pulled away from the pack into second place."

The varsity eight (3:12.6) won the silver, behind the Burnaby Aquatic Center Club of Vancouver, British Columbia (Canada's national development team, which finished at 3:07.7). After Wisconsin, the order was Philadelphia's Vesper Boat Club (less than a second behind Wisconsin), Philadelphia's College Boat Club (3:13.4), Yale (3:16.0) and Lake Washington Rowing Club. (3:22.8). Seattle Times reporter Dick Rockne described the celebration:

> The emotions of victory and defeat were in evidence. At the end of the last race yesterday, members of the University of Wisconsin's open eight were overcome with joy—after placing second. Their display of unabashed delight included a "victory lap" along the shore as, one by one, the girls passed stern to bow a bottle of champagne.
>
> Despite its second place, the Wisconsin crew's the national open-eight champion. After all, members of the winning crew were foreigners—Canadians all the way from Burnaby Rowing Club near Vancouver.[30]

Coach Mimier recalls being told by the twenty-five- to twenty-seven-year-olds in Burnaby's crew, which was always fast off the line, that they weren't worried about anyone but Wisconsin coming back on them. He also remembers some of Yale's rowers in Burnaby's boat, whom he'd cut at the prior summer's national's camp, were "after him" in this race.

UW's novice four (3:58) finished fourth in the senior four finals on Lake Merritt, behind College Boat Club's two entries (3:40.25 and 3:41.0) and the Lake Merritt Boat Club (3:47.89). The University of Minnesota, in fifth, and Pacific Lutheran, in sixth, finished out the final field.

Badger Carie Graves was named to her second U.S. national team, and Chris Cruz to her first, where both competed for the United States on summer tours to European rowing championships leading up to the 1978 Worlds in late fall.[31]

The Badger varsity eight started off their 1978–79 season with a big win in the fall at the Head of the Charles, their second consecutive outright win at the event! Wisconsin (17:47.3) defeated Penn (18:03.2), Vesper (18:09.3), and MIT (18:13.1). The boating: Monica Piaquadio (bow), Beth Ebert, Debbie Kelly, Barb Hasz, Amy Luchsinger, Margie Steuck, Janet Halvorson, Kristi Aserlind (stroke), and Chris Cruz (coxswain).

1979 novice 8 Eastern Sprints winner. The boating (order unclear vs. the photo): Gail Allen (bow), Connie George, Kris Thorsness, Chari Towne, Becky Stepien, Martha Roche, Ann Schachte, Heidi Grutzner (stroke) and Gail Ross (coxswain). Photo courtesy of UW Athletic Communications.

Saturday, May 5, in Madison, UW raced against the University of Minnesota, with the order of finish: Wisconsin, UW's 2V8 and Minnesota.

On Sunday, May 13, the Eastern Sprints, sponsored by the EAWRC, were held on Lake Waramaug, in New Preston, Connecticut. As described in the *WRA Newsletter* of June 1979:

> The frosh started badly and were down to the Princeton boat by open water with 750 meters to go. The well-conditioned crew responded, however, blazing past Princeton with 500 meters to go and winning by open water to keep their unbeaten record at the Sprints intact. (Wisconsin at 5:09.4; Princeton at 5:14.1; Northeastern at 5:20.4, and Yale at 5:22.4.)
>
> The 2V8 [also] struggled in the early going. When they finally began to swing, it was almost too late. Passing Dartmouth with only 100 meters to go, they won by a narrow margin. (Wisconsin at 5:10.1; Dartmouth at 5:10.6; Yale at 5:18.4, and Williams at 5:20.4.)
>
> The varsity women began the same as the 2V8 but managed to drive through the field to second with 500 meters to go. Yale responded to the chase, however, and held on to their ¾ length lead, keeping Wisconsin second. (Yale at 4:53.6; Wisconsin at 4:55.8; Radcliffe at 4:57.1; and Princeton at 4:57.6.)

The Badgers' novice eight victory was the fourth straight sprints triumph! (The

1978 sprint was canceled.) The novice gold medalist boating: Gail Allen (bow), Connie George, Kris Thorsness, Chari Towne, Becky Stepien, Martha Roche, Ann Schachte, Heidi Grutzner (stroke), and Gail Ross (coxswain).

The varsity silver medalist boating:[32] Janet Halvorson (bow), Kris Mesman, Amy Luchsinger, Barb Hasz, Jane Ludwig, Margie Steuck, Debbie Kelly, Kristi Aserlind (stroke), and Chris Cruz (coxswain).

June 10, Cal's undefeated Pacific eight winners (by 6 seconds over Washington) came to Madison and, on a weather-shortened course along the south shore of Picnic Point, the Badger eight defeated Cal by a seat and a half at the wire of the 1,000-meter course. In the 2V8 race, Cal prevailed, with the UW novices second and the Badger 2V8 a very close third.

At the NWRA's national open event in Detroit, Michigan on the 1000-meter Stony Creek Reservoir course, the regatta held its first "college event." The Badger varsity (3:09.6) took home a bronze behind Yale (3:06.3) and Cal (3:08.8); Wisconsin's novice eight, in the same open event (there was no novice event), finished fifth, just three seconds behind Princeton's varsity eight. The next day, on a less than 1,000-meter course, the novice eight won the "Senior" eight event (a kind of sub-varsity category for 2V8 rowers and new and/or smaller college programs).

Following the 1978–79 crew season, Jay Mimier resigned his head coaching position, after five and a half years, in order to pursue a legal career. Mimier had

1979 2V8 Eastern Sprints winner. The boating: Carol Rynning (bow), Polly Menendez, Sue Rutherford, Julie Hanson, JoAnn Berninger, Beth Ebert, Monica Piaquadio, Molly Duffy (stroke), and Martha Askins (coxswain). Photo courtesy of UW Athletic Communications.

MIMIER NAMED WOMEN'S CREW COACH   221

accomplished a good deal in his career as the first paid coach of the women's crew at Wisconsin. In addition to winning the National Championship against well-established club and national team development camp boats in 1975, Mimier had seen three of his rowers make the U.S. Olympic team and four other oarswomen represent the United States at World Rowing Championships. He had certainly gotten the Badger women off to a fast start in college rowing!

For many reasons, Mimier had long believed that a woman should coach the women's crew. As few male coaches had had much experience with coaching women, the early days created some awkward moments of discovery. Sometimes it was oars hitting women in the chest or wondering whether and how to train around an athlete's monthly menstrual cycle. Other times, the challenge arose from the unique calculus of factors inherent to the sport's early development—few experienced women coaches and a low pay scale, which attracted mostly young, healthy and single male rowers as coaches to a sport full of attractive and athletic young women near their ages. Such a mix often resulted in an inappropriate mix of coaching and romance. (Mimier and Ela would later marry, in 1982, and both would quickly say there was never a romantic coach-athlete relationship; they expressed strong opinions about the detrimental effects of such an association.) Experience and substantially increased future funding of women's athletics would serve to reconfigure these factors, but the pioneering days were filled with their own special coaching challenges.

13
Sue Ela—First Full-Time Women's Head Coach

I'm not looking for someone who can row in a good boat. I'm looking for someone who can row a not-so-good boat and make it good!—Attributed to Sue Ela by Shannon Daley ('94) in her letter to Ela at her spring 1998 retirement

With Jay Mimier's resignation, assistant coach Sue Ela was elevated to head coach of women's crew—for the first time a full-time position. Ela, born in Rochester, Wisconsin, on March 30, 1952, had not been an athlete in high school because there were no sports opportunities offered in her school at the time. Karen Ela, Sue's younger sister (who would join Sue as a rower at Wisconsin) enjoyed several more athletic opportunities at the same high school just three years later.

Coach Ela, who had been a member of the UW band when only men were invited into the marching band, thinks back and wonders—in the contemplation of life's choices—if she'd have been as interested in the band as in rowing at UW if she'd have been allowed to become a member of the marching band?[1]

Ela's 1989–90 co-captains would later describe her coaching style:

"As a coach, she's pretty quiet," said Kathryn Helke. "She doesn't say much, but she doesn't have to. We all know what she expects from us. She's not the kind of coach who stands by the tank [yelling] while you're rowing."

Anne Capelli continued, "Her actions speak louder than words. If she's got something to say, she says it, but she's not the type who goes screaming all the time."

Both captains chimed in unison about Ela's dedication to the team.[2]

To start the fall of 1979, Amy Luchsinger, the 1977–78 captain from Watertown, Wisconsin, was named as the novice openweight coach.

Over the summer, Badger rowers Peggy McCarthy (bow) and Carie Graves (stroke)

Sue Ela, coach 1979–98. Photo courtesy of UW Athletic Communications.

rowed for the U.S. National Team in the straight pairs and finished fifth in the 1979 Worlds in Bled, Yugoslavia.[3]

The major event at the start of the 1979–80 season was the Head of the Charles Regatta. The event had always been a budget challenge for both the men's and the women's crews. As the new head coach, the responsibility now fell directly on Ela to figure out how to manage her annual budget around the many "away" venues.

Luckily, she had other coaching friends around the country. For the Head of the Charles, she called her fellow National Team camp member Lisa Stone, the coach at Radcliffe, to ask if Wisconsin might row out of their Weld Boathouse and did she have any ideas on inexpensive housing for her crew in Boston during the regatta? Stone offered to have Wisconsin's rowers share dormitory rooms with her Radcliffe rowers!

Ela welcomed the offer, not realizing that her Radcliffe coaching connections—including future coaches Carie Graves and Liz O'Leary—would find her shelter at the Head of the Charles through 1999!

For the third consecutive year—a record no other college women's crew had accomplished before or since—the Badger varsity women again won the gold medal as the outright winner of the Head of the Charles, kicking off their 1979–80 season with another major triumph! Wisconsin finished at 17:27.0; Vesper at 17:31.2; St. Catharine's at 17:36.2, and New Haven R. C. at 17:40.2. The V8 boating: Kris Thorsness (bow), Heidi Grutzner, Jeanne Abbott, Chari Towne, Jane Ludwig, Barb Hasz, JoAnn Berninger, Kris Mesman (stroke), and Sue Alioto (cox).

On December 4, 1979, the women's crew decided it was finally important to make a special point with regard to their locker and shower arrangements with Athletic Director Elroy Hirsch. In coordination with local news outlets and media stations—many taking pictures for the evening news and the next day's papers—a group of roughly twenty-two women rowers went to the waiting room outside Hirsch's office and changed from their street clothes into their practice sweats. The move was in protest to the poor temporary locker conditions of the women as well as to the frequent but unkept promises to improve these facilities. All three local television stations featured the protest.[4]

Hirsch, who was out of town on December 4, commented several days later:

> The women were demonstrating in the wrong office. That situation has been in front of our administration for two years. We didn't have $250,000 to build a new crew house. Now we're looking at a place in Humphrey Hall to remodel. But you know how things move around here.[5]

History apparently proved, it would seem, that clothes changing, disrobing, and shower protests gets things done. Around March 15, 1980, the basement area of Humphrey Hall dormitory, near the boathouse, was converted to locker, shower, and lounge facilities for the women's rowing team. The space had formerly been the offices for the Agricultural School's short-course staff, which moved to space next to president E. B. Fred's home.

Slipping to third at the Eastern Sprints on Sunday May 11 at Lake Waramaug, the varsity rowed to this result: Penn, Radcliffe, Wisconsin, MIT, Yale, and Princeton. The 2V8 won its second consecutive gold, followed by Yale, Penn, Williams, Radcliffe, and MIT. Wisconsin's novice eight was fourth behind Princeton, Dartmouth, and Yale.

On Friday June 13, Cal visited Lake Mendota to race Wisconsin. In the varsity and 2V8 races, the June 14, 1980, *Wisconsin State Journal* described the race,

> The two races Friday were close for the first 400 meters, but Wisconsin boats began pulling ahead at the halfway mark of the 1,000-meter events. The Badger varsity led by a half-length at the 650 mark and stretched that to a length by the finish line.
>
> The Badgers (varsity) were clocked in 3 minutes, 14.34 seconds compared with California's 3:17.34.
>
> The Badger JV's swept down the course in 3:17.11, while their California counterpart rowed the distance in 3:21.80. Wisconsin's freshman boat also rowed in this race and finished third at 3:25.81.[6]

The varsity boating against Cal: Heidi Grutzner (bow), Janet Halvorson, Kay Jablonic (daughter of the men's coach), JoAnn Berninger, Chari Towne, Jeanne Abbott, Barb Hasz, Kris Thorsness (stroke), and Krista Graven (coxswain). The 2V8 boating: Gail Allen (bow), Barb Bradley, Megan Williamson, Julie Hanson, Becky Stepien, Martha Roche, Ann Schachte, Kris Mesman (stroke), and Sue Alioto (coxswain).

In 1980, after several years of college coaches talking of organizing some kind of "college only" national regatta, the NWRA agreed to host a series of college events during the two days prior their annual "open" national regatta. The first Women's National Collegiate Rowing Championship regatta (WNCRC) was held on June 18 and 19, 1980 in Oak Ridge, Tennessee. Over the following two days (June 20 and 21), the NWRA held their traditional open nationals, on the Clinch River in Oak Ridge.

1980 2V8 Eastern Sprints and NWRA winners. Courtesy of UW–Madison Archives, Image 11871-R.

The WNCRC had only nine varsity, two 2V8s, and three novice eight entries. The Badger novice eight (3:12.8), facing the Sprints-winning Princeton entry and highly touted Santa Clara, crossed the finish 1.5 seconds ahead of second place Princeton. The novice eight: Ann Boss (bow), Anne Hageman, Mary Borcherding, Alison Graves, Ellen Gandt, Theresa Gitter, Sue Dobrinski, Mary Vrabec (stroke), and Karen Smart (coxswain).

In the 1,000-meter 2V8 final, Wisconsin (3:15.2) blasted past Cal and won by five seconds. The 2V8 boating: Gail Allen (bow), Barb Bradley, Megan Williamson, Julie Hanson, Becky Stepien, Martha Roche, Ann Schachte, Kris Mesman (stroke), and Susan Alioto (coxswain).

In the tough varsity eight finals, Cal nipped Oregon State by 4/10ths of a second, with Wisconsin third. The varsity four finished third behind Cal and Washington. In the subsequent NWRA Championships—also in Oak Ridge—UW's "middleweight" (a category allowing a mix of open and lightweight rowers) four entry (3:39.30) brought home the team's only trophy from the regatta. The middleweight four boating: Gail Allen (bow), Barb Bradley, Becky Stepien, Heidi Grutzner (stroke), and Gail Ross (coxswain).

The senior eight contest of eighteen entrants saw Wisconsin's novice eight (the only novice in the company of varsity, 2V, and club crews) finish fourth, while the "senior" four (an experience-defined category between junior and elite—or those rowers with prior National Team experience) finished sixth among twenty entries. The elite eight was a seven boat final with cameras required to award Oregon State the gold by 0.18 seconds and Wisconsin the silver by 0.23 seconds over bronze-winner Cal.

For the second time, three Badger rowers—Chris Cruz, Carie Graves, and Peggy McCarthy—were selected to the 1980 Olympic squads. Sadly, they were unable to participate when the United States opted to boycott the 1980 Moscow Olympics. Graves was indicated as the 6-seat and McCarthy in the bow seat, both in the 8+. The U.S. Olympic committee honored Graves in 1981 as its Female Athlete of the Year.[7]

The 1980–81 season saw the crew's performance come to what might be considered a more normal level of results, after nearly ten years of outstanding national finishes. The varsity—defending their record of three consecutive outright wins—finished fifth at the Head of the Charles, behind winner St. Catharine's (17:58.3).

On January 13, 1981, the NCAA—seeing women's college athletics growing away from their control as the Association of Intercollegiate Athletics for Women (AIAW) landed its first cable TV contract to televise women's basketball—voted to "assimilate" many women's sports into their organization. With the vote, not only did 215 women immediately find jobs in the senior levels of the NCAA's key committees, such as the NCAA council and Executive and Infractions committees, but the organization also voted to sponsor national championships in several women's sports (but not yet rowing).

The NCAA's argument—that colleges would have a choice to be with either the AIAW or the NCAA—would turn out to be a red herring because most colleges found adding women's sports to their existing NCAA men's sports affiliation was simply too convenient. The AIAW would cease to operate by 1983.

While the Badgers won the April 25 Midwest Championships for the seventh consecutive year since becoming a varsity sport, the eight did not participate in the 1981 Eastern Sprints because of scheduling conflicts with final exams and the date set for the nationals in Oakland.

The WNCRC's were held on Lake Merritt in Oakland, California on May 20–21. Wisconsin's varsity eight (3:28.7) finished fifth, behind Washington (3:20.6), and the Badger novice eight also crossed fifth, behind winner Yale.

The coxswain's audio equipment in these days, for both men and women, was only one step above the "muzzle-like" megaphone strapped around the head. As Badger rower Sue Ela tells it, "Wisconsin's manager, Peter 'Jaccuzi' Gajenten, had rigged up a homemade amplifying device from Radio Shack equipment—for both the Wisconsin men's and women's crews—that wired a microphone in the megaphone of the coxswain to a couple of speakers along the inside of the shell gunwale. As the women's eight left the dock to practice before heats," Ela recalled, "the jerry-rigged speaker system stopped transmitting the coxswain's voice and picked up a local Sacramento radio station, broadcasting rock music throughout the boat!"

The NWRA's nationals were held in San Diego, June 15–18, where the varsity finished fifth.

> *The first U.S. women's Lightweight Rowing Camp was held July 12–August 1, 1981 in Minneapolis. The coaches were UW's Sue Ela and Rutgers's Jay Rechter. The camp was self-funded, as U.S.Rowing did not yet sponsor a lightweight camp (an official camp would be held the following summer). UW's Heidi Grutzner was a member of that summer's team, which won gold in the lightweight events at the Royal Canadian Henley.*
>
> *At the 1981 Worlds in Munich, Germany, Chris Cruz coxed the quad (a four-oared scull) to an eighth place. Carie Graves (6-seat) won a silver rowing in the eight.*

In the fall of the 1981–82 season, Wisconsin (17:04.2) finished fourth of forty-one crews at the Head of the Charles. Western Ontario (the Canadian National Team; 16:46.3), the 1980 Club (17:00.0, with former Badger Carie Graves at stroke), and Yale University finished ahead of the Badgers.

The following spring, the varsity eight finished fourth at the 1982 Eastern Sprints. UW's novice eight won their event, defeating favorite Boston University. As did the men's crew at Wisconsin, the women's crew improved over the spring as they got more water time.

Cal came to Madison for a dual meet, which, because of strong northwest winds and unrowable conditions on Lake Mendota, was switched to a 1,500-meter floating-start course on Lake Wingra. In the novice eight race, UW (5:08.26) defeated Cal's novices (5:20.43). Wisconsin put their varsity and second varsity eights in the second race ,and the order of finish was UW (5:08.79), Cal (5:19.08), and the Badgers' 2V8 (5:23.29).

In 1982, the college coaches—who made up the WNCRC—worked with the Association of Intercollegiate Athletics for Women in the organization of their annual college regatta, this time on Lake Waramaug. Since 1971 the AIAW had been an organizer of a growing number of women's athletic competitions and championships at the college level.

The national college regatta was run just after an historic storm in Connecticut, which dumped ten inches of rain, breaking state records, causing massive flooding, and limiting travel. Wisconsin's varsity lost its first heat but qualified for the finals by rowing in a delayed Sunday morning repechage (Yale and Washington went directly to the finals with a win in their first heats). Of the six boats in the repechage, only four would qualify for the finals. They were Boston University (5;15.0), Wisconsin (5:17.52), Stanford (5:17.76), and Cornell (5:20.28), with Cal and Dartmouth failing to qualify.

Sunday afternoon, the novice eight finals was the first to be rowed. The September *WRA Newsletter* described the race final:

> Wisconsin had proven its strength at the Eastern Sprints three weeks before by defeating the previously unbeaten Boston University frosh. Now the rivalry was alive again in a spirited drive by Boston University. The BU crew took a length lead and held off charges from Wisconsin to win the championship by 3.08 seconds.

The order of the novice eight finish was BU (5:05.00), Wisconsin (5:08.08), Cal (5:15), Smith (5:18.56), and Northeastern (5:27.97). The silver medal novice boating: Mandi Kowal (bow), Ann O'Connor, Teri Niemczyck, Deb Deppeler, Marge Suchy, Mindy Huitt, Kris Peterson, Kathy Place (stroke), and Mary Ackerman (coxswain).

In the second varsity eight event, Washington (5:08.7) defeated BU (5:14.76), Wisconsin (5:15.69), and Cornell (5:29.38). The bronze medal boating: Janet Bogdanow (bow), Mary Vrabec, Becky Stepien, Marcia Hageman, Nancy Froncek, Heidi Grutzner, Susan Offerdahl, Kim Woods (stroke), and Carla Landry (coxswain).

In the varsity final, the rough water necessitated splashguards, since the rain was already dropping a lot of water into the boat. The *WRA Newsletter* also described the 1,500-meter varsity race,

> After a Wisconsin false start, the second try saw a tight field of six off the line together. Washington took a slight lead before the 500, with Cornell dropping

back, the rest of the field tight. Wisconsin started at a 46 strokes per minute rating, dropping back to 39–40 for the rest of the race.

At 1,000 meters, it was Washington (leading) with Wisconsin, BU, and Yale making their moves. Stanford and Cornell were back. The last 500 meters was rowed very strongly by the Wisconsin women rowing in their new shell *Tenacious*. It was a chase for Washington, and a strong last 500, coupled with a fine sprint, left the Wisconsin crew soundly in possession of 2nd place.

The varsity order of finish: Washington (4:56.4), Wisconsin (4:59.83), BU (5:02.31), Yale (5:03.97), Stanford (5:05.41), and Cornell (5:20.31). Wisconsin's silver medal boating: Rose Morreale (bow), Alison Graves, Jenny Heinen, Chari Towne, Kris Thorsness, Susan Tietjen, Rachael Rodetsky, Mara Keggi (stroke), and Kim Santiago (coxswain).

The NWRA open nationals were held June 17–20, 1982, also on Lake Waramaug. Wisconsin remained on the East Coast—through the Yale crew's generous hospitality and that of the Keggi family—and practiced out of Yale's boathouse twice a day on the Housatonic River in Derby, Connecticut.

On the regatta's first day, Wisconsin again failed to qualify in their first heat and had to squeak through the repechage, where the photo finish took fifteen minutes to confirm. Wisconsin was the fourth of four to make the finals, with Yale and Vesper missing the cut.

In the finals on Sunday, Badger rower Alison Graves faced her sister, former Badger Carie Graves, now rowing for the Boston R. C., in the adjacent lane. In yet another photo finish, the national development camp boats placed first and third. The order of finish: College Boating Club (3:06.2), Washington/Lake Washington A (3:06.5), 1980 Club/Boston Rowing Club (3:06.94), Wisconsin (3:09.96), Pine Valley Rowing Association (3:10.0), and Washington/Lake Washington B (3:15.3).

Badger oarswoman Kris ("Thor") Thorsness, rowing 3-seat in the U.S. eight at the 1982 Worlds in Lucerne, Switzerland, won a silver medal. Russia won the gold.

Some time around the start of the 1982–83 season, UW rigger Jim Roper built the "shanty" office for the coaches of women's crew at the Babcock Street crew house, adjacent to the men's crew coaches office in the rowing tank room. The coaches office in the basement of Humphrey Hall had no windows and thus put the women's coaching staff at multiple disadvantages—unable to check the weather, to remain close to the athletes, nor to watch out for the safety of their athletes.

Beyond that, with the offices located right in the locker room, the coaches could seldom receive parents or reporters interested in the program. The new office—although without a ceiling and squeezed between the rowing tank and the men's crew office—addressed all of these challenges.

All across the country, coaches of women's crew had for some time been in more or less constant discussion on the subject of the current 1,000-meter course length being used for women's rowing and whether this was perhaps too short. While the Olympic distances for the women's events were still 1,000-meters, most collegiate courses were designed for the 2,000-meter lengths needed for the men's races. As a result, women's races at the same venues were often required to begin from the middle of the course and incorporate floating starts. As the debate continued, experiments tested the potential for lengthening the women's events.[8]

At the start of the 1982–83 season, UW finished fifth at the October 23 Head of the Charles Regatta on the Charles River between Boston and Cambridge, Massachusetts.

At the semester break, Coach Ela sought to take her athletes south to warmer weather and warmer water. Wisconsin historically waited three to five weeks longer than most other colleges for its local lakes to thaw. Since the early 1950s, the men's crew had often gone south during their semester breaks in January for the express purpose of getting water time to compensate for Wisconsin's long winters.

Ela remembers being frustrated at the constant chore of money raising. When she approached the Wisconsin Rowing Association, which had been "leaned upon" for some time to support the men's trips south, she was advised they did not have enough money to send both crews. As a young program, the women's crews did not yet have an older alumni base from which to seek economic support, so the women were forced to forgo a semester break training trip.

A regional regatta with eight schools attending, unofficially dubbed the Big Ten Championships, was organized on Madison's Lake Wingra on May 1—to be held the day following the Midwest Championships—but wound up being cancelled due to bad weather.

At the Eastern Sprints on Lake Waramaug May 15, Wisconsin's raced to a photo finish in its qualifying heat, but the video camera was down! Relegated in the controversy to the petite finals, UW won the event, finishing seventh overall. In the 2V8 Sprints event, Yale (5:04.5) prevailed over second-place Wisconsin (5:08.5). In the novice race, Princeton (5:09.9) also outraced second-place Wisco (5:13.3).

When the AIAW's sponsorship of national college championships for most college sports for women (but not rowing) was largely taken over by the NCAA—and the AIAW was in the process of disappearing—the college coaches for women's rowing awarded their annual regatta to UW. The Women's Collegiate Nationals were held June 2 and 3, 1983 in Madison on Lake Wingra's 1,500-meter course.

In the novice eight contest, Wisconsin faced the two boats that had beaten them earlier in the year, Princeton (at the Sprints) and Minnesota. The Badgers had beaten Minnesota at the Midwest Championships and then lost to them the following weekend in a dual meet in Minnesota. Another foe to watch was Yale, which UW had just beaten at the Sprints. The August 1983 *WRA Newsletter* described this most exciting race of the day:

> Princeton got off to a lead in the first five strokes as Minnesota started slowly and the rest of the field was very even among those crews. Wisconsin battled with Yale and Cornell staying dead even, for the most part, to the 500-meter mark. At that point, first place Princeton led fifth place Minnesota by a length with Wisconsin, Yale and Cornell fighting between them.
>
> And that was to be the largest difference between first and fifth through the whole race! Wisconsin edged past Cornell, while Yale fell behind Cornell by a seat. At the 1,000-meter mark, Princeton led by ⅓ length over Wisconsin. The Badgers had four seats on Cornell, with Yale and Minnesota trailing but both within a length of Princeton.
>
> Each crew [novice] took its sprint at a different time. As they did, each crew appeared to move briefly on the rest of the field. But the places didn't change, only the margins. Wisconsin raced to a close and gutsy second place, within a second of Princeton, and just barely a second ahead of Cornell on the 1,500-meter Lake Wingra course. (Cornell, Yale, and Minnesota followed.)

The 2V8 race was sparsely entered with Western Sprints champ Washington, "Dad" Vail Regatta champ Georgetown, and Wisconsin as the only participants. At the finish, Washington won by a half-length of open water, with Wisconsin second, and Georgetown never really a factor in third. Against a field of varsity rowers choosing to row in the fours at the Nationals, Wisconsin's boat—all four of whom had just raced in the 2V8 race—finished sixth.

The rainy varsity eight race was loaded with talent. The two fastest crews at the Eastern Sprints—Boston University and Dartmouth—were there, along with the two fastest at the Western Championships—Washington and Stanford—along with the Midwest champ Wisconsin. Cornell, which had been fifth at the Sprints, filled out the field.

Washington (4:57.5) won decisively, with Dartmouth and Wisconsin in a battle for second. By a 2/10 of a second margin, Dartmouth (5:03.2) nosed out the Badgers (5:03.4), who took home a bronze.[9] Stanford, BU, and Cornell followed.

The Badgers were looking to do better when the NWRA's open regional regatta was also held on their home course of Lake Wingra on June 4 and 5. An "albano buoy system" (a series of plastic cylinders bordering each lane and designed to muffle any wake between lanes) was constructed for the race course, the same system used at the collegiate nationals on Wingra.[10] In the varsity finals, Wisconsin's eight finished third and was awarded a bronze, behind winner Boston University.

The 1983 NWRA's[11] open nationals were held in Oak Ridge from June 14 to 17, where the Badgers finished third.

The NCAA had begun sanctioning (or regulating) a large number of collegiate women's sports, but not women's college rowing, and sponsoring national championship competition in several sports.

Over the summer of 1983, Badger oarswoman Mandi Kowal from Hayward, Wisconsin, was named to her first of five U.S. National Teams, this year in the lightweight category. The U.S. women's team won the exhibition events in the open lightweight and senior lightweight eight events at the Canadian Henley, even though it was not yet an officially sanctioned World's event. Kowal was in the bow in each case.

Kris Thorsness (bow seat) and Carie Graves (4-seat) were also selected, rowing to a silver (behind Russia) in the U.S. eight, at the 1983 Worlds competition held in Duisburg, Germany.

At the start of the 1983–84 season, Jane Ludwig, a high school soccer player from Pius XI High School in Brookfield, Wisconsin, replaced Amy Luchsinger as the novice coach. Luchsinger, after four successful years as UW's assistant coach, left to take the position of overall supervisor of the University of Michigan Rowing Club, which had been founded in 1976.

The Badgers started off their season with a third at the Head of the Charles, ahead of all other college crews and behind only the South Niagara R. C. (rumored to be Canada's elite women's eight) and the Boston R. C. (a women's National Team training group in Boston). The UW varsity boating: Mandi Kowal (bow), Carol Feeney, Katie Drissel, Kathy Place, Carolyn Potter, Susan Tietjen, Janet Bogdanow, Mara Keggi (stroke), and Kim Santiago (coxswain).

Over semester break, the women's crew, for the first time, left the frozen lakes of Madison and traveled south to Oak Ridge for practice on open water. On a shoestring budget, the team drove in two vans carrying two sectioned eight-oared shells. Captain Grutzner remembers stopping at a tollbooth when a truck ran into one of their boats, causing Ela to have a "stern" conversation with the errant truck driver.[12]

Not enough money was raised to take the novices to winter training that first year. Meals were just twice a day, with breakfast/brunch cooked at their Camp Tiyani Girl Scout lodging site. Forty women slept in cots at the camp. With the launch area a mile away, the athletes walked to and from their practices each day.

In the early '90s, Coach Ela's launch became a target for secret overnight paint-

232   FIRST FULL-TIME WOMEN'S HEAD COACH

1984 V8 Eastern Sprints winners. The boating (at the Sprints and the National Collegiate Regatta in Seattle): Mandi Kowal (bow), Kathy Place, Katy Drissel, Carol Feeney, Sarah Gengler, Susan Tietjen, Carolyn Potter, Mara Keggi (stroke), and Kim Santiago (coxswain). Photo provided by Sue Ela.

ings. One night, the crew clandestinely christened the *Honey Bun Mobile* (the name came from a waitress at a restaurant with the moniker "Quincy's—Home of the Big Fat Yeast Roll"). Future launches enjoyed many other incarnations.

The extra practice on the water became clearly apparent later in the spring, strengthening the crew for the coming season.

That spring, UW attended the San Diego Classic to compete for the Whittier Cup for the first time.[13] The Badgers (3:27.3) came away with a silver, with Washington (3:24.6) winning the gold. Behind these two came Yale (3:30.7), Cal (3:31.9), Stanford (3:33.3), and Oregon State (3:33.7).

At the 1984 Eastern Sprints, the varsity took a first, ending a seven-year gold drought at this event. The 2V8 finished fourth at the Eastern Sprints, and the novice eight was sixth.

The Sprints experience was memorable to many for the close airplane connection at LaGuardia Airport in New York. As the novice eight finished their race, they quickly loaded their boat, jumped into the van, and drove for New York. The 2V8 followed in the same manner. It was only when the varsity rushed onto the plane—and Badger manager Lynn Liberman (Class of '84) literally saw the door close behind her—that the twenty-three rowers who'd arrived ahead of the varsity eight learned the varsity had just won the final Sprints race! When several other Wisconsin travelers learned of the team's presence on the plane and the success of the varsity, they broke into song.[14]

In Seattle, at the 1984 WNCRC on June 2 and 3, the course length was set at 1,000-meters because the course lake was only that long. The Wisconsin varsity, leading at the 500-meter mark in a Schoenbrod, finished third to Washington (in an Empacher) and Radcliffe (in a Vespoli). Washington was 1.6 seconds ahead of Radcliffe, which was 1.9 ahead of Wisco, which, in turn, was 1.8 seconds ahead of Dartmouth.

Feeling as if the boat had let down her crew in the final 500, Coach Ela approached the Women's Intercollegiate Sports Club and asked for help.[15] With the Sports Club's approximately $8,500 contribution, Ela was able to purchase a new honeycombed Vespoli shell for $3,000 below list price, which price was part of the company's campaign to enlarge its customer base into the Midwest.

The 2V8 final, which under a new rule allowed schools not entered in the varsity event to substitute up to two varsity rowers in their 2V8 entry, both Princeton and Yale took such opportunity. The order of finish: Washington, Yale, Princeton, and Wisconsin. The 2V8 boating (at the Sprints and the national collegiate regatta in Seattle; one name missing): Janet Bogdanow (bow), Kathy Haberman, Marge Yankowski, Susan Bukolt, Suzanne Montesi, Susan Offerdahl, (7-seat), Carol Lewnau (stroke), and Amy Krohn (coxswain).

In the novice race, Cal won the gold, with Wisconsin sixth. The novice boating (at the Sprints and the national collegiate regatta in Seattle): Signe Hartmann (bow), Sue Fondrie (Lynn Ewig in the Sprints), Lisa Fahien, Sally Zentner, Gretchen Ahrnsbrak, Cindy Eckert, Elizabeth Olesch, Carol Chipman (stroke), and Stephanie McMahan (coxswain).

At the June 15–17 NWRA national open championships of 1984 in Oak Ridge, Tennessee, the Badgers won the Senior 8 event. Novice Sally Zentner and Cindy Eckert filled in for varsity rowers Kathy Place and Carol Feeney, and the 2V8 coxswain Amy Krohn steered the Senior eight entry.

In the Elite 8 (most competitive) event, Wisconsin ended in a photo finish for second. In the Senior 4+ event, the Badger entry finished with a bronze. The 4+ boating: Signe Hartmann (bow), Sue Fondrie, Kirsten Larson, Marge Yankowski (stroke), and novice coxswain Stephanie McMahan.

At the Montreal World's, where the non-Olympic rowing events were held, lightweight rowing was again offered an exhibition event in the lead-up to the sport's being added to the FISA World Championship format. Badger Mandi Kowal (5-seat) won the gold in the LW8 event.

At the 1984 Olympic Games in Los Angeles, Wisconsin rowers Carie Graves (4-seat), from Spring Green, Wisconsin, and Kris Thorsness (7-seat), from Anchorage, Alaska, won gold medals in the eight-oared event. Badger Chari Towne, from Wild Rose, Wisconsin, finished fifth rowing stroke seat in the straight pairs.[16]

Carie Graves, one of only two female three-time Olympians at UW (Suzy Favor Hamilton in track and field is the other), was among the first inductees (along with

UW Associate Athletic Director Kit Saunders-Nordeen) into the UW Women's Athletic Hall of Fame in 1984. When the UW Athletic Department as a whole initiated its own Hall of Fame in 1991, Graves was part of the initial inductee group and Saunders-Nordeen was inducted in 1998. The U.S. Olympic committee honored Graves a second time in 1984 as its Female Athlete of the Year.

At the start of the 1984–85 season, Wisconsin finished with a third at the Head of the Charles; the winning eight was South Niagara R. C. (18:36.0).

As the winner of the Midwest Championship, UW received a stipend to support their travel expenses in attending the San Diego Classic. The varsity registered another third at the San Diego Classic in early spring. The finish: Victoria (4:37.4), Washington (4:40.6), Wisconsin (4:44.7), Cal (4:52.3), Stanford (4:55.1), and UCLA (5:03.0). In spite of the sponsor stipend, UW's budget did not provide enough funding for Wisconsin's 2V8 and novice crews to participate.

The varsity and novice eights each had good days at the Eastern Sprints, with the varsity—just a seat behind Princeton—winning silver and the novice eight winning gold! The varsity boating: Mandi Kowal (bow), Cindy Eckert, Marge Yankowski, Kathy Haberman, Katy Drissel, Carol Feeney, Sara Gengler, Kathy Place (stroke), and Kim Santiago (coxswain).

In the WNCRC in Occoquan, Virginia, the 2,000-meter course was shortened to 1,500-meters, because flooding caused officials to be concerned about racing too close to an overburdened dam at the end of the course. The varsity finished second, and Minnesota was third to the winning Washington Huskies—the first instance anyone could remember when the eastern crews had been shut out of any medals. Wisconsin's novice eight (5:39.2), also on a 1,500-meter course, came through again, winning their second major gold medal of the season.

For the 1985 Worlds in Hazewinkle, Belgium, UW oarswomen Cindy Eckert, Sarah Gengler, and Mara Keggi were selected to represent the U.S. National Team. Gengler (4-seat) and Keggi (6-seat) finished fourth in the 8+. Lightweight women's events were formally added to the format of the world rowing championships in this year, following a final year of exhibitions the summer earlier in Montreal.

In the 1985–86 UW Women's Intercollegiate Athletics media guide, six of seven Badger Olympians mentioned were rowers.

In 1985–86, though the varsity began the season finishing "only" third at the Head of the Charles, the eight would go undefeated through the spring all the way through the Nationals in mid-June!

Jane Ludwig joined Sue Ela on March 1 to assist in coaching the women's openweight crew—anticipating Ela's maternity absence in late spring[17]—and led the varsity to an undefeated balance of the season.

The initial victory in the spring was also the Wisconsin's women's first win at

1985 novice 8 Eastern Sprints and WNCRC winners. The Badger frosh 8's partial boating: Sandra Mintz, Laura Graf, Annalise Melby, Mary Beth Blanding (stroke), and Yasmin Farooq (coxswain). Photo provided by Sue Ela.

the San Diego Classic. The race distance for women was now, in most cases, standardized at 2,000-meters. The finish: Wisconsin (6:28.5), Washington (6:35.4), Stanford (6:38.4), New Hampshire (6:42.3), British Columbia (6:43.0), and Minnesota (6:56.4). The boating: Kathy Haberman (bow), Laura Graf, Mary Beth Blanding, Katy Drissel, Carol Feeney, Carolyn Potter, Cindy Eckert, Sarah Gengler (stroke), and Yasmin Farooq (coxswain). UW's second varsity did not attend. At the 1986 Eastern Sprints, the Badger eight won their third Sprints title.

In the spring of 1986, the WNCRC championships, which remained an open regatta, was awarded to an organizing group—the Cincinnati Regatta—in Cincinnati, Ohio. The races were held on Harsha Lake near Cincinnati, and both the top men's and women's crews had been invited to settle their respective national championships.

In the men's case, this would be the first time in the season that all the top men's crews would ever get together, since Cal, the Pac-10 winner, had not attended the IRAs and neither, as was usual, had Harvard nor Yale. The course, designed by Bill Engemann, was the same for both the men and the women—2,000 meters in length.

Both the Badger women's varsity (6:53.28)—defeating Radcliffe in a photo finish—and the second varsity (7:04.4) won national titles and gold medals in their separate events. As if there wasn't enough to celebrate, the Badger men's eight also won their national title event at the same regatta for a complete Badger sweep!

A total of seven women rowers from Wisconsin were named to the U.S. National Team over the summer of 1986! Badgers, representing the United States at the 1986 Worlds in Nottingham, England, included still college-eligible athletes Cindy Eck-

Left: 1986 V8 Eastern Sprints and WNCRC winner. Rowing in a Vespoli christened the *Ne Pret* ("Born Ready"), the women's WNCRC varsity boating (right to left): Kathy Haberman (bow), Laura Graf, Mary Beth Blanding, Katy Drissel, Carol Feeney, Carolyn Potter, Cindy Eckert, Sarah Gengler (stroke), and Amy Krohn (coxswain). Photo courtesy of UW Athletic Communications.

Below: 1986 2V8 WNCRC winner. The boating: Rita Haberman (bow), Elizabeth Olesch, Lisa Fahien, Ann Maloney, Sandra Mintz, Marge Yankowski, Suzanne Montesi, Signe Hartman (stroke), and Yasmin Farooq (coxswain). Photographer unknown.

ert (bow seat in the eight, which placed fourth), and graduates Carol Feeney (4-seat in the 8), Sarah Gengler (7-seat in the 8), and Mara Keggi (4-seat in the 4+, which placed sixth), Mandi Kowal (3-seat in the LW4, which won the gold medal), Kris Thorsness (3-seat in the 8), and coxswain Kim Santiago (cox in the 4+).

In the 1986–87 season, Amy Luchsinger returned as novice coach, replacing Jane Ludwig, who had been hired by Smith College as their head coach. The UW rowing season started fast—with a second place finish at the Head of the Charles in the fall.

Anticipating another show of support and generosity from the UW Alumni Club of San Diego area, both crews (the men finished fourth) traveled to the San Diego Classic. The Wisconsin–Madison UW alumni in San Diego not only helped the crews by sponsoring one or more meals for the coaches and student-athletes,

FIRST FULL-TIME WOMEN'S HEAD COACH   237

but also sponsored three members of the UW band to travel to the regatta and bring the sound of Wisconsin rallying music to the shores of the race course. Many other university bands soon followed.

On April 4, the varsity openweight eight (5:45.95), on the 2,000-meter Mission Bay course, finished second to Washington (5:44.6), followed by Stanford (5:57.64), UCLA (5:58.03), Cal (6:01.2), and Minnesota (6:14.28).

On April 18–19, the women returned to Redwood Shores, California, a wonderful semiprotected racecourse off San Francisco Bay just south of the San Francisco International Airport. In the four-way contest with Cal, Radcliffe, and Princeton, Wisconsin raced in three dual meets, winning two and losing one. In the first contest, Wisconsin led most of the way until Radcliffe pulled ahead with less than 250 meters to go, rowing into a 30–35 mph headwind. Times at the finish were Radcliffe (7:05.22) and Wisconsin (7:07.22).

In the later Redwood Shores races, Wisconsin beat Cal (7:25 vs. 7:40) and Princeton (7:02.0 vs. 7:07.5) to end up tied with Radcliffe for second in the overall standings. Washington won all of their contests. In two 2V8 contests, Wisconsin defeated Cal and, later, Stanford.

On May 17 at the 1987 Eastern Sprints on Lake Waramaug in Connecticut, the women's varsity eight (6:45.39) was third behind gold medal winner Radcliffe (6:41.02) and silver medalist Yale (6:43.39). The frosh finished sixth behind Yale.

In the spring of 1987, in order to encourage the sport in various regions of the country, the WNCRC awarded its national regatta to Sacramento. The races were held on May 30. The Badgers failed to successfully defend their title. The finish, on a 2,000-meter course, was Washington (6:33.8), Yale (6:37.4), Radcliffe (6:40.2), and Wisconsin (6:40.6). Interestingly, the second varsity eight contest finished in the same order. The 2V8 boating: Emily Catlett (bow), Rachelle Bailey, Liza Behrendt, Ann Maloney, Lisa Fahien, Sandie Mintz, Rita Haberman, Sallie Stetzer (stroke), and Marguerite Burns (coxswain).

In the novice eight event, Yale (6:43.0) defeated Wisconsin (6:44.2) in a close one-two finish; Washington (6:56.3) and Cal (7:06.2) finished a distant third and fourth. The novice eight boating: Andrea Noeske (bow), Kathy Horn, Chris Berger, Gwen Weisbrod, Emily Dolan, Sylvia Hiller, Katherine Helke, Maura Clark (stroke), and Rachel Krook (coxswain).

At the June 13 Cincinnati Regatta at East Fork State Park in Bantam, Ohio, UW regained the taste of victory defeating a British national team entry by a boat length, with Minnesota fifteen seconds back in third place. The Badgers took home the Currie Invitational Cup. The boating: Margaret Calvert (bow), Laura Graf, Mary Beth Blanding, Katherine Helke, Sarah Jahnke, Kirsten Larson, Signe Hartmann, Cindy Eckert (stroke), and Yasmin Farooq (coxswain).

The NWRA (which merged into USRowing in 1986) saw its national regatta renamed the USRowing Regatta in 1987. The June 27–28 open national races were held in Indianapolis, Indiana, also the new home of USRowing (the NAAO's headquarters, a predecessor organization that merged into USRowing in 1986, had previously been headquartered in Philadelphia). Wisconsin, sending only a four (the rest lost to graduation) finished just out of the medals in fourth place. The boating: Sarah Jahnke (bow), Mary Beth Blanding, Signe Hartmann, Cindy Eckert (stroke), and Yasmin Farooq (coxswain).

Mandi Kowal (stroke), for the second consecutive year, won a gold medal in the lightweight straight four as one of the U.S. entries at the 1987 World Rowing Championships in Copenhagen, Denmark. For her successes, Kowal was named USRowing's Female Athlete of the Year in 1987[18] *and Sportswoman of the Year.*[19]

The 1987–88 season began with a change of novice coaches, with Mandi Kowal replacing Amy Luchsinger.

The openweight crew (16:59.51) again showed a fast start in the fall, with the top college finish at the Head of the Charles. Boston R. C. (16:18.30) and Lake Washington R. C. (16:42.28) finished ahead of Wisconsin.

Over the spring break, March 12–20, the women trained on open water again in Oak Ridge. The Badger varsity (6:48.48) won the Tom White Invitational Regatta during this period.

At the early spring's San Diego Classic on April 2, Wisconsin (7:09.50) again won silver and again behind Washington (7:02.38). After UW were Cal (7:14.1), Stanford (7:23.7), New Hampshire (7:29.4), and Minnesota (7:51.3).

At the April 16 and 17 Stanford Invitational's round of three dual races at Redwood Shores, California, Wisconsin (7:18.5) won their first contest against UCLA (7:20.5) and lost the next two to Brown (7:03.49 vs. 7:11.02) and to Yale (7:07.22 vs. 7:14.13). The Badger 2V8 defeated Cal in their first race and Brown in their second race, then lost to Yale.

At the April 31 Midwest Championship, Wisconsin's varsity again won the eight-oared contest. The varsity boating: Kathy Helke (bow), Mary Beth Blanding, Michelle Falivena, Sandra Minz, Sarah Janke, Maura Clarke, Katherine Yankula, Sallie Stetzer (stroke), and Yasmin Farooq (coxswain).

In the May 8 Eastern Sprints of 1988, the Badgers slipped to sixth place, but at the June 4 and 5 Women's National Collegiate Rowing Championships on a 2,000-meter course in Tioga, Pennsylvania, Wisconsin (6:52.97) finished sixth, behind winner Washington (6:41). The 2V8 finished sixth in the finals, and the frosh eight ended in fifth in the Petite Finals (eleventh overall).

Because the regatta was not particularly well organized, the WNCRC college coaches decided it best to award the regatta to one location for a two-year cycle. Their choice for the next two years was Madison.

Five Wisconsin oarswomen were named to the 1988 Seoul Olympics! The five Badgers were Cindy Eckert (Brookfield, Wisconsin), Sarah Gengler (Milwaukee), Mara Keggi (Middlebury, Connecticut), Kim Santiago (Monroe, Wisconsin), and Kris Thorsness (Anchorage).[20] Eckert (3-seat), Gengler (4-seat), and Santiago (coxswain)—all three in the coxed four—finished fifth. Mara Keggi, rowing 2-seat in the straight pair, finished sixth.

At the Worlds in Milan, Mandi Kowal, bow seat in the U.S. straight four, finished fourth.

At the start of the 1988–89 season, the Badger women (17:61) rowed to their fourth outright victory of the Head of the Charles in Boston, defeating the 1980 Club and Boston R. C.

Spring training was March 17–25 in Oak Ridge. In early April at the San Diego Classic, the eight (6:58.89) won a silver behind Washington (6:57.9). A close third was Cal (6:59.0), followed by Yale (7:00.5), UCLA (7:06.5), and Stanford (7:07.5). Two weeks later, at the Redwood Shores Invitational on April 16, UW finished fourth behind winner Radcliffe (6:39) and runner-up Stanford (6:37). For the varsity eight, the Eastern Sprints was less successful, where they finished sixth.

The WNCRC was held on Lake Wingra's 1,750-meter course in Madison. The organizational effort for hosting a regatta of this size and prominence was huge, and it kept Coach Ela and many others very busy! Ela drew on the regular organizers of the annual Midwest championships, and a new entity was formed for this specific two-year national collegiate championship effort, the Madison Championship Rowing Association, which included Bruce Wencel, Roger and Judy Rowell, Laurie Irwin, Sheila Parker, and many others.

The UW Athletic Department provided unusual support for a Madison rowing event, led by Tam Flarup and Marianne Runde, who not only helped organize the regatta but also developed the regatta program and the related artwork, including that on the program cover, fund-raiser posters, and specially designed medals. Former UW rowers also pitched in with assistance, including Jay Mimier, Kim Santiago, and Hal Menendez.

The varsity (5:37.5) won another silver medal. Cornell (5:34.9) won the championship and Stanford (5:38) was third with Washington (5:42.9) fourth. UW's boating: Laura Macaulay (bow), Tiffany Esher, Emily Dolan, Emily Canova, Carie Dunai, Gwen Weisbrod, Katherine Helke, Linda Baehmann (stroke), and Vivian Yuan (coxswain). Wisconsin's 2V8 won bronze behind Washington and Cornell.

In 1989, UW head women's crew coach Sue Ela was named USRowing's Woman of the Year, an honor given to "the woman who has made the greatest contribution to the advancement of women's rowing in the past year." Ela served as Director of the Women's National Collegiate Rowing Championship, which held its annual regatta in Madison in 1989 and would do so again in June 1990.

In the 1989–90 season, pressure from other colleges adding large numbers of women's crew program, including scholarships, began to have the natural effect—competition became even more fierce!

At the Head of the Charles in Boston, Wisconsin—which had placed first, second, or third in twelve of the last fifteen regattas, and fifth three times—slipped a bit farther this time to finish sixth.

Spring break training was held again in Tennessee from March 17 to 24. A fifth place finish followed at the April 7, 1990, San Diego Classic, when the Badgers (7:26.9) came in behind UCLA (7:19.1), Cal (7:19.5), Stanford (7:19.6), and Washington (7:24.8). The UW boating: Laura Macaulay (bow), Melissa Iverson, Emily Stoddard, Emily Canova, Tiffany Escher, Gwen Weisbrod, Katherine Helke, Linda Baehmann (stroke), and Vivian Yuan (coxswain).

At the May 18 Eastern Sprints in New Preston, Connecticut, the Badgers ended in seventh. The order of finish in the finals: Princeton, Cornell, Brown, Radcliffe, Boston University, and Northeastern. The varsity boating: Katherine Helke (bow), Gwen Weisbrod, Emily Stoddard, Maura Clarke, Carey Dunai, Linda Baehmann, Tiffany Escher, Melissa Iverson (stroke), and Erin Teare (coxswain).

The 2V8 (6:26.7) was sixth at the Sprints, behind Brown, Yale, Cornell, Radcliffe, and Princeton. The 2V8 boating: Jen Agger (bow), Amy Scott, Susan Basquin, Jodie Grabarski, Micaela Mejia, Emily Canova, Laura Macaulay, Susannah Galdston (stroke), and Vivian Yuan (coxswain). The varsity four with coxswain placed sixth.

The novice eight, seeded tenth of the eighteen entries, drew three-seed Radcliffe and four-seed Princeton in their qualifying heat. Rowing bow-ball to bow-ball with Radcliffe and Princeton, the Badgers bumped Princeton out the finals by nipping them for second in their qualifying heat. In the finals, the novice eight finished fifth, beating Rutgers, but behind Brown, Radcliffe, Cornell, and Yale. The freshmen boating: Catherine Ponti (bow), Laura Zirngible, Amy Nelson, Maureen ("Mo") O'Connor, Kristen Engen, Linnea Anderson, Sarah Mohs, Suzy Henry (stroke), and Wen Huang (coxswain).

The novice four (7:47.8) had the best Wisconsin finish of the 1990 Sprints by grabbing second in their final behind Princeton (7:42.1). UW's frosh four boating: Linda Specht (bow), Cathy Ponti, Andrea Mitchell, Traci Oleszack (stroke), and Chantel Smith (coxswain).

On June 2 and 3 in 1990, UW hosted their second consecutive collegiate championships (WNCRC) on Lake Wingra on a weed-shortened 1,500-meter course.

Many of the same volunteers threw in their support, plus new stalwarts, like Mary Nickel, joining the second year.

Unfortunately, the Wisconsin weather, beautiful on Friday, turned quickly nasty on Saturday and all races were postponed a day. The varsity race was finally held late Sunday afternoon as darkness arrived on the course. The varsity eight finish for second through fourth places was so close that a camera was needed to determine the places. Ela remembers the camera photo was brighter than actually watching the finish in person because the afternoon had become so dark.

The women's varsity eight results: undefeated Princeton (5:52.2) was first, followed by Radcliffe (5:54.2), Cornell (5:54.3), UCLA (5:54.7), Wisconsin (5:58.5), and Syracuse (6:02.7). In the 2V8 event, Wisconsin (6:11.4) took home the bronze behind Cornell (6:06.8) and UCLA (6:09.8). UW's V4 finished fifth behind winner UC–Santa Barbara.

In the novice events, UW's eight won the bronze behind Cornell and Radcliffe, and the fours were fourth when Northeastern, Radcliffe, and Pacific-Lutheran preceded them, in that order.

Kit Saunders-Nordeen retired June 30, 1990, after a twenty-six-year career at UW–Madison, including sixteen years with the Athletic Department. In 1974, Saunders-Nordeen had been named the first director of the UW Women's Athletic Department. In 1983, she was named Associate Athletic Director, taking over responsibility for the twenty-two men's and women's nonrevenue sports.

Former UW oarswoman Carol Feeney rowed 2-seat in the straight four, which finished fifth, and 2-seat in the eight in the 1990 Goodwill Games in Seattle. The eight, coxed by fellow Badger Yasmin Farooq, finished sixth.

Badger rowers Cindy Eckert (5-seat), Sarah Gengler (4-seat), and Yasmin Farooq (coxswain) in the eight finished second in the 1990 Worlds on Lake Barrington in Tasmania, Australia, behind Romania and ahead of East Germany. Eckert (2-seat) and Gengler (3-seat) also rowed to fifth in the straight four.

During the summer, after many years of depressed football revenues, five sports were cut from the UW sports program and crew budgets—both the women's and the men's—were capped for several years (the women's for six years until 1996–97 and the men's for eleven years until 2001–2).

To begin the 1990–91 season, Wisconsin come in seventh at the Head of the Charles race on October 21, a good finish considering three of the highest finishers were national crews or older rowers. The three fastest college crews finishing ahead of the Badgers were Boston University, Radcliffe, and Princeton. The coxed varsity four placed third and was the top college finisher in its event.

At the San Diego Classic, the varsity (7:03.1), competing for the Whittier Cup, rowed to a ninth behind one-two-three Boston University (6:47.0), UCLA (6:51.9), and Cal (6:58.4).[21]

On April 20, the women attended the Henley-on-the-Potomac Regatta in Washington D. C. The varsity eight (6:15.78) won a silver in the 2,000-meter final behind UCLA (6:12.48). The V8 boating: Laura McCaulay (bow), Kathy Ponti, Linnea Anderson, Amy Nelson, Emily Stoddard, Emily Canova, Maureen O'Connor, Melissa Iverson (stroke), and Becky Rosenberg (coxswain.)

At the 1991 Eastern Sprints, Wisconsin's varsity finished second in the Petite finals, while the V4+ won the silver behind Brown and ahead of Princeton, Radcliffe, Brown B, and Penn. Both the 2V8 and the frosh eight finished fifth. The V4+ boating: Kris Waschbusch (bow), Lynn Borek, Sue West, Andrea Mitchell (stroke), and Chantel Smith (coxswain).

Missing one of their top rowers, Emily Canova (replaced by Maureen O'Connor), the Badger eight finished eighth at the collegiate championships (WNCRC) in Cincinnati. The course for this annual championship was now fixed at 2,000 meters.

The 2V8 finished third with the boating: Jennifer Agger (bow), Jennifer Fenton, Melissa Plummer, Lori Kober, Sarah Mohs, Susie Henry, Kris Waschbusch, Micaela Mejia (stroke), and Erin Teare (coxswain).

The coxed open four entry from UW won the silver, with the boating: Pam Mork (bow), Mia Hospel, Sue West, Andrea Mitchell (stroke), and Chantel Smith (coxswain). For the first time ever, there was no freshman event at the college nationals.

Over the summer of 1991, four women from Wisconsin were named to the U.S. National Team racing at the Worlds in Vienna, Austria—including Cindy Eckert (4-seat in the straight four placing second), Carol Feeney (bow seat in the eight placing fourth), Sarah Gengler (4-seat in the eight), and Kim Santiago.

In the 1991–92 season, the Badgers slid to fifteenth at the Head of the Charles on October 20—their worst lowest finish ever by eight places. The boating: Maureen O'Connor (bow), Kris Waschbusch, Emily Stoddard, Amy Nelson, Linnea Anderson, Melissa Anderson, Kari Kartman, Cathy Ponti (stroke), and Wen Huang (coxswain).

At the San Diego Classic on April 4–5, the varsity eight (6:57.2) placed sixth to winner Washington (6:43.7). The 2V8 (7:08.7) was fifth to, again, winner Washington (6:51.1). The 2V8 boating: Mia Hospel (bow), Karen Mullen, Melissa Plummer, Sarah Mohs, Susie Henry, Pam Mork, Kim Zinniel, Kris Waschbusch (stroke), and Deanna Leslie (coxswain).

At the spring's Eastern Sprints on May 10, the rush to "hatchet" oars took full blossom (after the Badger men had been ambushed with the new design by Dartmouth at their annual Cochrane Cup on May 2). In the days after the Cochrane competition, Jablonic, Ela, and men's freshmen coach Dan Gehn put out emergency calls to generous alumnus from both crews and raised $4,000 to buy the new oars. With the generous help of Amy Luchsinger and her '79 teammates and Julie Hanson, the women were able to buy two sets of hatchet oars and keep up with their Eastern Conference competitors.

The women's eight (6:34.8)—which was seeded only twelfth among the eighteen university entries and had to best Northeastern and Penn to make the finals—finished sixth to winner Boston University (6:18.9), the eventual national champion in 1992. The 2V8 won the petite finals for seventh overall. The frosh eight ended in tenth, and the V4+ finished fifth to winner Radcliffe.

At the Women's National Collegiate Rowing Championships in Cincinnati on June 13, 1992 Wisconsin's eight finished fourth, ahead of Washington and UC–Davis but behind winner BU, Cornell, and Princeton. Wisconsin's V4+ was third behind Princeton and Kansas, while the UW open 4+, competing in a group of predominantly club entries, won the event's gold medal. The open pair event saw Wisconsin's Andrea Mitchell and Sandra Mintz also come away with the gold.

> *As happened in the 1988 Olympics, five women from UW–Madison again made the 1992 U.S. Olympic squad! At the 1992 Barcelona Olympics, UW rowers Cindy Eckert (2-seat) and Carol Feeney (4-seat) won the silver medal in the straight four. Badgers Yasmin Farooq, Sarah Gengler, and Kim Santiago were also named to the squad. Farooq (coxswain) and Gengler (5-seat) finished sixth in the eight-oared event. Feeney was later named USRowing's Female Athlete of the Year. In 1993 she was named the lightweight coach at Radcliffe.*

In 1992–93, the Wisco varsity went undefeated in fall intercollegiate competition. At the Bausch & Lomb Invitational of twenty-five teams in Rochester, New York, the Badgers, competing in an unusual regatta format that combined times from a three-mile head race and a 1,500-meter sprint, placed first with a total time of 29:43.51. The boating: Catherine Gunderson (bow), Karen Mullen, Kim Zinniel, Sarah Mohs, Denise Santina, Erica Plambeck, Linnea Anderson, Pam Mork (stroke), and Wen Huang (coxswain).

Although fourth among forty entries at the Head of the Charles, the result was the best finish among the college crews in the event. The varsity boating was the same as at the Bausch & Lomb Invitational. While in Boston, the Radcliffe crew kindly housed their Badger counterparts.

The Head of the Milwaukee/Tail of the Fox event was held on the Fox River in DePere, Wisconsin (due to construction in Milwaukee), and Wisconsin dominated the regional event.

Despite the crowded quarters at the Wisconsin boathouse and the occasional tensions at the coaches' levels, the two Wisconsin crews—the athletes on the women's openweight and the men's heavyweight squads—always seemed to get along pretty well. Catherine Gunderson wrote Coach Ela of one exchange between members of the two teams as they passed one another on campus during the fall,

> I remember a time I was walking up Bascom Hill in a stiff and slow manner. You had just put us through a hellish practice. A couple of the men's crew walked up and were lamenting about their own tough practice. I told them of the workout I had just been through. I said that I thought that the coaches had lost their minds. One of the men turned to me and said, "Yeah, but at least your coach is pregnant; what's Jabo's excuse?!"[22]

For six weeks in early 1993, Sean Tobin, who rowed for and graduated from Canisius College in New York in 1989, stood in for Coach Ela during her maternity leave.[23]

The crew departed March 5 for a week of two-a-day practices on the Clinch River in Oak Ridge. At the end of the week, the squad again competed in the Tom White Invitational in Oak Ridge. The major competition was Syracuse; the Badger finish is unknown.

April 3, at the San Diego Classic, the Badgers (7:05.9)—missing the finals after being seeded in the toughest qualifying heat—won the Petite Final over Syracuse, finishing seventh overall. Washington won the varsity event in 6:45.9. The varsity boating: Catherine Gunderson (bow), Karen Mullen, Shannon Daley, Sarah Mohs, Jodie Jenz, Erica Plambeck, Linnea Anderson, Pam Mork (stroke), and Wen Huang (coxswain).

In the Classic's 2V8 event, Wisconsin (7:22.56) finished fourth in the Grand Final behind Washington (7:12.1), Radcliffe (7:16.3), and Yale (7:17.2). The 2V8 boating: Susie Henry (bow), Andrea Mitchell, Sara Kouba, Jennifer Nelson, Melissa Plummer, Kathy Ponti, Mia Hospel, Amy Lambrecht (stroke), and Deanna Leslie (coxswain).

In the first Merrill Lynch Classic in Indianapolis, Indiana (which quickly became dubbed the "unofficial" Big Ten championship), the Badger women's eight won their event. When the Wisco men's varsity eight also won, Wisconsin took home the regatta's inaugural all-point trophy, scoring 172 points to Michigan's 158.

At the Eastern Sprints, the Badgers goal had been to be on the awards dock with all three eights. For the varsity, this did not occur, when they finished sixth.

At the WNCRC in Cincinnati, the novice four (7:55.81) won their 2,000-meter event. Wisconsin's varsity eight was seventh.

Melissa Iverson ('92) won a silver medal for the United States rowing bow seat in the straight four at the 1993 Worlds in Roudnice, Czechoslovakia. Iverson also rowed bow seat, and Yasmin Farooq ('88) coxed, in the U.S. eight that won a silver.

In the fall of the 1993–94 season, at the Bausch & Lomb regatta of twenty-five crews, the Badgers finished third, behind Radcliffe and Cornell.

At the Head of the Charles, with five buoy violations costing the boat a total of fifty seconds in penalties, the eight finished seventeenth. The varsity four, with one buoy violation, ended in tenth. Strong winds along the serpentine three-mile course made an even greater challenge for the coxswains.

Because of a late spring break, the women took a semester break trip (January 3–16), when they traveled to Cocoa Beach, Florida. Both women's and men's crews were assisted with financial support from alumnus (via the WRA) to help defray their winter training expenses.

At the 1994 San Diego Classic on April 9, Wisconsin (7:06.1) finished third behind Washington (6:57.9) and Cal (6:59.6). Behind these three were Penn (7:12.7), Oregon State (7:13.6), and Stanford (7:15.0).

On April 29 and 30, the Midwest Rowing Championship saw 1,200 competitors from forty-seven midwestern schools and clubs compete in a snow-covered event. A record 7.8" of snow fell in Madison, allowing only the heats to be run on Saturday. The frosh eight entries finished first and second. The boating of the first boat: Lisa Huhn (bow), Kitty Shonk, Kathy Topp, Janice Kupiec, Erica Mather, Aggie Zwierchowski, Kerry McEntee, Kendra Zink (stroke), and Liz Travers (coxswain).

The 2V8 also won, with the boating: Rebecca Ebert (bow), Jennifer Nelson, Amy Mathisen, Gina Utrie, Beth Huebner, Beth Traci, Karen Kleinmaier, Amy Lambrecht (stroke), and Jennifer MacLean (coxswain). The V8 won their twenty-second straight title as a varsity.

At the Eastern Sprints on May 8, Wisconsin's varsity missed qualifying for the finals by 0.5 seconds and won the Petite Final, for seventh overall. The 2V8 was also third in their qualifying heat and won the Petite's in 6:53.8 for seventh overall. The novice eight, second in their qualifying heats, finished fifth in the final at 6:53.8. The 2N8 (6:53.9) finished second in their final. As they did in the Eastern Sprints, the Badgers finished in sixth place at the Collegiate Nationals in Cincinnati.

Badger Yasmin Farooq coxed the U.S. eight to a silver in the 1994 Worlds in Indianapolis.

Before the start of the 1994–95 season, Mandi Kowal resigned as novice coach to accept the head coaching position at the University of Iowa and was replaced by Mary Lockyer Browning, a former coxswain, frosh coach, and graduate from the University of Massachusetts.

In the first major regatta of the season on October 23, Wisconsin (16:48.42) finished fifth at the Head of the Charles of 1994 in Boston behind winner Boston R. C. (16:07.4).

Semester break training (January 9–19) was, for the second time, in Cocoa Beach, Florida, and spring break training (March 11–19) was in Oak Ridge, Tennessee—only the third time a Wisconsin crew had found open water twice outside the state in one winter.

At the San Diego Classic on April 1–2, Wisconsin (7:10.9) finished in tenth place behind winner Washington (6:52.7), while the 2V8 (7:03.7) was fourth, also following winner Washington (6:52.6).

In a dual meet with Washington in Madison on April 22, Wisconsin's late spring thaw caught up with them as the eight (6:20.0) finished eleven seconds behind San Diego Classic winner Washington (6:09.7) on the 1,850-meter Lake Wingra course. The 2V8 (6:35.4) was third in their event, behind Washington A and B.

The Merrill Lynch Crew Classic April 15, 1995 featured primarily club crews from around the conference on a 2,000-meter course in Indianapolis. For the second straight year, the varsity eight (7:35.54) came away with the gold. Wisconsin's combined women's and men's result was a 231 score, which was followed by Michigan (132), Ohio State (113.5), Northwestern (50.5), and Purdue (38.5).

The Eastern Sprints were held May 21. Early in the season, Coach Ela had found she needed to further challenge her crew and bring their level of training intensity to a higher level. One of her challenges: "Third or better at the Easterns and we'll go to the Royal Henley Regatta."[24] With that challenge, the varsity won a bronze, behind Princeton and Brown. The 2V8 finished fifth. The novice eight finished third in the Petite Final, or ninth overall, and the four finished fifth.

At the 1995 WNCRC's 2,000-meter course in Cincinnati on June 9 through 11, the varsity (6:22.58) finished fourth, behind Princeton (6:11.98), Washington (6:12.69), and Brown (6:18.39). Following UW were, in order, Cornell (6:24.26), Washington State (6:34.16), and Stanford (6:37.69).

The 2V8 also finished fourth (6:31.1), behind Washington (6:25.9), Washington State (6:23.6) and defending champion Princeton (6:23.8), while the novice 4+ (7:18.2) won gold. The novice four gold medal boating: Becky Hoyt (bow), Jamie Scaletta, Deb Locke, Jane Kovacevich-Gilroy (stroke), and Leah Gassett (coxswain).[25]

Following the regular college season in the summer of 1995—and with funds raised from friends of women's rowing—the openweight varsity eight traveled for the first time to Henley Women's Regatta on the Thames river in London! The

1995 UW crew—winner of Royal Henley Regatta. The Henley champion boating: Kendra Zink (bow), Jodie Jenz, Melissa "Missy" McCrea, Jessica Hughes, Torrey Folk, Kathy Topp, Sarah Kacvinsky, Amy Mathisen (stroke), and Nicole May (coxswain). Coach Sue Ela is at far right. Photo provided by Sue Ela.

Wisconsin eight won their three elimination rounds—in a boat named *Ale* borrowed from the men of Yale—to qualify for the collegiate championship final. In headwind conditions on June 18, the Badgers (4:58) missed the course record by three seconds, defeating Georgetown in the final to win. The crew was awarded the Price-Waterhouse Cup as winner of the collegiate eights event. The victory was another milestone in the proud history of rowing at Wisconsin!

Yasmin Farooq coxed the U.S. women's eight to a gold medal at the 1995 Worlds in Tampere, Finland.

In 1995–96, Wisconsin, in a continuing quest to satisfy Title IX's compliance tests, elected to add lightweight women's crew to its athletic program—although it is not an NCAA sanctioned sport. By eventually adding seventy-five to one hundred lightweight women athletes to its student-athlete universe and establishing a roster management system, the university was able to satisfy the principal compliance criteria of "proportionate headcount equality" by roughly matching its female-to-male student-athlete proportions with the same gender ratio as exists in the school's undergraduate enrollment population.

Lightweight rowing programs are for athletes who naturally weigh 130 pounds or less. In comparison, the average size of an openweight rower might be 5'11" and around 160 pounds.[26] In a serious effort to understand weight management and its potential dangers, Coach Ela enlisted the input of the UW medical staff and the Athletic Department's nutritionist. The UW Health Sports Medicine Center was also engaged to begin tracking accurate comparative body measurements over time, including "Max VO_2" testing to measure how well these lightweight student-athletes take in, transport, and utilize oxygen in their cardiovascular system. The objective was to bring a measure of knowledge and caution to an athletic endeavor, which, like wrestling, bore risks of some athletes seeking to achieve unhealthy weight losses in order to compete.

In the first year of the new lightweight women's crew development, it was true that while budgets were somewhat limited, Wisconsin in any case elected to build its program quietly and slowly, without much first year fanfare.

Future lightweight competition would come most heavily from Princeton, Radcliffe, and Stanford as well as from Villanova, Mercyhurst, University of Central Florida, MIT, and Delaware.

Sue Ela, the openweight women's coach, took on oversight responsibilities for the newly formed lightweight women's crew. Anne Dinshah, formally named the lightweight novice coach, actually worked more as an assistant coach. The squad raced as novices in the fall and as a varsity in the spring.

Openweight Season Results

At the October 15, 1995 Bausch & Lomb Invitational in Rochester, New York, the Badgers (30:48.27), competed against thirty-one other boats and reclaimed the title last won in the 1992 inaugural regatta.

At the October 22 Head of the Charles of 1995, the varsity eight (17:11.88) finished seventh behind winner Rowing Canada (15:44, a record).

On March 30 and 31 at the 1996 San Diego Classic, the varsity won the silver medal. The finish: Washington (7:00.1), Wisconsin (7:00.74), Washington State (7:08.4), UMass (7:14.9), Northeastern (7:15.9), and Stanford (7:25.9).

In the Merrill Lynch Invitational on April 13 and 14, Wisconsin's varsity and 2V8 won the gold. The following week, the varsity (6:42.7) traveled to Seattle and lost to Washington.

At the Eastern Sprints on May 12, the varsity eight finished fourth, the 2V8 (8:08.9) was third, and the V4+ (9:03.7) was fourth. Wisconsin's varsity boating: Kendra Zink (bow), Anne Getka, Gina Utrie, Kathy Topp, Torrey Folk, Jessica Hughes, Sarah Kacvinsky, Amy Mathisen (stroke), and Meghan Phelan (coxswain).

On June 7–8, 1996, the WNCRCs were again held on a 2,000-meter course in Cincinnati. The varsity (6:52.54) finished third for a bronze, behind Brown (6:45.70) and Princeton (6:49.30). Washington (6:54.2) was fourth. UW's novice four (7:53.2) won a gold on a 2,000-meter course, easily defeating Colorado (8:08.99). The N4+ boating: Kirsten Hope (bow), Katie Hope, Ellen Rewolinski and Emily Liolin (stroke), and Tynille Rufenacht (coxswain).

Every Wisconsin entry medaled! The Badgers, for the first time, also won the Sprague Trophy for overall team supremacy, defeating four-time defending all-points titlist Princeton, which finished second. The trophy, first offered in 1988, was awarded to the school that scores the most total points in competition at the Cincinnati Regatta.[27]

Lightweight Season Results (1995–96)

Because the lightweight squad was just being formed, a lightweight eight did not participate in the Head of the Charles during the fall of 1995, although a LW4+ (21:03.89) competed and finished eighth.[28]

Thirty lightweight rowers and three coxswains traveled on their first Cocoa Beach semester break training trip. Among their many memories was seeing NASA's fifth space shuttle *Endeavor*, named after Captain Cook's first ship, launch from Cape Canaveral on January 11 early in the morning before practice.

At the San Diego Classic, the LWV8 finished fourth. The varsity order of finish: Villanova (8:18.2), Radcliffe (8:22.5), Western Washington (8:31.4), Wisconsin (8:38.4), UC–San Diego (8:45.7), and Humboldt (8:50.5). The UW 2V8 (7:37.6) finished third behind Washington (7:24.8) and Washington State (7:27.3).

In the Merrill Lynch Invitational, on April 13 and 14, Wisconsin's LWV8 won the gold. A month passed before the next race when, in the Eastern Sprints on May 12, the eight (8:44.0) was third, as was the LWV4+.

The Intercollegiate Rowing Association (IRA)—since 1895 the men's national collegiate competition and absent the NCAA's sponsorship—came the closest to a national college regatta. In 1996 the regatta agreed to sponsor their first lightweight women's national college championship. In the regatta in Camden, New Jersey, the LWV8 finished third. No LWV4+ event was held at the regatta.

At the WNCRCs in Cincinnati, on June 7 and 8, the LW8 finished is believed to have finished third. The boating is also uncertain. The LWV4 finished third at the WNCRC in Cincinnati.[29] The LWV4 boating: Jill Schindhelm (bow), Kim Johnson, Jodie Thistle, Jane Kraft (stroke) and Shannon Konyn (coxswain).

Following the 1995–96 season, Coach Ela, while remaining as head coach for both women's crews, filled the lightweight women's varsity coaching position, by hiring Sasha Stone. Anne Dinshah continued as the lightweight novice coach.

Following the 1996 season, Gina Utrie, a zoology major from Beaver Dam, Wisconsin, received the Remington Fellowship Program scholarship of $1,000, honoring the male and female student-athlete who graduates with the highest grade-point averages in their class.[30]

UW coach Sue Ela was presented with the award of varsity "Coach of the Year" by the EAWRC, which stated that the organization honored her for her "tenure, success, and commitment" to women's crew. The novice coach award was given to Radcliffe's Holly Hatton.

Yasmin Farooq and Melissa Iverson[31] were selected to the 1996 U.S. Olympic women's rowing squad competing in Atlanta. Farooq coxed the eight-oared entry to a just out of the medals fourth place finish. Lightweight women's rowing was introduced to the slate of Olympic events at the 1996 Atlanta Olympics.[32]

For the 1996–97 season, the National Collegiate Athletic Association (NCAA) agreed to sanction women's crew (openweight but not lightweight).[33] For the openweight rowers on Wisconsin's 120 member women's varsity squad, the NCAA's recognition only intensified the level of competition among the then fifty-three Division I schools with similar crew programs.[34]

The NCAA move brought many benefits to those colleges offering openweight crew—uniform rules of competition across the country, inclusion in the Directors' Cup calculation of comparative college athletic success, and a national championship sponsored by the NCAA (the women's national collegiate championship regatta cost an estimated $500,000 to $600,000 in 2002, which annual regattas rowing colleges no longer had to support on their own). In addition, schools with NCAA-sanctioned rowing programs are credited with one more sanctioned sport in the formulas allocating funds back to member colleges "from gate receipts at 87 NCAA-sponsored championships in 22 sports and from television and marketing rights contracts."[35]

The NCAA's sanction in rowing also comes with some considerable drawbacks. For example, the national championship is no longer an inclusive open college competition but rather—for budget reasons—an *invitational* (with vastly reduced numbers of colleges, clubs, and individual participants). The NCAA's championships also have fewer events. For example, the women's national NCAA regatta has only three events, the V8, 2V8, and the V4+, while the current men's IRA college national rowing championship format has eight heavyweight events. The IRA is, for all practical purposes, an open regatta, as a large number of participants are invited with limited prequalifying requirements.

In the year 1996–97, the UW women's openweight crew accomplished not only lifting the six-year-old budget cap on the program but also adding UW's first two and a half scholarship equivalents for the academic year beginning the fall of 1996. While NCAA rules allowed up to twenty scholarships, few offered that many in 1996–97, though funding was being increased. *USA Today*'s Peter Brewington reported, "Longtime powerhouse Washington is offering 12 scholarships this year, among the most in the USA, and will continue to upgrade. 'We need to stay ahead of the pack.' said Washington coach Jan Harville."[36]

The combination of Title IX influenced funding to women's athletics and the NCAA's recognition of women's crew as an intercollegiate varsity sport would have the result of creating large numbers of new Division I openweight college crew programs. The competition would soon become even more fierce!

The additional attention would influence many aspects of the sport. Recruiting would broaden to national and international searches for athletes, and pressures would increase on coaches in women's crew. For many women's rowing coaches and athletic departments, the criteria for measuring a program's excellence would become success at the conference, rather than at the national, level of the sport.

Openweight Season Results

In 1996–97, both Wisconsin's October 18 dual meet with Radcliffe and the October 20 Head of the Charles regatta were cancelled—the HOC for the first time in thirty-two years—because of gale-force winds and the threat of floods.

The spring season for the varsity would be one of some disappointment, logging an eleventh at the San Diego Classic, losing a dual meet against Washington in Madison, and slipping to tenth at the Eastern Sprints. The varsity boating: Kendra Zink (bow), Kiri Hope, Kate Hillman, Ellen Rewolnski, Suzanna Mork, Kathy Topp, Kati Hope, Torrey Folk (stroke), and Tynille Rufenacht (coxswain).[37]

In the 2V8 for the Media Trophy at the San Diego Classic, the Badgers were more successful, finishing second (7:20.16) to Washington, (7:18.1) and at the Eastern Sprints third (6:47.3) behind Princeton (6:40.6) and Yale (6:46.3). Also at the Sprints, the V4+ (7:41.3) won a bronze, following Princeton (time unknown) and Rutgers (7:36.1).

The NCAA sponsored its first national women's invitational openweight championship in 1997 on Lake Natoma in Sacramento, California. Ten schools were selected to compete for a team victory. Each team was then required to field two eights and a four. Nine additional schools, which were not competing for the team championship, were also selected.[38] On May 20, the NCAA announced the varsity eight event would have sixteen crews, the 2V8 event eight entries and the V4+ event sixteen entries.

Wisconsin, not having received an invitation, did not attend the inaugural NCAA event. "It will be hard not going to the nationals after having attended the nationals for the past twenty-two years, never having finished lower than eighth," lamented UW coach Sue Ela.[39]

With the NCAA's much reduced invitational field of nineteen colleges, the IRA's organizers offered to host an openweight event at their annual men's collegiate championship.

At the 1997 IRAs in Camden in May 29–31, the Wisconsin openweight eight (7:02.9) won a second place silver medal behind Boston University (6:59.9), as did the 2V8 (7:31.9) behind Boston College (7:31.8). UW's novice eight (7:33.3) finished just out of the medals at fourth, behind Radcliffe (7:23.1), Syracuse (7:25.5), and BU (7:27.2).

Wisconsin's combined women's and men's results (the men were awarded the men's IRA all-events Ten Eyck Trophy for the tenth time) won the inaugural award of the 1997 Robert E. Mulcahy III trophy at the IRAs. Wisconsin had 634.75 points, followed by BU (340.65), and Navy (284).

The Mulcahy Trophy—named after a former president and CEO of the New Jersey Sport and Exposition Authority—is an all-points award awarded to the school with the best combined results in the five women's eights events that year in the IRA (openweight, 2V, novice, lightweight varsity, and LW novice eights) and the eight men's heavyweight events (large and small boats) plus one lightweight eight men's event (which Wisconsin did not enter) at the IRA.

Wisconsin's women also won the Camden County Freeholder's Women's Overall Trophy. Wisconsin's commanding 634.75 points total was followed by Boston University's 340.65.

Lightweight Season Results (1996–97)

For the lightweights, as for the openweights, the season started with the weather and flood-threat ("storm of the century") cancellation of the 1997 Head of the Charles regatta in Boston.

At the spring's San Diego Classic, the eight (7:46.81), competing for the Black Mountain Cup, finished third, behind winner Radcliffe (7:32.9) and Villanova (7:39.44).

On May 3, at the Grand Valley Lightweight Invitational in Allendale, Michigan, the LW8 (7:47.6), the LW4 (9:16.6), the novice eight (9:16.6), and the N4+ (9:38.8) all finished first in their events against Grand Valley State.

At the Eastern Sprints, the varsity eight (6:52.8) finished third, behind Radcliffe (6:41.6) and Virginia (6:46.5). In the novice eight event, the order of finish was: Radcliffe (6:37.9), Princeton (6:39.2), Brown (6:41.1), Dartmouth (6:47.7), and Wisconsin (6:48.0). The LWV4+ was also third.

Because the NCAA does not sanction (regulate) lightweight women's crew, no "sponsored" national championship is held for the sport. The IRA, a men's national regatta for over one hundred years, generously offered to host a college lightweight women's championship event as part of their ongoing annual rowing regatta.

In the Camden IRAs, the LW varsity eight A boat (7:20.9) was third, behind Radcliffe (7:07.3) and Villanova (7:15.2).

The LW novice eight (7:52.8) was second behind Seattle Pacific (7:48.0).

At the beginning of the 1997–98 season, Mary Browning, the previous novice openweight coach, was named as the varsity openweight coach. Sue Ela kept the program's overall head coaching position. Former varsity assistant coach Linnea Anderson was named the novice openweight coach. As generally happened each year, starting with a group of more than eighty women trying out for the novice openweight squad in September, the coaching corps saw the group shrink to twenty-six by season's end. Maren Watson, previously a volunteer novice openweight coach, was appointed the novice lightweight coach.

Openweight Season Results

For another season, the openweight crew struggled to return to its previous national prominence in the face of a growing number of Division I openweight women's crew programs.

The varsity eight (32:12.0) traveled to Rochester for the Stonehurst Capital Regatta and finished third behind a strong Northeastern crew (31:09.2) and Yale (31:45.0); Syracuse and Purdue trailed.

At the Head of the Charles, the varsity eight (16:48.71) finished fifteenth (ninth among the college entries, the fastest of which was Brown at 16:19.38). After a collision under Weeks Bridge, UW's championship four finished sixth.

In the San Diego Classic, April 4–5, the finish in the Jessop-Whittier Cup final was Washington (6:28.10), Michigan (6:31.93), Northeastern (6:39.90), Radcliffe (6:40.12), Wisconsin (6:42.84), and Oregon (6:44.44). Two weeks later on April 18 in Seattle, the Badger eight (6:42.6) lost to both Washington's varsity (6:34.4) and 2V8 (6:40.7).

For the first time in the twenty-six years of the Midwest Championships (April 25), Wisconsin (6:52.46) failed to win first place and finished fourth, behind Michigan (6:35.14), MSU (643.41), and OSU (6:44.51). (Two Wisco varsity rowers did not compete because of a rib injury and the flu; both returned before the IRA Regatta.)[40]

At the May 10 Eastern Sprints in New Preston, Connecticut, the V8 was thirteenth, the 2V8 finished seventh overall, and the V4+ (8:30.70) was sixth in the Grand Final won by Rutgers (8:08.30).

Leading up to the IRAs, the openweight squad competed in the Lexus Central Sprints in Oak Ridge, a "year end" regatta in one of the NCAA's now four geographic regions. The regatta was used (although not sponsored by) the NCAA's selection committee in determining which colleges to invite to its national collegiate championship. Wisconsin's fourth place finish was not good enough to attract the much sought-after NCAA invitation to their Sacramento national college rowing championships.

At the May 27–29, 1998, IRAs in Camden, the Wisconsin women's openweight varsity eight (6:43.7) and 2V8 (6:53.8) won gold medals, and the novice eight (6:58.3, behind Cornell at 6:55.4) won silver among a total of four entries, with BU (7:04.0) third and Rutgers (7:10.1) fourth.

The varsity boating: Susanna Mork (bow), Molly Haning, Jyll Rademacher, Becky Hoyt, Laura Macfarlane, Elizabeth Havice, Kiri Hope, Kati Hope (stroke), and Tynille Rufenacht (coxswain).[41] Wisconsin won the all-points combined men's and women's Mulcahy Trophy for a second consecutive year at the 1998 IRAs.

Lightweight Season Results (1997–98)

The 1997–98 lightweight crew doubled in size and boated three eights for practice under coach Sasha Stone.

At the Stonehurst Capital regatta in Rochester, both the LW8 and LW4+ won gold medals. The eights defeated McGill, Western Ontario, and several others.

In the lightweight's first ever participation in an eight-oared event at the Head of the Charles (where the lightweight event was first introduced in 1980), the LW8 finished eighth in a field of twenty-three, after being unable to pass an unyielding crew. The LW4+ (19:32.93) had a great race, according to Coach Stone, finishing fifth out of an overall thirteen. Argonaut R. C. (18:55.04) was first.

At the Lexus Invitational, Virginia's LW8 (7:06.8) edged out Wisconsin (7:09.0), who were then trailed by Tennessee (7:15.6), Wisconsin's LWF8 A boat (7:28.7) and LWF8 B boat (7:51.3). Wisconsin won the LW4+ and were third in the Open 4+ event.

At the San Diego Classic, the varsity (7:04.65) finished fourth behind two fast first and second crews—Radcliffe (6:56.80) and Princeton (6:59.16). Villanova (7:03.11) was third.

On April 18, UW traveled to Princeton's Carnegie Lake to participate in competition, also attended by Virginia. Princeton (7:14.47) won the contest handily, with the Badgers (7:25.46) slipping past UVA by 0.27 seconds, their first defeat of the Cavaliers in two years.

At the 1998 Midwest Championships on Lake Wingra in Madison, eleven lightweight entries competed versus only four the year before. The LW8 (6:38.20) took first (and the LWN8 (6:42.16) took third in the varsity race, with Texas (6:40.80) sandwiched in between. The LW4+ (8:10.54) was third in their event, chasing Northwestern (8:00.60) and Kansas (8:05.85).

At the 1998 Eastern Sprints on May 10, the LW8 finish was Princeton (6:54.00), Radcliffe (6:58.30), Wisconsin (7:04.60), and Virginia (7:10.90). In the LW4+, Wisconsin was second after Radcliffe and in the LWN8 Wisconsin (7:15.50) also won the silver, behind Princeton (7:13.00).

At the IRAs on May 28–30 in Camden, the LW8 finished fourth and joined the UW men's and openweight women's crews as winners of the Mulcahy Trophy.

Following the 1997–98 season, Coach Ela resigned as the head coach of the two women's crew programs. No overall head coach was named to replace her. After helping to organize and raise funds to initiate the club rowing program at Wisconsin in 1972, rowing for two years as a club rower and one as a varsity rower, coaching the novices for tjree years and then the varsity for another nineteen years, Ela's career had spanned the entire history of organized competitive rowing for women at Madison!

In her three years as novice coach, Ela's eights won both Eastern Sprints and National open titles. Coach Ela's athletes (while head coach) included eight Olympians and many more U.S. National Team members. She led her squads to Royal Henley, Canadian Henley, and many other eights and small-boat titles. Ela is also credited with involvement in a coaching capacity for two international teams and the first Lightweight Development Camp in 1981. Along with the successes came the usual and extraordinary challenges of developing a program from scratch.

Tom Finkelmeyer interviewed Ela for the *Capital Times* and wrote:

"The first fifteen years I was coaching, it was a hard, steady climb for women's crew, always battling for credibility, funding, staffing, and raising money for equipment," said Ela. "We did all that and were still competing on a national level. Then, within the last three years, it has really exploded. It's an NCAA sport, there are scholarships available, and it's whole other level."[42]

Sue Ela is a true pioneer in the sport of women's college rowing. She was present at the beginning of so many stages of the Wisconsin women's rapid rise to national prominence, which included helping to give a fast start to a high-quality club rowing program at Wisconsin, and bringing home a national championship. She also worked with her coaching counterparts (including Mimier, who proposed the idea) to develop a college-only national regatta, and to move the women's racing distance from 1,000 meters to 2,000 meters. The University of Wisconsin, and the sport itself, owes Sue Ela a huge debt of gratitude for putting the sport on such a sound footing. "You were the visionary, the catalyst, the proud and positive leader. (The program) has flourished under you."[43]

14

The Competition Becomes Fierce!

When Coach Ela retired following the 1997–98 season, she was not replaced with a single coach overseeing both crews. While the Athletic Department gave more thought to how it wanted to structure the coaching staffs, Mary Browning was given the title of interim head coach of the openweights, with Carrie Davis as the assistant coach, and Amy Appleton (replacing Linnea Anderson) was named the novice coach.

Prior to joining the UW coaching staff for the 1993–94 season, Browning had served as the novice rowing coach at the University of Massachusetts. As a college athlete, she had coxed the men's varsity eight, which won the New England Championship in 1991. At the 1995 Head of the Charles, she coxed a composite crew of American and Danish rowers, winning the lightweight event. A year later, she coxed the Danish 4+ to her second Head of the Charles title.

Browning majored in Communications/Middle Eastern Studies, graduating cum laude from the University of Massachusetts–Amherst in 1991. She was also a member of Phi Beta Kappa.

Sasha Stone was also given the interim title as head coach of the lightweights; Maren Watson continued as the novice coach.

The NCAA, the sanctioning body for openweight collegiate crew, allowed a ceiling of up to twenty scholarships to each college's openweight program and, at about this time, UW's Athletic Department opted to allocate two of this twenty to its lightweight women's crew.

Mary Browning, coach 1997–2002. Photo courtesy of UW Athletic Communications.

Badger Mandi Kowal was named to the USRowing Hall of Fame in New York in 1998 (as was UW rower Robert Espeseth, Jr.).

In the 1998–99 season, the openweight crew showed improvement over the prior two years, while the lightweights did not have a particularly outstanding year.

Openweight Season Results

The openweights started their season slowly with a tenth at the October 18 Head of the Charles, followed by a sixth at the spring's San Diego Classic.

257

Improvement began to show on April 10 when, competing against Michigan and Ohio and the University of Iowa in Iowa City, the Badger eights swept the event with the varsity coxed four finishing second.

Against Washington on April 17 at 8:15 A.M. on Lake Mendota, the Huskies defeated both the varsity and 2V8. A week later, the Badgers traveled to New Haven and on April 24 rowed as a guest in the Radcliffe-Yale Case Cup competition. The order of finish in the varsity eight race was Radcliffe (6:27.8), Wisconsin (6:33.6), and Yale (6:51.7). The result was the same in the 2V8 contest, with the times of 6:41.1, 6:47.3, and 6:56.3, respectively.

The following day, the Badgers took on BU and Northeastern. In a strong head wind, the varsity (7:11.37) defeated Northeastern (7:12.61), BU (7:15.39), and visiting Texas (7:32.39). The order of finish in the 2V8 race: BU (7:29.5), Northeastern (7:32.7), Wisconsin (7:40.1), and Texas (8:05.1).

Former Badgers—Olympian and University of Texas head coach Carie Graves, and World Champion and Iowa head coach, Mandi Kowal—brought their crews to the Midwest Championships. Wisconsin's nationally ninth-ranked varsity, in a photo finish, knocked off eighth-ranked Michigan State, fifth-ranked Michigan, as well as Texas and Iowa.

At the 1999 Eastern Sprints on May 16, the varsity (6:14.10) finished fifth behind winner Brown (6:02.10). The 2V8, N8, and V4+ all finished second in the Petites (eighth overall). The novice coxed four (8:00.40) finished sixth.

The Sprints boatings—for the varsity: Kate Hammes (bow), Mary Collins, Tessa Michelson, Laura Macfarlane, Jyll Rademacher, Jenny Sturino, Kiri Hope, Kati Hope (stroke), and Meghan Phelan (coxswain) and in the 2V8: Jill Cartwright (bow), Val Bakken, Jena Cappel, Amy Thoreson, Kary Oetjen, Kate Crowley, Ellen Rewolinski, Acey Neel (stroke), and Tynille Rufnacht (coxswain).

1999 Royal Henley Regatta entry from UW. Photo courtesy of UW Athletic Communications.

The Badger varsity, then ranked sixth in the country, earned its first invitation to the three-event NCAA National Championships on Lake Natoma in Sacramento, on May 28–30. The national regatta of 1999 was the NCAA's third since initiating sponsorship of women's openweight rowing championships in 1997. As a "team" invitee, UW was allowed to send a V8, 2V8, and V4+ entry. The V8 ended up tenth, and the team finished tenth overall.[1]

The varsity then went to Royal Henley Regatta for the second time. With the help of many alums and a special Women's Sport Grant, ten rowers and two coaches made the trip. In the first single elimination match in the Championship event (UW had won the College event in 1995), the Badgers drew a very experienced British national team boat, which included several Olympic rowers, and lost by one and one-quarter lengths (about 4 seconds).

Lightweight Schedule Results (1998–99)

At the Stonehurst Capital Regatta in the fall, the LW8 finished first among seven competitors, and the LW4 finished second among six entries.

At the Head of the Charles on October 18, the LW8 crossed the line in seventh place among fifteen entries. The LW4+ entry of the Badgers finished thirteenth.

On Tuesday, October 27, the Wisconsin crews were shocked by the sudden death of junior Sarah Jean Gornick, stricken with a fatal strain of bacterial meningitis. She had been practicing early on Monday, preparing for the Head of the Elk, and passed away less than twenty-four hours later. A biochemistry major, Sarah hailed from St. Paul, Minnesota, and was a member of the Pi Beta Phi sorority. Always wearing ribbons in her hair, and red ribbons when competing, a new bow-loader four[2]—named *Red Ribbons*—was dedicated to Sarah's memory.

In a tragic coincidence, men's rower Jason "Lundy" Lundelius ('99) died the same day from injuries sustained several days earlier in a car/bike accident in Montana. Jason had been biking across the country.

Fourth-ranked nationally in the week's polls, Wisconsin traveled to Princeton on April 17 for a dual meet. The Badger varsity and novice eights lost to Princeton, although the LW4+ was first. The varsity boating: Sharone Cohen (bow), Dusty Darley, Kirstin Holbeck, Sara Borchardt, Tamara Miller, Angela Lay, Anna Vaughn, Sara Lyng (stroke), and Maureen O'Donnell (coxswain). The winning V4+ boating: Suzie Canney (bow), Kate Scheffler, Kathy Ushijima, Jenny Churas (stroke), and Angie Matten (coxswain). The next day against Villanova and Radcliffe, in Camden, Wisconsin's three eights—varsity, 2V8, and novice—were all second.

At the San Diego Classic, April 27–28, the finish was Villanova (7:33.1), Virginia (7:36.1), Wisconsin (7:42.4), UC–Davis (7:54.4), Humboldt (8:04.0), and UC–Davis (8:07.4).

At the May 16 Eastern Sprints on Lake Waramaug in New Preston, the varsity (6:49.1) finished fourth, behind winner Princeton (6:31.2). The LW4+ (7:32.9) was second, six seconds behind Georgetown. The novice eight, also finishing second, was nine seconds behind Princeton.

At the 1999 IRA's National Collegiate Lightweight Rowing Championships, May 27–29 in Camden, Wisconsin finished fifth.

Badger Torrey Folk ('97) rowed on the 1999 U.S. National Team at the Worlds in St. Catharine's, Canada, rowing 7-seat in the eight, which placed second.

For the season 1999–2000, Mary Browning was formally named the head coach of the openweight program. Maren Watson LaLiberty, MD, UW's lightweight novice coach, replaced Sasha Stone, as head coach of the lightweight women's program, and Sarah Haney replaced LaLiberty as the lightweight novice coach.

Coach LaLiberty, born in Minneapolis in 1961, graduated with a bachelor's degree in microbiology and Latin from the University of Minnesota in 1984. In 1992 she earned her MD from the University of Minnesota Medical School. Following a family-practice residency and a year of medical practice in Tennessee, LaLiberty moved to Madison in 1996, where she worked for three years at the Dean Clinic in Madison, Wisconsin.

Over the 1996–97 season, LaLiberty had worked as a volunteer coach with UW's openweight crew and the following year became novice coach of the lightweight women. Her prior coaching experience included being a volunteer coach in the summer of 1996 at the Oak Ridge (Tennessee) Rowing Association and, before that as head coach of the University of Minnesota women's Crew Club for the 1991–92 season.

Maren Watson LaLiberty, coach 1999 to 2004. Photo courtesy of UW Athletic Communications.

LaLiberty rowed for Minnesota from 1981 to 1983 and served as the team captain in 1983. She rowed in both the winning lightweight club eight at the 1982 Head of the Charles and in the 1983 NWRAs, winning the lightweight 4+ as coxswain. The following summer, LaLiberty finished fifth in the lightweight eight at the 1984 Worlds. From 1983 to 1987, she rowed with the Minnesota Boat Club of St. Paul and was a member of the lightweight eight that took first place at the 1983 Head of the Charles. She was a member of the lightweight pair that finished first at both the 1993 Head of the Charles and the 1994 U.S. Olympic Festival.

Beginning with the 1999–2000 season, the Big Ten Conference added openweight women's rowing—already an NCAA sanctioned sport—to its program of sponsored varsity sports, with six teams—Indiana, Iowa, Michigan, Michigan State, Ohio State, and Wisconsin (Minnesota added their name in 2001)—competing for the conference title. The first Big Ten-sponsored championship was be held on Lake Wingra on April 29, 2000.

Openweight Season Results

The Badgers (17:38.75), in their major fall schedule event at the 1999 Head of the Charles on October 23–24, finished ninth, behind winner Rowing Canada (16:31.41).

April 1–2 at the San Diego Classic, the varsity (6:59.7) finished sixth in the finals to winner Washington (6:38.4). The 2V8 finished second in the Petite Finals (eighth overall); Virginia (6:39.5) won the Grand Final. UW's novice eight (7:04.9) was fifth in the Sea World Trophy chase, behind Washington (6:46.8), Cal (6:54.9), Michigan (7:00.9), and Washington State (7:01.4).

The following weekend, after driving to Columbus, Ohio, to race Michigan and Ohio State, the event was cancelled when heavy rains flooded the race course. The next competition was in Seattle, where the varsity lost by eight seconds to the University of Washington but won the next day against Washington State University by seven and a half seconds.

At the Midwest Championships the varsity won their event, and the 2V8 boat finished fifth, also racing in the varsity eight event. The 2V8 boating: Erin Conlin (bow), Rachel Rogozinski, Acey Neel, Jessamy Flaherty, Tessa Michaelson, Tara Gedman, Erin Bye, Marianna Waters (stroke), and Tiffany Suda (coxswain). The varsity four won first place at the regatta, with the boating: Kylie Fredrickson (bow), Julianne Hertz, Brigid Myers, Carrie Byron (stroke), and Erin Buchanan (coxswain). The novice eight also finished first.

The first Big Ten Women's Rowing Championships was held on the 1,850-meter course on Lake Wingra on April 29. Temperatures were in the forties, with a slight crosswind. The Badger eight (6:25.33) finished fourth in the six-entry field, with the Wolverines of Michigan (6:15.9) finishing with the gold, Michigan State (6:18.27) with the silver, and Ohio State (6:23.07) with the bronze. The 2V8 (6:36.13) was fifth to Michigan's (6:24.88) victory.

In the third scored event, the Badger V4+ (7:15.92) won the gold, coming from behind to row through Michigan (7:17.94) with 100 meters to go. The novice eight, an unscored event, also won the gold.

On May 14 on Lake Waramaug, the varsity (6:53.3) placed tenth at the 2000 Eastern Sprints. The varsity eight boating: Jen Broerman (bow), Val Bakken, Kari Oetjen, Alyssa Vegter, Katie Hammes, Jenny Pofahl, Jyll Rademacher, Mary Collins (stroke), and Kate Edwards (coxswain).[3] The 2V8 finished fourth and the varsity four was fifth. The second varsity eight boating: Erin Conlin (bow), Acey Neel, Jessamy Flaherty, Rachel Rogozinski, Tessa Michaelson, Tara Gedman, Erin Bye, Marianna Waters (stroke), and Tiffany Suda (coxswain).[4]

The Badger novices at the Sprints finished as follows: the novice eight (7:07.30) in fifth place, second novice eight (7:30.90) in fourth, and the N4+ (8:12.5) finished first. The gold medal-winning novice 4+ boating at the Sprints: Betsy Lucas (bow), Chris Holland, Alana Burny, Heather Koch (stroke), and Cecile Bien (coxswain). The next year's Sprints were expected to move to Camden for a year. The openweight crew did not receive an invitation to the NCAA's college championship regatta in Camden.

Lightweight Season Results (1999–2000)

Every now and then, bite off more than you can chew.—H. Jackson Brown, Jr., in "Varsity Lightweight Women," in the Wisconsin Rowing Newsletter *(Summer 2000), written by lightweight women's crew coach Maren Watson LaLiberty*

At the Head of the Charles in Boston on October 24, 1999, the Badger eight finished fifth at 20:52.75 behind winner Arco Training Center (16:58.49). The LW4+ came in third at 19:39.75.

In the April 2 San Diego Classic's hunt for the lightweight varsity A. W. Coggeshall Cup, Wisconsin won the silver in this finish: Princeton (7:13.9), Wisconsin (7:28.7), Radcliffe (7:29.6), Villanova (7:30.6), UC–Davis (7:49.2), and Humboldt (7:57.7).

In a dual meet against Princeton, in Princeton on April 15, the UW varsity eight (7:01.08) defeated the Tigers, as did the LW4+ (8:03.20) and the novice eight—a Badger sweep! Coach LaLiberty remembers this day's work was especially important as "it was a confirmation" to all concerned, especially Wisconsin's athletes, that not only could Princeton be beaten but also Wisconsin's rather young lightweight program was strong at all levels.[5]

At the Eastern Sprints in New Preston on May 14, both the varsity LW8 (7:13.20) and the V4+ (8:09.60) finished second to Princeton (7:12.10 and 8:06.40, in their respective races).

The Badger novice LW8 (7:26.40) defeated Princeton (7:31.40) and won their event at the Sprints, while the novice four with coxswain (8:33.10) finished very well with a fifth in the varsity fours event, ahead of Georgetown (8:43.40). The frosh four boating: Julie Franzen (bow), Colleen Conway, Lindsey Carlstrom, Tessa Molter (stroke), and Clara Bien (coxswain).

The gold medal novice eight Eastern Sprints boating: Courtney Cowie (bow), Mary Rohlich, Andrea Winger, Kristin Hall, Jenny Nelson, Joni Wiebelhaus, Becca Flood, Hoda Ahmadi (stroke), and Jade Brueckner (coxswain). The frosh four boating: Julie Franzen (bow), Colleen Conway, Lindsey Carlstrom, Tessa Molter (stroke), and Clara Bien (coxswain).

At the 2000 IRAs in Camden, competing for the Camden County Freeholders Trophy, the varsity LW8 (7:12.36) finished third, behind Princeton (7:03.52) and Villanova (7:07.49). The varsity boating: Lindsay Gorsuch (bow), Sara Lyng, Kirsten Holbeck, Alison Frohberg, Stacey Langenecker, Angela Lay, Marisa Hoffman, Dusty Darley (stroke), and Maura O'Donnell (coxswain).[6] Wisconsin again won the all-points combined men's and women's (the lightweight eight event) Mulcahy Trophy at the 2000 IRAs.

Former Badger Torrey Folk rowed 5-seat in the U.S. eight-oared entry in the 2000 Sydney Olympics and finished sixth.

In the 2000–2001 season, the openweight crew experienced another difficult year—now facing eighty-seven Division I openweight crew programs—while the lightweights showed improvement over a fine previous year.

Openweight Season Results

At the 2000 Head of the Charles on October 21–22, the varsity (17:05.34) finished their highest in five years with an eighth overall (sixth among the college entries). The winner, Princeton (16:37.52), was the first college entry to win outright since Wisconsin in 1988.

Against Duke in a dual meet in Oak Ridge on March 25, the Wisconsin squad won all four of their contests, including the V8, the 2V8, the V4+, and the N8+.

The varsity skipped the April 7–8 San Diego Crew Classic and traveled to Cambridge to face Radcliffe and Brown. The Badgers finished third to both in four contests. The next day against MIT and BU, the Badgers did better, winning the 2V8 event, finishing second in the varsity eight and the N8 events. The V4+ came in third.

On April 21, Washington (6:44.7) came to Madison and defeated Wisconsin (6:57.4) in a dual meet.

At the second annual Big Ten Conference Openweight Women's Rowing Championships, held April 28 in Ann Arbor, the Badgers' finished fourth as a team, behind Michigan, Ohio State, and Michigan State. The Wolverines of Michigan again finished in first in the varsity eight contest in which UW finished fifth of seven entries. Wisconsin's 2V8 was third, the V4+ finished fifth, the 2V4+ won their contest, the N8 was fourth, and the N4+ won their event.

At the Eastern Sprints on May 13 in Camden, the varsity finished eleventh. The 2V8 ended in thirteenth place, the V4+ was second, the N8 finished twelfth, the 2N8 was second, and the only Badger winner of the day was the N4+. Wisconsin, for the fourth time in five years, missed receiving an invitation to the NCAA's college openweight national regatta.

Lightweight Season Results (2000–2001)

At the Head of the Charles, the LW8 (17:56.09) won the trophy for first place! Their teammates in the LW4+ were tenth in their event. The varsity boating: Joni Wiebelhaus (bow), Alison Frohberg, Kirsten Holbeck, Angel Lay, Marisa Hoffman, Becca Flood, Stacey Langenecker, Dusty Darley (stoke), and Maura O'Donnell (coxswain).

In the April 7–8 San Diego Classic, Wisconsin's lightweight eight won the A. W. Coggeshall Cup, with the finish in the following order: Wisconsin (7:20.7), Princeton (7:21.67), Villanova (7:48.03), UC–San Diego (7:54.22), University of Colorado (8:00.11), and University of Central Florida (8:00.69). The varsity boating: Margot Miller (bow), Ali Endress, Leah Hanson, Joni Wiebelhaus, Eileen Ruzicka, Kirstin Holbeck, Marisa Hoffman, Stacey Langenecker (stroke), and Maura O'Donnell (coxswain).[7]

At the Eastern Sprints on May 13, both the Varsity LW8 and the LW4+ won gold medals. The LW4+ boating: Angela Lay (bow), Lindsay Gorsuch, Courtney Cowie, Noelle Vitone (stroke), and Jade Brueckner (coxswain).

In the IRA's National Collegiate Lightweight Rowing Championship in Camden on June 2, 2001 (held with the men's IRA championships), the Badger varsity LW8 (6:53.36) finished second to Princeton (6:47.50). They were followed by Radcliffe (7:02.14), MIT (7:02.58), Villanova (7:05.86), and Mercyhurst (7:07.01).

On June 5, 2001, former UW women's head crew coach Sue Ela was inducted into the Madison Sports Hall of Fame.

The 2001–2 season was another in a series of transitional years for the openweight crew and another strongly contending year for the lightweight squad.

Openweight Season Results

In the 4.4-mile (where the regatta combines two course times—one northbound and one southbound over the same course) Milwaukee River Challenge on September 22, the varsity (22:22) finished second to Notre Dame (22:14). In the open 4+, UW's openweight entry (25:59) won within their category, ahead of the second place UW lightweight four B (26:10) and the third place UW lightweight A (26:21). The winning Open 4+ boating: Rochelle Jacques (bow), Alyssa Elver, Jeannete Moore, Erin Bye (stroke), and Erin Buchanan (coxswain).

At the Head of the Charles on October 21, the Badger eight (16:59.44) finished sixteenth, while the Open 4+ (19:15.72) was twelfth.

On March 30 the varsity took a full squad to race Northeastern and Rutgers on the Raritan River in New Brunswick, New Jersey. Winning five of five against Rutgers, the Badgers only prevailed in two of six against Northeastern with the V4+ and N4+ crossing first. The varsity, 2V8, frosh eight, and the N4+ all lost to Northeastern.

Again skipping the San Diego Classic, Madison hosted Iowa for a series of dual races on April 6. The Hawkeyes defeated the Badger varsity eight, while the Wisconsin 2V8 and N8 both won. On April 13 UW traveled to Washington's Montlake

Cut and lost to both Washington and Washington State. In Iowa City on April 20, the Badgers raced two successive 2,000-meter races on the Iowa River and lost first to Minnesota and then to Michigan State.

On May 4, at the third Big Ten Conference Championships in Lansing, Michigan, Ohio State won first place as a team, with Wisconsin finishing fourth for the third consecutive year. Results in each of the events: the V8 finished sixth (6:39.9 in the Petite final behind Iowa at 6:36.8; Ohio State won the Grand final in 6:29.5); the 2V8 was fourth; the V4+ won the silver (7:26.6 behind Michigan State at 7:25.9); the 2V4+ came in fifth; the N8 won a bronze, and the 2N8 finished first (at 7:02.6 over Iowa at 7:26.6).

At the Eastern Sprints, May 12, in Camden, the Badgers as a team were seventh. Results in each of the events: the V8 finished tenth; 2V8 was ninth; the V4+ won a gold medal (7:18.4, ahead of Princeton by over four seconds in the fifteen-crew race and followed by Cornell, Virginia, and BU); the N8 came in tenth; the 2N8 was 7th; and the N4+ also won a gold!

On May 19 on Melton Lake in Oak Ridge, the Badgers competed in their last race of the season, the Lexus Central Southern Sprints. The varsity finished tenth in an event won by Ohio State. The varsity boating: Amy Weatherby (bow), Jenny Pofahl, Alissa Adler, Rachael Rogozinski, Annie Trimberger, Elpi Pagitsas, Ashley Mays, Marianna Waters (stroke), and Erin Buchanan (coxswain).

In the 2V8 race, it was Michigan (6:51.5), Michigan State (6:53.8), Wisconsin (6:56.2), Ohio State (6:57.5), Notre Dame (6:59.1), and Iowa (7:05.7). The bronze-medal 2V8 boating: Erin Bye (bow), Betsy Lucas, Kylie Frederickson, Nicky Weir, Nikki Lennart, Tara Gedman, Alyssa Elver, Jeannette Moore (stroke), and Andrea Hayden (coxswain).

The varsity's low finish at the Central Sprints meant another year without an invitation to the NCAA championships, which were held in Indianapolis.

Lightweight Season Results (2001–2)

In a very strong year, the lightweight varsity crew went undefeated in major races of the 2001–2 season, except for their final two.

For the second consecutive year, Wisconsin's LW8 won the Head of the Charles; their time on the winding three-mile river dividing Boston and Cambridge was 16:49.090. The Badger LW4 was fourth.

The spring season began for the squad March 30, 2002, at the Petrakis Cup on the Trout River in Jacksonville, Florida. The LW8 finished first (at 7:03.8, the Badgers were twenty-five seconds ahead of second place!) defeating Delaware, Central Florida, and Embry-Riddle. Other Petrakis Cup regatta results included: the

LW2V8 in fourth place; LWV4+ won their event; the LWN8 finished second; the LWOpen 4+ was second; and the LWN4+ won a gold.

At the 2002 San Diego Classic's 2,000-meter Mission Bay course on April 6–7, Wisconsin's LW8 successfully defended their 2001 title, scoring another first over archrival Princeton (6:52.15 vs. 6:56.08). Later finishers included: UC–Santa Barbara (7:11.64), Queens (7:19.68), Stanford (7:28.73), UC–San Diego (7:35.12). The LW8 boating: Lindsay Gursuch (bow), Katie Bohren, Ali Endress, Eva Payne, Joni Wiebelhaus, Katie Sweet, Stacey Langenecker, Eileen Ruzicka (stroke), and Tessa Molter (coxswain).[8]

At the Knect Cup's 2,000-meter Cooper River course in Camden, New Jersey, on April 13, the Badgers won their third consecutive lightweight varsity trophy by beating four crews ranked in the top twelve nationally. In this one, Wisconsin (6:52.1) defeated second-place Radcliffe by 7.7 seconds. Other Badger finishes: the LW Open 4+ was fifth, LWV4+ finished second, and LWN8 ended in third. At the

2001 LW8 winner of the Head of the Charles. The boating: Eileen Ruzicka (bow), Joni Wiebelhaus, Katie Sweet, Eva Payne, Margot Miller, Stacey Langenecker, Lindsay Gorsuch, Leah Habson (stroke), and Jade Brueckner (coxswain). Coach LaLiberty is at the left. Photo by Brad Taylor.

Villanova Invitational the next day on the same course, Wisconsin again struck gold. The finish: Wisconsin (6:55.2), Princeton (7:01.5), and Radcliffe (7:06.4).

In the 2002 Eastern Sprints in Camden on May 12, Princeton (7:00.3) finally caught the Wisconsin LW8 (7:02.1), with Radcliffe (7:12.5), MIT (7:27.6), and Georgetown (7:37.9) following the leaders. The LWV4+ (8:05.1) reversed the trend, defeating Princeton (8:14.4) for the first time this year. Others in order of finish: Radcliffe (8:31.2), Wisconsin's LWN4+ (8:40.4), MIT (8:53.8). and Georgetown (9:09.0). The winning LWV4+ boating: Becca Bolz (bow), Nicole Olsen, Anne Porter, Jessica Neuville (stroke), and Sara Wolfgram (coxswain).

The LWN8 finished second at the Sprints, and the LWN4+, racing in the varsity event, finished fourth. The novice eight boating: Diane Martins (bow), Mary Jo Fait, Katherine Kludt, Jen Howard, Jenny Lockridge, Jessica Lee, Lindsay Rongstad, Maggie Heike (stroke), and Michelle Caraballo (coxswain).

At the IRAs in Camden, on June 1, 2002, for the National Collegiate Lightweight Rowing Championship—the last race of the season—Princeton (6:29.64) edged Wisconsin (6:30.07) by 0.43 seconds for the national title and the Camden County Freeholder's Trophy. The varsity eight boating: Leah Hanson (bow), Lindsay Gorsuch, Stacey Langenecker, Margot Miller, Eva Payne, Katie Sweet, Joni Wiebelhaus, Eileen Ruzicka (stroke), and Jade Brueckner (coxswain).

Badger Katie Hammes made the 2002 U.S. National Team, and raced in the 7-seat of the eight in the 2002 Worlds in Seville, Spain, placing fifth.

As the 2001–2 season ended, the coaching turnovers in women's crew at UW—which began in 1998–99 with Sue Ela's departure—continued. With the birth of her daughter, openweight head coach Mary Browning opted to resign and spend time with her family. The issue of how to best organize the two women's crews then had to be faced. Options included searching for a new openweight head coach, naming individual openweight and lightweight coaches with a head coach overseeing both crews, or identifying one head coach over both crews, without naming a varsity coach for either of the two crews individually.

On the recommendation of Maren LaLiberty, the third alternative was selected. LaLiberty became the single head coach of Women's Rowing. In the combined mode with no team-specific head coaches, LaLiberty named two "at large" Varsity Assistant Coaches—Jamie Whalen and Mitz Carr. Whalen had spent the prior twelve years coaching individuals and clubs around North America, while Carr had been a nationally competitive sculler. At the start of the 2002–3 season, two new novice coaches were named, in addition to the two new varsity assistant coaches.

Openweight Season Results

Under Coach LaLiberty's approach, the two women's programs trained together for the first time during the 2002–3 season. Marina Traub, an alumna of the University of Virginia with coaching experience at Cal and Loyola College in Maryland, was named the Novice Openweight Coach.

At the Milwaukee River Challenge on September 21, the openweight and lightweight teams created mixed crews and entered seven events, the best of which finished fourth on the 4.4 mile, two-way course through the center of the city. On October 20 at the Head of the Charles, the openweight eight finished fourteenth and the Open 4+ was 12th on the three-mile course. At the San Diego Classic April

5 and 6, the varsity eight finished a disappointing fifth in their heat and fourth in the Petite Final. The winning eight was Cal. At the Princeton Quad in Princeton, New Jersey, on April 12, 2003, the Badger varsity eight (7:29.79) was fourth to winner Radcliffe. The 2V8 was third, beating Cornell, while the novice eight and the varsity 4+ each finished second.

In the Big Ten Championships in Columbus, Ohio, on May 3, 2003, the varsity eight race had seven entries. The order of finish in the Grand Final (1st–4th) was: Michigan (6:27.8), Ohio State (6:30.4), Michigan State (6:31.1), and Iowa (6:35.7), followed in the Petite Finals (5th–7th) by Minnesota (6:34.8), Wisconsin (6:38.0), and Indiana (6:56.0). The varsity eight boating included Alissa Adler (bow), Julie Quoss, Amanda Frederick, Jeannette Moore, Annie Trimberger, Marianna Waters, Nikki Lennart, Erin Gladding (stroke), and Andrea Hayden (coxswain). The 2V8 ended fifth with the boating of Alissa Miller (bow), Nicky Weir, Jenny Tuffree, Leah Gordon, Chris Strasser, Shannon Gedman, Ashley Mays, Elpi Pagitsas (stroke), and Beth Redfearn (coxswain). The V4+ finished sixth.

But Badger spirits were lifted when the Novice 8, the second Novice 8 and the 2V4+ all won their finals. The N8 order of finish was Wisconsin (6:49.7), Michigan State (6:54.4), Minnesota (6:55.0), and Indiana (7:08.8). Wisco's N8 boating was Katie Culp (bow), Kat Piercy, Katie Pofahl, Bryanna Siefert, Kari Harman, Lindsey Bush, Katie Lawson, Emily Simonds (stroke), and Megan Bradshaw (coxswain). The 2N8 boating comprised Meghan Filbrandt (bow), Leanne Hughes, Carly Mulliken, Kim Ackerbauer, Claire Koch, Kirby Gallie, Megan Cotter, Lauren Baxter (stroke), and Megan Stevens (coxswain).

The final standings in the Big Ten regatta was Michigan (123), Michigan State (123), Ohio State (107), Iowa (99), Wisconsin (69), Minnesota (61), and Indiana (30). The three medal-earning finishes energized the Badgers' trip home and the strong novice finishes raised expectations for the future.

At the Eastern Sprints, held May 18 in Camden, New Jersey, the Varsity 8 finished a disappointing eleventh overall (fifth in the Petite Final) of seventeen entries. The 2V8 did better, finishing sixth in their Grand Final. Both the first Novice 8 and the N4+ finished fourth in their respective events.

The gold medal harvest was by the Badgers' 2V4 with coxswain and the second novice 8. The 2V4+ boating, which defeated, in order, Boston University, Yale, Cornell, Dartmouth, and Penn was Stacy Coy (bow), Martha Udelhofen, Sara Schreiner, Aliza Richman (stroke), and Courtney Carlovsky (coxswain). The 2N8 boating finishing ahead of Cornell, Dartmouth, Radcliffe, Northeastern, and Boston University included Meghan Filbrandt (bow), Kim Ackerbauer, Carly Mulliken, Leanne Hughes, Katie Pofahl, Kirby Gallie, Claire Koch, Lauren Baxter (stroke), and Megan Stevens (coxswain).

In the Willing Point Trophy, a measure of a team's overall finish, Radcliffe led the field of 18; Wisconsin was sixth. For another year, the openweight squad missed an invitation to the NCAA tournament, making the sprints competition the last of the season for the team.

Lightweight Season Results (2002–3)

Dusty Darley was named the Novice Lightweight Coach after competing as a lightweight rower at Wisconsin for four years (1998–2001)—the last as captain—and serving as a volunteer assistant coach in 2001–2. Darley graduated from UW–Madison with a B.A. in art history in 2001.

On October 20 at the Head of the Charles, the lightweight eight joined a field of twenty-four competitors in their category. Having won first place in each of the previous two years, the spotlight was on the Wisconsin women again. But in the end, the Badger eight took third, behind Radcliffe and Princeton.

At the San Diego Crew Classic on April 4, 2003, the varsity eight (7:07.76) prevailed in a field of nine, winning their third straight title and the A. W. Coggeshall Cup. Wisconsin's uwbadgers.com Web site, in a press release from UW Athletic Communications sportswriter Paul Capobianco, described the race,

> Under sunny skies, with temperatures in the upper 60s and a moderate cross wind, the Badgers posted a 1:46.94 over the first 500 and closed with a 1:45.29, the fastest 500 split of the race, to win the title by over 8.5 seconds. The Badgers, who defeated five other top-11 ranked teams, won the race on the 2,000-meter course in 7:07.76, with sixth-ranked Villanova second (7:16.28), third-ranked Stanford third (7:16.50), No. 5 Georgetown fourth (7:25.07), No. 10 San Diego State fifth (7:31.05) and No. 11 California sixth (7:35.34).

Claire Wallace (bow), Megan DeLonge, Katie Childs, Ali Endress, Lindsay Rongstad, Jessica Neuville, Eva Payne, Katie Sweet (stroke), and Tessa Molter (coxswain) made up the winning Wisco boating.

At the April 13 Knecht Cup, sponsored by Villanova, Wisconsin placed third, behind Princeton (6:58.3) and Radcliffe (6:58.7). Central Florida (7:16.7), Villanova and Delaware trailed.

The LWV4+ (8:27.6) did better, finishing a rather distant second behind Princeton (8:13.7) and ahead of Rhode Island (8:28.6), Radcliffe (8:31.5), Princeton B and Indiana. UW's boating: Diane Martins (bow), Jen Howard, Anne Porter, Jessica Lee (stroke), and Jade Brueckner (coxswain). Wisco's Novice LW8 (7:28) was also second, bowing to Princeton (7:16.9) while defeating Georgetown (7:33) and Penn State (8:31). The NLW8+ boating included Sarah Spolum (bow), Caroline Klocko, Sarah Schumaker, Shea Fetherston, Anaya Drew, Melissa Trinley, Kit Litzinger, Katie Smith (stroke), and Erin Specht (coxswain).

At the Eastern Sprints in Camden, New Jersey—with the collegiate openweights also rowing, in separate events—the Badger LW8+ finished third, the LW4+ was second and the LWN8+ was second. The varsity order of finish was: Princeton (7:06.40), Radcliffe (7:09.12), Wisconsin (7:14.02), Georgetown (7:27.58), and William and Mary (7:48.10).

The LWV4+ finish was: Princeton (8:14.50), Wisconsin (8:22.34), Radcliffe "A" (8:26.34), MIT (8:33.44), Radcliffe "B" (8:47.29), and Georgetown (8:48.70). Meanwhile, the Badger NLW4+ won the Petite Final over MIT. The Badger varsity four LW boating: Jen Howard (bow), Jessica Neuville, Diane Martins, Andrea Ryan (stroke), and Jade Brueckner (coxswain).

The lightweight women's college eights national championship ended the team's season. The event was held at the IRAs, largely a men's collegiate rowing season finale, in Camden on May 31. Wisconsin found its usual finishing position this season against the nation's best lightweight women's crews in the 2003 season —third place.

The Grand Final ended with Princeton (6:56.12) first, followed by Radcliffe (6:59.24), Wisconsin (7:02.31), Georgetown (7:05.48), Stanford (7:11.59), and Purdue (7:12.33). UW's varsity LW8+ boating was Claire Wallace (bow), Jessica Lee, Lindsay Rongstad, Megan DeLonge, Ali Endress, Andrea Ryan, Eva Payne, Katie Sweet (stroke), and Tessa Molter (coxswain).

Badger Katie Hammes rowed for the U.S. in the pairs (bow-seat) at the Milan, Italy, Worlds of 2003 and finished sixth.

The women's 2003–4 season began with more coaching changes. The "at large" designations disappeared when two coaches were replaced and team-specific assistant coaching assignments were formalized. It is probably an understatement to say that the impact of the annual coaching changes since 1999 created a sense of malaise, if not turmoil.

Though State of Wisconsin budget cuts were deep in many places over fiscal year 2003–4, especially in the University of Wisconsin system, a major commitment to all three of the crews at Wisconsin was solidified. Demolition of the old facility and construction of a new boathouse on the same site began in September of 2003. A larger facility had been sought for many years, because the single-crew facility, completed in 1968, became more and more overcrowded as two new women's crews were added. The substantial completion date was December 2004. A newer, more functional and attractive crew house is expected to improve recruiting for all three teams and with it, a return of the openweight program to a consistently high level of success.

Openweight Season Results

Nicole Borges joined the UW women's crew coaching staff as the assistant coach to lead the varsity openweights. Borges earned four rowing letters at the University of Washington through 2001 and rowed in several international regattas, including as a member of the Canadian National Rowing Team. She also coached at Vashon Island Rowing Club (2002–3) (off Seattle in the Puget Sound), assisted Washington's novice women and spent summers as a rowing instructor at the Toronto Boulevard Yacht Club in 1998 and 1999.

The Milwaukee River Challenge—a total of 4.4 miles in two legs—kicked off the fall crew season on Saturday, September 20. The Badgers raced five eight's in mixed boatings of lightweight and openweight rowers.

With good racing conditions, sunny skies and temperatures in the 60s, the order of finish in the eights was Iowa "A" (23:39), Wisconsin "A" (23:48), Wisconsin "C" (24:13), Iowa "B" (24:43), and Wisconsin "E" (24:45). Six four-oared boats, again with mixed lineups, were the Wisconsin entries to the small boat event, with the order of finish: Iowa "A," Wisconsin "A," Wisconsin "C," Iowa "B," Wisconsin "E," Wisconsin "F," and Picnic Point Rowing.

The big fall classic, the Head of the Charles on October 18 and 19, attracted 40 openweight entries. Wisconsin's Varsity 8 placed twelfth overall and eighth among college competitors. The four non-college entries—mostly national teams preparing for the Olympics coming up the following August—and the eight college finishers were: London Training Center (15:31.1), USRowing (15:49.6), Princeton Training Center (15:57.0), Yale (16:08.3), the Danish Roforeningen Kvik (16:12.1), Princeton (16:21.9), Brown (16:23.5), Radcliffe (16:31.4), Michigan (16:31.7), Stanford (16:32.5), Virginia (16:34.7), and Wisconsin (16:38.5). The Badger four entry was ninth in the overall field of 22 and sixth among the colleges.

On February 20, 2004, head coach Maren LaLiberty, in her second season, announced her resignation for personal reasons. Former UW coach Sue Ela was named interim director of Women's Crew, while Nicole Borges, then varsity assistant coach, and Marina Traub, then the novice coach, were given the job of co-coaching the varsity teams. In an interview in April, Ela answered a query on the turmoil that had resulted from ongoing coaching changes and temporary crew quarters, "I'm congratulatory . . . I think the team, the rowers have rallied around one another. They have learned to deal with adversity. I think as a staff, we've worked together to support one another and to support the team having the best possible season."

Competing for the Jessop-Whittier Cup at the San Diego Classic on April 3–4, the Badgers equaled their best finish since the 1998 season by coming in fifth (7:06.0), behind Cal (6:57.1), Washington (7:00.6), Tennessee (7:02.7), Washington

State (7:04.1), and ahead of USC (7:10.0) and Notre Dame (7:16.9). Wisco's 2V8 finished fourth and the Novice 8 was seventh.

The Big Ten Championships followed as the next big regatta. Held in Iowa City on May 1, Wisconsin demonstrated why it had climbed slowly in the national rankings over the previous several weekends of the season. The Badgers upset top-seeded Minnesota in the heats of the Varsity 4, and Wisconsin qualified all six of its boats for the grand finals.

The finals began with a UW victory in the Second Novice 8 event, their fifth consecutive win in the five years since this regatta had been staged. The finish: Wisconsin (7:10.5), Minnesota (7:11.0), Michigan State (7:16.3), Ohio State (7:20.4), and Michigan (7:41.1). UW's 2N8 boating was Jamie Genth (bow), Erica Hanson, Tegan Jones, Christen Stevens, Kelly Kwas, Suzie Benoit, Emily Boesen, Erin West (stroke), and Sonya Baumstein (coxswain).

The 2V8 finished third, the 1V4+ was second, the 2V4+ ended third, and the Novice 8 came in third. The Varsity 8 also finished third, which gave the Badgers enough points in the overall standing to finish second as a team, the school's highest-ever finish in the five-year-old Big Ten Championships. In the overall team standings for the Big Ten Regatta, Michigan (128) finished first, followed by Wisconsin (115), Ohio State (112), Michigan State (111), Minnesota (78), Iowa (42), and Indiana (27).

The UW women skipped the Eastern Sprints,[9] for only the second time since 1974, in order to focus on the South-Central regional regatta, an important opportunity to attract an invitation to the NCAA's three-event national championships. The NCAA divides the country into five rowing regions, each sending at least one team representative. After the first five teams are selected, seven additional "at-large" teams are chosen to send three boats each. Finally, four other schools are invited to send just a varsity eight entry to the race, which in 2004 was to be held in Rancho Cordova, California. There are no novice events in the NCAA-sponsored women's collegiate openweight rowing championship format.

In the South-Central regional finals, the V4+ finished second, the 2V8+ came in fourth, and the V8+ ended in fifth place. In the Badger V8+ boating were Nicole Weir (bow), Katie Culp, Julie Quoss, Christina Strasser, Bryana Seifert, Kari Harmon, Emily Simonds, Nikki Lennart (stroke), and Beth Redfearn (coxswain). As a result of the Badger openweights' showing at these Regionals, the squad received its first NCAA invitation since 1999 and only its second overall.

At the NCAA tournament from May 28 to 30, the Badgers rowed their best in the Varsity 4 with coxswain, finishing seventh overall. The Wisco V4+ boating: Malika McCormick (bow), Leah Gordon, Katie Pofahl, Kirby Gallie (stroke), and Megan Stevens (coxswain). The second Varsity 8 was second in their Petite Finals, finishing eighth overall. The 2V8 boating: Kim Ackerbauer (bow), Katie Karls,

Shannon Gedman, Amanda Frederick, Lindsay Bush, Jennifer Tuffree, Nicole Nelson, Katherine Lawson (stroke), and Meg Bradshaw (coxswain).

With the V8 finishing sixteenth overall, Wisconsin (with 19 points) as a team came in eleventh, behind leaders Brown (70), Yale (58), Michigan (52), Cal (51), Washington (43), Princeton (36), Virginia (36), Ohio State (33), Washington State (28), and Harvard (24).

Lightweight Season Results (2003–4)

Mary Shofner was hired as Varsity Lightweight Coach at the start of the fall of 2003, after spending two years as assistant coach for the University of Rhode Island. Shofner had rowed in college at the University of Central Florida. At Wisconsin she took over a program that had done very well in several recent seasons, but that had never achieved the pinnacle of their sport—winning a national championship.

At the Head of the Charles, the Badger lightweight eight finished third overall (of the fifteen entries) and second among the college competitors. The top six were Riverside Boat Club (16:47.78), Radcliffe (17:09.58), Wisconsin (17:11.44), Princeton (17:13.34), Hoya Boat Club (17:22.59), and Ottawa Rowing Club (17:37.64). Wisconsin's LW4+ was seventh of sixteen entries.

At the April 3–4 San Diego Classic, Wisconsin reeled in their fourth consecutive A. W. Coggeshall Cup, winning by an over-the-horizon margin of over seventeen seconds! The order of finish had Wisconsin (7:23.90) in the lead, followed by Stanford (7:40.98), University of Central Florida (7:47.63), Cal (7:51.33), Purdue (7:53.47), and San Diego State (7:53.91). Sponsored by the perennially loyal UW Alumni Association of San Diego, five members of the brass section of the Wisconsin Band played rallying music from the shore of Mission Bay, some 250 meters from the finish.

The Knecht Cup was held in Camden, New Jersey, on April 10 and 11, with over fifty schools attending. In the LW8+ finals, Wisconsin ended in third with the following order of finish: Princeton (7:06.2), Radcliffe (7:08.6), Wisconsin (7:08.9), Georgetown (7:18.3), University of Rhode Island (7:19.7), and Stanford (7:22.6). It was Princeton's second title in a row. The Badger V4+ (8:03.2) won their Knecht Cup event, defeating Georgetown (8:08.3), Radcliffe "A" (8:09.7), Princeton (8:17.6), St. Joe's (8:20.7), and Radcliffe "B" (8:26.7). UW's V4+ boating had Sarah Liefke (bow), Diane Martins, Candy Hansey, Claire Wallace (stroke), and Ashley Strobel (coxswain).

For their conference championships, the Badger lightweights returned to Camden on May 9 for the Eastern Sprints—the "conference" of UW's lightweight crew. It was a day to be remembered as all three Wisco entries earned a silver!

UW's Lightweight Eight—Winners of the IRA in 2004. Standing: Coach Mary Shofner, Andrea Ryan (bow), Anaya Drew, Mary Higgins, Ali Endress, Eileen Storm; crouching: Lindsey Rongstad, Katie Sweet, Eva Payne(stroke); foreground: Erin Specht (coxswain). Photo © SportGraphics.com.

Under sunny skies, westerly winds and temperatures in the mid-80s, the varsity eights of Radcliffe and Princeton jumped off to an early lead and held until the 1,500-meter mark, when the Badgers put on a gutsy sprint and surged ahead of the Tigers. Radcliffe (6:38.60) captured the gold. The followers were Wisconsin (6:41.47), Princeton (6:42.10), Georgetown (6:43.80), and MIT (6:44.60). The V8 line up for Wisconsin was Jessica Lee (bow), Anaya Drew, Mary Higgins, Ali Endress, Eileen Storm, Lindsey Rongstad, Katie Sweet, Eva Payne (stroke), and Erin Specht (coxswain).

In the N8+, the order of finish was Purdue (7:04.4), Wisconsin (7:14.99), Georgetown (7:19.96), and Radcliffe (7:30.5). Liz Hartje (bow), Alicia Albers, Joanne Scherwinski, Emily Sitek, Julie Nielson, Katy Klemme, Suzie Sagues, Faye Ehrich (stroke), and Erin O'Boyle (coxswain) were Wisconsin's N8+ boating. In the V4+, Wisconsin (7:38.90) finished behind Princeton (7:36.40), and ahead of Georgetown (7:43.14) and Radcliffe (7:48.91). The V4+ lineup for Wisconsin included Candy Hansey (bow), Diane Martins, Andrea Ryan, Claire Wallace (stroke), and Courtney Carlovsky (coxswain).

In the grand finale of the season—the lightweight women's eight event at the IRA regatta—the Badger women provided some needed pride and excitement to an otherwise disappointing regatta for the Badger heavyweight men, when they won their Grand Final event by almost twelve seconds! This was the event's largest margin of victory ever at the IRAs. Under overcast skies and cool temperatures, the Badgers (7:06.36) defeated Princeton (7:18.02), Radcliffe (7:19.04), Georgetown (7:25.59), Rhode Island (7:29.07), and Central Florida (7:43.77).

The margin of victory had at least one Web site commentator speculating that a Badger openweight rower had been slipped into the Badger lightweight's boating . . . a matter quickly disproven when earlier UW lightweight race rosters were e-mailed to the columnist.

The national championship UW boating—the program's first since starting in 1995—was Andrea Ryan (bow), Anaya Drew, Mary Higgins, Ali Endress, Eileen Storm, Lindsey Rongstad, Katie Sweet, Eva Payne (stroke), and Erin Specht (coxswain).[10]

The lightweight eight had not only added another crown to the school's long and proud rowing legacy, but the victory also added a strong statement—with the margin of victory adding a major punctuation mark—to the history of athletics at the University of Wisconsin.

Following a nationwide search for a new Wisconsin women's head coach, Bebe Bryans, former head coach at Michigan State, was brought on board in June 2004. The only coach at Michigan State since their varsity program began seven years previously, Bryans led the Spartans to five NCAA championship regatta appearances in the seven years of the regatta. Bryans, forty-six at the time of her hiring, had been named the Big Ten Rowing Coach of the Year in 2000 and 2003.

Prior to coaching at Michigan State, Bryans had served as the women's coach at Georgetown from 1992 to 1997, and before that at Mills College from 1988 to 1992. Over the summers of 1992 and 1993, Bryans was the head coach at the Junior World Championships. A 1986 graduate of San Francisco State University, Bryans was a ten-time Division II All-American in swimming.

Bryans's experience and indisputable record of success in her prior coaching responsibilities bodes very well for a resurgence in the prospects for women's rowing at Wisconsin. Assisting Bryans will be three of last year's four assistant coaches. The new face at the start of the 2004–5 season will be Amy Appleton, who coached for UW from 1998 to 2002. Appleton will take on responsibilities for the varsity openweight squad, while Nicole Borges will take over the responsibilities for the novice openweight squad.

Bebe Bryans, UW Women's Rowing Head Coach, 2004 to present. Photo courtesy of UW Athletic Communications.

The Last Piece

While college rowing, the oldest of college sports, has slipped from its position on the front pages of U.S. newspapers of a century ago—losing its preeminence to a proliferation of sports at all levels—rowing at the Olympics, the annual World Championships, and the Oxford-Cambridge "Boat Races" are watched by millions in Europe. It would be wonderful to see this trend reversed in the U.S. with more live coverage of the sport.

In Wisconsin, the future of rowing is well-grounded and secure. With the new crew house of over fifty thousand square feet largely completed in December of 2004, two highly regarded head coaches of the men's and women's programs and a continuing stream of smart, high-caliber athletes seeking a first-class education at UW–Madison, Badger rowing will further solidify its place among the top teams in national collegiate rowing.

The lack of scholarships at UW–Madison remains a challenge to the men's heavyweight and women's lightweight crew programs. Hopefully, clarification and evolution of Title IX—together with additional financial support—will help advance this issue and make Wisconsin even more competitive in the future. Ideally, the NCAA will find its way to sponsoring a national championship for men's crew and, in doing so, make its own contribution to a more level playing field. At this writing, the Pac-Ten is sounding as if they will be soliciting the NCAA to sanction men's crew and suggesting preliminarily a scholarship cap of the equivalent of 4.5 scholarships.

Endowments supporting all three of these teams would underpin a future longevity to this Olympic sport. Older generations of rowers will continue to support the younger. And the torch will be passed.

Rowing remains a unique combination of team and individual sport. Individuals look into themselves to find just how far they can go, while rowing together in an eight, a four, or a pair forces a person to achieve conformity beyond oneself in order to row powerfully and in perfect unity. Four years of practicing and competing together builds bonds of lifelong friendship among collegiate student-athletes. "Look around you," goes the coach's fall introduction to many novice rowers. "Many of those you see will be in your weddings and remain among the best friends you'll ever have over the rest of your lives."

To parents and supporters watching a start, the rumbling oarlocks as the shells work up to their settling pace, will always be in their ears. For those watching at the end, the surging excitement of urging a child or friend across the finish line will always be in their hearts. And to all who have competed for UW–Madison in the sport of intercollegiate rowing, may your mind forever hear the bold and boisterous shout of

Go Wisco!!

Appendix 1: "W" Winners

Appendix 2: UW Captains

Appendix 3: Boatings of the Fourteen UW Ten Eyck Trophy Victories

Notes

Bibliography

Index

Appendix 1
"W" Winners

Men's Crew "W" Winners, 1893–2004

YEAR	NAME	YEAR	NAME
1874 (intramural)	George P. Bradish*	1899	Louis W. Olson
1893	Harry B. Boardman	1899, 1900, 1901	William J. "Will" Gibson
1893	Chester C. Case		
1893	A. D. Daggett	1900	Francis. H. Crosby
1893	C. H. Howell	1900	William K. Herrick
1893	Herbert H. Jacobs	1900	Lynn A. Williams
1893	Henry H. Morgan	1900, 1901, 1902, 1903	Charles Harold Gaffin
1893	L. L. Worden		
		1901	Walter P. Hirschberg
1894	John D. Freeman	1901	Frederick A. Little
1894	W. W. Geisse	1901	T. F. Sawyer
1894	J. R. Richards	1901	T. E. VanMeter
1894	Percy Roberts		
1894	A. K. Sedgwick	1902	B. F. Lounsbury
		1902	John Q. Lyman
1895	Lee F. Austin	1902	William F. Moffatt
1895	Samuel Cady	1902	Glen Steere
1895	John Day		
1895	Curran C. McConville	1903	A. H. Bartlett
1895	Oscar Rohn	1903	Arthur H. Christman
1895	Marshall E. Seymour	1903	Arthur J. Quigley
1895	George P. Barth	1903, 1904	Albert B. Dean
1896	Walter A. Alexander	1904	Allen C. Abbott
1896	W. Dietrich	1904	Percy ApRoberts
1896	Harry C. Forrest	1904	Beverly B. Burling
1896	Walter Sheldon	1904	Morris F. Fox
		1904	Elbert L. Jordan
1897	Andrew R. Anderson	1904	E. V. McComb
1897	H. R. Chamberland	1904	John Church Potter
1897	H. A. Lake	1904	John R. Sawyer
1897	Joe Major	1904	Dwight C. Trevarthen
1897	J. F. A. Pyre	1904, 1905	Carl S. Reed
1897, 1898, 1899	William C. Sutherland		
1897	Merton L. Webber	1905	A. C. Boyle
		1905	T. L. Burke
1898	Harry R. Crandall	1905	G. G. Byden
1898	R. T. Logeman	1905	F. Ellis Johnson
1898	Lester C. Street	1905	Arthur H. Miller
1898, 1899, 1900	Alonzo A. Chamberlain	1905	D. W. Miller
1898, 1899, 1902, 1903	Israel Mather	1905	Earl B. Rose
		1905	Arthur H. Schumacher
1899	S. C. Welsh	1905	Robert G. Stevenson
1899	Joseph G. Dillon		

* Honorary "W" granted in 1912, per Athletic Department's *Centennial Media Guide of 1948*

YEAR	NAME	YEAR	NAME
1906	Max N. Bodenbach	1914	Bruce Tasker
1906	William Conway		
1906, 1907	Verl A. Ruth	1915	Charles W. Evert
		1915	Martin T. Kennedy
1907	Alfred W. Bechlem	1915	H. A. Lewis
1907	Benjamin F. Davis	1915	Harold L. Moffett
1907	George S. Hine	1915	Fred G. Mueller
1907	R. W. Lea	1915	Ralph A. Peterson
1907	William A. Winkler	1915	C. H. Schroeder
1907, 1908, 1909	Eugene A. Dinet	1915	Arno Wittich
1908	Lester Holford Levisee	1916	J. B. Brown
1908	Eugene J. Ryan		
1908	George C. Wilder	1920, 1921, 1922, 1923	Gerald Wade
1909	Ernest J. Steinberg	1921	Fred C. Prehn
1909	Rueben N. Trane	1921	George O. Toepfer
1909	Dexter H. Witte	1921, 1923	Everett H. Crozier
1909, 1910	Clarence N. Johnson	1921, 1923	Paul J. Okerstrom
1909, 1910, 1911, 1912	Robert L. Bowen		
		1922	Ed Hanley
1910	Robert Iakisch	1922	William F. Koch
1910	Henry W. John	1922	Charles B. Puestow
1910	Samuel Kerr, Jr.		
1910	William D. Richardson	1923	K. H. Fauerbach
1910	William O. VanLoon	1923	Raymond C. Klussendorf
1910	John W. "Jack" Wilce	1923	Don C. Newcomb
		1923, 1924	Ralph J. Schueutz
1911	John S. Corley	1923, 1924, 1925	Harold "Jack" Bentson
1911	Kenneth R. Hare	1923, 1924, 1925, 1926	Oscar W. Teckemeyer
1911	Karl L. Kraatz		
1911	L. E. Voyer	1924	Kenneth Gardner
1911, 1912	Kenneth S. Templeton	1924	Howard E. Johnson
1911, 1912	George F. Roberts	1924	E. M. Plettner
1911, 1912	Frank C. Wood	1924	G. C. Turner
1911, 1912, 1913	Marshall Graff	1924, 1925	Keith C. Sly
		1924, 1925, 1926	Henry C. McCormick
1912	John A. Fletcher	1924, 1925, 1926	Harold L. "Jerry" Coulter
1912	Charles M. Pollock	1924, 1925, 1926, 1927	Jefferson D. Burrus, Jr.
1912	Axel T. Sjoblom		
1912	Maurice C. Sjoblom	1925	Gordon Arey
1912 (1906)	Edward R. Richter	1925	William Gerhardt
1912, 1913, 1914	Hoy B. Clayton	1925	Eric Grunitz
1912, 1913	Ray L. Cuff	1925	C. J. Jax
		1925	Orville L. Jones
1913	Malcolm McFarland	1925	Richard V. Rhode
1913	Donald J. McLeod	1925, 1926, 1928	John C. McCarter
1913, 1914	Gustav Bohstedt		
1913, 1914	Carl H. Casberg	1926	Doesey A. Buckley
1913, 1914, 1915	Albert J. Dexter	1926, 1927	Allan B. Bibbey
		1926, 1927, 1928	Homer E. Kieweg
1914	John S. Gorley	1926, 1927, 1928	Lawrence Kingsbury
1914	Karl T. Schweitzer	1926, 1927, 1928	Franklin L. Orth

YEAR	NAME	YEAR	NAME
		1932	Robert O. Kettnet
1927	John E. Cullinane	1932	Oscar Olson
1927	Henry F. Hagemeister	1932, 1933	Paul O. Eckhardt, Jr.
1927	Oscar Woelfel	1932, 1933	Theo Eserkaln
1927, 1928	Dietrick Lunde	1932, 1934	Edward C. Helmke
1927, 1928	Foster C. Smith	1932, 1934	James F. McCain
1927, 1928, 1929, 1930	John L. Parks		
1927, 1929	Edwin J. Kesting	1933	Gordon R. Anderson
		1933	Almor A. Bartz
1928	Don B. Abert	1933	Sam D. Berger
1928	Frazier W. Bassett	1933	George Herro
1928	Phil Davis	1933	Ralph Hunn
1928	Lloyd R. Taylor	1933, 1934	Robert Kaska
1928	Robert A. Zentner	1933, 1934, 1935	Jack E. Cole
1928, 1929	Warren Drouet	1933, 1934, 1935	James Ivins
1928, 1929	Joseph David Horsfall	1933, 1934, 1935	Irving R. Kraemer
1928, 1929, 1930	Eugene Goodman	1933, 1934, 1935	Philip W. Rosten
1928, 1929, 1930	Jerome W. Sperling		
		1934	Victor Falk
1929	Duncan Beers	1934	Gerhardt A. Getzin
1929	Robert D. Evans	1934	Edward Le Veen
1929	Robert Jones	1934	James I. Weimer
1929, 1930	Max Goldsmith	1934	Casimer Zielinski
1929, 1930	Arthur J. Keenan	1934, 1935	Donald K. Gehrz
1929, 1930	Eldon M. Marple	1934, 1935	Otto Hibma
1929, 1930, 1931	Aaron J. Ihde	1934, 1935, 1936	Howard T. Heun
1929, 1930, 1931	William W. Lumpkin	1934, 1936	Lloyd Smith
1929, 1930, 1931	Louis E. Oberdeck	1934, 1936	W. Thomas Woodward
1929, 1930, 1931	Clifford B. Woodward		
1929, 1930, 1931	Harold H. Zabel	1935	Edward B. Barney
		1935	J. Crawford Crosland
1930	Fred G. Morton	1935	Charles Fiedelman
1930	Henry C. Weber	1935	Alfred Graef
1930	John A. Zeratsky	1935	Herbert Loomis
1930, 1931	George W. "Rip" Miller	1935	Phillip H. Seefeld
1930, 1931, 1932	William B. Hovey	1935	Clarke Smith
		1935, 1936	Frederic A. Benedict
1931	Henry A. Anderson	1935, 1936, 1937	Joe W. Brooks
1931	Orville G. Dutton	1935, 1936, 1937	W. L. Charles Burroughs
1931	Robert E. Jones	1935, 1936, 1937	Robert S. Heinze
1931	Richard C. Woodman	1935, 1936, 1937	Donald R. Heun
1931	John Zaylor		
1931, 1932	Harold Smedal	1936	Carl A. Burghardt, Jr.
1931, 1932	Sam B. Berger	1936	Ray L. Gaudette
1931, 1932	Robert M. Wells	1936	Richard Tinkham
1931, 1932, 1933	Roman P. Metz	1936, 1937	Richard M. Hofmann
1931, 1932, 1933	Herman A. Silbernagel	1936, 1937	Franz Ibisch
1931, 1932, 1933	Charles Tessendorf	1936, 1937	Stuart Olbrich
		1936, 1937, 1938	Arthur Robert Bridge
1932	Norwood T. Bryant	1936, 1937, 1938	Edwin J. Collins, Jr.
1932	Fred L. Emerson	1936, 1937, 1938	Ray Parker Pacausky
1932	Kenneth Hollander	1936, 1937, 1938	Donald C. Wiggins
1932	Robert Keown	1936, 1937, 1938	Robert W. Wolfe

YEAR	NAME	YEAR	NAME
		1941, 1942, 1946	Chester T. Knight
1937, 1938	Albert A. Pavlic	1941, 1942, 1947, 1948	A. LeRoy "Larry" Jensen
1937, 1938, 1939	Edmund J. Ryan		
		1942	Ralph Busch, Jr.
1938	John Davenport	1942	Robert L. Lowe
1938	Edgar Milhaupt	1942	Robert E. Moore
1938	Oscar Nerenberg	1942	William G. Phelan
1938, 1939	Donald Krause	1942	Roy C. Rom
1938, 1939	Wilfred H. Drath	1942	James H. Smythe
1938, 1939	Robert G. Hendy	1942, 1946, 1947	Carl A. Holtz
1938, 1939	Fred Kraatz	1942, 1946, 1947	Richard E. Mueller
1938, 1939	Walter Schultz		
1938, 1939	Harry Stroebe, Jr.	1943	Marshall Leard
1938, 1940	David W. Rendall, Sr.		
		1944	Harold Hamel
1939	John A. Beck	1944	Robert L. Lowe
1939	Victor Breytspraak	1944, 1946	Wayne Sanderhoff
1939	George Fraser		
1939	Lloyd J. Hughes	1945	Robert I. Rathcamp
1939	Robert Roederick	1945, 1946	Paul J. Kleinschmidt
1939	Robert J. Rosenheimer		
1939	Stanley F. Vaicelunas	1946	Andrew Allen
1939, 1940	William R. Goodier	1946	Joseph C. Binder
1939, 1940	John G. "Jack" Gunning	1946	Harold Danford
1939, 1940	Anthony Krancus	1946	William Horvath
1939, 1940	Lawrence E. Muskavitch	1946	Leon Jones
1939, 1940	John Rydell	1946	John Leverson
1939, 1940	Daniel Turner	1946, 1947	George H. Elder
1939, 1940, 1941, 1942	George Struck	1946, 1947	Gerald F. Gredler
		1946, 1947	Richard Kennedy, Jr.
1940	John D. Bates	1946, 1947	Fred R. Suchow
1940	Alexander Bodenstein	1946, 1947	Jacob M. Valentine, Jr.
1940	Richard Frazer	1946, 1947, 1948	Thomas A. Blacklock
1940	George N. Harris	1946, 1947, 1948	Ralph C. Falconer
1940	Wayne H. Weidemann	1946, 1947, 1948	Carlyle W. "Bud" Fay
1940, 1941	John Bruemmer	1946, 1947, 1948, 1949	Gordon T. Grimstad
1940, 1941	Frank T. Cameron	1946, 1947, 1948, 1949	Richard E. Tipple
1940, 1941	Harold E. Krueger	1946, 1948	Robert A. Hedges
1940, 1941	Clarence O. Schwengel		
1940, 1941, 1942	Thomas Thies	1947	Paul A. Honzik
		1947	Arthur Weise
1941	William Binney	1947, 1948, 1949	Frank L. Harris
1941	Howard E. Kaerwer, Jr.	1947, 1948, 1949	Donald J. Peterson
1941	Eugene Kleinschmidt	1947, 1948, 1949	Otto F. Uher
1941	Andrew Konopka		
1941	Thomas H. Lorenz	1948	George H. Crandall
1941	Donald C. Reek	1948	James Grootemaat
1941	Charles Willison	1948	John Mc Bratney
1941, 1944	Thomas W. McKern	1948	Floyd S. Nixon
1941, 1942	Robert C. Jenkins	1948	Robert Rath
1941, 1942	George A. Rea	1948, 1949	William D. Gittings
1941, 1942	Justin A. Walstad, Jr.	1948, 1949	Donn Linton
1941, 1942	James S. Yonk	1948, 1949, 1950	James C. Connell

YEAR	NAME	YEAR	NAME
1948, 1949, 1950	John C. Jung	1953, 1955	Jackson E. Goffman
1948, 1949, 1950	William R. Sachse	1953, 1955	Kenneth Runlee
1949	Paul M. Benson	1954	Thomas Butterbrodt
1949	Donald E. Haack	1954	David Nelson
1949	Earl L. Lapp	1954	Irwin Smith
1949, 1950	Norman Folts	1954, 1955	Stanley S. Smith
1949, 1950	John B. Gittings	1954, 1955	James E. Williams
1949, 1950	James Kress	1954, 1955, 1956	John G. Shaw
1949, 1950	Clifford F. Rathkamp	1954, 1955, 1956	Richard M. Smith
1949, 1950, 1951	Duane "Doc" Daentl	1954, 1955, 1956	Louis J. Uehling
1949, 1950, 1951	James B. Langdon	1954, 1955, 1957	James Urban
1949, 1950, 1951	Peter Wackman	1954, 1956	David Falk, Sr.
		1954, 1956	Foster Smith
1950	Frank M. Heuston	1954, 1956, 1957	Eugene "Gene" R. Huske
1950, 1951	Donald G. Heyden		
1950, 1951	Michael B. Torphy, Jr.	1955	Richard D. Center
1950, 1951, 1952	Delos Barrett	1955	Thomas D. Kussow
1950, 1951, 1952	Rollin B. Cooper	1955, 1956	Patrick Casey
1950, 1951, 1952	Robert Espeseth, Sr.	1955, 1956	Robert Farley, III
1950, 1951, 1952	Robert Y. "R. Y." Nelson	1955, 1956	Robert B. Graves
1950, 1951, 1952	James A. Schmidt	1955, 1956	Robert Madzar
		1955, 1956	Earle Olson
1951	Duane W. Hopp	1955, 1956, 1957	Allen H. Goldsmith
1951	John L. Schlick	1955, 1956, 1957	John L. Morgen
1951	James L. Van Egeren	1955, 1956, 1957	Dean R. Walker
1951, 1952, 1953	James C. Healy	1955, 1956, 1957, 1958	Richard O. Trummer
1951, 1952, 1953	Robert G. Hood	1955, 1956, 1958, 1959	Richard T. Ahner
1951, 1952, 1953	James T. Moran		
1951, 1952, 1953	Robert D. Roehrs	1956	David Slickman
1951, 1952, 1953	Victor H. Steuck	1956, 1957	Brian Bagley
1951, 1952, 1953	Donald L. Rose	1956, 1957	Norman Rasulis
		1956, 1957	William Yount
1952	Norbert Gehrke	1956, 1957, 1958	William L. Ehrke
1952	Robert S. Gittings	1956, 1957, 1958	Joe R. Irwin
1952	Richard Oehler	1956, 1957, 1958	John R. Koch
1952	William G. Priestley	1956, 1957, 1958	Thomas J. Prosser
1952, 1953	John Liesman	1956, 1957, 1958	Robert Larry Schmitt
1952, 1953	Edward C. Schleg	1956, 1958	Alan F. Clark
1952, 1953	Allen Wheeler		
1952, 1953, 1954	James H. Lorenzen	1957	Robert J. Mazur
1952, 1953, 1954	Virgil F. Trummer	1957	Terrol L. Rose
		1957, 1958	Ted Martens
1953	Richard L. Danner	1957, 1958	Donald Spring
1953	Maurice A. Johnson, Jr.	1957, 1958, 1959	Herbert L. Degner
1953	James C. King	1957, 1958, 1960	Alan Mess
1953, 1954	Jerry Finer	1957, 1959, 1960	Randall T. "Jabo" Jablonic
1953, 1954	Jerry D. Fink		
1953, 1954	William E. Mueller	1958	Philip Witte
1953, 1954	William A. Schneider	1958, 1959	Edgar Jacobi, Jr.
1953, 1954	John C. Severance	1958, 1959	Kenneth Olen
1953, 1954	James K. Winslow	1958, 1959	John Olson
1953, 1954, 1955	Carl E. Merow	1958, 1959	Robert Witte

YEAR	NAME	YEAR	NAME
1958, 1959, 1960	James H. Bowen	1964	George R. Emerson
1958, 1959, 1960	Courtney D. Freeman, Jr.	1964	Norbert Grisar
1958, 1959, 1960	Charles B. Pope	1964	George Thos. Kroncke
1958, 1959, 1960	Dale F. Sharpee	1964	Thomas O. Olson
1958, 1959, 1960	Palmer W. Taylor	1964	Charles A. Ruedebusch
1958, 1959, 1960	William A. Brauer	1964, 1965	Dennis W. Gillespie
		1964, 1965	Donald W. Mowry
1959	James Hanke	1964, 1965	Daniel W. Schwoerer
1959	Graham H. Hoffman	1964, 1965, 1966	Robert Boettcher
1959, 1960, 1961	Keith Herman	1964, 1965, 1966	Thomas G. Mitchell
1959, 1960, 1961	Phillip W. Mork	1964, 1965, 1966	Roger Seeman
1959, 1960, 1961	Ernest C. Smith	1964, 1965, 1966	Willard E. Witte
1959, 1961	Charles Laupp		
1959, 1961	Robert Schmidt	1965	Robert Krolnik
		1965	Lloyd S. Smith
1960, 1961	Steve Ballou	1965, 1966	David J. Storm
1960, 1961	John Hanson	1965, 1966	James H. Tonn
1960, 1961	Stephen Marsh	1965, 1966, 1967	William R. Clapp
1960, 1961, 1962	David W. Novak	1965, 1966, 1967	Neil C. Halleen
1960, 1961, 1962	Charles Temp	1965, 1966, 1967	John D. Halleran
1960, 1962	John P. Shaffer	1965, 1966, 1967	John I. Norsetter
		1965, 1966, 1967, 1968	Michael D. Danley
1961	Robert R. Burke		
1961	(John) Doug Haag	1966	Alan R. Horner
1961	James A. Kurtz	1966, 1967	Steven J. Bergum
1961, 1962	Denis Betzhold	1966, 1967	Gregory M. Farnham
1961, 1962	Gary L. Jacobson	1966, 1967	Donald E. Lange
1961, 1962	Douglas V. Knudson	1966, 1967	Bruce Larson
1961, 1962	William J. McIntire	1966, 1967	David J. Quam
1961, 1962, 1963	Donald C. Erbach	1966, 1967, 1968	David J. Ivaska
1961, 1962, 1963	Bernard A. Losching	1966, 1967, 1968	John C. Lorenz
1961, 1962, 1963	Douglas R. Reiner	1966, 1967, 1968	Arnold S. Polk
1961, 1963	David G. McClyman		
		1967	William D. Blakely
1962	John C. Albright	1967	Thomas W. Sy
1962, 1963	Jonathan W. Greenfield	1967, 1968	Leo Burt
1962, 1963	Allan G. Heggblom	1967, 1968	Kent A. Kautzer
1962, 1963	Lawrence S. Hurwitz	1967, 1968	Alan L. Whitney
1962, 1963	Benjamin G. Porter	1967, 1968, 1969	Guy W. Iverson
1962, 1963	Michael Wilhelm	1967, 1968, 1969	Gary H. Jacobson
1962, 1963, 1964	Victor R. Johnson, Jr.	1967, 1968, 1969	Douglas A. Sahs
1962, 1963, 1964	Benton Logterman		
1962, 1963, 1964	Jonathon T. Stoddard	1968	Philip L. Fitzgerald
1962, 1963, 1964	Marvin F. Utech, Jr.	1968	Edward Goldschmidt, Jr.
		1968	George W. Jackson
1963	Rodney W. De Spirito	1968	Ronald W. Kuehn
1963	Thomas Willett	1968	James G. Ozark
1963, 1964	Edward Beimborn	1968	Kenneth A. Struckmeyer
1963, 1964	Kent W. Carnahan	1968	Lewis Turner, Jr.
1963, 1964	James Hafemeister	1968, 1969	William J. Evans, III
1963, 1964, 1965	Steve Goodman	1968, 1969	Gary H. Jacobson
1963, 1964, 1965	Thomas H. Haworth	1968, 1969	David J. La Luzerne
		1968, 1969, 1970	Greg A. Margulies

YEAR	NAME	YEAR	NAME
1968, 1969, 1970	Timothy C. Mickelson	1972	Michael T. Leadholm
1968, 1969, 1970	Joseph E. "Jay" Mimier	1972	Robert M. Stern
1968, 1969, 1970	Phillip E. Resch	1972	Mark O. Swanby
1968, 1969, 1970	Robert E. Rottman	1972	Mark Tomczak
1968, 1970	Robert H. Gibbs	1972, 1973, 1974	Loren P. Bartz
		1972, 1973, 1974	James C. Swanson
1969	James V. Barager	1972, 1974	Kenneth E. Nelson
1969	Michael D. Lohius		
1969	Patrick R. Pollock	1973	Theodore C. Blodgett
1969	Richard P. Purinton	1973	Charles R. Herdeman
1969	Phillip T. Schaefer	1973	James R. McNett
1969	Richard Zondag	1973	John C. Osborn, Jr.
1969, 1970, 1971	Robert A. Blakely	1973	Gary Weyers
1969, 1970, 1971	Robert B. Fick, Jr.	1973, 1974	William J. Klinger
1969, 1970, 1971	Thomas J. Flammang	1973, 1974	James F. Ricksecker
1969, 1970, 1971	Thomas E. Hertzberg	1973, 1974, 1975	Eric L. Aserlind
1969, 1970, 1971	Steve A. Salter	1973, 1974, 1975	James R. Dyreby, Jr.
1969, 1970, 1972	Stewart G. MacDonald, Jr.	1973, 1974, 1975	Robert D. Espeseth, Jr.
1969, 1971	Charles T. Allen	1973, 1974, 1975	James T. Kirsh, Jr.
1969, 1971	Larry C. Utter	1973, 1974, 1975	Louis S. Schueller, Jr.
		1973, 1974, 1975	Douglas B. Trosper
1970	Andrew L. MacKendrick	1973, 1974, 1975, 1976	John R. Storck
1970	Allen G. Philipsen		
1970	Timothy E. Sanders	1974, 1975	Arno F. Werner
1970, 1971	Welden A. Peterson, Jr.	1974, 1975, 1976	John O. Bauch
1970, 1971	Douglas D. Stitgen	1974, 1975, 1976	Ross B. Graves
1970, 1971, 1972	David A. Tomfohrde	1974, 1975, 1976	Joseph M. Knight
1970, 1971, 1972	John William Vegter	1974, 1975, 1976	John C. Mercier
		1974, 1976	Karl F. Newman
1971	Alan B. Anderson		
1971	Daniel Barrington	1975	David P. Eloranta
1971	Edward Biggins	1975	Peter R. Hamilton
1971	Curt L. Carpenter	1975	Christopher G. Hayes
1971	James Drewry	1975	Daniel Kammer
1971	Gary Hill	1975	Craig J. Kaplan
1971	Dale Jacobson	1975	Donald F. Kraft
1971	Michael D. Malak	1975	William C. Norsetter
1971	Mark A. Schmidt	1975	Laurence W. Trotter, II
1971	Thomas Shimshak	1975	Randall H. Zondag
1971	Walter E. Tamminen, Jr.	1975, 1976	James W. Freeman, Jr.
1971	Richard C. Zielinski	1975, 1976	Paul R. Gebel
1971, 1972	David R. Kairis	1975, 1976	Harold A. J. Menendez
1971, 1972	Robert J. Koca	1975, 1976	Frederick A. Robertson
1971, 1972	Bruce A. Niedermier	1975, 1976	James Sullivan
1971, 1972	Kevin J. Ruesch	1975, 1976, 1977	Paul G. Askins
1971, 1972	M. Nicholas Schroeder	1975, 1976, 1977	Tom S. Schuchardt
1971, 1972	Scott R. Springman		
1971, 1972	Paul O. J. Ziebarth	1976	Nestor Dominguez
1971, 1972, 1973	Robert Eloranta	1976, 1977	Mark C. Boyle
1971, 1972, 1973	Gerard C. Phelan	1976, 1977	Edward Jackson
1971, 1972, 1973, 1974	John Bosio	1976, 1977	Patrick Litscher
1971, 1974	Michael Gross	1976, 1977	Allen Teter
		1976, 1978	Trent Carlson

MEN'S CREW 'W' WINNERS   287

YEAR	NAME	YEAR	NAME
1976, 1978	Paul Smith	1981, 1982	Mark B. Hallett
1976, 1978, 1979	Dave Moecher	1981, 1982	Val Runge
		1981, 1982	Charles Williams
1977	Donald Dey	1981, 1982, 1983	Brian Frohna
1977	Clayton Ryder III	1981, 1982, 1983	Mark Johnson
1977	Paul Schroeter	1981, 1983	Robert Raymond
1977, 1978, 1979	Michael J. Gasper		
1977, 1978, 1979	William Olsen	1982	William Baker
		1982	Blaine Renfert
1978	David Krmpotich	1982, 1983	Paul Egelhoff
1978	David Kufahl	1982, 1983	Greg S. Gaskill
1978	John Rooney	1982, 1983	Thomas Martell
1978	Dave Schultz	1982, 1983, 1984	Brian Christensen
1978	Michael Stemo	1982, 1983, 1984	Richard Hallett
1978, 1979	Joel Bertocchi	1982, 1983, 1984	John Heinrich
1978, 1979	Jay Starr	1982, 1984, 1985	Robert C. Hougard, Jr.
1978, 1979	Daniel Wilms		
1978, 1979	David Zwieg	1983	Frederick R. Suchy
1978, 1979, 1980	Allan Erickson	1983	Michael Zupke
1978, 1979, 1980	Paul Lambert	1983, 1984	Matthew Brown
1978, 1979, 1980	Kenneth Lawrence	1983, 1984	Stuart Krause
1978, 1979, 1980	John Olson	1983, 1984	William Meyer
1978, 1980	Swift C. Corwin, Jr.	1983, 1984	Dean Vogel
1978, 1980	Michael Gitter	1983, 1984, 1985, 1986	Mark A. Berkner
1978, 1980	Christopher Landry	1983, 1984, 1986, 1987	Michael Risse
		1983, 1985	Hans E. Borcherding
1979	Vern Frol	1983, 1985, 1986, 1987	David Evenson
1979	Peter R. Gajentan		
1979	Phillip T. Healy	1984	Sandie Pendleton
1979	Mike Kleckner	1984	Gregory Polston
1979	Chris Lesbines	1984	Michael Schultz
1979	Bill Supernaw	1984	Scott Williams
1979	Mike Vrabec		
1979, 1980, 1981	Ned Kline	1985	Patrick Duray
		1985	Scott Gobeli
1980	Matthew Franke	1985	John Hallett
1980	Curtis Jelinek	1985	Daniel Hilliker
1980	Thomas Kirk	1985	Robert Knickrehm
1980	Frank Remington	1985	John Murer
1980	James D. Seefeldt	1985	Randall Reiner
1980	Donald Tipple	1985	Kurt Rongstad
1980, 1981	John Jablonic	1985	Samuel Huntington
1980, 1981, 1982	Aaron Jacob	1985	James Periard
1980, 1981, 1982	Steve Manicor	1985, 1986	Michael A. Farrar
1980, 1981, 1982	Daniel Royal	1985, 1986	Duncan Kennedy
1980, 1981, 1982	Brian Steinbrecher	1985, 1986	Patrick McDonough
1980, 1981, 1982	John H. Streur	1985, 1986	Tom Thornton
		1985, 1986	Tom Tryon
1981	Douglas Berninger	1985, 1986, 1987	Joseph Cincotta
1981	Konrad "K. C." Opitz	1985, 1986, 1987	Daniel Gehn
1981	Daniel J. Ripp	1985, 1986, 1987	Kevin McAleese
1981	Steve Shenkenberg	1985, 1986, 1987	Raymond Mejia
1981	Steve Zellmer	1985, 1986, 1987	David Rugolo

YEAR	NAME	YEAR	NAME
1985, 1986, 1987, 1988	Steve Adamski	1989, 1990, 1991	Greg Myhr
1985, 1986, 1987, 1988	William Filip	1989, 1990, 1991	Daniel O'Shea
1985, 1986, 1987, 1988	Bryan Griesbach	1989, 1990, 1991	Paul Savell
1985, 1986, 1987, 1988	Christopher Johnson	1989, 1990, 1991	Mark Sniderman
1985, 1986, 1987, 1988	Jon Jonsson	1989, 1990, 1991, 1992	George Cadwalader
1985, 1986, 1987, 1988	John Tucker		
		1990, 1991	James Almquist
1986	Mike Cain	1990, 1991	Atri Amin
1986	Ken Pettit	1990, 1991	David Bormett
1986	Chris Schulte	1990, 1991	Adam Burke
1986, 1987	Eric Moeller	1990, 1991	Fraser Hewson
1986, 1987, 1988	Scott Lynch	1990, 1991	Eric Kafka
1986, 1987, 1988, 1989	Brandon Foss	1990, 1991	Eric Mueller
1986, 1987, 1988, 1989	Timothy Greger	1990, 1991	Patrick O'Connell
1986, 1987, 1988, 1989	Gregory Werner	1990, 1991	Aari Roberts
		1990, 1991	Matt Simon
1987	Mark Burnett	1990, 1991	Patrick Van Derhei
1987	Andreas Demakoulos	1990, 1991, 1992, 1993	Patrick Wright
1987	David Evensen		
1987, 1988	Greg Larson	1991	Jason Berkin
1987, 1988	Scott Paulman	1991	Michael Check
1987, 1988, 1989	Kurt Borcherding	1991	Nicholas Donovan
1987, 1988, 1989	Todd Williams	1991	Brian Folz
1987, 1988, 1989, 1990	Luke Astell	1991	Steve Krakora
1987, 1988, 1989, 1990	Dave Guhl	1991	Shawn Kriewaldt
1987, 1988, 1989, 1990	David Hautanen	1991	Kevin Krueger
1987, 1988, 1989, 1990	Paul Stevens	1991	Hayes Miliani
1987, 1988, 1989, 1990	Patrick Wolf	1991	Dylan Morss
1987, 1989	Timothy Wike	1991	Dean Olson
		1991	Patrick Stoa
1988	Andrew Bassak	1991	Charles Stollenwerk
1988	John Hill	1991, 1992	Mark W. Sniderman
1988	Patrick Mc Donough	1991, 1992, 1993, 1994	Colin Dicke
1988, 1989	Stephen White		
1988, 1989, 1990	Edward "Fitz" Dunne	1992	Dennis Schrag
1988, 1989, 1990	Michael Fisher	1992, 1993	James Farmer
1988, 1989, 1990	Todd Hinrichs	1992, 1993, 1994	Jason Barnett
1988, 1989, 1990, 1991	Steve Hatton	1992, 1994	Roger Norenberg
1988, 1989, 1990, 1991	Robert Palmer		
1988, 1989, 1990, 1991	Bill Shenkenberg	1993	Luke Bogdanowicz
1988, 1989, 1990, 1991	Brett Welhouse	1993	Michael Call
		1993	Anders Gilchrist
1989, 1990	Matthew Dahl	1993	Todd Korb
1989, 1990	Jonathan Henry	1993	Paul Melstrom
1989, 1990, 1991	Andy Berns	1993	Paul Nicholas
1989, 1990, 1991	Geoffry Caan	1993	Sean Phelan
1989, 1990, 1991	Kirk Everett	1993	Ryan Quint
1989, 1990, 1991	John Feller	1993	Jonathan Schaefer
1989, 1990, 1991	Jeff Freitag	1993	Aaron Stegner
1989, 1990, 1991	Jim Howery	1993, 1995	Andrew Hardacre
1989, 1990, 1991	Matt Imes	1993, 1995	Brendan Riley
1989, 1990, 1991	Jason Macek	1993, 1995	Roderick Wagner
1989, 1990, 1991	Rick Mollgaard		

MEN'S CREW 'W' WINNERS

YEAR	NAME	YEAR	NAME
1994	Gavin Bardes	1997	Mark Lee
1994	Bradley Behlke	1997, 1998	Duncan Roberts
1994	Alexander Flakas	1997, 1998	Nikolai Wedekind
1994	Samuel Hanks	1997, 1998, 1999	Dylan Cappel
1994	Tony Montabon	1997, 1998, 1999	Jeffrey Maples
1994	Timothy Mueller		
1994	Justin Schaefer	1998	Nathan Alwin
1994	Ryan Torgerson	1998	Matthew Darga
1994	William Weiske, III	1998	Zachary Franzen
1994	Marian Zincke	1998	Steven Neumann
1994, 1996	Tariq Pasha	1998	Timothy Teske
1995, 1996, 1998	Matt Baldino	1998, 1999	Mark Danahy
		1998, 1999	Thomas Flint
1995	David Berger	1998, 1999	Michael Leonardi
1995	Kristopher Dressler	1998, 1999	Ira Simpson
1995	Thompson Godfrey	1998, 1999	Ryan Westergaard
1995	Nathan Keeney	1998, 1999	Patrick Woerner
1995	Brendan Riely	1998, 1999, 2000	Justin Baumann
1995, 1996	Jeff Miller	1998, 1999, 2000	Matthew "N. J." Noordsij-Jones
1995, 1996	Timothy Storm		
1995, 1996	Neal Wiebelhaus	1998, 1999, 2000	Gabe Rudert
1995, 1996, 1997	Benjamin Pofahl	1998, 1999, 2000	Matthew Smith
1995, 1996, 1997, 1999	Brian Hertzberg		
1995, 1997	Nathan Dowd	1999	Peter Dietrich
1995, 1997	Jason Rezell	1999	Brian Epstein
		1999	Matthew Fischer
1996	Barish Edil	1999	David Hwang
1996	Erik Haslam	1999	Patrick Martino
1996	John Hockers	1999	Alexander Palmer
1996	Todd Jinkins	1999	Jon Susa
1996	Michael Kraehnke	1999, 2000	Gabriel Rudert
1996	Andy Lederer	1999, 2000	Ryan Van Schyndel
1996	Andrew Lischefski	1999, 2000, 2001	Joel Berger
1996	Isham Martin	1999, 2000, 2001	David Kaplan
1996	Doug Prochaska	1999, 2000, 2001	Reed Kuehn
1996	Samuel Rasmussen	1999, 2000, 2001	Dirk Peters
1996	Philip Rechek	1999, 2000, 2001	John Remington
1996	Benjamin Rikkers	1999, 2000, 2001	Jeremy "Maurice" Whitish
1996	Stanley Savage	1999, 2000, 2001, 2002	Alan Geweke
1996	Brett Zriny	1999, 2001	Scott Alwin
1996, 1997	Aaron Berger	1999, 2001	Ed Golding
1996, 1997	Paul Bolstad		
1996, 1997	Peter Denk	2000	Joel Bock
1996, 1997	Andrew Spakowitz	2000	John A. Cummings
1996, 1997, 1998	Edward Kakas, III	2000	Matt Rehm
1996, 1997, 1998	Nicholas Latona	2000	Peter Vitko
1996, 1997, 1998	Alexander Ressi de Cervia	2000, 2001	Brian Bauer
1996, 1997, 1998	Nicolis Schilling	2000, 2001	Daniel Chin
1996, 1997, 1998	Matthew Tucker	2000, 2001	Aric Montanye
1996, 1997, 1998, 1999	Paul Tegan	2000, 2001	Michael Seelen
1996, 1997, 1998, 1999	Nelson Williams	2000, 2001	Michael Stahlman
1996, 1997, 1999	Kristian Knutsen	2000, 2001, 2002	Samuel McLennan

YEAR	NAME	YEAR	NAME
2000, 2001, 2002	Benjamin Kaker	2002, 2003	Paul Daniels
2000, 2001, 2002	Nicholas Kitowski	2002, 2003	Daniel Mueller
2000, 2001, 2002	John O. Taylor	2002, 2003, 2004	Micah Boyd
2000, 2001, 2003	David Farnia		
2000, 2002	Matthew Kennedy	2003	Ross Hart
2000, 2002	Craig Miller	2003	Joe Peplin
2000, 2003	Mike Anderson	2003	Dave Shore
		2003, 2004	Alexander Cockerill
2001	Zachary Gutt	2003, 2004	Mike Lucey
2001	Ken Price		
2001, 2002	Nathaniel Altfeather	2004	Anders Boyd
2001, 2002	Brian McDonough	2004	Jason Devlin
2001, 2002, 2003	Peter Giese	2004	John Dyreby
2001, 2002, 2003	Beau Hoopman	2004	Mike Kuklinski
2001, 2002, 2003	Ryan Kipp	2004	Tyler Resch
2001, 2002, 2003	Eric Knecht	2004	Kyle Schaible
2001, 2002, 2003	Peter Nagle	2004	Mike Tupek
2001, 2002, 2003	Michael Niemczyk	2004	Peter Turney
		2004	Shawn Wanta

Women's Crew "W" Winners, 1975–2004

YEAR	NAME	YEAR	NAME
before 1975*	Janet (Vogel) Blackstad	1979	Monica Piaquadio
before 1975*	Jessica Bulgrin	1979, 1980	Barbara A Hasz-Paul
before 1975*	Deb Crozier		
before 1975*	Kathy (Lhost) Galles	1980	Jeanne Abbott
before 1975*	Liesel Geyer	1980	Judy (Kelly) Abbott
before 1975*	Cynthia (Phelan) Holden	1980	Susan (Ahoto) Alioto
before 1975*	Susan Hurley	1980	Jeanne Ayivorth
before 1975*	Chris Kunz	1980	Kristine Mesman
before 1975*	Judy Marohl	1980	Kay M. (Jablonic) Opitz
before 1975*	Kathy Plager	1980, 1981	Joanne Berninger
before 1975*	Donell Rogness	1980, 1981, 1982	Kris "Thor" Thorsness
before 1975*	Mary K. Schuette	1980, 1981, 1982	Chari Towne
before 1975*	Allison Snyder	1980, 1981, 1982	Heidi J. (Grutzner) Martell
before 1975*	Kathy (Smith) Wutke		
		1981	Gail S. Allen
1975**	Sue Ela	1981	Martha Askins
1975	Carol Milner	1981	Ellen Gandt
1975	Barbara A. Schaefer	1981	Polly Menendez
1975	Elizabeth M. Zanichkowsky	1981	Gail Ross
1975, 1976	Carie Graves	1981	Becky Stepien
1975, 1976	Jackie (Major) Zoch	1981	Julie M. (Hanson) Van Cleave
1975, 1976, 1977	Beth M. (Traut) Bosio		
1975, 1976, 1977	Mary Connell-Eloranta	1981, 1982	Therese M. Gitter
1975, 1976, 1977	Karen J. Ela		
1975, 1976, 1977	Mary Grace Knight	1982	Jenny Heinen
1975, 1976, 1977	Deb Oetzel	1982	Susan Offerdahl
1975, 1976, 1977, 1978	Peggy A. (Bailey) McCarthy	1982	Rachel M. (Rodetsky) Reed
		1982	Kristin A. Smith
		1982	Kim Woods
1976, 1977, 1978	Carolyn A. Hegge	1982, 1983	Alison Graves
		1982, 1983	Rose (Morreale) Marchuk
1977, 1978	Sue Bott	1982, 1983, 1984	Mara W. (Keggi) Ford
1977, 1978	Lois (Harrison) Schloss	1982, 1983, 1984	Susan Tietjen
1977, 1978, 1979	Kristi M. Aserlind	1982, 1983, 1984, 1985	Kim Santiago
1977, 1978, 1979	Christina A. Cruz		
1977, 1980	Krista Graven	1983	Julie (Brasser) Barnett
		1983	Anne Hageman
1978	Barb C. Bradley	1983	Marcia Hageman
1978	Susan (Hutkowski) Dennis	1983	Carla Landry
1978, 1979	Debbie (Kelly) Hunter	1983	Ann M. Slewitzke
1978, 1979	Amy Luchsinger	1983	Mary Vrabec
1978, 1979	Margaret M. (Jennerman) Steuck	1983, 1984	Lynn C. Liberman
		1983, 1984	Amy Schuler
1978, 1979, 1980	Janet C. (Halvorson) Raphael	1983, 1984	Janet (Bogdanow) Wanamaker
1978, 1979, 1980, 1981	Jane Ludwig	1983, 1984, 1985	Mandi E. Kowal
		1983, 1984, 1985	Kathryn M. Place

* Honorary Letters were awarded January 30, 2005, to those who rowed in 1972-1974.

** "W's" awarded for the first year in 1974–75, per Badger Report of 5/22/75. Sue Ela rowed in the first eight-oared boats in 1972, 1973, 1974, and 1975.

YEAR	NAME	YEAR	NAME
		1989, 1990, 1991	Suzanne West
1984	Carol Lewnau	1989, 1990, 1991	Linda N. Baehmann
1984	Kristin Peterson		
1984, 1985, 1986	Sarah (Gengler) Dahl	1990	Anne Capelli
1984, 1985, 1986	Katy Drissel	1990	Tina Schoenwald
1984, 1985, 1986	Carol Feeney	1990, 1991	Emily (Catlett) Plesser
1984, 1986	Carolyn (Potter) Liepzig	1990, 1991, 1992	Melissa Iverson
		1990, 1991, 1992	Emily Stoddard
1985, 1986	Kathleen Haberman		
1985, 1986	Amy C. Krohn	1991	Carrie Peters
1985, 1986	Suzanne Montesi	1991	Ulrike Rudolph
1985, 1986	Marge Yankowski	1991	Lucia Thoenig
1985, 1986, 1987	Cynthia Eckert	1991	Laura Zirnigible
		1991, 1992	Amy (Nelson) Clark
1986	Rita Haberman	1991, 1992	Maureen "Mo" O'Conner
1986	Linda Kiltz	1991, 1992	Cathy Ponti
1986	Elizabeth Olesch	1991, 1992	Becky Rosenberg
1986, 1987	Laura Graf	1991, 1992, 1993	Linnea Anderson
1986, 1987	Signe Hartmann	1991, 1992, 1993	Sarah Mohs
1986, 1987	Ann Maloney	1991, 1993	Mia Hospel
1986, 1987	Sandy Mintz	1991, 1993	Karen Mullen
1986, 1987, 1988	Mary Beth "MB" Blanding	1991, 1993	Kim Zinniel
1986, 1987, 1988	Yasmin Farooq		
1986, 1987, 1988	Lisa (Fahien) Uldrich	1992	Kari Kartman
		1992	Lori (Badke) Kober
1987	Kirstin Larson-Becker	1992	Kris Waschbusch
1987, 1988	Margaret Calvert	1992, 1993	Wen Huang
1987, 1988	Michelle D. (Falivena) Farley	1992, 1993, 1994	Catherine H. Gunderson
		1992, 1993, 1994	Pamela E. Mork
1987, 1988	Sarah A. Jahnke	1992, 1993, 1994	Erica L. Plambeck
		1992, 1994	Deanna L. (Leslie) Kelly
1988	Chris Berger		
1988	Sallie Stetzer	1993	Nora Buckley
1988	Katherine L. Yankula	1993	Denise Della Santina
1988, 1989, 1990	Maura Clarke	1993	Suzie Henry
1988, 1989, 1990	Carey A. Dunai	1993	Andrea Mitchell
1988, 1989, 1990	Katherine Helke	1993	Melissa (Waldvogel) Plummer
1988, 1989, 1990	Gwen K. Weisbrod		
		1993	Katherine Smilikis
1989	Megan Crowley	1993, 1994	Shannon Daley
1989	Emily Dolan	1993, 1994, 1995	Sara J. (Kouba) De Tienne
1989	Mary Dyer	1993, 1994, 1995	Jodie (Jenz) Sloan
1989	Stephanie Hansen		
1989	Amy Martin	1994, 1995	Beth S. (Traci) Hatton
1989	Vivian Yuan	1994, 1995	Karen Kleinmaier
1989, 1990	Jen Agger	1994, 1995	Amy Lambrecht
1989, 1990	Tiffany Escher	1994, 1995	Melissa A. (McRae) Schmidt
1989, 1990, 1991	Emily (Hahn) Canova		
1989, 1990, 1991	Susannah Gladston	1994, 1995, 1996	Sarah M. Kacvinsky
1989, 1990, 1991	Laura J. Macaulay	1994, 1996	Tamara J. (Dinkel) Schilling
1989, 1990, 1991	Micaela (Mejia) Pond	1994, 1995, 1996, 1997	Kendra M. Zink
1989, 1990, 1991	Linda Specht		
1989, 1990, 1991	Erin Teare	1995	Heather Maclean

WOMEN'S CREW 'W' WINNERS

YEAR	NAME	YEAR	NAME
1995	Tracey Maloney	1997, 1999	Ellen M. Rewolinski
1995	Sarah A. Markwart		
1995	Nicole May	1998	Jena Cappel
1995	Amy (Lambrecht) Ruddell	1998	Molly Haning
1995	Jennifer "Nif" (Nelson) Saracevic	1998	Tamara Miller
		1998	Emily Morrison
1995	Kitty Shonk	1998, 1999	Amy (Thoreson) Pierce
1995, 1996	Jessica (Hughes) Breedlove	1998, 1999	Stacy Roessel
1995, 1996	Beth M. Huebner	1998, 1999	Jenny N. Sturino
1995, 1996	Amy Mathisen	1998, 1999, 2000	Valerie S. Bakken
1995, 1996, 1997	Torrey A. Folk	1998, 1999, 2000	Mary B. Collins
1995, 1996, 1997	Kathy E. Topp	1998, 1999, 2000	Angela S. Lay
		1998, 1999, 2000	Sara M. Lyng
1996	Claire Cornelius	1998, 1999, 2000	Jyll M. Rademacher
1996	Sara L. Cox-Landolt	1998, 1999, 2000, 2001	Althea "Acey" C. Neel
1996	Tara L. (Zabkowicz) Darga	1998, 1999, 2001	Carrie J. Byron
1996	Becky Ebert		
1996	Ann Getka	1999	Sarah Borchardt
1996	Nicosia (Herink) Hoenninger	1999	Jenny Churas
		1999	Sharone Cohen
1996	Lisa Huhn	1999	Kate Crowley
1996	Paisley Pingree-Hawkins	1999	Angela Mattern
1996	Charil Reis	1999	Ellen Rewolinski
1996	Gina A. Utrie	1999	Amy Skolaski
1996, 1997	Kara J. Conway	1999, 2000	Jennifer L. Englander
1996, 1997	Laurie S. Norcross	1999, 2000	Katie A. Hammes
1996, 1997, 1998	Emily Farrell	1999, 2000	Tessa Michaelson
1996, 1997, 1998	Suzannah Mork	1999, 2000	Sara E. Webb
1996, 1997, 1998	Kate (Hillmann) Ruffing	1999, 2000, 2001	Dusty J. Darley
1996, 1997, 1998, 1999	Meghan B. (Phelan) Fetherston	1999, 2000, 2001	Kirstin Holbeck
		1999, 2000, 2001	Gidge C. Myers
1996, 1998	Becky C. Hoyt	1999, 2000, 2001	Maura K. O'Donnell
		1999, 2000, 2001	Kary A. Oetjen
1997	Jane E. Kraft	1999, 2000, 2001	Tiffany L. Suda
1997	Sarah L. Marty	1999, 2000, 2001, 2002	Jenny E. Pofahl
1997	Jill Schindhelm		
1997	Heidi Woefel	2000	Katie A. Barofsky
1997, 1998	Maura Clark	2000	Nicole M. Moen
1997, 1998	Elizabeth Havice	2000	Karin Swanson
1997, 1998	Shannon Konyn	2000	Jordan S. Uffen
1997, 1998	Jane Kovacevich-Gilroy	2000	Alyssa Vegter
1997, 1998	Jodie (Thistle) Poetter	2000	Betsy A. Wild
1997, 1998	Rebecca N. Stuckman	2000, 2001	Jen B. Broerman
1997, 1998, 1999	Jill Baumgartner	2000, 2001	Kate I. Edwards
1997, 1998, 1999	Jill V. Cartwright	2000, 2001	Marisa Hoffman
1997, 1998, 1999	Christy Codner	2000, 2001	Noelle M. Vitone
1997, 1998, 1999	Kati L. Hope	2000, 2001, 2002	Alison A. Frohberg
1997, 1998, 1999	Kiri L. Hope	2000, 2001, 2002	Tara E. Gedman
1997, 1998, 1999	Kim Johnson	2000, 2001, 2002	Lindsay Gorsuch
1997, 1998, 1999	Laura M. Macfarlane	2000, 2001, 2002	Stacey M. Langenecker
1997, 1998, 1999	Amy B. Nemson	2000, 2001, 2003	Erin Gladding
1997, 1998, 1999	Tynille R. Rufenacht	2000, 2002	Erin L. Conlin
1997, 1998, 1999	Anna C. Vaughn		

YEAR	NAME	YEAR	NAME
2001	Courtney Cowie	2003	Betsy Ann Lucas
2001	Rebecca Flood	2003	Diane Martins
2001	Heather D. Koch	2003	Jessica Neuville
2001	Emily M. Peterson	2003, 2004	Megan DeLonge
2001	Molly J. Rennebohm	2003, 2004	Amanda Frederickson
2001	Katie Shea	2003, 2004	Shannon Gedman
2001, 2002	Meredith Blair	2003, 2004	Leah Gordon
2001, 2002	Alana Burney	2003, 2004	Jessica Lee
2001, 2002	Erin E. Bye	2003, 2004	Nikki Lennart
2001, 2002	Alyssa Elver	2003, 2004	Alissa Miller
2001, 2002	Leah Hanson	2003, 2004	Eva Payne
2001, 2002	Margaret S. Miller	2003, 2004	Julie Quoss
2001, 2002	Sara Stahlman	2003, 2004	Lindsay Rongstad
2001, 2002, 2003	Jadrian Brueckner	2003, 2004	Christina Strasser
2001, 2002, 2003	Jeannette M. Moore	2003, 2004	Katie Sweet
2001, 2002, 2003	Annie Trimberger	2003, 2004	Jenny Tuffree
2001, 2002, 2003	Marianna Waters	2003, 2004	Claire Wallace
2001, 2002, 2003	Joni Wiebelhaus	2003, 2004	Nicole Weir
2001, 2002, 2003, 2004	Alexandra Endress		
2001, 2002, 2004	Eileen (Ruzicka) Storm	2004	Kim Ackerbauer
		2004	Meghan Bradshaw
2002	Clara Bien	2004	Lindsay Bush
2002	Katie Bohren	2004	Courtney A. Carlovsky
2002	Erin E. Buchanan	2004	Katie Culp
2002	Kylie L. Fredrickson	2004	Meghan Cummings
2002	Chelle M. Jacques	2004	Anaya Drew
2002	Rachel "Rogo" Rogozinski	2004	Colleen Gosa
2002	Amy Weatherby	2004	Candice Hansey
2002	Sarah Weis	2004	Katie Harmon
2002, 2003	Alissa Adler	2004	Mary Higgins
2002, 2003	Ashley Mays	2004	Kate Lawson
2002, 2003	Tessa Molter	2004	Malika McCormick
2002, 2003	Elpi Pagitsas	2004	Elizabeth Redfearn
2002, 2003	Aliza Leah Richman	2004	Andrea Ryan
		2004	Heidi Sallach
2003	Katie Childs	2004	Bryana Seifert
2003	Stacy Lynn Coy	2004	Emily Simonds
2003	Erin Gladding	2004	Erin Specht
2003	Andrea M. Hayden	2004	Meghan Stevens

Appendix 2
UW Captains

Men's Crew Captains, 1892–2005

YEAR	NAME	SEAT	YEAR	NAME	SEAT
1892	Charles C. Case		1933	Charles Tessendorf /	7
	8/27/92—first Varsity race	S		Herman A. Silbernagel	6
1893	Charles C. Case	S	1934	Edward C. Helmke[h]	4
1894	Herbert H. Jacobs	5	1935	Philip W. Rosten[i]	B
1895	Oscar Rohn	7	1936	Howard T. Heun	S
1896	Walter A. Alexander	2	1937	Robert S. Heinze /	2
1897	Lee F. Austin	6		Donald R. Heun	S
1898	Curran C. McConville	S	1938	Edwin S. Collins, Jr.	S
1899	William C. Sutherland	6	1939	Edmund J. Ryan[j]	5/S
1900	Andrew R. Anderson	7	1940	Jack Gunning	Cx
1901	William J. Gibson	5	1941	Harold Krueger	S
1902	Charles H. Gaffin	7	1942	William Phelank	7
1903	Robert G. Stevenson	4	1943	Carl A. Holtz[l]	S
1904	Elbert L. Jordan	6	1944	None-intramural only	NA
1905	Arthur H. Miller	5	1945	None-intramural only	NA
1906	Beverly B. Burling	B	1946	Carl A. Holtz[m]	S
1907	Benjamin F. Davis	4	1947	Carl A. Holtz	S
1908	George C. Wilder	7	1948	LeRoy "Larry" A. Jensen[e]	5
1909	Eugene A. Dinet	5	1949	Dick Tipple	3
1910	Reuben N. Trane	3	1950	Cliff Rathkamp	B/7
1911	Karl L. Kraatz	7	1951	Duane Daentl	Cx
1912	Charles M. Pollock	6	1952	Robert ("R. Y.") Nelson	S
1913	Maurice C. Sjoblom /	3	1953	Victor Steuck	4
	Donald J. McLeod[a]	[b]	1954	Virgil Trummer-Subs. /	2
1914	Arno Wittich	7		Jim Lorenzen	B
1915	None-intramural only	NA	1955	William Schneider	6
1916	None-intramural only	NA	1956	Robert Graves[n]	3
1917	John L. Mitchell[c]	NKn	1957	Dean R. Walker	5
1918	None-intramural only	NA	1958	Joe Irwin	7
1919	None-intramural only	NA	1959	James Bowen	4
1920	None-intramural only	NA	1960	Courtney Freeman	7
1921	Arthur Samp /	3	1961	Phillip Mork	B
	George O. Toepfer[d]	3	1962	William McIntyre	6
1922	George O. Toepfer[e]	B	1963	Douglas Reiner	7
1923	Howard E. Johnson[f]	S	1964	Victor Johnson	2
1924	Ralph J. Schueutz	B	1965	Kent Carnahan /	7
1925	Oscar Teckemeyer	S		Dennis Gillespie	B
1926	Harold L.(Jerry) Coulter	Cx	1966	Willard Witte	Cx
1927	Jefferson Burrus (Fall?) /	6	1967	Bill Clapp /	B
	Franklin Orth (Spring?)[g]	S		John Halleran	B (JV)
1928	Franklin Orth	S	1968	David Ivaska	Cx
1929	Warren Drouet	5/S	1969	Douglas Sahs	4/B
1930	Eugene Goodman-Subs.		1970	Phillip Resch	5
1931	Louis E. Oberdeck	6	1971	Tom J. Flammang	S
1932	Harold Smedal	5	1972	John Vegter	4

YEAR	NAME	SEAT
1973	Bob Eloranta /	B
	Scott Springman	5
1974	Jim Swanson	2
1975	Doug (Bill) Trosper	Sb
1976	John Bauch	5/B
1977	Tom Schuchardt	S
1978	Paul Smith	Cx
1979	Michael "Mike" J. Gasper	6
1980	Allan Erickson	S
1981	Thomas Kirk	Cx
1982	Aaron Jacob	6
1983	Mark B. Hallet	3
1984	Matt Brown	5
1985	Bob Hougard	4
1986	Tom Tryon	3
1987	Kevin McAleese	S
1988	Pat McDonough	2
1989	Todd Williams	5
1990	Todd Hinrichs	7
1991	Nick Donovan	B
1992	Greg Myhr	3
1993	Jim Farmer /	7
	Pat Vander Hei	B
1994	Martin Zincke	5
1995	Thompson Godfrey	NKn
1996	Neal Wiebelhaus	Bow
1997	Aaron Berger	6
1998	Nelson Williams	5
1999	Jeff Maples	6
2000	Matt Smith	S
2001	Alan Geweke	7
2002	Beau Hoopman	7
2003	Micah Boyd	5
2004	Alex Cockerill	S
2005	Ryan Schwend /	
	Peter Turney	

[a] Capt. Sjoblom resigned the spring of 1913 due to heart problems; succeeded April 18, 1913, by McLeod (*The Badger,* 1915 (pgs. 307-18) and *Daily Cardinal,* April 19, 1913).

[b] No. 3 in the Varsity Four at final IRAs.

[c] Bob Hood/Jim Almquist list; probably should be "Non-intramural only." Mitchell was found in the 1918 *Badger* (p. 153) as captain of his freshman ('15) crew, commodore in 1918 and president of the Mendota Crew Club in 1917 and '18.

[d] *1991 Banquet of Champion Program* (March 2, 1991) and the *1923 Badger Yearbook* lists George O. Toefper as the captain in 1921, who may have replaced Samp after an injury.

[e] Per Duane Daentl *IRA Program of 1948,* Mr. Jensen signed his name as "LeRoy."

[f] Bob Hood/Jim Almquist's database lists Charles Puestow.

[g] Source of Burrus unclear. *1991 Banquet of Champion Program* (March 2, 1991) lists Franklin Orth.

[h] Source: March 2, 1991 UW crew banquet program. Fred Emerson, awarded a "W" in 1934, was never a UW crew captain-in spite of such affirmation in "In Memoriam," *WRA Newsletter,* December 1992 (p. 6). According to crew historian, crew mate and Phi Gamma Delta fraternity brother of Emerson, Paul O. Eckhardt, Jr., in a November 3, 2000 telephone interview, Emerson was never elected captain.

[i] Ralph Hunn was initially elected captain for 1934-35, but gave it up when offered the position of coach. *1991 Banquet of Champion Program* (March 2, 1991) lists Howard Heun and Philip "Rosrow" (a misspelling, per Jom Mott's "W" Club membership roster.). *The Badger,* 1936 (p. 254) indicates Rosten as the 1934-35 captain.

[j] 1991 Banquet of Champion Program (March 2, 1991) lists "Eugene;" first name, per Jim Mott's "W" Club membership roster is "Edmund." The *IRA Program of 1939* indicates 'Edmund.'

[k] Source: *History of Crew as a Wisconsin Sport,* a monograph by the UW Sports News Service, Art Lenz, Editor, 1946 (15 pp.).

[l] Elected but did not serve because of WW II interruption (*New York Times,* September 19, 1942, p. V-7).

[m] Yearbook shows Chester Knight (B), who may have been a "fall" season captain (Bob Hood advises there were sometimes "fall" and "spring" captains).

[n] *Row Wisco* of February 7, 1996 (p. 3.), lists John Morgen (in obituary article) as captain in 1956; *Wisconsin Athletic Reviews* of 1955 and '56 lists Robert Graves as captain-elect for 1956.

Women's Crew Captains, 1972–2005

YEAR	OPENWEIGHT CAPTAIN	LIGHTWEIGHT CAPTAIN[a]
1972	The club president was also captain—Kathy Wutke[b]	
1973	The club president was also captain—Kathy Wutke[b]	
1974	The club president was also captain—Cindy Holden[b]	
1975	Carie Graves[c]	
1976	Carie Graves	
1977	Mary Connell	
1978	Peggy McCarthy	
1979	Amy Luchsinger	
1980	Jane Ludwig	
1981	Julie Hanson	
1982	Heidi Grutzner	
1983	Rose Morreale	
1984	Mara Keggi	
1985	Kathy Place	
1986	Katy Drissel	
1987	Signe Hartmann	
1988	Yasmin Farooq	
1989	Gwen Weisbrod / Katherine Helke	
1990	Annie Capelli / Katherine Helke	
1991	Rebecca Rosenberg / Laura Macaulay	
1992	Kris Waschbusch / Melissa Iverson	
1993	Sarah Mohs	
1994	Catherine Gunderson	
1995	Jodie Jenz	
1996	Sarah Kacvinsky / Beth Huebner	
1997	Torrey Folk	Kim Johnson / Kelly Peterson
1998	Kate Hillmann	Amy Nemson / Anna Vaughn
1999	Meg Phelan	Sara Lyng / Sharone Cohen
2000	Val Bakken	Noelle Vitone
2001	Kate Edwards	Dusty Darley
2002	Brigid Myers	Stacey Langenecker
2003	Elpi Pagitsas / Marianna Waters	Jadrian ("Jade") Brueckner
2004	Chris Strasser / Nicky Weir	Megan De Longe
2005	Shannon Gedman / Beth Redfearn	Katie Sweet

[a] First lightweight year is 1995–96.
[b] Club Sport from spring 1972 through spring of 1974.
[c] In the transition to a varsity sport, the club president acted as captain.

Appendix 3
Boatings of the UW Ten Eyck Trophy Victories

UW's First IRA/Ten Eyck Trophy — IRAs of June 1–3, 1972

Event	Varsity 8+	JV 8+	Freshman 8+	Pairs -
Points for First[a]	8	6	6	0
UW's finish	3	2	1	3
Bow seat	Stern, Robert	Ricksecker, Jim	Espeseth, Bob	Weyers, Gary
2	Vegter, John ©	Koca, Robert	Melis, Gary	
3	Eloranta, Bob	Osborn, John	Schueller, Lou	
4	Bartz, Loren	Klinger, Bill	Blodgett, Ted	
5	Springman, Scott	Nelson, Ken	Schultz, Dale	
6	Ziebarth, Paul	Neidermeier, Bruce	Dyreby, Jim	
7	Phelan, Gerald	Gross, Mike	Kirsch, Jim	
Stroke	Tomoforde, David	Swanson, Jim	Trosper, Doug	Herdeman, Charles
Coxswain	Bosio, John	Malak, Mike	Kammer, Daniel	

Event	Varsity 4+	Freshman 4+
Points for First[a]	0	0
UW's finish	No Entry	6
Bow seat		Piotrzkowski, Winston
2		Toraason, Larry
3		Kraft, Don
Stroke		Jens, Tom
Coxswain		Meili, Stephen

[a] Points for first place under the Ten Eyck event-weighting scoring system.
© Captain

TEN EYCK TROPHY VICTORIES

UW's Second IRA/Ten Eyck Trophy — IRAs of May 31, and June 1 and 2, 1973

Event	Varsity 8+	JV 8+a	Freshman 8+	Pairs -
Points for First[b]	8	6	6	0
UW's finish	1	1	1	No entry
Bow seat	[c]Eloranta, Bob (Co-Capt)[d]	Aserlind, Eric	Graves, Ross	
2	Swanson, Jim	McNett, Jim	Storck, John	
3	Ricksecker, Jim	Kirsch, Jim	Rose, Reinhardt	
4	Bartz, Loren	Blogett, Ted	Newman, Carl	
5	Phelan, Jerry	Weyers, Gary	Mercier, John	
6	Espeseth, Bob	[c]Klinger, Bill	Trotter, Larry	
7	Schueller, Lou	Osborn, John	Knight, Joe	
Stroke	Dyreby, Jim	Trosper, Doug	Bauch, John	
Coxswain	Bosio, John	Malak, Mike	Werner, Arno	

Event	Varsity 4+	Freshman 4+
Points for First[b]	0	0
UW's finish	No Entry	9[e]
Bow seat		Melcher, Chris
2		Valentine, Jake
3		Zondag, Randy
Stroke		Koehler, Jim
Coxswain		Kaplan, Craig

[a] Osborn, John, boating of 2V8 from an e-mail dated August 8, 2002.
[b] Points for first place under the Ten Eyck event-weighting scoring system.
[c] Denotes a senior.
[d] Scott Springman was the other co-captain.
[e] "Badger Rowers Win It All," The *Milwaukee Journal*, June 3, 1973, p. 5. UW had only four entries in the six events.

UW's Third IRA/Ten Eyck Trophy — IRAs of May 30 and 31, and June 1, 1974

Event	Varsity 8+	JV 8+	Freshman 8+	Pairs -
Points for First[a]	72	54	54	18
UW's finish	1	1	2	8
Bow seat	Aserlind, Eric	Kirsh, Jim	Schroeder, Bob	Eloranta, Dave
2	Swanson, Jim ©	Knight, Joe	Hayes, Steve	
3	Newman, Karl	Bauch, John	Boyle, Mark	
4	Bartz, Loren	Mercier, John	Graff, Roger	
5	Schueller, Lou	Nelson, Ken	Robertson, Fred	
6	Espeseth, Bob	Graves, Ross	Wolf, Doug	
7	Ricksecker, Jim	Storck, John	Schroeder, Paul	
Stroke	Dyreby, Jim	Trosper, Doug	Schuchardt, Tom	Freeman, Jim
Coxswain	[b]Bosio, John	Malak, Mike	Shea, Gary	

Event	Varsity 4+	Varsity 4 w/out	Freshman 4+	Pair +
Points for First[a]	36	40	27	18
UW's finish	2	No entry	5	No entry
Bow seat	Gabel, Paul		Schroeder, Bob	
2	Norsetter, Bill		Horward, Dave	
3	Stern, Bob		Schink, Steve	
Stroke	Klinger, Bill		Teter, Al	
Coxswain	Werner, Arno		Kramer, Larry	

[a] Points for first place under the Ten Eyck event-weighting scoring system.

[b] Denotes a senior.

© Captain

UW's Fourth IRA/Ten Eyck Trophy[a] — IRAs of May 29–31, 1975

Event	Varsity 8+	JV 8+	Freshman 8+[b]	Pairs -
Points for First[c]	72	54	54	18
UW's finish	1	3	2	No Entry
Bow seat	Aserlind, Eric	Kraft, Don	Schultz, Steve	
2	Schuchardt, Tom	Cleary, John	Kufahl, Dave	
3	Kirsh, Jim	Boyle, Mark	Dey, Don	
4	Mercier, John	Zondag, Randy	Litscher, Pat	
5	[d]Schueller, Lou	Storck, John	Rasmussen, John	
6	[d]Espeseth, Bob	Teter, Al	Jackson, Ed	
7	Fred Robertson	Schroeder, Paul	Schultz, Dave	
Stroke	[d]Dyreby, Jim	Norsetter, Bill	Moecher, Dave	
Coxswain	Greg Askins	Menendez, Hal	Smith, Paul	

Event	Varsity 4+	Varsity 4 w/out	Freshman 4+[e]	Pairs +
Points for First[c]	36	40	27	18
UW's finish	3	1	7	5
Bow seat	Trotter, Larry	Sullivan, Jim	Folts, Dave	Gebel, Paul
2	Hamilton, Pete	Eloranta, Dave	Frol, Vern	
3	Trosper, Doug ©	Freeman, Jim	Carlson, Mark	
Stroke	Bauch, John	Knight, Joe	Ambrose, John	Graves, Ross
Coxswain	Werner, Arno		Carlson, Trent	Kaplan, Craig

[a] "Badger Crew Wins National Title," *Wisconsin State Journal*, June 1, 1975 (undated clipping from Margaret Drewes), shows Frosh eight cox was Trent Carlson, Don Dey (stroke), and Ed Jackson (No. 6), and Frosh 4 + cox was Paul Smith, Nester Dominguez (stroke), and Don Miller (No. 3).

[b] "Badger Crew Wins National Title," *Wisconsin State Journal*, June 1, 1975, lists lineup as S. Schultz (bow), Kufahl, D. Schultz, Litscher, Rasmussen, Jackson, Moecher, Dey (stroke), and Trent Carlson (cox).

[c] Points for first place under the Ten Eyck event-weighting scoring system.

[d] Denotes a senior.

[e] The *Milwaukee Journal* of June 1, 1975, quotes Jablonic describing John Ambrose as having broken his toe Thursday while playing Frisbee. On Saturday, the Frosh 4+ was UW's only boat not to make the finals. Jablonic planned to replace Ambrose with Nestor Dominguez or Vern Frol.

© Captain

UW's Fifth IRA/Ten Eyck Trophy[a] — IRAs of May 31 and June 1 and 2, 1979

Event	Varsity 8+	JV 8+	Freshman 8+	Pairs +
Points for First[b]	72	54	54	18
UW's finish	2	2	1	No Entry
Bow seat	Wilms, Dan	Vrabec, Mike	Berninger, Doug	
2	Olsen, Bill	Starr, Jay	Steinbrecher, Brian	
3	Kline, Ned	Ripp, Dan	Williams, Charles	
4	Zwieg, Dave	Jablonic, John	Jacobs, Aaron	
5	Lambert, Paul	Olson, John	Shenkenberg, Steve	
6	Gasper, Mike ©	Seefeldt, John	Streur, John	
7	Erickson, Allan	Remington, Frank	Royal, Dan	
Stroke	Moecher, Dave	Lawrence, Ken	Supernaw, Bill	
Coxswain	Bertocci, Joel	Kirk, Tom	Manicor, Steve	

Event	Varsity 4+	Varsity 4 w/out	Freshman 4+	Pairs -
Points for First[b]	36	40	27	18
UW's finish	No Entry	3	4	No entry[c]
Bow seat		Corwin, Jr., Swift	Betzig, Bob	
2		Tipple, Don	Schten, Karl	
3		Jelinek, Curt	Schemel, Phillip	
Stroke		Gitter, Mike	Runge, Val	
Coxswain			Galowich, Dave	

[a] Boatings based on Al Erickson fax of January 19, 2001. The boatings in the *Wisconsin State Journal* article of May 31, 1979, Sports, p. 3. is not correct.

[b] Points for first place under the Ten Eyck event-weighting scoring system.

[c] Butler, Tom, "Jablonic savors heroic efforts," *Wisconsin State Journal*, June 6, 1979, Sports. Only five boats taken to the IRAs by Wisconsin in 1979. Pat Frayne did not make the trip because of an injury.

© Captain

TEN EYCK TROPHY VICTORIES

UW's Sixth IRA/Ten Eyck Trophy[a] — IRAs of May 30 and 31, and June 1, 1980

Event	Varsity 8+	JV 8+	Freshman 8+	Pairs -
Points for First[b]	72	54	54	18
UW's finish	4	No entry	2	1
Bow seat	Erickson, Allan ©		Ellis, David	Remington, Frank
2	Jacob, Aaron		Renfert, Blaine	
3	Ryder, Ky		Davies, James	
4	Jablonic, John		Raymond, Bob	
5	Jim Seefeldt		Adams, Timm	
6	Lambert, Paul		Frohna, Brian	
7	Streur, John		Baker, Bill	
Stroke	Landry, Chris		River, Vince	Jelinek, Curtis
Coxswain	Kirk, Tom		Rafson, Bob	

Event	Varsity 4+	Varsity 4 w/out	Freshman 4+	Pairs+
Points for First[b]	36	40	27	18
UW's finish	1	5	11	6
Bow seat	Steinbrecher, Brian	Corwin, Jr., Swift	Keepers, John	Zellner, Steve
2	Royal, Dan	Tipple, Don	Heyden, Marc	
3	Kline, Ned	Borcherding, Steve	Pendleton, Sandie	
Stroke	Lawrence, Ken	Gitter, Mike	Kay, Tim	Bucher, Scott
Coxswain	Franke, Mathew		Pelkey, (Dan)	Matesek, Dave

[a] Boatings of winning Pairs and Varsity 4+ are sourced from the *1987 UW Crew Guide* and *Banquet of Champions Program,* March 2, 1991. Other boatings from Al Erickson fax of January 19, 2001; varsity 8 reflects "lineup shuffle for finals." Frosh 4+ from WRA's *Open Water,* August 1980, p. 1., where no first names and no seats were identified. First names were obtained from the 1979–80 Crew Roster. The coverage of Bob Snyder, "Red-letter day for Sailors" *Syracuse Herald-Journal,* June 2, 1980, Sports, C-2. had Wisco's Pair+ in sixth, not fourth, as did the *Capital Times* of June 2, 1980, p. 9 (from Professor Ihdes's records in the Archives of the Memorial Library).

[b] Points for first place under the Ten Eyck event-weighting scoring system.

© Captain

UW's Seventh IRA/Ten Eyck Trophy[a] — IRAs of June 5–7, 1986

Event	Varsity 8+	JV 8+	Freshman 8+	Pairs -
Points for First[b]	108	81	81	18
UW's finish	3	1	4	2
Bow seat	Moeller, Eric	Tucker, John	Williams, Todd	Hallett, John
2	Evenson, David	Greisbach, Brian	Wike, Tim	
3	Schulte, Christopher	Tryon, Tom ©	Foss, Brandon	
4	Berkner, Mark	Murer, Jonathan	Larson, Greg	
5	Gehn, Dan	Risse, Michael	Campbell, Peter[c]	
6	Kennedy, Duncan	McDonough, Patrick	Borcherding, Kurt	
7	Hanson, Bryan	Thornton, Thomas	Werner, Gregory	
Stroke	McAleese, Kevin	Cincotta, Joe	Anderson, Jim	Gobeli, Scott
Coxswain	Mejia, Ray	Farrar, Michael	White, Stephen	

Event	Varsity 4+	Varsity 4 w/out	Freshman 4+	Open 4+
Points for First[b]	36	36	27	18
UW's finish	2	No entry	2	1
Bow seat	Raia, Frances		Askelson, Mark	Righini, John
2	Burnett, Mark		Ebert, Jerry	Lynch, Scott
3	Paulman, Scott		Schober, Tom	Johnson, Chris
Stroke	Huntington, Sam		Adamski, Steve	Farrar, Chris
Coxswain	Rugolo, Dave[d]		Lindsay, Mike	Farrar, Michael

[a] Boatings as per the May 31, 1986, Cochrane Cup *Navy Sports Program*, except Varsity and JV eights and Open 4+, which source is the *1987 UW Crew Guide* (March 2, 1991 crew banquet program shows Tryon and Risse reversed in 2V8). Coxswain Michael Farrar is one of a very few rowers participating in more than one IRA event and perhaps the only one to win two golds in the same IRA. He and brother Chris (Op4+) may also be the only brothers to win golds as stroke and coxswain.

[b] Points for first place under the Ten Eyck event-weighting scoring system.

[c] *1988 UW Crew Guide* incorrectly lists Ray Mejia as the cox of the Op4+ and also, incorrectly, lists the F8 boating as the 2V8 boating.

[d] E-mail of April 12, 2004, from Mike Farrar and confirmed by Dave Rugolo in an e-mail of April 14, 2004.

© Captain

TEN EYCK TROPHY VICTORIES

UW's Eighth IRA/Ten Eyck Trophy[a] — IRAs of June 4–6, 1987

Event	Varsity 8+	JV 8+	Freshman 8+	Pairs -
Points for First[b]	108	81	81	18
UW's finish	2	2	2	3
Bow seat	Tucker, John	[c]Moeller, Eric	Shenkenberg, Bill	Lynch, Scott
2	Patrick McDonough	James Anderson	Dunne, Fitz	
3	[c]Risse, Michael	Knickrehm, Rob	Kriewaldt, Shawn	
4	[c]Evensen, Dave	Raia, Frank	Bakken, Bill	
5	Gehn, Dan	Williams, Todd	Hoffman, Phil	
6	[c]Kennedy, Duncan	Paulman, Scott	Meissner, Jerry	
7	[c]Hanson, Bryan	[c]Thornton, Tom	Hinrichs, Todd	
Stroke	McAleese, Kevin ©	[c]Cincotta, Joe	Wolf, Pat	Huntington, Sam
Coxswain	Mejia, Ray	[c]Rugulo, Dave	Bull, Chris	

Event	Varsity 4+	Varsity 4 w/out	Freshman 4+	Open 4+
Points for First[b]	36	36	27	18
UW's finish	1	4	3	3
Bow seat	Stevens, Paul	[c]Burnett, Mark	Wilson, Mark	Bassack, Andrew
2	Borcherding, Kurt	Larson, Greg	Berrghahn, Marcus	Guhl, Dave (Fr)
3	Werner, Greg	Foss, Brandon	Schamens, Scott	Hautanen, David (Fr)
Stroke	Wike, Tim	Adamski, Steven	Tennessen, Andrew	Dunai, Steve
Coxswain	Lindsay, Michael		Fisher, Mike	Demakopoulos, Andreas

[a] Boatings as per the *Navy Sports Program* for the Walsh Cup of 1987; JV-8 and Varsity 4+ from *Banquet of Champions Program* for the March 2, 1991 crew banquet, except the cox for the varsity 4+ is Michael Lindsay, and not Stephen White, per the *Row Wisco Newsletter* of April 15, 1987, p. 6.

[b] Points for first place under the Ten Eyck event-weighting scoring system.

[c] Denotes a senior (per *1987 UW Crew Guide*).

© Captain

UW's Ninth IRA/Ten Eyck Trophy[a] — IRAs of June 2–4, 1988

Event	Varsity 8+	JV 8+[b]	Freshman 8+[c]	Pairs -[d]
Points for First[e]	108	81	81	18
UW's finish	3	2	3	1
Bow seat	Wolf, Pat	Anderson, Jim "Earl"	Donovan, Nicholas	Gregor, Tim
2	Adamski, Steve	[f]Bassak, Drew	Henry, Jon	
3	Williams, Todd	Larson, Greg	Feller, John	
4	Borcherding, Kurt	Werner, Greg	White, Jeff	
5	[f]Gehn, Dan	[f]Paulman, Scott	Arbogast, C. (Lincoln)	
6	Hinrichs, Todd	Dahl, Matt	Stoa, Pat	
7	[f]Tucker, John	[f]McDonough, Pat ©	Hatton, Steve	
Stroke	[f]Lynch, Scott	Dunne, Edward "Fitz"	Olson, Dean	Foss, Brandon
Coxswain	[f]Mejia, Ray	White, Steve	Ling, C. (Roy)	

Event	Varsity 4+	Varsity 4 w/out[g]	Freshman 4+	Open 4+
Points for First[e]	36	36	27	18
UW's finish	4	5	2	3
Bow seat	Stevens, Paul	[f]Periard, Jim	Palmer, Rob	Askelson, Mark
2	Astell, Luke	Dunai, Steve	Roberts, Ari	Pirrozola, Josh
3	Hautanen, David	[f]Filip, Bill	Meisner, Dan	Almquist, Jim(Fr)
Stroke	Meisner, Jerry	Wike, Tim	Truman, James	Jonsson, Jon (Fr)
Coxswain	Lindsay, Michael		Welhouse, Brett	Fisher, Mike

[a] Boatings largely taken from the Midwest Championships, "Wisconsin's crews don't disappoint," *Wisconsin State Journal*, May 1, 1988, Sports, p. 1, as amended by Pat McDonough's e-mail of August 12, 2001.

[b] Tim Wike's December 11, 2001 e-mail provided the JV8 boating and were confirmed in June 2004 telephone calls with Drew Bassak and Fitz Dunne; Steve White's e-mail of July 10, 2004 confirmed the 4-seat.

[c] December 11, 2001 e-mail from Jim Almquist, amended by phone call with Drew Bassak on June 4, 2004.

[d] *Banquet of Champions Program* for the March 2, 1991, UW crew banquet.

[e] Points for first place under the Ten Eyck event-weighting scoring system at the time.

[f] Denotes senior or last year of competition.

[g] Tim Wike e-mail of December 11, 2001, questioned whether Jim Philip might have been in the 2-seat.

© Captain

TEN EYCK TROPHY VICTORIES

UW's Tenth IRA/Ten Eyck Trophy — IRAs of May 30 and 31, and June 1, 1997

Event	Varsity 8+	JV 8+	Freshman 8+	Pairs -
Points for First[a]	108	81	81	18
UW's finish	4	3	2	3
Bow seat	Darga, Matt	Roberts, Duncan	Smith, Matt	Woerner, Pat
2	Ressi, Alex	Danahy, Mark	Rudert, Gabe	
3	Tucker, Matt	Neumann, Steve	Hagen, Mitch	
4	Maples, Jeff	Hertzberg, Brian	Marlotte, Rob	
5	Pofahl, Ben	Berger, Aaron ©	Cummings, John	
6	Kakas, Chris	Westergard, Ryan	Cappel, Dylan	
7	Wedekind, Nik	Tegan, Paul	Moody, Jed	
Stroke	Williams, Nelson	Leonardi, Mike	Callahan, Dennis	Bolstad, Paul
Coxswain	Knutsen, Kristian	Spakowitz, Andrew	Torgerson, Rolf	

Event	Varsity 4+	Varsity 4 w/out	Freshman 4+	Open 4+
Points for First[a]	36	36	27	18
UW's finish	6	4	2	4
Bow seat	Lee, Mark	Sensenbrenner, Lee	Noordsij-Jones, Matt	Bock, Joel (Fr)
2	Rezell, Jason	Fisher, Matt	Fulghum, Craig	Privett, Buck
3	Schilling, Nic	Epstein, Brian	Pollack, Zack	Simpson, Ira
Stroke	Flint, Tom	Dank, Peter	Baumann, Justin	Teske, Tim
Coxswain	Hwang, David		Dymond, Devin	Dowd, Nathan

[a] Points for first place under the Ten Eyck event-weighting scoring system.

© Captain

UW's Eleventh IRA/Ten Eyck Trophy — IRAs of May 29–31, 1999

Event	Varsity 8+	JV 8+	Freshman 8+	Pairs -
Points for First[a]	108	81	81	18
UW's finish	5	5	6	2
Bow seat	[b]Westergard, Ryan	Price, Ken	Neil, Kevin	Bock, Joel
2	Bauer, Brian	Baumann, Justin	McLennan, Sam	
3	Gewecke, Alan	Golding, Ed	Farnia, Dave	
4	Cappel, Dylan	Danaly, Mark	Peters, Dirk	
5	Cummings, John	Van Schyndel, Ryan	Cronk, Spencer	
6	[b]Maples, Jeff ©	Altfeather, Nate	Obuchowicz, Dave	
7	Moody, Jed	Leonardi, Mike	Stahlman, Mike	
Stroke	Smith, Matt	Flint, Tom	Kitowski, Nick	Woerner, Pat
Coxswain	[b]Knutsen, Kristian	Hwang, David	Taylor, John	

Event	Varsity 4+	Varsity 4 w/out	Freshman 4+	Open 4+
Points for First[a]	36	36	27	18
UW's finish	1	1	1	1
Bow seat	Rudert, Gabe	Fisher, Matt	Miller, Craig	Chin, Dan (Fr)
2	Alwin, Scott	Noordsij-Jones, Matt	Kohl, Louis	Epstein, Brian
3	Berger, Joel	Seelen, Mike	Montanye, Aric	Pollack, Zach
Stroke	Tegan, Paul	[b]Simpson, Ira	Rehm, Casey	Anderson, Kevin
Coxswain	Gutt, Zach		Okada, Vince	Whitish, Jeremy

[a] Points for first place under the Ten Eyck event-weighting scoring system.
[b] Denotes a senior.
© Captain

TEN EYCK TROPHY VICTORIES   311

UW's Twelfth IRA/Ten Eyck Trophy — IRAs of June 1–3, 2000

Event	Varsity 8+	JV 8+	Freshman 8+	Pairs -
Points for First[a]	108	81	81	18
UW's finish	8	5	3	2
Bow seat	Geweke, Alan	[b]Baumann, Justin	Welsh, Ian	Miller, Craig
2	Golding, Ed	Price, Ken	Hoopman, Beau	
3	Bauer, Brian	[b]Pollack, Zack	Daniels, Paul	
4	[b]Cappel, Dylan	Kuehn, Reed	Mueller, Daniel	
5	Peters, Dirk	McLennan, Sam	Harrison, Dan	
6	[b]Cummings, John	Alwin, Scott	Giese, Pete	
7	[b]Hertzberg, Brian	Kitowski, Nick	Peplin, Joe	
Stroke	[b]Smith, Matt ©	Farnia, Dave	Nagle, Pete	Berger, Joel
Coxswain	Whitish, Jeremy	Gutt, Zachary	Franklin, Adam	

Event	Varsity 4+	Varsity 4 w/out	Freshman 4+	Open 4+
Points for First[a]	36	36	27	18
UW's finish	1	1	1	1
Bow seat	Kaker, Ben	Seelen, Mike	Shilling, Travis	Vitko, Peter
2	Montanye, Aric	[b]Noordsij-Jones, Matt	Fruechtl, James	Anderson, Mike (Fr)
3	Obuchowicz, Dave	Remington, John	Kemper, David	[b]Rudert, Rudy
Stroke	Chin, Dan	[b]Bock, Joel	Knecht, Eric	Stahlman, Mike
Coxswain	Kaplan, David		Shore, David	Taylor, John

[a] Points for first place under the Ten Eyck event-weighting scoring system.
[b] Denotes a senior or end of eligibility.
© Captain

UW's Thirteenth IRA/Ten Eyck Trophy — IRAs of May 31 and June 1 and 2, 2001

Event	Varsity 8+a	JV 8+	Freshman 8+	Pairs -
Points for First[b]	108	81	81	18
UW's finish	8	3	5	3
Bow seat	[c]Bauer, Brian	Kitowski, Nick	Cockerill, Alex	Niemczyk, Mike
2	McDonough, Brian	[c]Price, Ken	Cox, Derek	
3	Peters, Dirk	Mueller, Daniel	Schaible, Kyle	
4	Geweke, Alan ©	McLennan, Sam	Turney, Pete	
5	Giese, Pete	Altfeather, Nate	Boyd, Anders	
6	[c]Golding, Ed	Daniels, Paul	Egelhoff, Eric	
7	Hoopman, Beau	[c]Alwin, Scott	Dyreby, John	
Stroke	Nagle, Pete	[c]Kuehn, Reed	Boyd, Micah	Peplin, Joe
Coxswain	Taylor, John	[c]Gutt, Zachary	McDermott, Andrew	

Event	Varsity 4+	Varsity 4 w/out	Freshman 4+	Open 4+
Points for First[b]	36	36	27	18
UW's finish	2	1	4	1
Bow seat	Montanye, Aric	Stahlman, Mike	Hilsabeck, Brad	Shepard, Ben (Fr)
2	Knecht, Eric	[c]Seelen, Mike	Skye, Harrison	[c]Berger, Joel
3	Kaker, Ben	Hart, Ross	Devlin, Jason	Vitko, Peter
Stroke	Chin, Dan	[c]Remington, John	Kuhn, Mattias	Miller, Craig
Coxswain	[c]Kaplan, David		Burcham, Robert	[c]Whitish, Jeremy

[a] In the first two IRA heats, the varsity boating was Nagle (bow), Giese, Bauer, Hoopman, Golding, McDonough, Geweke, Peters (stroke), and Taylor (cox). The lineup was changed for the semis and the finals.

[b] Points for first place under the Ten Eyck event-weighting scoring system.

[c] Denotes a senior; Reed Kuehn had a year of eligibility remaining, but graduated and attended medical school in Maryland.

© Captain

TEN EYCK TROPHY VICTORIES

UW's Fourteenth IRA/Ten Eyck Trophy — IRAs of May 30 and 31, and June 1, 2002

Event	Varsity 8+	JV 8+	Freshman 8+	Pairs -
Points for First[a]	108	81	81	18
UW's finish	2	4	13	2 (& 5)[b]
Bow seat	Nagle, Pete	[c]Stahlman, Mike	Treibwasser, Mike	[c]Vitko, Peter
2	[c]McLennan, Sam	Boyd, Anders	Burnett, Ed	
3	[c]McDonough, Brian	[c]Kitowski, Nick	Stepak, Amir	
4	Giese, Pete	Cockerill, Alex	Bunnow, Kyle	
5	Boyd, Micah	[c]Altfeather, Nate	Okoh, Jemre	
6	Mueller, Daniel	[c]Geweke, Alan	Podbregar, Chris	
7	Hoopman, Beau	[c]Kaker, Ben	Lehman, Eric	
Stroke	Daniels, Paul	Niemczyk, Mike	Schwend, Ryan	[c]Miller, Craig
Coxswain	[c]Taylor, John	Burcham, Robert	Meader, Garrett	

Event	Varsity 4+	Varsity 4 w/out	Freshman 4+	Open 4+
Points for First[a]	36	36	27	18
UW's finish	3	1 (& 2)[b]	8	4
Bow seat	[c]Chin, Dan	Kipp, Ryan	Borchert, Blake	Pesavento, Anders (Fr)
2	Turney, Pete	Schaible, Kyle	Hardenbergh, Scott	Dyreby, John
3	Knecht, Eric	Devlin, Jason	Wagstaffe, Joe	Wanta, Shawn
Stroke	[c]Montanye, Aric	Hart, Ross	Kelp-Lenane, Nate	Farnia, Dave
Coxswain	Lucey, Mike (Fr)		Feinberg, Andrew	Berman, Jaron

[a] Points for first place under the Ten Eyck event-weighting scoring system.

[b] In the second Badger 2-entry, which placed fifth, the boating was Brad Hull (bow) and Dirk Peters (stroke); the second Badger V4-entry, which placed second and won the silver, the boating was Connor Sabatino (bow), Tyler Resch, Mike Anderson, and Joe Peplin (stroke).

[c] Denotes a senior or fourth-year of eligibility.

Notes

Introduction

1. In 1982, the Big Ten Conference began awarding its medal to the top male and female student athlete at each university.

Prologue

1. Arthur Hove, *The University of Wisconsin: A Pictorial History* (Madison: University of Wisconsin Press, 1991), 38.

2. Ibid., 8.

3. J. F. A. Pyre, *Wisconsin* (New York: Oxford University Press, 1920), p. 186. Both a rower and a tackle on the football squad in the 1890s, Pyre participated in two historic athletic contests for the university, including the first "extramural" crew race (and victory) in 1892 and, in football in 1894, the first victory over archrival University of Minnesota. Pyre (Class of '92), who was still playing football in graduate school in 1896 (one year before receiving his PhD.), caught the eye of UW president Charles Kendall Adams in 1893 after Adams read an article written by Pyre in a college publication. Soon after, Adams offered Pyre a position in the English Department at a salary of $1,000 per annum. See Charles Foster Smith, *Charles Kendall Adams: A Life-Sketch*, (Madison: University of Wisconsin, 1924), 58.

4. Hove, 10.

5. Ibid., 8.

6. Pyre, 310.

7. Ibid.

8. Don Kopriva and Jim Mott, *On Wisconsin! The History of Badger Athletics* (Champaign, Ill.: Sports Publishing, Inc., 1998), 3.

9. Hove, 39.

10. Merle Curti and Vernon Carstensen, *The University of Wisconsin: A History 1848–1925*, vol. 1 (Madison: University of Wisconsin Press, 1949), 693.

11. Jim Feldman, *The Buildings of the University of Wisconsin* (Madison: The University Archives, 1997), 87–88.

12. Reuben Gold Thwaites, *The University of Wisconsin: Its History and Its Alumni* (Madison, Wisc.: J. N. Purcell, 1900) 250–51.

13. Pyre, 315.

14. Curti, 693.

15. C. V. P. Young, *Courtney and Cornell Rowing* (Ithaca, N.Y.: Cornell Publications Printing Co., 1923), 31.

16. Hove, 39.

17. "The Crews at Poughkeepsie," *New York Times*, June 21, 1896, p. 3.

1. The First Race as a "Varsity"

1. "Varsity" in the chapter title refers to the first Wisconsin crew race that was not an intramural contest, rather competition against a club or school from outside the UW.

2. Adams Makes Crew a Priority

1. Margaret K. Look, *Courtney, Master Oarsman—Champion Coach* (Interlaken, N.Y.: Empire State Books, 1989).

2. "University Boat-House Company," *The Badger*, 1894, p. 131.

3. Don Kopriva and Jim Mott, *On Wisconsin! The History of Badger Athletics* (Champagne, Ill.: Sports Publishing Inc., 1998), p. 2. The date of 1874 is based on a 1912 letter of Wisconsin alumnus C. B. Bradish in which he recounts his father's telling him that "he rowed on the first crew Wisconsin ever had" in 1874. Baseball, recording its first game on April 30, 1870, was discontinued at Wisconsin in 1990. Athletic Department records show that the father, George P. Bradish, was awarded an honorary "W" in 1912.

4. In a May 6, 1952, interview in the *Wisconsin State Journal*, Walter Alexander (captain in 1896) remembered, from his 2-seat, the 1895 race against the Delawares, "Half-way down the lake, we heard an oar snap, but we kept in rhythm and won. But when we sailed past the finish buoy, we all shouted, 'Who broke the oar?' Would you believe it . . . it was Myron Weber [5-seat], the lightest man on our crew. And it was the first time any of us ever pulled hard enough to break an oar."

5. Bob Kane, in his book *Good Sports: A History of Cornell Athletics* (Ithaca, N.Y.: 1992), 6, refers to Professor Waterman Thomas Hewett, author of the 1905 volume, *Cornell University: A History*, who quotes John Ostrom's (1877 crew captain at Cornell) tart comment about the Harvard-Yale withdrawal to their own dual meet: "They withdrew to have their own dual union where victory was assured for one instead of probable defeat for both."

3. The Badgers' First Collegiate Opponent

1. Thomas Corwin Mendenhall (1910–98), once president of Smith College, grew up in Madison and was the son of UW's Physics Department Head, Professor Charles E. Mendenhall and his wife, Dr. Dorothy R. Mendenhall.

2. In older texts, the word "varsity" is often preceded by an apostrophe.

3. Reuben Gold Thwaites, *The University of Wisconsin, Its History and Its Alumnus* (Madison: J. R. Purcell, 1900) 246.

4. *The Big Ten Athletic Calendar 1909 (Wisconsin Edition)* (Chicago: Inter-College Publishing Co., 1909), 146. The *Wisconsin State Journal* of July 6, 1896, p. 1, described the opponent as the St. Paul Boat Club.

5. *Minneapolis Tribune*, July 5, 1896, p. 3.

6. "The Crews at Poughkeepsie," *New York Times*, June 21, 1896, p. 3.

5. Wisconsin's First IRA Victory

1. D. Hayes Murphy is believed to have been the older brother of W. K. Murphy, the 2-seat oarsman in the freshman boat of 1900.

2. "Cudworth Beye, Frank Lloyd Wright, and the Yahara River Boathouse, 1905," *Wisconsin Magazine of History* 72, no. 3 (spring 1989): 163–98.

6. Last of the Sculler Coaches

1. Malcolm Alama, *Mark of the Oarsmen* (Syracuse, N.Y.: Eastbrook Printing Inc., 1963).

2. After the IRA moved from Poughkeepsie to Marietta, Ohio, in 1950 and 1951 and eventually to Syracuse, N.Y., in 1952, the Syracuse Rowing Alumni Association would persuade the regatta stewards to create a new team trophy in honor of their long time head coach, Jim Ten Eyck. The University of Wisconsin would later become one of the most successful college crews at winning the Ten Eyck team trophy awarded each year at the IRAs.

3. Gordon Newell, *Ready All* (Seattle: University of Washington Press, 1987), 43.

4. J. F. A. Pyre, *Wisconsin* (New York: Oxford University Press, 1920).

5. Jim Feldman, *The Buildings of the University of Wisconsin* (Madison: The University Archives), 1997, 87–88.

6. UW yearbooks in the early 1900s were usually two years delayed in covering crew. Two reasons led to this delay: first, the crew seasons usually finished after the school year had ended and second, the junior class organized and wrote the yearbook during this period and usually didn't publish the book until late in or after their senior year.

7. Vail Obituary, *Wisconsin State Journal*, October 8 1928.

8. Tom Butler, *Wisconsin State Journal*, ca. June 7, 1984, upon "Dad" Vail's posthumous induction into the Madison Sports Hall of Fame.

9. Arthur Hove, *The University of Wisconsin: A Pictorial History* (Madison: University of Wisconsin Press, 1991), 125.

UW History—1925–1946

1. Arthur Hove, *The University of Wisconsin: A Pictorial History* (Madison: University of Wisconsin Press, 1991), 187.

7. Never Giving Up

1. From a January 8, 1979, letter in the archives of the UW's Memorial Library. The letter is part of a bequest (Accession 1998/070) of the late UW chemistry professor Aaron Ihde, a Wisconsin rower (1929–31) who later kept in close touch with Murphy, his former coach.

2. Peter J. Coleman and Paul Hass, "The President Wore Spats," *Wisconsin Alumnus*, March 1965, 9–12.

3. Patent #2,748,964 was issued to Murphy on June 5, 1956 (having been applied for on April 13, 1953), dealing with the "loading and compacting of material in a refuse truck." Letter of November 25, 2001, from George Rea.

4. "Wisco" is frequently used by ship-to-shore announcers, and by Badger supporters cheering from shore, as a sharper and more audible shorthand for "Wisconsin." The word, used generally and perhaps anachronistically, is believed to be used exclusively by fans and officials at rowing events involving the three Wisconsin crews. Coach Jablonic remembers the word's use beginning with the arrival of a women's crew in the boathouse.

5. "First Pro Football Telecast—1939," an undated NBC Sports release provided by the Yale University crew archivist via fax on September 20, 2000.

6. Robert F. Kelley, Adams Cup Regatta, *New York Times*, May 17, 1942. Copyright © 1942 by The New York Times Co. Reprinted with permission.

7. While records are sketchy and do not fully cover races after the school year, Drewes's boats did fall to a small number of non-intramural opponents.

8. Eastern Intercollegiate Regatta (later the Eastern Sprints). *The Evening Capital*, May 13, 1946. Reprinted with permission of Capital-Gazette Newspapers.

9. *Wisconsin Football Facts Season of 1948 and Centennial Sports Review 1848–1948*, 86, plus an unlabeled, undated United Press newspaper article in the 1946 scrapbook of Carlyle Fay.

10. Allison Danzig, Lake Cayuga race, *New York Times*, June 2, 1946. Copyright © 1946 by The New York Times Co. Reprinted with permission.

11. Northwest Maritime Regatta, *Seattle Post-Intelligencer*, June 24, 1946. Reprinted with permission of the Seattle Post-Intelligencer.

12. *Wisconsin Football . . . and Centennial Sports Review 1848–1948*, 86.

13. Telephone interview with Dick Tipple on July 2, 2002. Jean Holtz, in an October 23, 2003, interview, confirms Sikorsky had leased Walz a helicopter to try out for coaching.

14. William N. Wallace, letter of September 12, 2000.

15. Interview with William Wallace, September 26, 2000.

8. Sonju Solidifies the Program

1. Bob Wolf, "Sonju Expects to Strike It Rich Again," *Milwaukee Journal*, May 17, 1948.

2. Yale-Wisconsin race, *New Haven Sunday Register*, May 8, 1949. Reprinted with permission of the New Haven Register.

3. Robert F. Kelley, "That's Poughkeepsie," *IRA Regatta Official Program*, June 25, 1941, Board of Stewards, Intercollegiate Rowing Association, 9, 22. Reprinted with permission of the IRA Stewards.

4. From an interview with Duane Daentl, November 17, 2000, described in *A History of Men's Crew at Wisconsin—Research Notes for the Hard Core Enthusiast*, unpublished research notes of Brad Taylor dated November 17, 2001, 196.

5. Daniel J. Boyne, *The Red Rose Crew* (New York: Hyperion, 2000), 3.

6. Malcolm Alama, *Mark of the Oarsmen* (Syracuse, N.Y.: Estabrook Printing Inc., 1963). Randy Jablonic in the 3-seat remembers the stroke rate more likely at 32–33 than 40.

7. Adams was an idol of Coach Jablonic, especially his emphasis on land-based training. Jabo believed that an athlete can push himself harder on land (and on an erg), including working so hard as to fall down. In a boat, however, an athlete often feels others would complain if he passed out.

8. Arnie Burdick, 1964 IRA Freshman Race, *Syracuse Herald American*, June 21, 1964. The Herald Company ©1964 Syracuse Herald American.

9. Boyne, 28.

10. Allison Danzig, "Wisconsin First in Rowing Upset," *New York Times*, June 19, 1966. Copyright © 1966 by The New York Times Co. Reprinted with permission.

11. Coach Jablonic remembers that in the late 1950s, Norm Sonju's assistant James Williams declined a small salary and instead suggested a banquet, which was held for the varsity rowers at a steakhouse on State Street. Earlier banquets were held in the late 1920s and '30s, but the consistency of such an annual event is unclear.

9. "Jabo" Takes Over

1. The "Worlds" refers to the annual World (Senior) Rowing Championships sponsored by FISA (Fédération Internationale des Sociétés d'Avrion in French, or International Federation of Rowing Associations in English). FISA also sponsors an annual Junior Worlds for rowers under 23-years of age.

Formed June 25, 1892, FISA is the oldest international sports federation in the Olympic movement. Headquartered in Lausanne, Switzerland, FISA is empowered by its member National Rowing Federations (USRowing in the U.S.), the National Olympic Committees and the International Olympic Committee to govern the sport of rowing and manage its development.

In years where there are the summer Olympic Games, a subset of FISA's rowing events are held as part of the Olympic Games that year and those rowing events not "sponsored" by the Olympic Committee at the Games are competed for at a reduced event FISA World (Senior) Championships before the Olympics that summer.

FISA is managed by a Council of 21 members, which in turn appoints an Executive Committee and an Executive Director and are supported by a permanent staff of 10 (see also *www.worldrowing.com*).

2. Don Selje, "Crew Alumni Offer Solution to Athletic Department Woes," *Badger Herald*, 5 April 1971, 10.

3. Annie Burdick, 1975 IRA varsity race, *Syracuse Herald American*, June 1, 1975. The Herald Company © 1975 Syracuse Herald American.

4. Paul Jirak, "I.R.A.," *The Oarsman*, 11, 3 (May/June 1979), p. 45. Reprinted with permission of USRowing.

5. The rules of the Open 4+ event state that at least one novice and one varsity rower must be included among the four oarsmen.

6. A bronze plaque dedicated to Vail hangs in the Hall of Fame Room of Monona Terrace. The list of honorees is accessible at *www.espn1070.com/hallfame.html*.

7. Norman Hildes-Heim, 1986 IRA varsity race, *New York Times*, June 15, 1986. Copyright © 1986 by The New York Times Co. Reprinted with permission.

8. William Wallace, 1989 Eastern Sprints varsity race, *New York Times*, May 14, 1989. Copyright © 1989 by The New York Times Co. Reprinted with permission.

9. Michael Jaffe, "Rude Red Crushes Crimson," *Sports Illustrated*, June 25, 1990. Reprinted courtesy of Sports Illustrated. Copyright © 1990 Time Inc. All rights reserved.

10. Ratio, in a stroke cycle, is the proportion of time on the drive to the proportion of time on the recovery. A "one and one ratio" is when the time spent on the drive is equal to that on the recovery. A "reverse ratio" is sometimes asked for by a coach during early season practice sessions to train a rower to feel what's wrong when the boat and the rower are too slow on the drive and too fast on the recovery.

11. Pioneer Years of Badger Women's Crew

1. "Ladies' Crew Rows," *Daily Cardinal*, May 5, 1896, 1.

2. "Another Women's Crew," *Daily Cardinal*, May 6, 1896, 1.

3. *Daily Cardinal* undated, likely early May of 1896.

4. "Outing Clubs for Women," *Daily Cardinal*, April 29, 1901, 1.

5. "Three Girls' Crews Out," *Daily Cardinal*, May 18, 1901, 1.

6. "Junior Girls' Crew," *Daily Cardinal,* May 22, 1901, 1.

7. "Personnel of Girls' Crews," *Daily Cardinal,* May 22, 1901, 1.

8. The "Lucie Case ('04)" and the "Ms. Case" rowing 2-seat in the sophomore crew of 1901 may have been the same person and may have been related to avid rower and four-sport letterman Chester C. Case, the UW men's crew captain in 1892–93.

9. Katherine "Kit" Saunders, "The Governance of Intercollegiate Athletics" (Ph.D. diss. University of Wisconsin–Madison, 1977), 44.

10. Mike Murphy in an April 4, 1982, letter to UW professor Aaron Ihde ('31), a former Badger oarsman.

11. Alpha Gamma Delta, *The Badger* 1935, 289.

12. "Wisconsin Women's Crew," *WRA Newsletter,* March 1974, 3.

13. Bruce Niedermeier, in a telephone interview April 15, 2003, did not remember the exact conversation.

14. Kit Saunders Nordeen, from typed notes given the author April 12, 2003.

15. Saunders, 12. The AIAW, organized in 1971, provided a governing body and leadership for excellence in women's intercollegiate athletic programs. By the 1981–82 academic year, more than 700 colleges and universities were members of AIAW, which conducted 41 national championships in 19 different sports. In the spring of 1982, AIAW, for one year, organized the national championship for intercollegiate women's crew. When the NCAA "assimilated" (initiated sponsorship) of many intercollegiate women's sports after 1981, the AIAW lost significant funding, membership and influence to the NCAA and ceased to operate in 1983.

16. Bonnie Ryan, "Kathy Wutke, Pals Win Crew for Girls," *Capital Times,* May 23, 1972, Sports.

17. Saunders, in her 1977 thesis (pp. 49–50), remembers securing $18,000 from the Intramural Recreation Board for all women's sports in 1973–74, $7,000 less than was needed and requested. When she approached Campus Administration and obtained the incremental funding, the Board was "so annoyed" they "actually considered revoking their original allocation of $18,000."

18. Saunders, notes of April 11, 2003.

19. "Girls in a Crew Racing Shell at UW? Sue Ela, Rochester, is Among the First," *Standard Press* (Rochester, Wisc.), July 10, 1972, 4. (Reprinted with permission of the Burlington Standard Press.)

20. Debbie Erdman, "Women's Rowing Club—a launch to success," undated news clipping, probably in the *Wisconsin State Journal,* sometime from January to March of 1972. Reprinted with permission of the Wisconsin State Journal.

21. A barge is three to four inches wider then the typical racing shell so as to make the craft somewhat more stable. The wooden boat also had a stabilizing keel and floor boards to prevent novice rowers from stepping through the hull.

22. *Capital Times,* two photo captions confirm the varsity and 2V8 boatings, May 23, 1972.

12. Mimier Named Women's Crew Coach

1. Bruce Neidermeier, "Boston Regatta Victory for Crew," *Badger Herald,* an undated news clip from around October 22, 1972.

2. Daniel J. Boyne. *The Red Rose Crew* (New York: Hyperion, 2000), 33.

3. Randy Jablonic, in a telephone interview of February 28, 2003.

4. Bruce Niedermeier, in a telephone interview April 15, 2003.

5. Aaron Ihdes, notes taken on the 1973 Midwest Sprint Regatta Program, UW–Madison Archives, Ihdes Accession 1998/070, Box 2 of 2.

6. Interview with Coach Ela on March 26, 2003.

7. The National Women's Rowing Association (NWRA) was established by supporters of women's rowing, including Ed Lickess, in 1962 and hosted its first "open" national championship in 1966 in Seattle, Wash. Before 1980, few colleges had women's rowing programs and thus there were no college-only national championships. The NWRA, formed to encourage women's rowing at all levels, sponsored open national championships in the third weekend in June, which pitted women's college crews against clubs and U.S. and foreign Olympic training center entries (many with older and more experienced rowers). As more colleges initiated women's crew programs, a desire emerged to organize an annual college-only national championship, with common rules regarding eligibility. The Women's Collegiate National Rowing Championships (WCNRC) were first held in the spring of 1980 on the Clinch River in Oak Ridge, Tenn., jointly with the NWRA's open that year. A "college event" had been introduced at the NWRA's regatta the previous year.

8. Boyne, 40.

9. Jay Mimier, journals and records.

10. Mimier, which differs from Boyne (32), who writes of Graves' rowing in the 6-seat on an 800-meter course.

11. Ann Beckman, "Enthusiastic UW Crew Women Battle the Obstacles," *Capital Times,* 10 May 10, 1974, 21. Reprinted with permission of the Capital Times, Madison, Wisconsin.

12. William B. Blankenburg, "1000 Meters of Agony," *Milwaukee Journal Insight,* August 25, 1974, 20–29. Reprinted with permission of William B. Blankenburg. Mimier's records indicate Radcliffe won the heat.

13. Blankenburg, 23.

14. Saunders, 49. Saunders had been the Advisor/Director of the Women's Recreational Association since 1967 and the Coordinator of Women's Sports, an activity organized in 1970 with a budget of $2,000 allocated to women's sports in 1971–72, according to Saunders's thesis.

15. Tamara J. Flarup, UW–Madison Women's Intercollegiate Athletics, UW Sports News Service press release, January 3, 1978, 2.

16. Saunders, 61.

17. Adding the two Midwest wins as a club sport, UW won twenty-seven consecutive Midwest Championship eights contests.

18. Beseck Lake is one mile from Middlefield and six miles from Middleton, Conn.

19. Boyne, 56.

20. Kit Saunders, letter dated June 30, 1975, to Mary Grace Knight.

21. Boyne, 189.

22. Donald A. Bluhn, "A Long Journey Leads Women Crew to Loss," *Wisconsin State Journal*, undated news clipping from the spring of 1976.

23. Judith Burns, "Women's crew steers toward equity," *Daily Cardinal*, May 20, 1976. Reprinted with permission of the Daily Cardinal.

24. "UW Women and Men Take Thirds at Huge Head of the Charles," *WRA Newsletter*, October 1975, 1. Reprinted with permission of the Wisconsin Rowing Association.

25. Nancy Saslow, "Graves stands alone in team sport," *Daily Cardinal*, 2 March 2, 1976.

26. "UW women's crew wins preliminary," *Wisconsin State Journal* of June 1976 lists Carie Graves, Jackie Zoch, Peggy McCarthy, and Debbie Oetzel as the four UW rowers selected for Olympic tryouts. The coxswain candidate was Beth (Traut) Bosio.

27. A protest similar to Yale's 1976 action occurred on the Madison campus in 1971. John Aehl, in an article "Improves with age Wisconsin women mark 17th year," in the *WRA Newsletter* of August 1990 (12), quoted Mary Rouse, currently a UW Assistant Vice Chancellor, in describing a story from 1971. The UW had a "Shower Protest" by several women, who were unhappy there "were no locker rooms or showers for women in the shell—the Camp Randall Memorial Sports Center. A group of women wrote letters and tried to negotiate peacefully for improvements, for two years. No luck. So we lost patience and one day about 10 of us went into part of the men's locker room, admired the beautiful facilities, and showered. The police were called, but no one was arrested. The next day a guard was posted at the locker room, but it was embarrassing enough going in there once, and we had no intention of doing it again. A week later, construction began on a women's locker room."

28. Mimier notes of March 13, 2003.

29. Ibid.

30. Dick Rockne, "Let's Hear It for Wisconsin Rah! Rah!" *Seattle Times*, June 18, 1978.

31. Jay Mimier, in an interview April 8, 2003, said neither rower was able to participate in the November 1–5, 1978, Worlds in Lake Karapiro, New Zealand, as both had conflicts—Graves with her coaching responsibilities at Radcliffe, and Cruz with her academic career in the graduate school in engineering.

32. Mimier notes of March 13, 2003.

13. Sue Ela

1. Sue Ela interview, March 5, 2003. Michael F. Lorenz, Associate Director of the UW Band, in an e-mail of May 6, 2003, advised, from the UW Marching Band's history, *Songs to Thee,* that the band department in 1971 had removed the qualifications for Marching Bands, which had previously read, "Open to all male students." Lorenz continued that, prior to 1974, there were no serious inquiries about membership by female students. In 1974–75, Paula Schultz (trumpet) and Ann Thurber (saxophonist) were the first women to join the Marching Band.

2. Tricia Dearing, "Ela Awarded 'Woman of the Year' by USRA," *Daily Cardinal*, December 11, 1989, 4–5.

3. The website www.RowingHistory.net lists U.S. National and Olympic Team rosters, boatings, and results. Under "U.S. Rowing Team 1900–2001," and "Senior & Lightweight Women 1967–2001." At March 1, 2003, information was included through the 2002 Worlds in Seville, Spain.

4. Rob Zaleski, "UW crew wins dressing room," *Kenosha News,* October 15, 1980, whose historical report had the incident outside the office of Assistant Athletic Director Otto Breitenbach.

5. "Crew gripes are to wrong person," *Milwaukee Journal,* (December 8, 1979), part 2, p. 3. The article also said AAD Breitenbach kept his door closed during the December 4 demonstration. © 2004 Journal Sentinel Inc., reproduced with permission.

6. Wisconsin–Cal race description from *Wisconsin State Journal,* June 14, 1980. Reprinted with permission of the Wisconsin State Journal.

7. Daniel J. Boyne. *The Red Rose Crew* (New York: Hyperion, 2000), 202.

8. In an April 21, 2004, telephone interview, UW rower and

now head coach for women's rowing at the University of Iowa, Mandi Kowal describer a 2000-meter lightweight exhibition race at an internationally sanctioned regatta in Montreal in which she participated. From that race forward, standard distance of 2000-meters seemed to be set for most women's rowing.

9. *WRA Newsletter,* August 1983, 8.

10. In an April 21, 2004, telephone interview, Mandi Kowal remembered participating in the preparation of this regatta with a group of women athletes by stringing buoys—the first 150 meters and the last 100 meters of each lane's markers—through the trees beside the crew house and painting them the regulation red required to communicate these beginning and ending lane distances to rowers and coxswains.

11. The NWRA merged in 1986 with the Philadelphia-based National Association of Amateur Oarsmen (the NAAO, established in 1872) to form the United States Rowing Association ("USRowing"). The U.S. Olympic Committee recognizes USRowing as the national governing body for the sport of rowing in the U.S. USRowing selects, trains, and manages the teams, which represent the United States in international competition, including the World Championships, Pan American Games, and Olympics. USRowing moved its headquarters to Indianapolis, Indiana, in the 1985.

12. Heidi (Grutzner) Martell, in a letter sent at the time of coach Ela's spring 1998 retirement.

13. The website www.crewclassic.org lists results and winning boatings at the San Diego Classic.

14. Lynn Liberman, undated letter to coach Ela at her spring retirement in 1998.

15. Formed in the fall of 1975, the "WIS Club" was a 300 member booster club in 1982, raising funds from dues and fund raisers for the purpose of supporting awards banquets, travel budgets, advertising, and a scholarship toward the development of women's athletics at UW, according to the 1981–82 UW Women's Intercollegiate Athletics media guide. Kit Saunders, in her 1977 thesis (p. 60) referenced earlier, describes the WIS Club as "the first booster club for women's athletics in the Big Ten and probably the first in the country."

16. Jay Mimier's notes suggest the bow seat, whereas www.RowingHistory.net indicates the 2-seat.

17. The happy day for Ela's family turned out to be May 1, 1986, with the birth of daughter Julia.

18. Sue Ela, notes of February 26, 2003.

19. Paul Capobianco, *Wisconsin Women's Rowing 2002–2003,* media guide, UW Sports Information Office, Madison, 25.

20. Ibid., 23.

21. The website www.crewclassic.org indicates Wisconsin finished ninth; third was indicated in the 2002–3 UW media guide for women's crew.

22. Cathy Gunderson, in an undated personal letter to Coach Ela at her spring 1998 retirement.

23. Son Michael was born January 18, 1993.

24. Jodie Jenz (2-seat), "A Tribute to Sue From Her '95 Crew," an undated letter at the spring 1998 retirement of coach Ela.

25. Mary Browning, note received May 5, 2003.

26. *Wisconsin Men's & Women's Intercollegiate Rowing 1998–99* media guide, Sports Information Office, 9.

27. Winners since 1988 include Washington (1988), Cornell (1989), Radcliffe (1990–91), Princeton (1992–5), and Wisconsin (1996), UW Athletic Board Notes VII, no. 6, UW Sports Information (June 14, 1996): 4.

28. "Women's Rowing," *1995–96 Wisconsin Women's Athletics* annual review and *Row Wisco* newsletter dated February 7, 1996, p. 3. The boating may have been lighter openweight rowers or UW alumnae.

29. Results and boatings taken from a signed poster in the crew coach's office.

30. Capobianco, 23. The Remington Fellowship honors the memory of professor Frank J. Remington, a longtime law school faculty member at UW–Madison, who died in 1996. During his career at Wisconsin, Remington served as Faculty Athletics Representative to the NCAA, Big Ten Conference, and was a longtime member of the NCAA Committee on Infractions.

31. While Iverson is not listed in the www.RowingHistory.net records of Olympians, Mary Browning, on May 5, 2003, advised Iverson was an alternate.

32. *Wisconsin 1995–96 Men's & Women's Intercollegiate Rowing,* media guide, p. 7.

33. The NCAA apparently steers clear of lightweight women's rowing in part because of their discomfort, as in wrestling, with the need to develop highly refined weight-management regulations.

34. Peter Brewington, "NCAA wades into women's rowing," *USA Today,* April 1, 1997, 8C.

35. Miles Brand, "College Presidents Lead Charge for N.C.A.A. Reform," *New York Times,* April 6, 2003, Sports, 7.

36. Ibid.

37. Wisconsin Women's Sport's Information's weekly news summary, May 12, 1997, 4.

38. From the *Wisconsin Men's & Women's Intercollegiate Rowing 1998–99* media guide (12). The selection of individual boats is based on a combination of late-season performance, regional rankings, results against boats already selected, re-

sults against regionally ranked boats, and results from major regattas. One team from each of three geographic regions is selected, and the remaining six teams are selected at large. A minimum of four eights are also allocated to participants from Division II and III.

39. *Wisconsin State Journal,* May 19, 1997.

40. Jason Wilde, "Streak ends at 25 for women's varsity eight," *Wisconsin State Journal,* April 30, 1998.

41. Browning notes of May 5, 2003. Boating was believed to be correct.

42. Todd Finkelmeyer, "Ela Bids Emotional Farewell," *The Capital Times,* April 23, 1998.

43. Tam Flarup in a personal e-mail to coach Ela, dated March 21, 1998 (used with permission).

14. The Competition Becomes Fierce!

1. The 2V8 and V4+ were unavailable from either UW sources or the NCAA website as of the date this manuscript was completed.

2. A "bowloader" is a four-oared shell which, for better weight distribution, positions the coxswain forward in the boat, rather than in the rear as in an eight.

3. Browning's notes of May 5, 2003, suggest Oetjen and Broerman may have been interchanged.

4. Browning notes of May 5, 2003.

5. Interview with coach Maren LaLiberty in her office on April 3, 2003.

6. Dusty Darley, e-mail of March 1, 2004.

7. The website *www.crewclassic.org* gives this boating for 2001.

8. The website *www.crewclassic.org* gives this boating for 2002.

9. As the Big Ten has now superceded the WEARC/Eastern Sprints as the UW openweights "conference," UW may be precluded by Big Ten rules from participating in the Sprints in the future. UW was a founding member of the EAWRC and its membership may be assumed by UW's lightweight program.

10. Details of UW's crew races—weather, times, boatings, and other commentary—are available online at www.uw-badgers.com. Historical information about races since 2002 is also available.

Bibliography

Alama, Malcolm R. *Mark of the Oarsmen*. Syracuse, N.Y.: Syracuse Alumni Rowing Association, 1963.

Boyne, Daniel J. *The Red Rose Crew: A True Story of Women, Winning, and the Water*. New York: Hyperion Press, 2000.

Bradley, U. T. *The "Dad" Vail Story*. Winter Park, Fla.: The Rollins Press, Inc. 1961.

Curti, Merle, and Vernon Carstensen. *The University of Wisconsin: A History, 1848–1925*. 2 vols. Madison: University of Wisconsin Press, 1949.

Dauzing, Allison and Peter Brandwein. *Sport's Golden Age*. New York: Harper & Brothers, 1948.

Eckhardt Jr., Paul O. "Wisconsin, Where They Row," *The Wisconsin Alumnus,* vol. 49, no. 9, 1948.

Feldman, Jim. *The Buildings of the University of Wisconsin*. Madison: The University Archives, 1997.

Gill, Alison. *The Yanks at Oxford*. Sussex, England: The Book Guild Limited, 1991.

Hartsuff, Gregg. *Michigan Crew: The First Twenty Years*. Ann Arbor, Mich.: Braun-Brumfield, Inc., 1996.

Hove, Arthur. *The University of Wisconsin: A Pictorial History*. Madison: University of Wisconsin Press, 1991.

Kane, Bob. *Good Sports: A History of Cornell Athletics*. Ithaca, N.Y.: Cornell University Press, 1992.

Kelley, Robert F. *American Rowing*. New York: G. P. Putnam's Sons, 1932.

Kopriva, Don, and Jim Mott. *On Wisconsin! The History of Badger Athletics*. Champaign, Ill.: Sports Publishing, Inc., 1998.

Lemmon, Jim. *The Log of Rowing at the University of California, Berkeley, 1870–1987*. Berkeley, Calif.: Western Heritage Press, 1989.

Look, Margaret K. *Courtney, Master Oarsman—Champion Coach*. Interlaken, N.Y.: Empire State Books, 1989.

Mendenhall, Thomas C. *The Harvard-Yale Boat Race, 1852–1924*. Mystic, Conn.: Mystic Seaport Museum, 1993.

Newell, Gordon. *Ready All!: George Yeoman Pocock and Crew Racing*. Seattle: University of Washington Press, 1987.

Pocock, Stanley Richard. *"Way Enough!"* Seattle: BLABLA Publishing, 2000.

Pyre, J. F. A. *Wisconsin*. New York: Oxford University Press, 1920.

Saunders, Katherine. "The Governance of Intercollegiate Athletics." Ph.D. thesis, University of Wisconsin–Madison, 1977.

Smith, Charles Foster. *Charles Kendall Adams, A Life Sketch*. Madison: University of Wisconsin Press, 1924.

Stewart, Robert. *Rowing . . . The Experience*. Philadelphia: Boathouse Row Sports, Ltd., 1988.

Telander, Rick. *From Red Ink to Roses*. New York: Simon & Shuster, 1994.

Thwaites, Reuben Gold. *The University of Wisconsin, Its History and its Alumni*. Madison: J. N. Purcell, 1900.

Topolski, Daniel and Patrick Robinson. *True Blue*. London: Doubleday, 1989.

Young, C. V. P. *The Cornell Navy*. Ithaca, N.Y.: Taylor and Carpenter, 1907.

———. *Courtney and Cornell Rowing,* Ithaca, N.Y.: Cornell Publications Printing Co., 1923.

Index

Many rowers are named in the text's listings of boatings or the photo captions, or in the appendixes of captains, Ten Eyck boatings, and letter-winners. An estimated 5,000+ student-athletes have rowed at UW (including 1,300 men's and women's winners of the "W") from 1892 to 2005.

Adams, Charles Kendall (UW President), 9, 10, 19–24, 41, 42
Adams Cup Regatta (Boston), 77
AIAW (Association of Intercollegiate Athletics for Women), 194, 226, 228, 230
Alexander, Walter, 28, 29, 33, 64–65, 67, 102, 190
All-American football team, first, 8
Alvarez, Barry, 89

Bascom, John, 5, 6
Bausch & Lomb Invitational, UW's first attendance at, 244. See also Stonehurst Capital Regatta
Berry Crate Crew/Race, 11, 34–39, 78, 102
betting of the shirts, origin, 46, 48
Beye, Cudworth, 42
Big Ten Conference, origins, 24
Big Ten Conference Medal. See Conference Medal of Honor
Big Ten Openweight Women's Rowing Championship, first, 260
Birge, Edward A. (founder of Madison Boat Club), 21
Black Mountain Cup (San Diego), 253. See also Coggeshall Cup, A. W.
boathouses at UW. See UW boathouses
Boston Globe Trophy, 134, 137
Bradish, C. B., 4
Bradley, U. T., 105, 108
Brooklyn Dodgers, 82
Browning, Mary, 247, 254, 257, 260
Bruhn, Milt, 194, 200
Bryans, Bebe, 275
Burt, Leo, 120

Callow, Russell "Rusty" S., xviii, 60–61, 69, 81, 90, 105, 112
Callow Award (Rusty), 183
Camden (New Jersey), IRA move to, 169
Camden County Freeholders Women's Overall Trophy, first, 253
Camp, Walter, 55
Camp Randall, acquired, 8
Cappel, Dylan, 176, 179, 182
Case, C. C. "Jimmy," 8, 14, 15, 17, 22
catching a crab, 72
Central Hudson Steamboat Co., fire, 49
Central Intelligence Agency, 86
Chapman, Tom, 121
cheese ambassadors, 82, 84
Chicago Navy, 10, 13–18, 19, 22
Cincinnati Collegiate Invitational Championship, first, 150
Clark, Chris H., xv, 68, 152, 171–72, 174, 176–78, 180, 181–85
Coach of the Year (EARC/EAWRC), UW honorees, 183, 204, 251
Cochrane Cup, first, 114
Coggeshall Cup, A. W. (San Diego), 262, 264, 273. See also Black Mountain Cup
College Crew of the Year Award (*Rowing News*), 183
Conference Medal of Honor (Big Ten): first UW winner, xviii, 57; list of UW rower winners, 143
Conibear, Hiram, 48–49, 58
course change, 1,000 to 2,000 meters, 230, 236
Courtney, Charles E., 9, 19–20, 22, 23, 43, 49, 50, 52–53, 56–57, 99
Cregier, Commodore Dewitt C. (Chicago Navy), 13, 14, 17, 18
crew commodore, 28–29
Crew Cut Day, 105
Culver Academy, 70, 73

"Dad" Vail Regatta, origins, 60, 69
Daily Cardinal, founded, 8
Danzig, Allison, 75, 83, 107

Day, John F., 28, 131
Dayne, Ron, 174
Derby Day (Yale), 95–96
Drewes, Curt, 62–63, 73–74, 78, 79, 94, 101, 133, 144, 168, 195, 196, 199
Dyreby, Jr., James "Jim" R., 132, 136, 137, 138, 141–43, 144; bio, 142–43

EARC (Eastern Association of Rowing Colleges): first Eastern Sprints, 76, 78–81, 85, 92
Eastern Intercollegiate Regatta, 1946. See EARC
Eastern Sprints. See EARC; EAWRC
EAWRC (Eastern Association of Women's Rowing Colleges): first Eastern Sprints for UW crews, 210, 259
Eckhardt, Jr., Paul O., 67–69, 95–96; bio 68
Ela, Sue, xv, xvii, 194–97, 199, 200, 201, 202, 205, 206, 208, 210, 212, 216, 217, 218, 222, 223, 227, 230, 232, 234, 235–36, 240–42, 244, 245, 247–49, 250–51, 252, 254, 256, 257, 264, 267, 271
Elms, The (UW boarding house at Poughkeepsie Regatta), 51
Emerson, Fred, 121, 134
Espeseth, Jr., Robert, 132, 136, 138, 141, 142–43, 144, 150, 152, 159 170, 257

FISA (Federation of International Rowing Associations [English]), 234, 317 chap. 9 n. 1
Fish, Hamilton, 27
Fisher Cup, 131
Frank, Glenn (UW President), 62, 66–67

Geweke, Alan, 182
Goes, Clifford "Tip," 102, 103, 122
Gornick, Sarah Jean, 259
Governor's Cup, 199
Grand Valley Invitational (Allendale, Michigan), first, 253

Graves, Carie 107, 189, 202–4, 205–9, 211–16, 218, 219, 223–24, 225, 226, 227, 229, 232, 234, 235, 241, 258; bio 203–4
Green Bay Packers, join NFL in 1922, 57

Harvard–Yale Boat Race, first, xviii, 5, 26
Head of the Charles Regatta (Boston): first, 117, 199; map, 137; UW's first attendance, men, 120; UW's first attendance, women, 199–200, 255
Helms Foundation Sports Hall of Fame (rowing). *See* National Rowing Foundation
Heun, Howard, 70–72
Hirsch, Elroy "Crazylegs," 93, 127, 129, 139, 224, 244
Holtz, Carl A., xv, 77, 80–82, 85, 173, 179; bio 76
Honey Bun Mobile, 232–33
Hoopman, Beau (first UW Men's Olympic gold medal winner), 173, 174, 175, 178, 179, 180, 181, 182, 185, 186, 189
Humphrey Hall, 224–25
Hunn, Ralph, 62, 70–72, 74

Ihde, Aaron J., 129
Intercollegiate Conference of Faculty Representatives, 24. *See also* Big Ten Conference
IRA (Intercollegiate Rowing Association) Regatta: UW's first attendance, 31, 250, 253. *See also* Poughkeepsie Regatta

Jablonic, Randall T. "Jabo," xv, 61, 90, 92, 93, 108. 109, 110–16, 121, 122, 124–26, 128, 131–33, 136–37, 139–45, 149–52, 155, 157, 160–62, 164–65, 166, 169–70, 172, 173, 184, 189, 194–96, 199–200, 213, 244, 245
Jablonic Boat Fund Endowment, 189
Jablonic Cup, first, 174
Jessop-Whittier Cup. *See* Whittier Cup
Johnson, Howard "Howie," 59

Kelly, Jr., John "Jack" B., 93
Kletsch, Alvin, UW's first athletic coach, 8
Knecht Cup (New Jersey), 266, 273

Lac La Belle. *See* Oconomowoc
Lake Cayuga (New York), 9, 20, 56–57, 83
Lake Harsha (Ohio), 164, 236
Lake Minnetonka (Minnesota), 23, 24, 32
Lake Onondaga (New York), 61, 94, 105, 106, 115, 116, 118, 121, 130, 162
Lake Quinsigamond (Massachusetts), 44, 184, 217
Lake Saltonstall (Connecticut), 11, 28, 29–31
Lake Saratoga (New York), 31
LaLiberty, Maren Watson, xv, 257, 260, 262, 267, 266, 269, 271
Leopold, Aldo, 76
Lightweight Development Camp, first, 227
Lightweight Women's Rowing, introduced at UW, 248–49
Lincoln Park Boat Club, organized, 13
Louis, Joe, 75
Ludwig, Jane (interim head coach), 235–36
Lundelius, Jason "Lundy," 259
Lurline Boat Club. *See* Minnesota Rowing Club

MacDonald, Stewart (first UW Olympic rower), 123, 126, 127, 133
Madison Boat Club, founded, 6
Madison Championship Rowing Association, 240
Madison Sports Hall of Fame, 152, 166, 264
Marietta Regatta, 101–4
Marietta Trophy, 97
Marston, Amos T., 22–23
Maytag, Fred L., 67
McConville, Curran C., 28, 32–33, 34, 38, 40, 64, 73, 131
Memorial Library archivist, xvi
Memorial Union, 3, 5, 34, 61, 64, 65, 93, 104
Mendota, The, 94, 101
Merrill Lynch Classic, first, 245
Mickelson, Tim (first UW Olympic medallist), 126, 127, 133
Mickey's Dairy Bar, 93–94, 140
Midwestern Athletic Conference, 24. *See also* Big Ten Conference
Midwest Rowing Center, 122

Midwest Rowing Championship (Madison), first, 134
Milwaukee River Challenge, first, 264
Milwaukee Sentinel Cup, 139
Mimier, Jay, 127, 200–201, 202, 208–11, 213–19, 222, 223, 240, 256
Minnesota Boat Club (a.k.a. St. Paul's), 23, 24, 32, 197
Minnesota Rowing Club (formerly Lurline Boat Club), 23
Morrill Act (land grant legislation), 3
Mucks, Arlie, 130
Mulcahy Trophy (Robert C.), first, 253
Murphy, George W. "Mike," 58, 62, 64, 65, 67–70, 192, 193
Murphy (George W.) Endowment Fund, vii, 68

NAAO (National Association of Amateur Oarsmen), 239
National Intercollegiate Regatta (Long Beach, California), 70
National Intercollegiate Varsity Eight Rowing Championship. *See* Cincinnati Collegiate Invitational Championship
National Rowing Foundation and NRF Hall of Fame, 76, 85, 109, 116, 122, 144, 203
National "W" Club, 129, 207. *See also* Appendix 1
Nation's Cup. *See* Under-23 Worlds
NCAA (National Collegiate Athletic Association): "assimilation" of AIAW sports, 226–27, 230; first openweight championship, 251, 252; potential sponsoring of men's heavyweight crew, 276; UW's first invitation, 258
Neil, Doug, 195–96, 199–200
Northwest Maritime Regatta (Seattle), 84, 93
Nova, Lou, 75
NWRA (National Women's Rowing Association): established in 1962, 318 chap. 12 n. 7; merger into USRowing, 239; UW's first regatta attendance, 202, 206

Oconomowoc (Wisconsin), 10, 13–16, 17, 18
Oconomowoc Yacht Club, 13, 28

O'Dea, Andrew, 11, 23–26, 28, 31–32, 40, 42–43, 71, 72, 103, 143, 190, 191–92
O'Dea, Patrick, 24–26, 28, 71, 103, 108, 110, 115
Old Nero, 102
Olympics. *See* U.S. Olympic Committee/Olympics
Orth, Franklin, 16, 64, 127
Oxford–Cambridge Boat Race, first, xviii

Pabst, Frederick (captain), 22
Parker, Harry, 140–41, 201, 213, 216
Peck, Commodore Ferdinand "Ferd" W., 13, 14–16
Peck, George W. (governor), 14, 18
Pen & Mike Club (Madison). *See* Madison Sports Hall of Fame
Phi Gamma Delta, 68, 96, 103
pickle boat, 75, 110–12
Pocock, George, 49, 58, 67, 84, 93, 101, 105, 128
Pollock, Charles, 51
Polo Grounds, 75
port and starboard rigging, 115
Poughkeepsie Regatta (Hudson River): beginnings, 26–27, 98; essay 98–101; map/photo 35, 54; UW's first attendance, 27, 31–32
Poughkeepsie Regatta Trophy, 97, 105, 114
Purdue University, 80, 103, 105, 114
Price-Waterhouse Cup, at Royal Henley Regatta, 248
Pyre, J. F. A., 4, 16–17, 22, 55–56

Ratzeburg Rowing Club (Germany), 115–16
Rea, George, 62–63, 69, 77–78, 129–30, 193
Red Gym/Red Armory, 10, 17, 18, 21, 24, 65, 76, 91, 105, 159
Reed, Carl S., 143–44
repechage regatta format, 161
Richter, Pat, 89
Rollins College (winter training site, Winter Park, Florida), 105, 107, 108
Rom, Roy, 76, 78, 82, 83, 85
Rose, Don (*Daily Cardinal* reporter), 104–6
Royal Henley Regatta: UW men's participation, 40, 122, 136–37, 157, 166; UW women's participation, 247–48, 258–59

San Diego Classic: first, 134; UW's first attendance, 137, 233, 250
Saucerman, W. T., 7, 17, 22
Saunders-Nordeen, Katherine "Kit," 194, 195, 207, 211–12, 216, 235, 242
Schlitz Trophy/Schlitz Beer Company, 23, 32, 136
Scholastic Rowing Regatta, 81
Schreiner, Dave, 76
Schueller, Jr., Louis "Lou," 132, 136, 138, 141, 142–43
Schultz, Dale (Wisconsin state senator), 132
scullers, 106
seat numbering, 113
Seattle Invitational Sprint Regatta. *See* Northwest Maritime Regatta
Shalala, Donna (UW president), 89
"Sing a Song of College Days," vi
Slavin, "Paddy," 23
Smelstor, Sister Marjorie, 194–95
Sonju, Norm, 40, 60, 61, 68, 76, 85, 90–92, 93, 97, 101–9, 113–15, 117, 118, 119, 122–24, 133, 157, 173, 188
sorority races (1933–1934), 193
Spanish-American War, 31
Sprague Trophy, 250
St. John's Military Academy, 40, 73, 78
Stephenson, Senator Isaac, 42–43
Stonehurst Capital Regatta (Rochester, NY), 254, 255, 259. *See also* Bausch & Lomb Invitational
Stuhldreher, Harry, 62, 69, 72, 73, 74, 78, 91, 103
Sullivan, John L., 23
sweepswingers, 106
Sweetland, Edwin R., 49

Taylor, John, 176, 178, 179, 180, 181
Ten Eyck, David, 44
Ten Eyck, Edward Hanlan "Ned," 44–46, 48, 49, 69, 73, 83, 93, 109
Ten Eyck, James B. "Captain Jim," 44
Ten Eyck, Jr., James A., 45–46
Ten Eyck, Sr., James A "Jim," 11, 45–46, 49, 50, 52–53, 56, 57, 61, 73, 93, 99
Ten Eyck Trophy, 44, 61, 97, 105, 133
Thoma, Harry, 65

Thorsness, Kris "Thor" (first UW women's Olympic gold medal winner), 189, 204, 220, 221, 224, 225, 229, 232, 234, 235, 237, 240
Title IX, 130, 133, 198
Tobin, Sean (interim head coach), 245
Trilling, Blance M., 192
Trochos, The, 6

Under-23 Worlds, 117, 171, 176, 182
University Boat Club, 8, 21
University Boat-House Company, formed 1892, 21
U.S. Coast Guard Academy, exercise to Madison, 131
U.S. Olympic Committee/Olympics: early selection camps, after "set" crews, 117, 210, 213, 227, 256, 257
USRowing, 169, 170, 239, 241, 244, 257, 317 chap. 9 n. 1
UW Athletic Association, formed, 8
UW Athletic Hall of Fame, 76, 143, 173, 189, 203, 235
UW boathouses: first (1893), 21; second (1967–68), 117, 122; third (2004), 175, 270
UW Women's Athletic Department, 207, 242

Vail, Harry Emerson "Dad," 11, 32, 33, 50, 55, 58, 59, 60–61, 62, 116, 152
VO_2 tests, 249

Walker, Dean (first UW competitor in Olympics), 107, 127
Walsh, Charles S. "Buck," 60, 79
Walsh Cup (Navy), first, 121
Walz, Allen W. "Skip," xv, 62–63, 69, 74–76, 78–80, 82, 83–87, 91, 92, 95, 106, 114, 130, 144, 160
Watson, Maren. *See* LaLiberty, Maren Watson
W Cup, 86
Western Conference, 24. *See also* Big Ten Conference
Western Conference Medal. *See* Conference Medal of Honor
westerners, UW as, 31
Western Regatta, 15
Whittier Cup (San Diego Classic), 233
Wilce, Jack, 47–48
Williams, Ted, 69

Willing Trophy, 269
Winnipeg Boat Club, 57
Winter Park (Florida). *See* Rollins College
Wisconsin Alumni Association (WAA), 3, 130; UW alumni clubs, 26, 72, 96, 103, 108, 110, 130, 237–38
Wisconsin Crew Corporation. *See* Wisconsin Rowing Association
Wisconsin Idea, 11
Wisconsin Rowing Association, xv, xvi, 29, 34, 64–65, 68, 73, 81, 129–30, 137, 144, 151, 173, 213, 230

WNCRC (Women's National Collegiate Rowing Championship), first, 225
Wolman, J. Martin "Murph," 65
Women's Athletic Association, 192–93
Women's Athletic Department, 210
Women's Intercollegiate Sports Club, 234
Women's Recreational Association, 194, 195

Women's Rowing Club, 195
Women's Sport Grant, 259
Wopat, Tom, 128
"Worlds," 317 chap. 9 n. 1
Wright, Frank Lloyd, 42
Wutke, Kathy, 193–97, 199, 200, 201

Yahara River, 25, 42, 67, 72, 109
Yale University (UW's first collegiate opponent), 28–30